COMPLEX LITIGATION: PROBLEMS IN ADVANCED CIVIL PROCEDURE

by

JAY TIDMARSH
Professor of Law
Notre Dame Law School

ROGER H. TRANGSRUD
Senior Associate Dean for Academic Affairs and
Oswald Symister Colclough Research Professor of Law
George Washington University Law School

CONCEPTS AND INSIGHTS SERIES

NEW YORK, NEW YORK
FOUNDATION PRESS
2002

Cover Design: Keith Stout
Cover Photo: Photograph of Johns-Manville Employee Frank Russo, Handling Asbestos (1949) from the Bill Ravanesi exhibit, Breath Taken: The Landscape and Biography of Asbestos, see www.bumc.bu.edu/SPH/Gallery

COPYRIGHT © 2002 By FOUNDATION PRESS
395 Hudson Street
New York, NY 10014
Phone Toll Free 1–877–888–1330
Fax (212) 367–6799
fdpress.com

ISBN 1–56662–885–7

 TEXT IS PRINTED ON 10% POST CONSUMER RECYCLED PAPER

To Mom and in memory of Dad

— J.T.

To Darryl and Cindy

— R.H.T.

PREFACE

We thank Kathleen Bradley, Jody Klontz, Gloria Krull, Lois Plawecki, and Debbie Sumption for their assistance in the preparation of this manuscript, and Jesse Schomer for research and editorial assistance.

TABLE OF CONTENTS

CONCEPTS AND INSIGHTS SERIES

COMPLEX LITIGATION: PROBLEMS IN ADVANCED CIVIL PROCEDURE

Chapter 1

COMPLEX LITIGATION
IN PERSPECTIVE

A fair question, which you might have asked when you first read the title of this book, is: What exactly is "complex litigation"? The problem is that no one really knows — or more accurately perhaps, various definitions don't agree. Complex civil litigation has an "I-know-it-when-I-see-it" quality. Nearly everyone agrees that matters like the massive asbestos litigation, the AT&T antitrust suit, or the remedial phase of a school desegregation suit are complex. But trying to find a common thread that both describes these cases and distinguishes them from the run-of-the-mill car crash is difficult.[1]

The answer to the question "What is complex litigation?" is more than an academic one. The phrase "complex litigation" has a talismanic quality to it; once a court is convinced that a case is "complex," it often becomes more innovative and aggressive in developing methods to resolve the dispute. Since various methods of resolution can lead to different outcomes for the litigants, a critical dimension in the success (or failure) of a case is whether a lawyer can convince a court that the case is or is not complex.

Having said this much, we will for now eschew any formal definition of "complex civil litigation." The only way truly to develop an understanding of the subject is to see the various ways in which the problem of complexity manifests itself. Thus, this entire book can be seen, at one level, as an attempt to work out a definition of the subject. After the various manifestations of complexity have been explored in the following eight chapters, we will return in a final chapter to synthesize what we have learned.

---

1. For two articles that define "complexity" but also take account of other possible definitions, see Jay Tidmarsh, *Unattainable Justice: The Form of Complex Litigation and the* *Limits of Judicial Power*, 60 GEO. WASH. L. REV. 1683 (1992); and Jeffrey W. Stempel, *A More Complete Look at Complexity*, 40 ARIZ. L. REV. 781 (1998).

For the present, therefore, let us define "complex civil litigation" broadly and intuitively: "Complex cases" are cases in which the procedural system that we have established does not function well to resolve a dispute. This intuitive understanding of complex litigation immediately puts "complex" and "ordinary" litigation into opposition. It also forces us to consider exactly what the "ordinary" procedural system is, and why it is that this system fails to work in some cases.

A. THE ASSUMPTIONS OF THE AMERICAN PROCEDURAL SYSTEM

Modern procedural systems tend to share certain common values, such as accuracy of outcome, finality, and the employment of reason in the determination of facts and law. But these values, which may rule out some procedures such as ordeals or wagers of law, do little to put flesh on the bones of a procedural system; put differently, it is possible to design many different procedural systems that give effect, more or less, to these values. In order to further develop its own procedural system, each culture appeals to certain additional norms or assumptions that may not fully specify the procedural system, but that nonetheless frame in the main components of that system.

Looked at in broad perspective, there are eight fundamental assumptions on which the civil procedural system of modern America is based: due process, adversarialism, efficiency, jury trial, pretrial factual development, transactionalism, and trans-substantivity.

1. Due Process. The fundamental cornerstone of American procedure is the notion of due process. "Due process" is a complex notion, meaning different things in different contexts. In one sense, due process requires, before a judgment can deprive a person of his or her interests in life, liberty, or property, that the person be extended notice of the judicial proceeding and an opportunity to be heard in that proceeding;[2] in this sense there is affinity between the notion of due process and the adversarial system, which is a strong method of ensuring an affected individual's opportunity to be heard. Beyond that affinity, however, the due process clause has also been understood to state a limited constitutional preference for adversarial procedure.[3] A third understanding of due process is a guarantee that the adjudicator will use reason (and reason-enhancing procedures) to arrive at judgments.[4] In still another sense, due

---

2. Mullane v. Central Hanover Bank & Trust Co., 339 U.S. 306 (1950).

3. Hansberry v. Lee, 311 U.S. 32, 40 (1940); Goldberg v. Kelly, 397 U.S. 254 (1970); Joint Anti-Fascist Refugee Comm. v. McGrath, 341 U.S. 123, 170 (1951) (Frankfurter, J., concurring).

4. *In re*: Japanese Elec. Prods. Antitrust Litig., 631 F.2d 1069 (3d Cir. 1980).

process expresses a preference for the use of procedures that minimize the sum of litigation costs and error costs.[5]

Two of these aspects of due process — adversarialism and efficiency — have come to mean much more than their constitutional minimum, and are critical assumptions in their own right.

2. Adversarialism. Our system is essentially an adversarial one, in which the litigants and their lawyers are placed in control of such central tasks as the selection of parties, claims, and court system; the accumulation of evidence; and the presentation of evidence and arguments to the decisionmaker. The decisionmaker is neutral and passive, and is supposed to render a decision based only the information that the litigants and their lawyers present. The parties themselves are even more passive. They provide information, comply with the remedy, monitor their lawyers' work, and pay their lawyers' fees; otherwise, they are inactive. This adversarial system is different from the world's other major procedural system — the civil law (or inquisitorial) system — in which the decisionmaker is much more active in shaping the case and accumulating the evidence.

Over the years there have been numerous strong defenders of the adversarial system, and many detractors. Its proponents argue that the adversary system, which places the incentive for developing information in the hands of those with the largest stake in the outcome, is the best vehicle for determining the truth; that the system acts as a check on the power of the wealthy; that it acts as a democratic check on the power of the judiciary; and that it best guarantees the fundamental personal right to make autonomous decisions such as whether, when, and where to sue another and how best to prosecute or defend against a claim. Opponents of the adversarial system argue that it can obfuscate the truth; that information can be more efficiently obtained by judicial officers; that the adversarial system provokes litigiousness, an unduly contentious attitude toward litigation, and needless expense; that the strong protection of one litigant's autonomy can often cause serious harm to the interests of others who have not yet chosen to litigate; and that, at least in the system's present form, litigants are too removed from critical litigation decisions to regard the notion of litigant autonomy seriously.[6]

---

5. Mathews v. Eldridge, 424 U.S. 319 (1976). This understanding of due process is especially consonant with the law-and-economics account of procedure. *See infra* n.7 and accompanying text.

6. For a more detailed review of some of these arguments and for further sources, see JAY TIDMARSH & ROGER H. TRANGSRUD, COMPLEX LITIGATION AND THE ADVERSARY SYSTEM 13-27, 120-26 (1998).

3. Efficiency. A third fundamental assumption of modern American procedure is efficiency. At one level, it is difficult to disagree with the notion that a procedural system should be as costless as possible; the costliness of litigation can often distort a person's incentives to act in socially appropriate ways, can force some plaintiffs with small but meritorious claims to decide not to sue, and (conversely) can blackmail some defendants into settling claims that lack merit purely in order to avoid litigation expenses.

One branch of this desire for efficient procedure is located in the law-and-economics approach to civil procedure. In this account, an ideal procedural system would render perfectly accurate judgments without cost. In the real world, however, procedural protections are costly, and judgments are sometimes wrong. In general, the more procedural protections there are, the less errors there will be; the fewer procedures, the more errors. Since errors in judgment inflict social costs (they induce parties to act in non-optimal ways due to the possibility of an inaccurate judgment), the "best" procedural system is one in which the sum total of the direct costs of litigation and the indirect costs of erroneous outcomes is at its lowest point.[7]

Many people, however, resist an undue emphasis on efficiency. Some assert that claims of distorted incentives and blackmail are overdrawn. Others reject the law-and-economics project generally, or else argue that too much zeal in trying to make the system run efficiently sacrifices other rights and values — such as litigant autonomy, individualized adjudication of claims, restrained judicial power, and jury trial — that are not easily quantified.

4. Jury Trial. The fourth cornerstone in American procedure is jury trial. To some extent this assumption is one of constitutional stature; the Seventh Amendment of the United States Constitution guarantees federal litigants a right to jury trial in "suits at common law, where the value in controversy shall exceed twenty dollars." Although this right has never been made applicable to state courts under the Fourteenth Amendment, 49 of our 50 states have similar, if not greater, jury trial rights in their own courts.

In ways that might not be immediately apparent, the existence of jury trial has had four ripple effects throughout our procedural system. First, because juries are drawn from the community and because it is inconvenient to keep recalling them, jury trial essentially commits a procedural system to a single climactic trial event in which all issues are resolved. This uniquely common law method of trial should be contrasted with the continuous trial method of most

---

7. *See* RICHARD A. POSNER,   (4th ed. 1992). ECONOMIC ANALYSIS OF LAW 549-50

civil law systems, in which discrete issues are determined in a series of separate hearings by a career judge who is well-versed in the law and often well-versed in the nature of the disputed transaction, and further proceedings in the case hinge on the outcome of the early hearings.

Second, a climactic trial event requires a procedural commitment to some across-the-board method of narrowing issues and/or discovering the facts before the trial begins. Expecting the parties to commence a trial with no knowledge of the legal issues or the facts is a poor way to ensure rational and efficient adjudication. Nor, our procedural ancestors thought, was it an appropriate way to constrain a fallible human institution like the jury. For much of the common law's history, the method through which the jury was constrained was the writ system. This system emphasized the narrowing of issues (in a rather draconian way), and did a poor job of assisting the parties in the development of facts; its emphasis on narrowing issues also frequently prevented a dispute involving multiple claims or parties from being resolved in a single action.

Third, since the jury is not knowledgeable about the particulars of the case or the law, and is arguably easily swayed by passion and prejudice, strict rules of evidence must govern the trial event.

Finally, the existence of jury trial resulted in the development of a parallel procedural system to handle cases in which the jury system worked poorly or in which the common law judges refused to become involved. Thus, alongside the common law jury system sprouted a system of equity, which relied in significant ways on the procedures of the civil law: No juries were used, pleading rules were more relaxed, techniques for the discovery of facts were available, and a continuous trial method was often employed. Equity also developed more generous rules for joining multiple parties and claims in one suit, thus making more likely the granting of complete relief. But equity was largely limited to the granting of injunctions; most circumstances in which the plaintiff sought damages, and even some in which he or she sought injunctive relief, required resort to the courts of law. It was impossible to join both legal and equitable matters in one proceeding.

Over the centuries, some of the distinctions between "law" (i.e., jury-tried actions) and "equity" (i.e., judge-tried actions) began to break down. When the Federal Rules of Civil Procedure were created in 1938, the Rules finally collapsed law and equity into a single system.[8] The Rules were premised on the existence of the common

---

8.   F.R.CIV.P. 2 ("There shall be   action.'").
one form of action to be known as 'civil

law's single climactic trial, but otherwise adopted many of equity's features. Still today, however, the Seventh Amendment right to jury trial has been understood to apply only to actions "at law," so that the factual issues on which a party is entitled to a jury depends on whether the action is considered to be a "legal" or an "equitable" one.

   5. *Pretrial Factual Development.* The heritage of next three cornerstones of our modern procedural system lies in the system of equity. The fifth assumption is the commitment to a short pleading stage followed by the pretrial development of factual issues. Contrary to the common law, which employed an intricate pleading stage to narrow issues for trial, equity's pleadings were (in theory, at least) simpler, and pleading mistakes were less critical. Taking this notion to an extreme, and borrowing further from the lessons of some states that had adopted the concept of "code pleading,"[9] the drafters of the Federal Rules required only "notice pleading," under which a plaintiff was suppose to provide only "a short and plain statement" of the basis of jurisdiction, the nature of the claim, and the relief requested.[10] The defendant's answer was comparably short.[11] Since the complaint and answer typically closes the pleadings stage,[12] federal pleadings today do a poor job of narrowing the issues and developing the facts for trial.

   To address this deficit, the drafters put into place a battery of devices to discover the relevant facts — interrogatories, requests for the production of documents, depositions, and physical or mental examinations.[13] They also developed a few weak issue-narrowing devices — the motion to dismiss, the request for admission, and the motion for summary judgment.[14] The discovery devices borrowed from (and expanded on) comparable devices available in equity, and the general tilting of the pretrial process from an issue-narrowing process to a fact-discovery process is consistent with equity as well.

   6. *Judicial Discretion.* The sixth assumption of our modern procedural system is a strong preference for judicial discretion. The roots of this preference lie in the system of equity, in which substantive merit rather than procedural nicety was supposed to dictate

---

   9. For a well-known work on code pleading, which somewhat overlooked the intricacies of code pleading in many states, see CHARLES E. CLARK, HANDBOOK OF THE LAW OF CODE PLEADING (1928). Professor Clark was a principal draftsman of the Federal Rules of Civil Procedure.

   10. F.R.CIV.P. 8(a). There are a few exceptions to this rule. *See* F.R.CIV.P. 9(b), (g).

   11. F.R.CIV.P. 8(b), (c).

   12. F.R.CIV.P. 7(a).

   13. *See* F.R.CIV.P. 30-35. Another tool that is sometimes regarded as a discovery device is the Rule 36 request for admission. On balance, however, it is probably better understood as an issue-narrowing device.

   14. *See* F.R.CIV.P. 12(b), 36, 56.

outcomes. This preference for merit over form — substance over procedure — became one of the rallying cries of procedural reformers in the early part of this century.[15] The method by which this preference was to be given effect was to create general, open-textured rules that imbued judges with significant discretion.[16] The belief was that rigid rules had led to excessive adversarialness and gamesmanship by lawyers, and that expert judges entrusted with discretion to implement general rules would ensure that substantive justice was accomplished.

This belief took hold with a vengeance in the Federal Rules, in which nearly a third of all the Rules (and well more than a third of the critical ones) explicitly or implicitly authorize judges to use discretion in their implementation.[17]

7. *Transactionalism.* The seventh assumption is "transactionalism" — in other words, the basic unit of litigation is the transaction or series of transactions out of which the legal claims and defenses arise. Organizing litigation around the transaction may seem both obvious and insignificant, but it is neither. For much of our common law history, the litigation unit was the writ — or in somewhat anachronistic modern parlance, the substantive theory of recovery. Thus, two entirely unrelated breach of contract claims could be brought together, while breach of contract and tort claims that arose out of the same set of historical events could not. Moreover, due to the limitations of the writ system, it was often difficult to join other parties — whether plaintiffs, defendants, or others with an interest in the outcome of the case — at common law. Equity had a contrary view, and prided itself on the ability to bring together all of the related equitable claims and all of the parties with an interest in the outcome of the case. As long as equity and law remained distinct, however, equity could not achieve the complete joinder of related claims and parties.

At the same time that the Federal Rules abolished the distinction between law and equity, they permitted the joinder of all claims arising out of the parties' transaction (as well as many that did not).[18] The 1938 Rules also allowed fairly liberal joinder of parties, but with some important restrictions. Many of these restrictions were eliminated in the 1966 amendments to the Federal Rules, when the rules of party joinder were changed to create more opportunities

---

15. Roscoe Pound, *The Decadence of Equity*, 5 COLUM. L. REV. 20 (1905).

16. Roscoe Pound, *Some Principles of Procedural Reform*, 4 ILL. L. REV. 388 (1910).

17. Stephen N. Subrin, *How Equity Conquered Common Law: The Federal Rules of Civil Procedure in Historical Context*, 135 U. PA. L. REV. 909 (1987).

18. *See* F.R.CIV.P. 13(a)-(b), 18.

for persons affected by a transaction to join in one case.[19] Although sensible in the main, we shall see that this impulse has created some of the most enduring problems of complex litigation.

   8. Trans-substantivity. The eighth and final assumption — "trans-substantivity" — was a new creation of the Federal Rules of Civil Procedure. This assumption responded to the reality that the various common law writs had developed distinct procedures, and equity had developed still other procedures, to resolve their respective causes of action. The basic idea of trans-substantivity is that the same procedural rules should be applied regardless of the substantive theory of recovery. Although it is a logical and desirable feature in a procedural system that organizes itself around transactions rather than substantive theories of recovery, trans-substantivity also aspires to a far more profound goal — the like procedural treatment of like cases. Put somewhat differently, different procedural rules should not result in different substantive outcomes for similarly situated parties.

   Fundamentally, trans-substantivity rests on a proposition that is hardly controversial among modern proceduralists, yet rarely is acknowledged in an explicit way: Procedural rules can affect substantive outcome (i.e., when applied to two hypothetically identical transactions, two different systems of procedure can result in different outcomes). The fact that procedure is not outcome-neutral in this sense is an unpleasant fact, and one with which procedural thinkers must be constantly concerned. As we shall see, it is not easy to design a system of one-size-fits-all procedural rules. Thus, a critical question in the design of any procedural system is which sort of differences in outcome we are willing to tolerate. Are we willing to allow two people injured in the same transaction to receive different, outcome-determinative procedural rules? How about people similarly injured in factually indistinguishable but historically separate transactions? How about treating a single claimant's tort and contract theories in procedurally different ways that cause the contract claim to succeed but the tort claim to fail? How about — and here we come to the immediate rub — developing different procedural rules for "complex" and "ordinary" cases that have the indirect and undesirable effect of making it easier (or harder) for the plaintiff in the "complex" case to win?

   Summary. Obviously these eight principles do not spell out each and every detail of our present procedural system. Nor are they entirely consistent with each other; for example, the desire for

---

   19. *See* F.R.CIV.P. 14, 19-24. Often these additional parties can assert additional claims and join additional parties. *See* F.R.CIV.P. 13 (g), (h).

efficiency in adjudication may conflict with the right to jury trial or a strong commitment to the adversary system. Likewise, in certain ways both judicial discretion and transactionalism makes the achievement of trans-substantivity harder. For now, we will not attempt a lexical ordering of the principles; instead, we will see how, in various ways, complex litigation poses problems for the full realization of these principles, and often brings the various principles into conflict with each other.

B. THE ROADMAP

The best method that we know to explore the problems that complex litigation poses for our procedural system is to examine the various phases of litigation and to see the ways in which complexity can manifest itself. In the first phase of the litigation, which we loosely call the "structural phase," the parties struggle to determine the structure of the litigation: who the participants will be, which court system (state or federal) will take jurisdiction of the case, and which court within that system will hear the case. In the second phase of the litigation, the "pretrial phase," the issues are narrowed for trial and the facts relevant to those issues are discovered. In the third phase, the "trial phase," certain issues, claims, and/or cases are definitively determined. Then, in the final "remedial phase," the remedy that flows from the trial is declared and implemented.

These four phases — from structure to pretrial to trial to remedy — are often intertwined, especially in complex litigation. Moreover, end-of-the-day matters such as trial management or remedial difficulties often influence theoretically antecedent structural and pretrial matters. These realities should be kept constantly in mind as we examine each of the phases of complex litigation in the following chapters.

Chapter 2

STRUCTURAL COMPLEXITY:
INTRA-DISTRICT CONSOLIDATION

In an adversarial system, you would expect that the tasks of choosing the party structure, the court system, and the courtroom would be performed by the parties rather than by the court. The American adversarial system bears out that expectation, and allocates the primary responsibility for these functions to the plaintiff. As a result, the plaintiff is often said to be "the master of the complaint."[1] In many complex cases, however, this approach to structuring the litigation creates serious, and sometimes crippling, problems.

The reason is that many complex cases involve hundred or thousands of plaintiffs and hundreds or thousands of defendants. Each plaintiff, left to his or her own devices, will seek the most privately advantageous court, court system, and party structure. In some cases, the plaintiff's goal will be to effect the complete joinder of all parties in one court; in other cases, the plaintiff's goal will be to effect something less than complete joinder. Even if the plaintiff wants to achieve optimal joinder, however, a panoply of rules — for instance, rules of subject matter jurisdiction, territorial jurisdiction, and venue — can frustrate the realization of this goal. In either event, the plaintiff will not achieve the level of joinder that would be regarded as socially optimal.

"Social optimality" carries two sometimes inconsistent meanings. The first meaning equates with efficiency; society prefers a litigation "package" that is large enough to prevent the needless re-litigation of questions common to many or all of the individual cases yet small enough to avoid unworkable pretrial, trial, and remedial problems in the case. Put differently, the economically ideal litigation package is the one that minimizes the sum of the re-litigation costs in future

---

1. *See* The Fair v. Kohler Die &   (Holmes, J.).
Specialty Co., 228 U.S. 22 (1913)

cases and the pretrial, trial, and remedial costs in the present case.[2]

The second meaning of social optimality equates with, for lack of a better phrase, "remedial equity." An aspect of the trans-substantive desire to treat like cases alike, "remedial equity" seeks to ensure that like-situated litigants receive both an equitable share of the remedy in the present case and also an equitable share of the remedy in relation to similarly situated individuals who are not parties to the present case. This latter concern — an equitable remedy in relation to nonparties — has two parts: a concern that present parties will, by virtue of being first, get too much remedy; or the obverse concern that later litigants will be able to undo the remedy that the parties labored to obtain in the original litigation. The first of these concerns can occur with either injunctive or monetary relief, the latter concern primarily with injunctive relief. One way to avoid the problem of remedial inequity is to join all similarly situated litigants in the original litigation, yet that approach threatens to skew litigation incentives and outcomes. Case studies have suggested that, until litigation "matures" through a series of individual trials and settlements, aggregation often favors one side or the other; in particular, aggregation of related cases at a very young stage may benefit defendants, while aggregation of related cases in an "adolescent" stage (i.e., after plaintiffs have achieved early breakthrough victories) may favor plaintiffs.[3] Moreover, experimental studies have shown that aggregation helps plaintiffs with weak cases and hurts plaintiffs with strong cases in terms of damages, and have generally (though not entirely) pro-plaintiff effects in terms of liability.[4]

Therefore, before we even begin to examine specific rules concerning the structure of the litigation, we see how structural complexity brings into conflict aspirations such as adversarialism,

2. This, of course, is simply the marginal cost understanding of the Hand Formula, put into procedural terms. *See* RICHARD A. POSNER, ECONOMIC ANALYSIS OF LAW 549-50 (4th ed. 1992). To use Judge Calabresi's phrase, this formula minimizes some of the "tertiary" accident costs. GUIDO CALABRESI, THE COSTS OF ACCIDENTS 225 (1970). Understood in this way, the formula in the text is somewhat inaccurate, since the ultimate social goal is to minimize the overall sum of accident costs, accident prevention costs, and tertiary accident costs. It might be possible that higher procedural (tertiary) costs will lead to lower accident costs or accident prevention costs. For our purposes, however, we can ignore this refinement.

3. *See* Francis E. McGovern, *Toward a Functional Approach for Managing Complex Litigation*, 53 U. CHI. L. REV. 440 (1986); Francis E. McGovern, *An Analysis of Mass Torts for Judges*, 73 TEX. L. REV. 1821 (1995).

4. *See* Irwin A. Horowitz & Kenneth S. Bordens, *The Effects of Outlier Presence — Plaintiff Population Size, and Aggregation of Plaintiffs on Simulated Civil Jury Decisions*, 12 L. & HUM. BEHAV. 209 (1988).

efficiency, trans-substantivity, and transactionalism. There is no easy or pat way to resolve these conflicts. The point from which we begin — whether a strong belief in the notion of litigant autonomy that underlies the adversarial system, a strong preference for efficiency, or a strong preference for the like treatment of like parties — might well determine the point at which we end.

Nor is the resolution of these conflicts a minor task. Structuring a large multi-party multi-forum suit in an optimal fashion is one of the signature problems of complex litigation. Its importance cannot be underestimated. This signature problem has multiple levels. For the moment, assume that we are capable of defining and then determining the socially optimal aggregation in related litigation. If we further assume that plaintiffs, exercising their rights as masters of the complaint, have already or will in the future bring separate suits, then the only way to achieve optimal aggregation is to have aggregation devices that can:

- Consolidate in one suit all the separate cases filed in the same courtroom or courthouse;

- Transfer to one courtroom all the cases filed in the same court system but in other districts or divisions of that system;

- Remove the cases filed in other court systems (or otherwise enjoin their separate prosecution) and place them into the court system in which the other cases have been aggregated; and

- Respond to litigation that has not yet been filed.

The first three types of devices operate on cases that have already been filed in dispersed forums — the problem of geographical dispersion. The fourth type of device responds to a somewhat different problem — temporal dispersion. Even if a way can be found to aggregate all geographically-dispersed cases, no aggregation solution can be complete if next week an entirely new group of plaintiffs can file suit on the same issues. Thus, some method of resolving the cases of *potential* plaintiffs is also essential. These potential plaintiffs break into two groups: those who have presently ripe claims but have not yet filed suit ("present claimants") and those whose claims have not yet ripened to the point that they can sue ("future claimants"). Complex cases often involve present claimants who sit on the sideline and watch the course of ongoing litigation; some complex cases (especially latent injury mass torts) also involve future claimants. Two responses to deal with present and future sideline-sitters suggest themselves: either force the joinder of the sidelines-sitters in a single case, or preclude the sideline-sitters from raising certain claims or defenses in future litigation.

If we represent the socially optimal level of aggregation by a point, then the entire set of doctrines required by structural difficulties might be represented schematically as a pyramid:

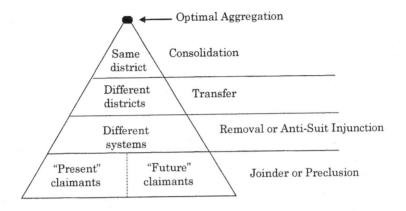

In attempting to accomplish this task of funneling litigation to an optimally aggregated point through consolidation, transfer, removal, injunctions, joinder, and preclusion, a host of doctrines that you might have encountered elsewhere — subject matter jurisdiction, territorial jurisdiction, venue, joinder under Rules 19, 20, and 24,[5] and claim and issue preclusion — come into play. But a series of doctrines that you are less likely to have encountered — Rule 42 consolidation, *forum non conveniens*, multidistrict transfers, anti-suit injunctions, abstention, stays, interpleader, class actions, and bankruptcy — are also critically important.

Over the course of the next four chapters, we move from the simplest to the hardest aggregation questions: from intra-district consolidation to intra-system aggregation to intersystem aggregation to aggregation of nonparties with present claims, and finally aggregation of non-litigants with future claims. As you explore these questions, keep in mind that the quest to achieve an optimal level of aggregation is not necessarily subject to a single answer. If the plaintiff(s)' private incentives for packaging match the socially optimal packaging of the case, the issue is whether the rules that determine the court and party structure are themselves adequate; in other words, are the rules both broad enough to achieve the desired

5. Here we refer to the Federal Rules of Civil Procedure. Most states have comparable rules of civil procedure. Since the federal system enjoys certain advantages as a forum for aggregation, it is most profitable to study the Federal Rules.

packaging and narrow enough to repulse the defendant(s)' efforts to defeat optimal packaging? Conversely, suppose that a plaintiff's private incentives vary from the socially optimal packaging. Here, the basic issue is whether the defendant(s) and/or the court should be able to overcome the plaintiff's strategic choice; in other words, are we required to accept a less optimal structure chosen by the plaintiff(s) when our rules permit a more optimal structure? This latter issue requires an examination not only of the relevant structural rules but also of the relative values of the adversary system, litigant autonomy, transactionalism, and trans-substantivity.

How important, ultimately, is the socially optimal packaging of a case? Are gains in efficiency of adjudication an adequate reason to change the plaintiff's right to choose a forum? Is the prevention of remedial inequity an adequate reason?

We begin our examination of these questions with the problem of intra-district consolidation. Consolidating cases separately filed in a single district brings into play four distinct doctrines: subject matter jurisdiction, territorial jurisdiction, venue, and consolidation. The first three doctrines determine whether a court in this system and in this district can properly entertain a case brought by the present plaintiff(s) against the present defendant(s). We will come back to these doctrines in Chapters 3 and 4 (on intra-system and intersystem consolidation, respectively). For now we will assume that the court has jurisdiction over the subject matter and the parties, and is also a proper venue for the case. This brings squarely into play the court's power to consolidate cases properly before it.

In the federal system, the basic rule permitting consolidation is Federal Rule of Civil Procedure 42(a), which provides:

> When actions involving a common question of law or fact are pending before the court, it may order a joint hearing or trial of any or all the matters in issue in the actions; it may order all the actions consolidated; and it may make such orders concerning proceedings therein as may tend to avoid unnecessary costs or delay.[6]

A parsing of the rule indicates only a single necessary requirement:

---

6. Prior to the creation of Rule 42, federal courts had held that they had inherent power, both in law and equity, to consolidate cases in the same district. Johnson v. Manhattan Ry. Co., 289 U.S. 479 (1933); Daniel J. Meador, *Inherent Judicial Authority in the Conduct of Litigation*, 73 TEX. L. REV. 1805 (1995).

"a common question of law or fact." Beyond that, the use of the word "may" suggests that the court retains broad discretion to consolidate cases — for pretrial purposes, for trial purposes, or for both — in appropriate circumstances.[7]

Since a single common question of law or fact is not a high threshold, the critical issue is usually whether the circumstances are appropriate for consolidation. For instance, suppose that two cases both alleging injury from the same fraudulent securities registration are filed in the same district. Should they be consolidated? Most of us would intuitively say "yes." Now suppose that the two victims of asbestos exposure, who worked for the same company but during different time periods and in different occupations, file separate suites in the same court. Should these cases be consolidated? Many of us might be less certain about the answer to this question. What if the two plaintiffs worked for different companies? What if there were two thousand, instead of two, plaintiffs?

As a general matter, courts have tended to answer these types of questions by asking whether consolidation would "promote judicial economy."[8] Increasingly, however, courts are recognizing that economy is not the only issue, and "[c]onsiderations of convenience and economy must yield to a paramount concern for a fair and impartial trial."[9] Relevant concerns in determining economy and fairness include "the specific risks of prejudice and possible confusion" if separate cases are consolidated, "the risk of inconsistent adjudications of common factual and legal issues" if the cases are not consolidated, "the burden on parties," "the length of time required to conclude multiple suits as against a single suit," and "the relative expense" of the consolidated and non-consolidated alternatives.[10] Thus, the appropriateness of consolidation cannot be answered without some sense of the pretrial and trial techniques that could be employed to resolve a large consolidated action — matters that we take up in Chapters 6 and 7.

7. *See* Johnson v. Celotex Corp., 899 F.2d 1281 (2d Cir.), *cert. denied*, 498 U.S. 920 (1990) ("The trial court has broad discretion to determine whether discretion is appropriate.").

8. Katz v. Realty Equities Corp. of New York, 521 F.2d 1354, 1358 (2d Cir. 1975).

9. *Johnson*, 899 F.2d at 1285.

10. Hendrix v. Raybestos-Manhattan, Inc., 776 F.2d 1492, 1495 (11th Cir. 1985). In the asbestos context, *Hendrix*, *Johnson* and other cases have relied on a standard set of criteria to determine whether the balance favors consolidation: (1) the existence of a common worksite, (2) similarity of plaintiff occupations, (3) similarity in time of exposure, (4) types of diseases suffered by plaintiffs, (5) whether plaintiffs were living or deceased, (6) status of discovery in each case, (7) whether the same counsel represented the parties in each case, and (8) types of cancer suffered by plaintiffs. *See Johnson*, 899 F.2d at 1285.

The case law on consolidation is mixed. For instance, in *Katz v. Realty Equities Corp. of New York*,[11] a case most noteworthy for its holding that a judge could order a single complaint to be filed in actions that were consolidated, the court found no abuse of discretion in the consolidation for pretrial purposes of twelve securities actions that arose out of a series of transactions allegedly designed to defraud the public. Likewise, in *Hendrix v. Raybestos-Manhattan, Inc.*,[12] the courts upheld consolidation for trial of the cases of four asbestos plaintiffs who worked out of the same union hall (frequently on the same jobs), who were exposed to asbestos during the same time frame, who suffered the same illness, and who had the same doctors and lawyers. In *Johnson v. Celotex Corp.*,[13] the bubble was stretched a bit farther: The cases of two asbestos workers who worked at the same jobsite, who suffered from asbestosis, and who were represented by the same lawyer were consolidated for trial, even though their exposures occurred during different time periods, the plaintiffs had different occupations, and one plaintiff had died of his exposure while the other remained alive.

On the other hand, *Malcolm v. National Gypsum Co.*[14] reversed as an abuse of discretion the trial consolidation of 48 asbestos cases involving plaintiffs injured in various New York powerhouses. The court thought that, due to different worksites, occupations of plaintiffs, times of exposure, and types of diseases involved, the district court had gone "too far in the interests of expediency and [sacrificed] basic fairness in the process.[15] Specifically, the court mentioned the possibility of jury confusion. While Rule 42 was "designed to achieve efficiency," the court cautioned that it was not intended to "compromis[e] a litigant's right under the Seventh Amendment to a jury trial."[16] Furthermore, in *In re: Repetitive Stress Injury Litigation*,[17] the court granted writs of mandamus against the pretrial consolidation of 44 cases against defendants that made or distributed products that allegedly caused an array of repetitive stress injuries. The only commonalities among the cases operated at a high level of generality, a fact which led the court to observe that "[t]he systemic urge to aggregate litigation must not be allowed to trump our dedication to individual justice."[18]

It is difficult to draw definite lessons from such an array of cases. No easy distinction reconciles them all. For instance, it is tempting

11. 521 F.2d 1354 (2d Cir. 1975).

12. 776 F.2d 1491 (11th Cir. 1985).

13. 899 F.2d 1281 (2d Cir.), *cert. denied*, 498 U.S. 920 (1990).

14. 995 F.2d 346 (2d Cir. 1993).

15. *Id.* at 354.

16. *Id.*

17. 11 F.3d 368 (2d Cir. 1993).

18. *Id.* at 373 (quoting *In re Brooklyn New York Asbestos Litig.*, 971 F.2d 831, 853 (2d Cir. 1992)).

to say that consolidation should be used primarily in small-stakes securities litigation like *Katz*, in which it makes little economic sense to bring individual suits and the argument for individualized justice is therefore the weakest. But consolidation was allowed in large-stakes tort cases like *Hendrix* and *Johnson*. It is tempting to suggest that consolidation should be easier in "mature" litigation in which the lack of novel issues should make joint treatment especially efficient. But *Malcolm* suggests that maturity is not dispositive, and the lack of maturity in *Katz* was not an insuperable barrier. It is also tempting to suggest that consolidation is possible as long as the plaintiffs consent to consolidation, but that line clearly does not work, for the plaintiffs consented in *Malcolm* and *Repetitive Stress Injuries*. Another idea is that pretrial consolidations, as opposed to trial consolidations, should be easier to obtain, yet *Repetitive Stress Injuries* refused to permit even pretrial consolidation. A final way to reconcile cases is to argue that the number of consolidated action matters: two, four, or twelve actions can be consolidated, but forty-four or forty-eight cannot. But this line suggests that consolidation is least helpful when it is most needed — when hundreds of cases threaten to create great inefficiencies or serious remedial inequities.

Thus, even the "simple" case of intra-district consolidation raises hard questions of the proper roles of efficiency, litigant autonomy, jury trial, judicial discretion, transactionalism, and (to the extent that consolidation is easier in some types of cases than others) trans-substantivity. In Chapter 5 we will return to another method for achieving intra-district consolidation by means of the joinder of related parties' claims in one case, rather than through the consolidation of cases that are separately filed. For now, however, we see that even the simplest form of aggregation is surprisingly difficult. This augurs poorly for the harder aggregation questions to which we now turn.

Chapter 3

STRUCTURAL COMPLEXITY: INTRA-SYSTEM AGGREGATION

Large-scale litigation often involves the filing of different cases in different courts within a single court system.[1] Cases are filed in different courts for two reasons: structural limitations and strategic choices.

A. STRUCTURAL LIMITATIONS ON INTRA-SYSTEM AGGREGATION

Two types of structural impediments prevent plaintiffs who would otherwise be willing to file their cases in a single court from doing so: First, there may not be a single court that has territorial jurisdiction over all of the plaintiffs or all of the defendants, and second, venue rules may make it impossible to join all related cases in a single court. For instance, suppose Smith, a citizen of New Hampshire, is injured in Maine by asbestos manufactured in North Carolina by XYZ Co., a citizen of New York. XYZ does no business in New Hampshire. Jones, a citizen of California, is injured in Arizona, by asbestos manufactured by QRS Corp., a citizen of Oregon, in its Idaho plant; QRS does no business in California. Assume as well that XYZ does business only on the eastern seaboard, and QRS only on the West Coast. Finally, assume that the efficiencies of consolidated treatment of the two cases would make it desirable to handle them together; the cases will raise common factual issues regarding the conduct of the asbestos industry, and the same lawyer represents both Smith and Jones. Where can Smith bring suit? Where can Jones bring suit? Is there any forum within the system in which both claims may be filed together?

---

1. In this context a "single court system" refers to either the federal court or the state court system. Hence, a case filed in state court in Maine is in the same system as a case filed in state court in Hawaii, while cases filed in state court in Maine and federal court in Maine are not.

Rules of territorial jurisdiction and venue limit the ability of a court to hear cases that have no connection to the court. For instance, it seems intuitively correct to say that a state court in Kansas could not hear Smith's case against XYZ or Jones's case against QRS even if the plaintiffs wanted a Kansas forum; while it would not be unfair to force Smith or Jones to submit to the jurisdiction of a Kansas court (after all, they voluntarily chose to bring their cases there, so they could be deemed to have waived any claims of unfairness), it would be quite unfair to XYZ or QRS to force them to defend a case in a state with which they have no connection. Moreover, the inefficiencies of trying these cases in a distant Kansas forum would, in most cases, make the idea very unappealing.

Territorial jurisdiction and venue doctrines respond to these concerns of unfairness and inefficiency. Doctrines of territorial jurisdiction determine which courts have the authority to hear a case involving certain plaintiffs and defendants. The doctrines can be described many different ways. A common division is to break the matter into a court's power to adjudicate everyone's interest in a piece of property located within the court's territorial boundaries (*in rem* jurisdiction), a court's power to adjudicate a defendant's personal liability (*in personam* jurisdiction), a court's power to adjudicate the plaintiff's and defendant's relative interests in property located within the court's territorial boundaries (*quasi-in-rem* jurisdiction), and a court's power to adjudicate a defendant's personal liability up to the extent of the defendant's interests in property located within the court's territorial boundaries (a different form of *quasi-in-rem* jurisdiction). But recent trends in Supreme Court jurisprudence have made these divisions less relevant, especially in the *quasi-in-rem* area;[2] and in any event, in most complex cases the defendant's liability (and hence the jurisdiction) is personal. Thus, for our purposes a more useful description is to distinguish between general and specific jurisdiction. The defendant's presence or level of activity may be so great in some states that the courts of that state are regarded as having a *general* power to adjudicate disputes involving the defendant, including disputes that have no specific connection to the state. In other states, however, a defendant's activities within the state are more limited, so that it might be fair to allow the court to hear disputes relating to those *specific* activities but not to hear disputes arising from activities unrelated to activities within the state.

If jurisdiction over a party is specific rather than general, and the claim is brought in the state court system, the question whether

2. Shaffer v. Heitner, 433 U.S. 186 (1977).

a defendant's activities are adequate enough to establish territorial jurisdiction is a two-fold one: first, whether a state statute or rule authorizes such jurisdiction; and second, whether the due process clause of the Fourteenth Amendment permits this jurisdiction. The answer to this latter inquiry is found in the Supreme Court's well-known "minimum contacts" test,[3] which in recent years has required an inquiry into questions of "power" (or a defendant's "purposeful availment" of a state's rules) and "convenience."[4]

Although there may be no constitutional necessity for them to do so, the federal district courts have (with only a few exceptions[5]) adopted the territorial jurisdiction rules of the state in which the district is located.[6] The effect of territorial jurisdiction rules, therefore, is to limit the number of courts that can hear a particular case. In our hypothetical, XYZ could certainly be sued by Smith in a New York state or federal court for any claims (general jurisdiction); would also be amenable to suit in North Carolina (either general jurisdiction if the company's presence is great enough, or specific jurisdiction with respect to products made in North Carolina); and might be subject to suit in Maine (specific jurisdiction, in which issues of the Maine's "long-arm" statute and XYZ's level of contacts are relevant). Suit in New Hampshire (specific jurisdiction) is more problematic, given the more attenuated nature of the state's relationship to XYZ, though the Supreme Court has not yet held on these facts that jurisdiction is impermissible. Similarly, QRS could be sued by Jones in Oregon and Idaho, might be suable in Arizona, and is arguably suable in California. Notice that there is no court that overlaps the two cases and has power to adjudicate the claims against both defendants.

The rules of venue operate in a similar way, but with a somewhat different purpose — to allocate a case to an appropriate courthouse within a single court system. At the federal level, for instance, there are a total of 94 geographically defined districts. The rules of venue determine which districts are proper "venues" for a case and which are not. At the state level, no similar system of allocating cases among the courts of the various states exists. Although most states have developed a doctrine of *forum non conveniens* to dismiss those

---

3. International Shoe Co. v. Washington, 326 U.S. 310 (1945).

4. World-Wide Volkswagen Corp. v. Woodson, 444 U.S. 286 (1980); Burger King Corp. v. Rudzewicz, 471 U.S. 462 (1985); Asahi Metal Indus. Co. v. Superior Court of California, 480 U.S. 102 (1987).

In many cases, transitory physical presence within a state also can vest a court with jurisdiction over the person. Burnham v. Superior Court of California, 495 U.S. 604 (1990).

5. *See* F.R.CIV.P. 4(k)(1)(B)-(D), 4(k)(2).

6. F.R.CIV.P. 4(k)(1)(A).

cases when the venue of a particular state is regarded as too inconvenient, this is a doctrine of refusal rather than a doctrine of acceptance.[7]

The federal venue rules used to limit significantly the number of federal district courts that could hear a case. Liberalizing amendments in the late 1980's and early 1990's expanded the number of federal courts with venue. For cases based only on a federal court's diversity of citizenship jurisdiction,[8] venue is proper in the district in which any defendant resides (as long as all defendants reside in one state), or any district in which a "substantial part of the events or omissions giving rise to the claim occurred."[9] In the event that no district meets either of these criteria, then venue is proper in any district in which "any defendant is subject to personal jurisdiction at the time the action is commenced."[10] For all other cases within a federal court's jurisdiction,[11] the first two methods for determining venue are the same as for a diversity case — any defendant's district of residence if all defendants reside in one State, or any district in which a "substantial part" of the activities in the case occurred.[12] The third proper venue is a bit different; if neither of the other two methods of determining venue results in the selection of a proper venue, then venue is proper in any district "in which any defendant may be found."[13]

As a result of the recent amendments to the venue statute, territorial jurisdiction and venue have been brought in much closer alignment. This is most obvious in the default provisions of §§ 1391(a)(3) and (b)(3), in which the absence of any other suitable venue automatically lodges the venue in a federal court with territorial jurisdiction over the defendants. With regard to corporate defendants, another alignment occurs: According to § 1391(c), a corporation is "deemed to reside" for purposes of §§ 1391(a)(1) and

7. Courts of a single state may have venue rules that determine the particular county or counties in which a case may be heard, and thus are comparable to the rules of the federal system. Since our focus is on the state courts as a single system, see *supra* n.1, these rules need not be specifically considered.

8. 28 U.S.C. § 1332. For a description of this jurisdiction, see *infra* at pp. 46-48.

9. 28 U.S.C. §§ 1391(a)(1), (a)(2).

10. 28 U.S.C. § 1391(a)(3).

11. The main font of this jurisdiction, federal question jurisdiction, is described *infra* at pp. 44-46.

12. 28 U.S.C. §§ 1391(b)(1), (b)(2).

13. 28 U.S.C. § 1391(b)(3). This phrase encompasses situations in which a federal court has jurisdiction over a defendant, as in (a)(3), but it also includes a limited number of other situations. *See* 15 CHARLES A. WRIGHT ET AL., FEDERAL PRACTICE & PROCEDURE § 3802.1 (Supp. 2002). Thus, (b)(3) is somewhat broader than (a)(3).

(b)(1), "in any judicial district in which it is subject to personal jurisdiction at the time the action is commenced."[14] Thus, to use our hypothetical, venue in a case against XYZ lies in at least one of the federal districts in New York and at least one of the federal districts in North Carolina, as well as possibly in the federal districts in Maine and New Hampshire.

Venue rules operate together with territorial jurisdictional rules, rather than in derogation of them; both sets of rules must be satisfied in order for a court to hear a case. In some situations, therefore, the venue rules can contribute to the forced dispersal of related cases. Consider these three scenarios:

(1) Assume that Smith has lung cancer, and believes that his cancer resulted from his exposure both to XYZ's asbestos and to cigarettes. The cigarettes were made by Black Lung Co., which is incorporated and headquartered in Virginia. Black Lung markets its products in Massachusetts, Vermont, and New Hampshire. Smith buys the cigarettes in New Hampshire. Using a minimum contacts analysis,[15] it would seem that Black Lung cannot be sued in Maine, nor in New York or North Carolina. Unless XYZ is amenable to suit in New Hampshire, which is uncertain, there seems to be no federal court that can hear the entire case.

(2) Suppose that XYZ sells its asbestos to a distributor in Maine (JKL) that supplies industries in Maine and New Hampshire, and JKL distributes the asbestos to a local Maine retailer (MNO). Smith wants to sue XYZ, JKL, and MNO in one case, alleging state law claims. In this situation, the United States District Court for the District of Maine would be the only court in which venue is clearly proper; all three defendants "reside" in the state (§ 1391(a)(1)), and a "substantial part" of the case arose in Maine (§ 1391(a)(2)).[16] So far, so good. But now suppose that Green, a citizen of New Jersey, works at a Brooklyn shipyard using asbestos made by XYZ, and distributed

---

14. For states that have more than one federal judicial district, § 1391(c) makes provision for the residency of corporations that have sufficient contacts with a State as a whole, but insufficient contacts with one or more of the federal judicial districts within the State. Essentially, a corporation is resident only in those districts which, if it were a State, would have territorial jurisdiction over the defendant. If there is no such district, then residency exists in the district with the "most significant contacts."

15. *See supra* nn.3-4 and accompanying text.

16. Section 1391(a)(3) would not apply, since jurisdiction exists under (a)(1) and/or (a)(2). Jurisdiction might exist in North Carolina, since the manufacture of the asbestos occurred there. Since there would appear to be no territorial jurisdiction over MNO, and arguably over JKL, in North Carolina, however, a federal court in North Carolina would not appear to be an appropriate forum.

and sold by a Brooklyn distributor (DEF) and a Brooklyn retailer (GHI). In Green's case, the only federal forum that has territorial jurisdiction over XYZ, DEF, and GHI and venue over the case is the United States District Court for the Eastern District of New York. Even though it might be advantageous to adjudicate the facts underlying XYZ's liability only once, territorial jurisdiction and venue rules will keep the cases of Smith and Green apart.

(3) In the hypothetical with which this section began, the cases of Smith against XYZ and Jones against QRS could benefit from joint handling. As we have seen, no court would have jurisdiction over both defendants or venue to hear a consolidated case.

It is possible to respond to these three scenarios by saying that (1) the Black Lung situation is an outlier; in a time of national marketing, some state is likely to have minimum contacts with both of the defendants; (2) joining together the cases of Smith and Green is undesirable; the Maine distributor and retailer have no interest in Green's case, the New York distributor and retailer have no interest in Smith's case, and the possibility that New York law might apply in Green's case and Maine law in Smith's case makes the joint treatment of the two cases undesirable; and (3) similarly, the consolidation of the cases of Smith and Jones is undesirable.[17] The second and third of these responses are, of course, built upon assumptions concerning both choice of law and the inefficiency or unfairness of consolidated treatment that may prove false in a significant number of cases. The first response may also often prove inaccurate, at least when regional distributors, local retailers, and local medical professionals are attractive additional defendants. The simple fact is that territorial jurisdiction and venue rules can prevent a single court from hearing all aspects of a controversy.

B. Strategic Behavior

Until now, we have focused on how rules of territorial jurisdiction and venue can force the dispersal of the controversy across numerous forums within a single system. But the dispersal of cases across courts within a single system is often the result of strategic choices made by plaintiffs. Assuming that XYZ has harmed five people who lived in five different states, each of the putative plaintiffs (who are, recall, the masters of their complaints) will look for the court that provides the greatest chance of a favorable outcome — in other

---

17. On the choice of law question, see Jay Tidmarsh & Roger H. Trangsrud, Complex Litigation and the Adversary System ch.7 (1998); American Law Institute, Complex Litigation: Statutory Recommendations and Analysis ch.6 (1994).

words, the court that provides the best combination of substantive law, procedural law, convenience, and practical considerations such as docket speed, judicial attitude, and jury sympathy. It can be expected that these five plaintiffs might choose to bring their cases in a number of different districts.

This fact is the dark flip-side of the expansion of the rules of territorial jurisdiction and venue. In a hypothetical world in which only one court had jurisdiction over XYZ and venue for the case — say, the Western District of North Carolina — there would be no dispersal problem; all cases against XYZ would be filed in that court.[18] In the real world, however, expansive rules of territorial jurisdiction and venue give each plaintiff the choice of multiple forums. For instance, Smith would seem to be able to sue XYZ in New York and North Carolina, probably in Maine, and possibly in New Hampshire. Even if we assume that all four of the other plaintiffs decide that it is most advantageous for them to sue XYZ in North Carolina, Smith can still bring suit in Maine if it is advantageous for him to do so. Indeed, unless all five plaintiffs are represented by the same lawyers, the odds that all five plaintiffs will choose one forum in which to bring their cases are high, and as the number of different plaintiffs and plaintiffs' lawyers increases beyond five, the odds grow higher. The adversarial focus on private interests can lead to choices that, from a public perspective, are unwise.

Again, therefore, if optimal aggregation is to occur, mechanisms to permit the aggregation of cases filed in different courts within a single system must be developed. Such mechanisms, however, interfere with two of the foundational assumptions of our procedural system: the autonomy of each plaintiff to bring suit in the forum of his or her own choosing and, to the extent that outcomes in aggregated cases differ from those in non-aggregated cases, the like procedural treatment of like cases. The critical questions are when such mechanisms already do — and when they should — override our preferences for adversarial control and trans-substantivity.

C. RESPONSES

Three types of responses can achieve the consolidation of related cases located in various courts of the same system: changes in settled rules of territorial jurisdiction and venue, negative responses such as dismissals or stays of litigation in all forums other than a

---

18. Of course, there would be serious problems with such a draconian rule. Such a rule would make impossible the aggregated handling of separate cases against XYZ and QRS, and would also probably be unworkable if Smith wanted to sue multiple defendants.

designated forum, and positive responses that affirmatively transfer all cases within a system to a designated forum. As we shall see, all three types of response have been employed, though the patchwork of available doctrines still leaves significant gaps in achieving the goal of intra-system aggregation.

1. Changing Settled Rules

One possible solution to the problem of aggregation-frustrating rules of territorial jurisdiction and venue is to legislate special rules. In a few instances Congress has permitted federal courts to use "nationwide service of process" — in other words, to permit any federal court to obtain jurisdiction over a defendant as long as the defendant has minimum contacts with the nation as a whole. Among the types of cases in which nationwide service of process is permissible are Clayton Act antitrust claims,[19] certain securities claims,[20] RICO claims,[21] ERISA claims,[22] and statutory interpleader actions.[23] Additionally, in cases based on federal law in which the defendant does not have minimum contacts with any state, but does have minimum contacts with the country as a whole, nationwide service of process is permitted under the Federal Rules of Civil Procedure.[24] Despite occasional calls for a change,[25] however, there is not presently a general statute or rule authorizing nationwide service of process in other cases that would benefit from aggregated handling.[26]

More expansive rules of territorial jurisdiction would not, of course, be sufficient. Special venue rules would also need to be legislated. The statutes presently authorizing nationwide service of process often include special venue provisions. For instance, venue in a securities case is available in "any district wherein the defendant is found or is an inhabitant or transacts business,"[27] and interpleader actions can be brought in "the judicial district in which one or more of the claimants resides."[28] Note that the latter form of venue statute is more helpful to the cause of aggregation than the former: In the

19. 15 U.S.C. § 22.

20. 15 U.S.C. § 78aa.

21. 18 U.S.C. § 1865(d).

22. 29 U.S.C. § 1451(d).

23. 28 U.S.C. § 2361.

24. F.R.CIV.P. 4(k)(2).

25. ALI, *supra* n.17, § 3.08.

26. A nice question is whether a federal court can exercise territorial jurisdiction over a defendant on a claim for which there is no nationwide service of process, as long as the defendant is properly before the court on a related claim for which there is nationwide service of process. Some courts have been willing to exercise "pendent personal jurisdiction" over defendants with regard to the related claims. *See* TIDMARSH & TRANGSRUD, *supra* n.17, at 274.

27. 15 U.S.C. § 78aa.

28. 28 U.S.C. § 2361.

XYZ-QRS situations, the latter form of venue allows venue in either the federal court in New Hampshire (Smith's residence) or the federal court for the district in California in which Jones resides; the former venue statute might still not provide a single venue for the entire controversy.

One of the oft-cited advantages of federal courts as a forum for aggregated litigation is the ability of Congress to create such service of process and venue statutes. No state legislature acting on its own initiative could, within the constraints of the Fourteenth Amendment, do so. Thus far, however, Congress has shown little interest in the issue.[29]

Rather than waiting for legislative change, the courts themselves could attempt a different solution to the problem of aggregation-frustrating jurisdictional and venue rules by creating special interpretations of the rules that apply to complex litigation. For instance, in the QRS-XYZ situation, a court could reconceive the relevant minimum contacts to be the contacts of the entire asbestos industry to the state of Maine. Thus, QRS, which admittedly had no direct contacts with Maine, could be seen as participating in an industry that did have such contacts; its absorption of a market share in other parts of the country made the Maine market more desirable or available for its competitors. This generous understanding of territorial jurisdiction, at least in the context of corporate defendants, could then carry over under §§ 1391(a)(1) and (c) to establish the necessary venue as well.[30]

There are a few cases that suggest just such a willingness to rethink jurisdiction and venue rules for complex cases. The most noteworthy is *In re DES Cases*,[31] in which Judge Jack B. Weinstein, one of the country's leading scholars on the subject of complex litigation, thoroughly critiques the inadequacy of present rules of territorial jurisdiction in mass tort cases, and proposes abrogation of the present rules in favor of a two-step inquiry: a forum state's

---

29. The constitutionality of a nationwide service of process statute for claims based on state law is not entirely certain. *Cf.* ALI, *supra* n.17, at 155 ("The power of Congress to supply a federal national-contacts long-arm statute for use in complex cases seems clear."). It is also not clear that Congress could delegate authority to the states to create nationwide service of process rules, or that the states could, by interstate compact, develop nationwide service of process rules.

30. With non-corporate defendants, a court would probably need to develop a generous understanding of the "substantial part" language of §§ 1391(a)(2) and (b)(2).

31. 789 F. Supp. 552 (E.D.N.Y. 1992) *appeal dismissed,* 7 F.3d 20 (2d Cir. 1993). A similar, also interesting opinion was written in the related state litigation. *In re* New York County DES Litigation, 202 A.D.2d 6, 615 N.Y.S. 2d 882 (1994).

"appreciable interest in the litigation" and the defendant's inability to show that it "is unable to mount a defense in the forum state without suffering relatively substantial hardship."[32] This proposal, however, was in the alternative, and therefore dicta. Moreover, *DES Cases* involved *sui generis* New York tort law that in some situations made a manufacturer responsible for injuries that it did not cause, as long as it manufactured identical goods for use in the national market. Most states would not impose such liability; hence, *DES Cases* is more interesting as a blueprint for future change than as an edifice built upon present law.

In any event, statutory or judicial changes to territorial jurisdiction and venue rules help only to overcome the structural impediments to aggregation in our present system. They do not address the problem of aggregation-frustrating strategic choices; indeed, to the extent that these changes open up more potential forums, they increase the opportunity for aggregation-frustrating strategic behavior. At the same time, these changes would create special procedural rules in a subset of cases, raising questions of fairness. Whether other solutions — such as dismissals, stays, or transfers — can accomplish the same ends with less violence to our preferences for litigative autonomy and "like treated alike" procedure is the issue to which we now turn.

2. Dismissals and Stays

Another alternative to accomplish the aggregation of cases dispersed throughout a single court system is to use dismissals or stays. The idea of a dismissal is that the court or courts in which cases are inconveniently located dismiss them, hopefully causing the plaintiffs to re-file in a more convenient forum. Stays come in two types. First, a court in which a case was inappropriately located (from an aggregation viewpoint) can stay itself from proceeding with the case before it; or, second, a court in which all the cases should appropriately be aggregated can issue a stay that prevents the cases from proceeding in any other forum.

The dismissal and the two types of stay are indirect methods of aggregation. None of the techniques effects an aggregation *per se*; they merely render impossible the maintenance of disaggregated litigation and then rely on the self-interest of the plaintiff to re-file in the appropriate forum. The basic effect of a dismissal and of a stay of the first type (a self-stay) is the same; the only difference is whether the court retains jurisdiction over the case in the event that something untoward happens in the aggregated forum. The second

32. 789 F. Supp. at 587.

form of stay, however, is more advantageous than either the dismissal or the self-stay in several ways; in particular, rather than relying on the coordinated efforts of multiple judges to divest themselves of cases pending before them, the second type of stay requires only a single order of a single judge in the appropriate forum.

The devices of dismissal and stay are thus capable of dealing with the problem of strategic plaintiff choices that result in dispersed litigation, but they are relatively powerless to overcome structural impediments to single-forum aggregation. For instance, neither a dismissal nor a self-stay confers territorial jurisdiction or venue on the desirable forum; if we assume that Kansas is the most desirable forum for the aggregation of asbestos cases, dismissing Smith's case against XYZ in Maine or self-staying Jones's case against QRS in Arizona does not give a court in Kansas the power to hear the case against either XYZ or QRS. Conversely, the second type of stay, which precludes plaintiffs from maintaining a suit elsewhere than in a designated forum, vests no omnipotence in the issuing court; assuming that a court in Kansas issued an order precluding the maintenance of asbestos cases in any other forum, only plaintiffs and defendants over whom the court had jurisdiction would be required to obey the order.[33] Thus, effective use of the dismissal or the self-stay requires congenial defendants that accede to the orders of a court that has no jurisdiction over them, and the second form of stay requires both congenial plaintiffs and congenial defendants.

Of course, even when these problems can be overcome, other conceptual difficulties arise. Under what theory can an admittedly appropriate forum choice by a plaintiff be overridden by the defendants? May the court override the plaintiff's choice even if the defendants do not object to the forum? In particular, are convenience or the court's interest in aggregated handling sufficient reasons for dismissals or stays?

a. Forum Non Conveniens *Dismissals.* As these questions and concerns suggest, intra-system dismissals and stays tend to be ineffective in aggregating large-scale litigation. To begin with, the dismissal device — called, most typically, a dismissal on *forum non conveniens* grounds — has little remaining vitality at the federal level; as we shall see shortly, more recently enacted statutes that permit one federal court to transfer a case directly to another federal

---

33. It is axiomatic that orders from a court that has no jurisdiction over a party do not bind that party. For a case in which a court refused to issue the second type of stay due to a lack of jurisdiction over plaintiffs, see *In re* General Motors Corp. Pick-Up Truck Fuel Tank Prod. Liab. Litig., 134 F.3d 133 (3d Cir. 1998). On the question of territorial jurisdiction over plaintiffs, see *infra* ch.5, nn.191-201 and accompanying text.

district court have made *forum non conveniens* unnecessary in most cases. In fact, today *forum non conveniens* has importance in only two situations. The first is the field of transnational litigation, in which a federal or state court might feel that it is an inconvenient forum in comparison to a foreign court.[34] The second situation involves cases brought in state court. Despite the drafting of a model Uniform Transfer of Litigation Act in 1991, the states have not yet adopted interstate transfer mechanisms akin to those in federal system, so *forum non conveniens* dismissals remain the primary vehicle for handling inconveniently located state court litigation.[35]

Even where it is still operative, the *forum non conveniens* doctrine was not developed and has not evolved with the particular needs of complex litigation in mind. As the Supreme Court has said, "a plaintiff's choice of forum should rarely be disturbed"; only when there exists either "oppressiveness or vexation to a defendant . . . out of all proportion to plaintiff's convenience" or "considerations affecting the court's own administrative and legal problems"[36] can a court dismiss a case on *forum non conveniens* grounds. The Supreme Court has developed a list of "private interest factors" that should be considered in answering the first question, and a list of "public interest factors" to help answer the second.[37] Some states use a somewhat different list of factors, though they may not make a practical difference.[38]

When a court does grant a *forum non conveniens* dismissal, it can attach to the dismissal certain conditions that ameliorate the hardship to the side disadvantaged by the dismissal.[39]

---

34. Piper Aircraft Co. v. Reyno, 454 U.S. 235 (1981).

35. A few states have maintained an "open courts" tradition in which the *forum non conveniens* doctrine does not operate, or at least is narrowly construed. The most noteworthy of these states was Texas, though in 1991 it enacted a limited *forum non conveniens* statute. *See* TEX. CIV. PROC. & REM. CODE § 71.051.

36. *Reyno*, 454 U.S. at 241 (quoting Koster v. Lumbermans Mut. Cas. Co., 330 U.S. 518, (1947)).

37. Gulf Oil Corp. v. Gilbert, 330 U.S. 501, 508-09 (1947). The private factors include the ease of obtaining evidence in the two forums, the availability and costs of witnesses in the two forums, and other "practical prob-lems that make trial of a case easy, expeditious and inexpensive." Public interest factors include court congestion, "the local interest in having localized controversies decided at home," the desirability of having the trial in a forum whose law will apply or which avoids unnecessary choice of law difficulties, and the unfairness of burdening citizens of a disinterested state with jury duty. *Id.*

38. *See, e. g.*, LA.C.C.P. 123 (dismissal appropriate when the claim is predicated on acts occurring outside of state, and "the convenience of parties and witnesses" and "the interests of justice" require dismissal).

39. *See In re* Union Carbide Corp. Gas Plant Disaster, 809 F.2d 195 (2d Cir. 1987).

b. Kerotest *Stays.* In a few instances a court will stay its own proceeding in favor of related litigation in another court in the same system. In the federal system, such a stay is sometimes called a "*Kerotest* stay," after the case in which the Supreme Court first accepted the idea.[40] Like many cases that have successfully invoked the doctrine, *Kerotest* involved a patent infringement claim in which the patent owner and the alleged infringer filed suits against each other in different districts. The usual presumption in the *Kerotest* situation in that the second-filed case is stayed in favor of the first-filed case, although there are exceptions.[41] Some state courts have developed a doctrine akin to the *Kerotest* stay, and stay a case in favor of litigation in a court of another state.[42]

The *Kerotest* stay has traditionally been used only when the parties and the essential claims in the two cases are the same. The stay has been little used when the parties in the two cases are different, as they often are in complex litigation. Courts have never extended the *Kerotest* stay so that a court hearing Jones's case against QRS would stay its hand in favor of the court hearing the case between Smith and XYZ.

c. Anti-Suit Injunctions. The second form of stay, in which one court enjoins related proceedings in other courts, is far less cumbersome than a *forum non conveniens* dismissal or the *Kerotest* stay, and far more certain of achieving the objective of single-forum aggregation. Thus far, however, this second form, which is sometimes called an "anti-suit injunction," has been used only in the circumstances in which the *Kerotest* stay would have been proper.[43] Thus, as an aggregation device, the anti-suit injunction is no panacea. Moreover, the anti-suit injunction raises certain comity problems that a self-stay does not. First, some courts, arguing that "considerations [of judicial economy] should rarely if ever lead to such broad curtailment of the access to the courts," have been reluctant to permit such injunctions except in "extreme circumstances."[44] Second, it is one thing for a court to stay its own hand, but quite another thing for a court to warn another court of equal stature off the field. Hence, some courts have suggested that the anti-suit injunction should not

---

40. Kerotest Mfg. Co. v. C-O-Two Fire Equip. Co., 342 U.S. 180, 183 (1952) (permitting a stay as an exercise of "wise judicial administration, giving regard to conservation of judicial resources and comprehensive disposition of litigation").

41. William Gluckin & Co. v. Int'l Playtex Corp., 407 F.2d 177 (2d Cir. 1969); Kahn v. General Motors Corp.,

889 F.2d 1078 (Fed. Cir. 1989).

42. *See* TIDMARSH & TRANGSRUD, *supra* n.17, at 437, 470.

43. *See, e.g.,* Schauss v. Metals Depository Corp., 757 F.2d 649 (5th Cir. 1985).

44. Span-Eng Associates v. Weidner, 771 F.2d 464, 468, 469 (10th Cir. 1985) (quotations omitted).

be liberally used, even in situations in which it might be applied.[45] Third, anti-suit injunctions have not always been heeded in the enjoined court, a fact which increases friction and creates complex full faith and credit problems.[46] Indeed, when both forums issue anti-suit injunctions, the ensuing staredown can create true nightmares for the litigants.[47] Finally, the anti-suit injunction has led, predictably, to the issuance of "anti-anti-suit injunctions," in which a court orders the parties not to seek an anti-suit injunction in any other courts.[48]

As an additional complicating fact, the exact authority for the issuance of anti-suit injunctions is unclear. For federal courts the apparent authority is the All Writs Act.[49] Whether a judge has the *sua sponte* power to issue such a stay, or rather must wait (in keeping with classical adversarial theory) for a motion from a party, has not been explored in detail in the cases.

Like *forum non conveniens*, self-stays and anti-suit injunctions are of less practical importance in the federal court system than they once were. The reason is that various transfer mechanisms can more directly achieve the aggregation that dismissals and stays achieve only indirectly. But *forum non conveniens* dismissals and the various stays remain relevant to the problem of intra-system aggregation. They are the only game in town for the aggregation of cases located exclusively in state courts and cases that are transnational in character. Moreover, they suggest a potentially broad power, so far untapped, to supplement and smooth over some of the deficiencies in federal courts' transfer powers. Whether these powers should be tapped depends, of course, on one's perspective on the relative importance of individual control of litigation and the efficiency of aggregated handling.[50]

---

45. Asset Allocation and Mgmt. Co. v. Employers Ins. Co., 892 F.2d 566 (7th Cir. 1989); Laker Airways Ltd. v. Sabena, Belgian World Airlines, 731 F.2d 909 (D.C. Cir. 1984).

46. *See* Mahan v. Gunther, 278 Ill. App. 3d 1108, 663 N.W.2d 1139 (1996).

47. *Laker Airways*, 731 F.2d 909.

48. Owens-Corning Fiberglas Corp. v. Baker, 838 S.W.2d 838 (Tex. App. 1992).

49. 28 U.S.C. § 1651(a) ("The Supreme Court and all courts established by Act of Congress may issue all writs necessary or appropriate in aid of their respective jurisdictions and agreeable to the usages and principles of law.").

50. For recent articles on aspects of dismissals and stays, see Martin H. Redish, *Intersystemic Redundancy and Federal Court Power: Proposing a Zero Tolerance Solution to the Duplicative Litigation Problem*, 75 NOTRE DAME L. REV. 1347 (2000); James P. George, *Parallel Litigation*, 51 BAYLOR L. REV. 769 (1999).

3. Transfers

A transfer takes a case from the docket of one court within a system and moves it to the docket of another court within that same system. Among the reasons that a party or parties might want to transfer a case are easier access to witnesses or evidence, convenience for the moving parties, inconvenience to other parties, and securing a better judge or jury pool. Not all of these are noble reasons, nor are they all reasons that the federal transfer statutes expressly countenance. In an adversarial system any rule designed for one purpose can be manipulated for private ends.

Our particular concern is whether transfers can be used to achieve optimal single-forum aggregation when cases are dispersed over several forums. As mentioned above, state courts have not thus far developed interstate transfer mechanisms, nor are there transnational transfer mechanisms. The only functional transfer mechanisms exist on the federal level, a fact which is sometimes cited as one of the advantages of the federal system as a forum for complex multi-party litigation.

There are two main transfer provisions, and a third mechanism that may be yet prove to be valuable for aggregation.[51]

a. *Section 1404 Transfers.* The first transfer provision is 28 U.S.C. § 1404. Enacted in 1948 and superceding the old doctrine of *forum non conveniens*, § 1404 permits one federal court to transfer a case to another federal court "where it might have been brought." The standard stated for transfer in § 1404(a) is "[f]or the convenience of parties and witnesses, in the interest of justice." In their subsequent exposition of this statute, courts have considered a wide array of convenience and justice considerations and balanced them against countervailing considerations, including the plaintiff's interest in his or her chosen forum.[52] Although one of the parties usually moves for a § 1404(a) transfer, it has also been understood that the judge has a *sua sponte* power to order transfer.[53] Once the case is transferred, the transferor court has nothing more to do with the case.

Section 1404(a) has occasionally been used with success in complex litigation.[54] It has some noteworthy features: a direct power

---

51. Other transfer powers exist, though none regularly affects the aggregation of dispersed litigation. *See* 28 U.S.C. § 1406 (permitting court to transfer improperly venued case to a proper venue); 28 U.S.C. § 1412 (permitting bankruptcy case to be transferred "in the interest of justice or for the convenience of the parties").

52. *See* WRIGHT ET AL., *supra* n.13, §§ 3847-54.

53. *Id.*, § 3844.

54. *See, e.g., In re* Joint E. and S. Dists. Asbestos Litig., 769 F. Supp. 85 (E. & S.D.N.Y. 1991).

of transfer rather than an indirect power of dismissal or stay, a set of standards flexible enough to encompass optimal aggregation, and a *sua sponte* judicial power to override adversarial gamesmanship. For several reasons, however, § 1404(a) is not the solution to the problem of intra-system aggregation.

The first problem is § 1404(a)'s provision that the case can be transferred to another district "where it might have been brought." In *Hoffman v. Blaski*,[55] the Supreme Court held that this phrase meant that a case could be transferred only to a district in which venue would have been proper when the case was first filed. *Hoffman v. Blaski* further held that the defendant's willingness to consent to the transfer to an improper venue was irrelevant. Thus, to use the XYZ-QRS hypothetical, if we were to assume that the most logical forum for aggregation was the United States District Court for the District of Kansas, neither the case against XYZ nor the case against QRS could be transferred under § 1404(a), since the District of Kansas was not a proper venue in either case. Similarly, if we assume that Smith's case against XYZ is properly filed in the United States District Court for the Western District of North Carolina, and that it would be proper to aggregate the cases against XYZ and QRS, the cases against QRS could not be transferred under § 1404(a) to the Western District of North Carolina, even if QRS consented to the transfer. Despite trenchant criticism, *Hoffman v. Blaski* has never been overruled.

A second, related problem is that transfer cannot be made to a district that lacks territorial jurisdiction over the defendant. This rule, most notably stated in *Foster-Milburn Co. v. Knight*[56] by Judge Learned Hand, has never been expressly endorsed by the Supreme Court, but after *Hoffman v. Blaski* it seems the likeliest conclusion.[57]

We encountered the third problem in the material on *forum non conveniens* and the *Kerotest* stay: Section 1404(a) requires that the transfer motion be made in the court from which transfer is sought (the "transferor" court). This is not a great burden when only a few cases must be transferred. With widely dispersed litigation, however, the burden of filing hundreds of transfer motions is significant, and successful aggregation depends on the willingness of dozens of federal judges, acting independently, to agree about the convenience and justice of coordinated handling in a single forum.

---

55. 363 U.S. 335 (1960).

56. 181 F.2d 949 (2d Cir. 1950).

57. *See* WRIGHT ET AL., *supra* n.13, § 3845. After the convergence of territorial jurisdiction and venue in the recent amendments to § 1391, this problem is less acutely felt than in olden days, but it is still occasionally an impediment.

From an aggregation perspective, § 1404(a) transfers have some utility; most particularly, the ability of a court to grant a motion *sua sponte* can overcome the problem of aggregation-dispersing strategic choices by the parties. Nevertheless, § 1404(a) does not overcome significant structural impediments to aggregation (i.e., territorial jurisdiction and venue), and it lacks a single decisionmaker for aggregation decisions.

b. Section 1407 (Multidistrict) Transfers. At this point the second transfer mechanism — multidistrict litigation (MDL) transfer under 28 U.S.C. § 1407 — enters the picture. Section 1407 was created in 1968, largely in response to the filing of large numbers of dispersed antitrust actions. The statute established the Judicial Panel on Multidistrict Litigation, which is comprised of seven sitting federal judges. According to § 1407(a), this Panel is empowered, whenever "civil actions involving one or more common questions of fact are pending in different districts, to transfer the cases "to any district for coordinated or consolidated pretrial proceedings." Section 1407(a) also provides the standard under which such transfers should occur: "[T]ransfers for such proceedings will be for the convenience of the parties and witnesses and will promote the just and efficient conduct of such actions." The Panel is given the authority to sever any claim by or against any party and remand that claim to the original forum.

According to § 1407(c), the Panel can act either *sua sponte* (by issuing a "show cause order") or on the motion of a party. Under rules of procedure that the Panel has developed, the Panel also has provided for the transfer of related actions that are subsequently filed (usually called "tag-along actions").[58]

The Panel itself does not handle an MDL case; instead, it chooses a federal district court (the MDL "transferee" court) that will handle an MDL case. The transferee court is responsible for all further pretrial proceedings in the transferred cases. The transferee judge presides over discovery, which needs now be done only once rather than multiple times in each forum, and renders a single consistent ruling on all pretrial matters — including case-dispositive or claim-dispositive motions. "[A]t or before the conclusion of such pretrial proceedings" for a particular case, 28 U.S.C. § 1407(a) provides that the Panel shall remand the case or cases to the transferor forum, "unless [they] shall have been previously terminated." As a general proposition, the transferee court's pretrial rulings travel back to the transferor forum.

---

58. *See* Rules of Procedure of the   tion 1.1, 7.4, 7.5.
Judicial Panel on Multidistrict Litiga-

Until now, we have studied rules that were not written with structural complexity in mind, and we have seen how courts have pressed those rules into the service of aggregation. For the first time, the MDL statute presents us with a device written specifically for the aggregation of dispersed litigation. At first blush, the statute seems to do a good job of overcoming the hurdles to intra-system aggregation while avoiding some of the shortfalls of other aggregation devices.

First, there are no limits on the forum to which the cases can be transferred. The Panel is not limited just to districts that have territorial jurisdiction over all the defendants or venue over the entire case.[59] Thus, if it makes sense to "multidistrict" the XYZ-QRS case in the United States District Court for the District of Kansas, it can be done.

Second, strategic behavior by the parties is also no barrier. The Panel has a *sua sponte* power to order transfer; it need not await a motion by the parties.

Third, the MDL statute provides a single, centralized decisionmaker that can transfer all related litigation; motions for dismissals or stays need not be filed in multiple forums. Transfer of subsequently filed cases can also be handled efficiently. Moreover, since the Judicial Panel is distinct from the transferee court and is usually comprised of judges well-versed in complex litigation, the comity problems associated with a transferee court's order to stay proceedings in other forums are avoided.

Fourth, the standards under which transfer occurs are flexibly stated, so the Panel has the discretion to ensure that only the cases truly meriting aggregation receive it. Section 1407(a) lists three prerequisites to transfer: at least one common question of fact, convenience of parties and witnesses, and promotion of the just and efficient conduct of the action. In practice, these factors have not been treated equally, nor has the Panel been consistent in applying them. The "commonality" requirement has not proven to be a significant hurdle in most circumstances, although there are a few Panel decisions suggesting that the common factual questions must predominate over individual ones in order for MDL transfer to be appropriate. The "convenience" requirement is an important one, but this issue is often passed over quickly in the Panel's transfer opinions, with the most relevant convenience considerations being the elimination of duplicative litigation, the reduction of repetitive discovery costs, and the conservation of the parties' resources. The

---

59. See WRIGHT ET AL., *supra* n.13, § 3862; *In re* Aviation Prod. Liab. Litig., 347 F. Supp. 1401 (J.P.M.L. 1972).

critical question is convenience in the aggregate; individual inconvenience can be tolerated as long as overall convenience is achieved.[60] The final prerequisite of § 1407(a) — the "just and efficient conduct" requirement — is the central issue in most transfer decisions, since it encompasses within its ambit both of the earlier prerequisites. The Panel has never attempted a complete list of all the factors it considers in making its determination of justice and efficiency. Among the factors the Panel frequently cites, however, are the number of cases involved; the reduction of costs; the ability to coordinate overlapping class actions; the elimination of inflicting pretrial rulings; the readiness of some or all of the cases for trial; the availability (and efficacy) of other mechanisms for coordinate handing of the cases, including voluntary cooperation; and the parties unanimous opposition (or unanimous consent) to transfer.[61]

A fifth strength of the MDL transfer is that the aggregated case is usually handled by a judge with some experience and skill in handling large-scale litigation. Indeed, in many of the proceedings before the Panel, the critical question dividing the parties is not *whether* to transfer the case, but *where*. The Panel will never transfer an MDL proceeding to an unwilling federal judge, and will attempt to find a judge both with experience in this particular type of litigation and with talent for handling big cases. The Panel also considers the location of parties and evidence and the situs of the injuries in choosing a transferee venue. But often two or three, and sometimes more, judges in different districts fit this general description. Since each judge has somewhat different attitudes toward this type of case and toward managing large-scale cases in general, different parties believe that they will have an advantage appearing before one judge or a disadvantage appearing before another. Hence, they often litigate the question of who the MDL judge should be.[62] Although it is typical for the Panel to choose a judge from the transferee district, sometimes the Panel will choose a judge from a different district and have that judge designated to sit in the transferee forum.

The litigation over *whether* to multidistrict and *where* to multidistrict underscores the fact that MDL transfers are controversial devices. Until now, we have painted the MDL picture in a fairly rosy way: single-forum aggregation that avoids needless expense and fosters consistency in the pretrial rulings of related cases. In

---

60. For a critical appraisal of the first two factors, see TIDMARSH & TRANGSRUD, *supra* n.17, at 510-12.

61. *See id.*

62. *See, e.g., Aviation Prod. Liab. Litig.*, 347 F. Supp. 1401; *In re* Silicone Gel Breast Implants Prod. Liab. Litig., 793 F. Supp. 1098 (J.P.M.L. 1992).

fact, MDL transfers raise numerous problems that make some commentators and lawyers far less enthusiastic about the device as it is presently constituted.

The first problem is endemic to all devices that seek to affect a plaintiff's forum choice: MDL transfer violates the plaintiffs' adversarial ability to control the litigation. Of course, §1407 does so in a less severe way than other devices, since the transfer is only for "pretrial proceedings." Nonetheless, most litigation ends during the pretrial process, whether through settlement or dismissal. Moreover, in deciding whether to transfer, the Panel considers only the overall benefits and costs of aggregation; transfer is appropriate even when it imposes excessive costs on certain individuals. Indeed, in many cases, the person most benefitted from consolidated handling is the defendant, who otherwise would have to engage in the same discovery again and again. Thus, an MDL transfer portends a shift in power from the plaintiff, who can use an inconvenient forum against a defendant, to the defendant, who can now use an inconvenient transferee forum against a plaintiff.

Shifts in the dynamics of litigation are not the only concern. More generally, as the often pitched battle over the transferee judge shows, the identity of the transferee judge can have a significant effect on the outcome of a case. A trial judge possesses a plethora of pretrial powers that might affect the outcome of the litigation.[63] One of those powers is the ability to appoint a lawyer to represent the interests of the transferred plaintiffs — a lawyer not necessarily of the plaintiff's choosing, and one whom the plaintiff will often never meet. The focus of the MDL judge and lawyers must necessarily be on the overall litigation picture; small, but often important, details of individual cases will be overlooked. Moreover, an MDL pretrial often takes longer to complete than the pretrial phase in any single individual litigation; even though the total time for handling all cases goes down, the complexities of a large-scale aggregation means that the pretrial phase is often longer, more cumbersome, and more expensive than the factual phase of individual litigation. If it occurs early in the litigation cycle, an MDL transfer can also deprive plaintiffs of the opportunity to perfect their cases against a defendant through trial and error.[64] Moreover, studies suggest that aggregated

---

63. On these powers, see *infra* ch.6.

64. The leading work on this concept, often referred to as the "maturity" issue, has been done by Francis McGovern. Professor McGovern suggests that litigation goes through several cycles: first, an initial cycle in which defendants win most cases; second, a breakthrough cycle in which plaintiffs adjust to defense strategies and start to achieve widespread victories; and third, a "mature" cycle in which plaintiffs and defendants finally achieve an equilibrium. *See* Francis E. McGovern, *An Analysis of Mass*

litigation may lead to different outcomes than individually controlled litigation. Some of those changes favor plaintiffs and others favor defendants; whichever occurs in a particular case, the aggregation of cases in an MDL proceeding cannot be viewed as an outcome-neutral event.[65]

A related criticism is the very flexibility of the MDL standards that seemed to have been one of its strengths. For the reasons we have just seen, a decision to multidistrict is one of the most critical in the litigation, but the Panel's discretion is only loosely constrained. Nor has the law developed in the Panel's opinions been an especially useful check. The simple fact is that Panel decisions ordering transfers (or refusing to order transfers) often border on the perfunctory. Very little information about the Panel's views on "commonality," "convenience," and "just and efficient conduct" emerges from most decisions. Many of the factors we have just described are never consciously mentioned. Lawyers and academics might hope for better guidance on, and a more intellectually honest appraisal of, one of the most critical decisions in the litigation.

This problem is perhaps best represented by the Panel's well-known treatment of the asbestos litigation. In 1977, when 103 asbestos cases were pending in the federal courts, the Panel proposed to multidistrict the federal asbestos litigation, but backed off in light of the unanimous opposition of plaintiffs and defendants.[66] Over the course of the next fourteen years, as the number of federal asbestos cases skyrocketed upward, the Panel refused to multidistrict federal asbestos cases on four more occasions. Finally, in 1991, faced with more than 26,000 pending federal asbestos cases, the Panel consolidated the cases in a single transferee forum over the opposition of many but not all parties.[67] The 1991 decision is one of the Panel's lengthiest and most thorough, analyzing both the failures of individual litigation and the need for the consolidated handling of the asbestos controversy. The problem was that by 1991 there was very

---

Torts for Judges, 73 TEX. L. REV. 1821 (1995). Obviously, aggregation at different points of this cycle can affect the outcome of the case.

65. *See* Irwin A. Horowitz & Kenneth S. Bordens, *The Effects of Outlier Presence, Plaintiff Population Size, and Aggregation of Plaintiffs on Simulated Civil Jury Decisions*, 12 L. & HUM. BEHAV. 209 (1988) (size of plaintiff group strengthens weaker cases and makes plaintiffs more likely to recover, but reduces awards to

plaintiffs with stronger cases). This study involved simulated jury verdicts, not actual decisions made by MDL courts. Its results, however, are suggestive of the outcome-affecting potential of MDL aggregation.

66. *In re* Asbestos and Asbestos Insulation Materials Prod. Liab. Litig., 431 F. Supp. 906 (J.P.M.L. 1977).

67. *In re* Asbestos Prod. Liab. Litig. (No. VI), 771 F. Supp. 415 (J.P.M.L. 1991).

little additional pretrial work to be done in asbestos cases; all the relevant information had been discovered. The MDL transfer did generate a large number of individual settlements, as well as a failed global settlement effort,[68] but consolidation for such purposes seems to stretch the purpose of the MDL proceeding. As of this writing, more than a decade later, the asbestos MDL is still ongoing.

The opposite story can be told of the silicone gel breast implants litigation. After a couple of significant successes in individual trials, breast implant cases were filed in many federal forums. Despite the relative immaturity of these cases, and perhaps responding to its failure in the asbestos litigation, the Panel consolidated the first 78 cases shortly after they first appeared in the federal system in 1992;[69] more than 10,000 tag-along cases ultimately followed. This litigation has resulted in settlements approaching $1 billion for thousands of claimants and has spun off a bankruptcy that is likely to deliver an additional $4 billion to thousands more claimants. This seems a notable success for an MDL litigation that is only ten years old. The problem is that the early plaintiff victories appear to have been something of an anomaly, and today it is still not clear that breast implants have significant long-term health effects. The multi-districted breast implants litigation seems to have been driven more by the fear of avoiding another asbestos catastrophe than by the science.

Of course, most of these criticisms are not unique to MDL aggregation; we raise them here because MDL aggregation is the first effective aggregation device we have seen, so it is important to appreciate the negative potential of MDL consolidations.

The MDL transfer statute can also be attacked from an opposing perspective: as an inadequate response to the need for aggregation. As mentioned, MDL transfers are designed to be used only for "pretrial proceedings." Once pretrial proceedings conclude, the cases are, according to § 1407(a), to be remanded to the transferor forums. Frequently, however, it would be more efficient for the transferee judge, who has handled the case up to that point, to continue to handle the case through trial rather than remand the cases to dozens of transferor judges who have little familiarity with the case.

Prior to 1998, the transferee judge often finessed this problem by using § 1404 to "self-transfer" those cases that "might have been brought" in the MDL district to the MDL district. Although this move seemed to fly in the face of § 1407(a)'s limitation that transfers

---

68. *See* Amchem. Prod., Inc. v. Windsor, 521 U.S. 591 (1997), considered *infra* ch.5, nn.100-02, 172-76, 280-86 and accompanying text.

69. *Silicone Gel Breast Implants*, 793 F. Supp. 1098.

be made only for pretrial purposes, the argument was generally accepted that the MDL transferee judge sat in the place of the transferor judge, and thus could invoke § 1404 just as the transferor judge could. This self-transfer power was limited by *Hoffman v. Blaski* and *Foster-Milburn*;[70] but the Panel, in selecting an appropriate MDL transferee forum, often venued the litigation to a district "where [the multidistricted cases] might have been brought." Although this self-transfer was the subject of occasional academic criticism,[71] it became an accepted part of MDL practice.

In 1998, however, the Supreme Court halted the practice. In *Lexecon Inc. v. Milberg Weiss Bershad Hynes & Lerach*,[72] the Court held that an MDL transferee judge does not have the power to self-transfer under § 1404. At the time of this writing, there is legislation pending in Congress to overturn the rule in *Lexecon* and to give the Judicial Panel (rather than the transferee judge) the power to order a transfer for trial purposes as well. From the viewpoint of aggregation, such a transfer power would be most desirable if it also sidestepped the *Hoffman v. Blaski* and *Foster-Milburn* limitations on § 1404(a) transfers. On the other hand, such a power would create an even greater inroad on the plaintiff's right to control the litigation — and even greater concerns for the outcome-determinative effects of transfer.

The debate over the excesses or inadequacies of the MDL process can easily overlook the amount of aggregation work that the MDL statute already performs on a regular basis. Large antitrust and securities cases are routinely multidistricted. So are many consumer suits and mass torts. It is likely that a lawyer who regularly litigates complex matters will sooner or later encounter a multidistrict situation.

    c. Inherent Power Transfers. In addition to §§ 1404(a) and 1407(a) transfers, courts may enjoy the ability to transfer cases as part of their inherent power to control litigation on their docket. Thus far, however, this power is more theoretical than real. In *In Re Joint Eastern and Southern Districts Asbestos Litigation*,[73] Judge Weinstein transferred cases from the Southern District of New York to the Eastern District of New York. He ultimately used § 1404(a) as the vehicle for transfer, but not before he dangled the intriguing possibility that § 1404 might not "exhaust[ ] the power of courts within the same circuit to consolidate cases pending in different

---

70. *See supra* nn.55-56 and accompanying text.

71. *See, e.g.,* Roger H. Trangsrud, *Joinder Alternatives in Mass Tort Litigation,* 70 CORNELL L. REV. 779,

809 (1985).

72. 523 U.S. 26 (1998).

73. 769 F. Supp. 85 (E. & S.D.N.Y. 1991).

districts for trial."[74] The source of this additional power, presumably, was the All Writs Act, which gives courts the power to issue writs "necessary in aid of their respective jurisdictions."[75] Presumably as well, the power could be exercised *sua sponte*. No case of which we are aware has yet utilized this power, which Judge Weinstein's dicta carefully limited to intra-circuit transfers.

If it existed, such a power might smooth over some of the bumps in §§ 1404 and 1407. Of course, the "bumps" in these statutes are also a strong argument against inherent power; district courts should not easily override the limits on intra-system transfer that have been crafted by Congress and the Supreme Court. Whatever the ultimate fate of the concept of inherent power, the need to consider it suggests that the "bumps" in our present transfer powers make the intra-system aggregation process less than optimal.

D. CONCLUSION

Our last remark about transfer is generally applicable to our present patchwork of intra-system aggregation tools: The tools are inadequate. To begin with, any realistic system of intra-system aggregation requires a centralized transfer power sufficiently broad to overcome both structural impediments, such as territorial jurisdiction and venue, and strategic litigant choices. At present, the transfer power is available only at the federal level, not at the state or transnational level. The present all-purpose transfer power, § 1404, contains a *sua sponte* dimension that permits the court to overcome strategic litigant choices, but the power is decentralized and cannot overcome structural impediments. The multidistrict transfer statute, § 1407, is centralized, and does overcome both structural impediments and strategic choices. But it is limited only to pretrial transfers, and its rules seem overly malleable.

More significantly, as we have now seen, the concept of "optimal aggregation" is hardly non-controversial. It eliminates (or at least alters) a litigant's right to bring and control litigation in a forum of his or her choosing, it invests tremendous power in a single judge, it is more expensive and litigation-prolonging for some litigants, and it affects the outcome of the litigation. As we shall see in succeeding chapters, these are not the only costs of aggregation.

Therefore, aggregation is not an unadulterated good. Given that fact, we can no longer pretend that bigger aggregation is necessarily better aggregation. "Optimal" aggregation means something far more complex and intricate, and can be achieved only through the

---

74. *Id.* at 88.　　　　　　　**75.** 28 U.S.C. § 1651(a), quoted in full *supra* n.49.

balancing of procedural variables (such as adversarialism, efficiency, transactionalism, and trans-substantivity) together with structural and substantive concerns.

One of the structural concerns, about which we have thus far spoken little, is federalism. This is the concern which we now address more directly.

Chapter 4

STRUCTURAL COMPLEXITY: INTERSYSTEM AGGREGATION

So far we have examined two powers of courts: first, to aggregate cases filed in the same district; and second, to aggregate cases filed elsewhere in the same system. In both situations, we found important limits on present aggregation doctrines. We now turn to a third aggregation issue: the aggregation of cases filed in different court systems (i.e., some in state court and some in federal court). In this area lie some of the most intractable limits on aggregation.

The fact that some cases are filed in the state court system and other related cases are filed in the federal court system should not be a surprise. Parties seeking to maximize their chances of success will choose the court system that provides the best melange of laws, procedures, personnel, and convenience, and the best choice for one litigant is not necessarily the best choice for another. As long as we operate within a litigation model that allows plaintiffs the autonomy to locate the case in the forum they find most desirable, related cases are likely to end up being dispersed between the state and federal court systems. Therefore, as we did in the last chapter, we begin with an examination of structural limitations and strategic behaviors that prevent optimal aggregation, and then turn to the responses that are available to overcome these barriers and achieve intersystem aggregation.

Before we begin this detailed examination, however, two basic observations are in order. First, the primary structural impediments derive from the fact that federal courts are courts of "limited jurisdiction"; in other words, unless a particular case is the one of the types of cases that a federal court has the power to adjudicate, the case must be heard in state court. As we have already seen, federal courts have certain advantages in terms of intra-system aggregation. Hence, the limits on federal jurisdiction make it more difficult to aggregate related cases in the system most likely to achieve significant intra-system aggregation.

Second, there are two important strategic barriers to intersystem aggregation, and both are related to the fact that the plaintiff is master of his or her complaint. On the one hand, as we shall see, plaintiffs often can manipulate their claims in order to locate their case in state court, thereby avoiding the intra-system aggregation powers of the federal system. On the other hand, the fact that a case is eligible to be filed in one court system does not mean that it must be filed there. For the most part, federal jurisdiction is "concurrent"; with the exception of a few circumstances in which federal jurisdiction is "exclusive," the plaintiff retains the choice to file a case over which a federal court has jurisdiction in a state court. Without some power of intersystem aggregation, related cases will remain dispersed among the federal and state courts.

A. STRUCTURAL LIMITATIONS ON INTERSYSTEM AGGREGATION

The federal courts' subject matter jurisdiction derives from two sources. The first is the United States Constitution. It is settled doctrine that federal courts cannot exercise judicial power unless the Constitution grants it.[1] The grants of jurisdiction — nine in total number — are contained in Article III of the Constitution. For our purposes, the critical grants are federal question jurisdiction, which permits federal courts to hear "all Cases, in Law and Equity, arising under this Constitution, the Laws of the United States, and Treaties made, or which shall be made, under their Authority";[2] and diversity jurisdiction, which permits federal courts to hear "Controversies . . . between Citizens of different States; . . . and between a State, or the Citizens thereof, and foreign States, Citizens or Subjects."[3]

The second source is an enabling statute that grants jurisdiction. It is generally thought that the federal district courts' Article III jurisdiction is not self-executing; Congress must also enact legislation authorizing a federal court to hear cases involving this subject matter.[4] Although Congress cannot give the federal district courts more jurisdiction than the Constitution allows, it can give less.

---

1.   Marbury v. Madison, 5 U.S. (1 Cranch) 137 (1803).

2.   U.S. CONST., art. III, § 2.

3.   *Id.* The jurisdiction apparently granted to entertain suits by private citizens of one state against states was removed in the Eleventh Amendment. The exact boundaries of the Eleventh Amendment and the more general question of the ability to sue states in federal or state court, are complicated problems beyond the scope of the present book. *See generally* RICHARD H. FALLON, JR., ET AL., HART & WECHSLER'S THE FEDERAL COURTS AND THE FEDERAL SYSTEM 1041-1105 (4th ed. 1996); *id.* Supp. 2000, at 80-152.

4.   *See* Sheldon v. Sill, 49 U.S. 441 (1850). The statement in the text

A party seeking to invoke the jurisdiction of a federal court must demonstrate the existence of *both* constitutional *and* statutory jurisdiction. Hence, it is important to study the limitations of both Article III and the jurisdictional statutes that Congress has enacted.

On the federal question side, *Osborn v. Bank of the United States* long ago held that Article III "arising under" jurisdiction exists as long as a federal question "forms an ingredient of the original cause."[5] This test, sometimes called the "potential ingredient" test, has been understood to mean that, as long as an issue of federal law *might be* raised in a case, Article III "arising under" jurisdiction exists — even if the issue of federal law is never actually litigated. For example, in *Osborn*, the federal court had constitutional jurisdiction to hear the case because the defendants in the case *might* have contested the ability of the Bank of the United States to sue or be sued (in other words, *might* have raised a question arising under the federal law that established the Bank) — even though the defendants in the case never in fact raised a challenge to the Bank's legal capacity.

Under *Osborn's* formulation, the scope of federal jurisdiction is great indeed. In a modern world rife with federal legislation and regulation, very few cases would lack a potential federal ingredient. For instance, it is possible that Smith, the asbestos victim, might claim a violation of federal rules on permissible asbestos exposure limits, or XYZ, the asbestos manufacturer, might defend by saying that some of its asbestos was used for military purposes. Since Article III jurisdiction hinges on what claims or defenses the case might raise before the litigation commences, rather than on the claims or defenses the litigation does in fact raise, *Osborn* seems to give constitutional jurisdiction over the case to the federal courts. Despite frequent criticism of *Osborn*, the Supreme Court has never wavered from its holding.[6]

---

is something of a simplification, and reads *Sheldon v. Sill* in the way most favorable to plenary congressional power to regulate lower federal court jurisdiction. The question of Congress's ability to regulate the jurisdiction of lower federal courts has spawned a vast literature, some of which contends that Congress cannot limit the jurisdiction of lower federal courts in some or all cases. *See* HART & WECHSLER, *supra* n.3, at 354-73. This section follows the main line of academic thought.

5.   Osborn v. Bank of the United

States, 22 U.S. (9 Wheat.) 738, 824 (U.S. 1824). In *Osborn*, Congress had passed a statute giving the federal courts statutory jurisdiction over all cases involving the Bank of the United States. Hence, the critical issue in the case was one of the scope of Article III jurisdiction.

6.   *See* American National Red Cross v. S.G., 505 U.S. 247 (1992). For some of the criticism of *Osborn*, much of which attempts to ground the case on a better intellectual foundation, see HART & WECHSLER, *supra* n.3, at 891-907.

Much of this breadth, however, is eliminated by 28 U.S.C. § 1331, the statutory grant of federal question jurisdiction that applies to most federal question cases. This statute reads remarkably like the Article III grant: "The district courts shall have original jurisdiction of all civil actions arising under the Constitution, laws, or treaties of the United States." It would be reasonable to infer, therefore, that § 1331 is coextensive with the constitutional grant.

In two significant ways, however, § 1331 has been construed more narrowly. First, the federal question in the case must appear on the face of a well-pleaded complaint; federal defenses to state-law claims do not satisfy the statutory half of federal question jurisdiction.[7] Second, statutory federal question jurisdiction exists only when federal law is the basis of the plaintiff's claim, or when a state-law claim necessarily involves a construction of federal law.[8] In essence, this second limitation means that *Osborn*'s potential federal ingredient is not enough for a federal court to assert § 1331 jurisdiction. An actual federal ingredient is also required — not as a matter of the Constitution, but as a matter of statutory law.

Since the Constitution is so much more capacious, it is always possible for Congress to expand statutory federal question jurisdiction beyond the well-pleaded complaint rule and the actual federal ingredient test. In certain circumstances, Congress has done so, either making a federal defense a sufficient federal question for jurisdictional purposes or (as in *Osborn* itself) passing a specialized jurisdictional grant that extends jurisdiction to the constitutional maximum. These statutes, however, are rare. If Smith wishes to sue XYZ on a state-law asbestos claim in federal court, the limits of § 1331 will prevent Smith from asserting federal question jurisdiction.

Hence, the scope of diversity jurisdiction becomes important. Like federal question jurisdiction, diversity jurisdiction has two components: a constitutional part and a statutory part. Like federal question jurisdiction, the general diversity statute, 28 U.S.C. § 1332, roughly tracks the language of Article III.[9] And like federal question jurisdiction, the statutory grant is much narrower than the Article III grant.

---

7. Louisville & Nashville R.R. Co. v. Mottley, 211 U.S. 149 (1908). A limited exception to this rule exists in certain cases of federal pre-emption of state claims. *See* Metro. Life Ins. Co. v. Taylor, 481 U.S. 58 (1987).

8. Merrell Dow Pharm., Inc. v. Thompson, 478 U.S. 804 (1986). After *Merrell Dow*, there seems to be little, if anything, left of "necessary construc-tion" federal question jurisdiction. *See* HART & WECHSLER, *supra* n.3, at 926-33. Thus, in almost all cases, federal question jurisdiction exists only when a plaintiff asserts a federal cause of action.

9. For a detailed analysis of the present statutory grant, see HART & WECHSLER, *supra* n.3, at 1524-26.

To see how this is so, suppose that Smith, a citizen of New Hampshire, wishes to sue TUV, an asbestos retailer and also a citizen of New Hampshire, on a state-law claim. The question is whether the Article III diversity grants would empower a federal court to hear Smith's case against TUV. Since both Smith and TUV have common, rather than diverse, citizenship, the answer obviously is "No"; neither constitutional nor statutory jurisdiction would seem to exist. Next, assume that Smith wants to sue XYZ, a citizen of New York. Here, the requisite diversity of citizenship, both constitutional and statutory, would just as obviously exist. Now comes the tricky part. Suppose that Smith wants to sue both TUV and XYZ in one case.[10] In this situation there is "minimal" diversity, which means that at least one plaintiff is of a different citizenship than at least one defendant. There is not, however, "complete" diversity, which means that *all* of the plaintiffs have different citizenship than *all* of the defendants.

In *State Farm Fire & Casualty Co. v. Tashire*,[11] which involved a statute that gave federal courts interpleader jurisdiction when minimal diversity was present, the Supreme Court held that Article III of the Constitution requires only "minimal" diversity — only one defendant must be diverse from one plaintiff. Long before *Tashire*, however, the Court had held, in *Strawbridge v. Curtiss*,[12] that the general diversity statute (now § 1332) required complete diversity. The Court has never retreated from its holding in *Strawbridge*.[13] Therefore, as with federal question jurisdiction, the statutory grant of diversity jurisdiction is much narrower than the constitutional grant.

There also exists a second statutory limit in § 1332: the matter-in-controversy limitation. Presently set at an amount in excess of $75,000, this requirement is designed to keep relatively small-stakes state-law cases out of federal court. But the matter-in-controversy requirement has led to some complications. For instance, one plaintiff who has two unrelated claims against a defendant can "aggregate" the amounts in controversy on each claim to meet the $75,000 limit.[14] But if two plaintiffs with related claims, each for $50,000, want to sue the same defendant, they may not "aggregate" their amounts in controversy to satisfy the more than $75,000 limit

10. This hypothetical assumes that there are rules under which Smith can join both TUV and XYZ in one suit. We examine joinder rules *infra* ch.5.

11. 386 U.S. 523 (1967).

12. 7 U.S. (3 Cranch.) 267 (1806).

13. As we shall see *infra* n.36, however, the complete diversity rule has been somewhat modified in the class action context.

14. Edwards v. Bates County, 163 U.S. 269 (1896).

unless they have a joint claim.[15] With respect to claims for money damages, the matter-in-controversy from each plaintiff's viewpoint is the relevant issue; the total amount of damages from the viewpoint of the defendant is not. With respect to claims for injunctive relief, however, the rule may be the opposite. Although the Supreme Court has never definitely decided the question, and although the courts of appeals have staked out at least four distinct positions,[16] the leading view looks at the matter-in-controversy from the viewpoint of either party, thus focusing on the total value of the injunction.

In determining whether plaintiffs' claims exceed the statutory amount in controversy, federal courts apply the "legal certainty" test: Unless it can be determined to a legal certainty that the amount in controversy does not exceed $75,000, federal jurisdiction is established.[17] Events subsequent to the filing of the case (for instance, the dismissal of one of the plaintiff's two $50,000 claims) do not affect the court's jurisdiction.[18]

As with federal question jurisdiction, Congress has occasionally enacted specific jurisdictional grants that ease the complete diversity and matter-in-controversy requirements. The most noteworthy is statutory interpleader, 28 U.S.C. § 1335. With statutory interpleader, which we consider in greater detail later, only minimal diversity among claimants is required, and the matter in controversy is an insignificant $500.

These basic rules of jurisdiction encounter a further difficulty in multiclaim or multiparty lawsuits. Suppose, for instance, that Smith, a citizen of New Hampshire, wishes to sue TUV, also a citizen of New Hampshire, on two claims, one a federal question claim and the other a related state-law claim. Obviously, if Smith had filed two separate suits, the federal court would have jurisdiction over the

---

15. Pinel v. Pinel, 240 U.S. 594 (1916); Troy Bank v. G.A. Whitehead & Co., 222 U.S. 39 (1911). Some courts have permitted the aggregation of punitive damages on the theory that, under the relevant state's law, they were a joint claim. See Allen v. R & H Oil & Gas Co., 63 F.3d 1326 (5th Cir. 1995).

16. The positions are: (1) value of the injunction to the plaintiff; (2) value of the injunction to the defendant; (3) value of the injunction to either party, and (4) value of the injunction to the party seeking to justify federal jurisdiction. Although some observers believe that the third posi-

tion is presently most favored, see ERWIN CHEMERINSKY, FEDERAL JURISDICTION § 5.3.4 (3d ed. 1999), the first position has been strongly emerging in recent decisions. See JAY TIDMARSH & ROGER H. TRANGSRUD, COMPLEX LITIGATION AND THE ADVERSARY SYSTEM 20 (Supp. 2000). Shortly before this book went to press, the Supreme Court granted certiorari in a case that may finally determine the question. See Ford Motor Co. v. McCauley, 122 S. Ct. 1063 (2002).

17. St. Paul Mercury Indem. Co. v. Red Cab Co., 303 U.S. 283 (1938).

18. Id. at 293.

federal question case but not the state-law case. Suppose, though, that Smith wants to bring the two claims in one case. Smith could probably do so in state court (which usually has concurrent jurisdiction over the federal claim). Can Smith also file the entire case in federal court, with one claim lying within the federal court's jurisdiction and one claim not?[19] This situation is referred to as a question of the federal courts' "pendent" jurisdiction.

A related, but different problem arises when additional claims or parties are involved. Suppose that Smith sues TUV in federal court only on the federal question claim, but TUV also has a state-law claim against Smith. May TUV assert that counterclaim in the federal proceeding, or must TUV file a separate action in state court? What if TUV wants to implead a New Hampshire citizen as a third-party defendant if that person is liable under state law to TUV? Suppose that Smith decides to sue XYZ in federal court on a federal question or state-law theory exceeding $75,000 (recall, XYZ has different citizenship from Smith). May Smith also assert a state-law claim against TUV? The first two of these situations typically were said to involve a federal court's "ancillary" jurisdiction; the last situation involved the court's "pendent party" jurisdiction.

Prior to 1990, the rules for each of these forms of jurisdiction had become fairly well settled. For pendent jurisdiction, a federal court could assert jurisdiction over a non-federal claim as long as the federal question within the court's jurisdiction was not frivolous, the original and pendent claims arose out of "a common nucleus of operative fact," and the claims "would ordinarily" be tried together. Federal courts retained the discretion not to exercise this jurisdiction in some situations.[20] With respect to ancillary jurisdiction, a federal court could exercise jurisdiction over counterclaims, third-party claims, cross-claims, or claims in intervention as long as there existed a "logical dependence" of the ancillary claim on the original one and the party asserting the ancillary claim did not voluntarily enter federal court.[21] In contrast, pendent party jurisdiction was disfavored; the Court required a clear congressional statement permitting such jurisdiction, and never found a statute of sufficient clarity.[22]

One of the conceptual problems of pendent and ancillary jurisdiction was the lack of statutory authority for their exercise.

---

19. Under F.R.CIV.P. 18, a plaintiff in federal court can assert as many claims against a defendant as he or she has. But Rule 18 addresses only the issue of claim joinder, not the issue of jurisdiction. *See* F.R.CIV.P. 82 (Federal Rules cannot expand federal jurisdiction).

20. United Mine Workers v. Gibbs, 383 U.S. 715, 725 (1966).

21. Owen Equipment & Erection Co. v. Kroger, 437 U.S. 365 (1978).

22. *See* Finley v. United States, 490 U.S. 545 (1989).

Even though pendent and ancillary jurisdiction made sense from the standpoint of "judicial economy, convenience, and fairness,"[23] they constituted an intellectually uncomfortable exception to Congress's purported power to specify statutorily the scope of federal jurisdiction.

In 1990 Congress eased this discomfort by enacting legislation designed to give federal courts the statutory authority to hear certain pendent, ancillary, and pendent party claims. This statute, 28 U.S.C. § 1367, established something called "supplemental" jurisdiction, which was a new umbrella term designed to cover all three forms of jurisdiction. The statute is complicated, and contains a number of unintended ambiguities (some of which we examine in Chapter 5). But the basic sense of the statute is this: For cases that are based, in whole or in part, on a federal question, § 1367(a) gives federal courts jurisdiction over all supplemental claims (whether pendent, ancillary, or pendent party) as long as the original and supplemental claims "are so related . . . that they form part of the same case or controversy under Article III of the United States Constitution." In this situation, Congress has authorized jurisdiction to the constitutional maximum, which is generally assumed to be *Gibbs*'s "common nucleas of operative fact."[24] For cases based solely on diversity jurisdiction, however, the rule is different; § 1367(b) does not permit supplemental jurisdiction over claims when "exercising supplemental jurisdiction over such claims would be inconsistent with the jurisdictional requirements of section 1332" (i.e., complete diversity and individual fulfillment of the requisite matter-in-controversy).

The fate of the former rules for pendent, ancillary, and pendent party jurisdiction varies under § 1367. Pendent claims will not generally be subject to the restrictive limitations of § 1367(b), but must satisfy the more generous *Gibbs*-like test of § 1367(a).[25] Many ancillary claims based on state law, such as counterclaims, cross-claims, and third-party claims, are also excluded from the operation of § 1367(b), though they must still meet the § 1367(a) test. In contrast, claims in intervention in pure diversity cases now must

---

23. *Gibbs*, 383 U.S. at 726.

24. *See* Rodriguez v. Pacificare of Texas, Inc., 980 F.2d 1014 (5th Cir.), *cert. denied*, 508 U.S. 956 (1993). It is important to note that § 1367(a) does not generally permit federal courts to exercise jurisdiction to the constitutional maximum. Rather, at least one claim must lie within federal jurisdiction under ordinary jurisdictional rules (which, for § 1331 claims, re-

quire a federal question arising under the well-pleaded complaint).

25. Cases in which the claim within original federal jurisdiction is a federal question are analyzed under § 1367(a). Cases in which there are two separate state-law claims, one of which is $75,000 or less, fit within the aggregation rules described *supra* n.15 and accompanying text, and need no supplemental jurisdiction.

pass the § 1367(b) test. Finally, under § 1367(a), jurisdiction can be asserted to the constitutional limit over pendent party claims in cases raising at least one federal question, but many pendent party claims in pure diversity cases would still be barred — though we shall see in Chapter 5 that an important ambiguity in § 1367(b) may create a couple of important exceptions to this bar.[26]

Following the lead in *Gibbs*, § 1367(c) gives federal courts the discretion to decline to exercise supplemental jurisdiction in certain situations, including cases with complex questions of state law or a predominance of supplemental claims.

This thumbnail sketch of federal jurisdiction suggests the intricacy of the subject, and shows that the attempt to aggregate related cases in a federal forum may meet a serious stumbling block.

B. STRATEGIC BEHAVIOR

These jurisdictional rules also provide plenty of play for litigants who, for strategic reasons, wish to avoid the federal forum. Suppose that Smith has two claims against XYZ, one federal and one based on state law; both claims are worth $100,000. Further assume that Smith has only a state law claim (also worth $100,000) against TUV. If Smith wants the entire controversy to be heard in federal court, he simply asserts both state-law and federal claims against XYZ, and then asserts the state-law claim against TUV. The federal court has jurisdiction over the claims against XYZ under §§ 1331 and 1332, and jurisdiction over the claim against TUV under § 1367(a). Recall that § 1367(b) comes into play only if Smith's case is based entirely on diversity, which it is not.

Now suppose that Smith wants the case to be located in state court. Smith has numerous options. Most obviously, he can sue only TUV; the lack of diversity of citizenship would keep the case in state court. Next, Smth could sue only XYZ in state court, pleading only the state-law claim and limiting the request for damages against XYZ on the state-law claim to $75,000.[27] Smith can also sue both XYZ and TUV in state court, and simply refuse to plead the federal claim; in this case, there is no complete diversity. Finally, assuming that the state court has concurrent jurisdiction over the federal claim, Smith can simply assert all of his claims against both defendants in state

---

26. *See infra* pp. 75-76, 152-54.

27. The plaintiff's limitation of damages in order to avoid federal jurisdiction is a time-honored tactic, though federal courts will not always honor the tactic if the case is removed to federal court before the plaintiff limits the damages. *See* De Anguilar v. Boeing Co., 47 F.3d 1404 (5th Cir. 1995); *In re* Gen. Motors Corp. Pickup Truck Fuel Tank Prod. Liab. Litig., 1993 WL 147245 (E.D. Pa.).

court and hope at least one defendant is happy enough with the state forum that it will refuse to permit the suit to be removed to federal court.[28]

Manipulating claims to obtain a state or federal forum is one of the most significant powers that a plaintiff in the American system enjoys. As "master of the complaint," a plaintiff cannot be forced to plead claims that would invoke federal jurisdiction, even when those claims are viable. As with intra-system aggregation, the plaintiff's autonomy to control the litigation is generally thought to outweigh the desire for efficiency in intersystem aggregation.

The present litigation system also encourages a second type of strategic behavior: duplicative litigation. Assume that Smith is not sure whether the state or federal forum will be better for his case. Might he be able to file the identical lawsuit in both state and federal court? Similarly, might he be able to file a case alleging only state-law claims against XYZ and TUV in state court, and simultaneously file a case alleging state-law and federal claims in federal court? Might Smith sue XYZ in federal court and TUV in state court?[29]

Although there might seem to be something wrong with duplicative litigation tactics, no rule absolutely prevents it. Indeed, dual filings of related (and sometimes identical) cases are commonplace in litigation, whether complex or routine. Any attempts at optimal aggregation must account for this reality.

C. RESPONSES

As with intra-system aggregation, three responses to structural and strategic barriers to aggregation are possible: changes in settled understandings of the jurisdictional rules, dismissals or stays of cases located in the non-optimal forum, and transfer of cases from a non-optimal forum to an optimal forum.

1. Changing Settled Rules

Like territorial jurisdiction, subject matter jurisdiction is a combination of constitutional and statutory rules. Unlike territorial jurisdiction, the constitutional rules (potential federal ingredient and

---

28. For a fuller discussion of removal and its limits, see *infra* nn.78-87 and accompanying text.

29. In some types of litigation one party may sue another party in one forum, and the second party sues the first party in a different forum.

The phenomenon is most typical in patent, construction, and insurance litigation, but can also occur in any case in which a declaratory judgment is possible. For the federal Declaratory Judgment Act, see 28 U.S.C. §§ 2201-02.

minimal diversity) are broad enough that it seems unnecessary to revamp them in order to achieve widescale aggregation.[30] The real problems with subject matter jurisdiction are the stingy, aggregation-frustrating interpretations given to § 1331 (well-pleaded complaint and "arising under" rules) and § 1332 (complete diversity and per-plaintiff matter-in-controversy rules). These interpretations are not the product of congressional action; rather they have resulted from judicial glosses. Hence, two different avenues are available to change the rules: congressional action or judicial refinement of the glosses.

In a few instances, Congress has acted. One instance is statutory interpleader, which requires only minimal diversity. Congress has also provided for federal jurisdiction over certain other large-scale cases, including state-law cases involving fraud in the sale of securities[31] and class actions involving Y2K liability.[32] But these statutes are useful only in limited situations. Congress has failed to enact broader legislation that would create federal jurisdiction for multistate, multiparty mass torts[33] and state court class actions.[34]

Since Congress rarely acts in the jurisdictional arena, a more promising avenue for jurisdictional reform in large-scale cases would appear to be judicial action that burnishes the present judicial glosses a bit. The Supreme Court's decisions contain some helpful language. For instance, in *Merrell Dow*, the Court acknowledged that the scope of § 1331 liability is not some "automatic test" with a "'single precise definition'"; rather, the interpretation of § 1331 involves

> "'a welter of issues regarding the interrelation of federal and state authority and the proper management of the federal judicial system.' . . . We have consistently emphasized that, in exploring the outer reaches of § 1331, determinations about

---

30. In academic circles, there have been some proposals to replace *Osborn's* potential ingredient test with a concept known as "protective juris-diction." Thus far, the Supreme Court has not accepted the invitation. *See* Verlinden B.V. v. Cent. Bank of Nigeria, 461 U.S. 480 (1983). Some formu-lations of the "protective jurisdiction" concept would be even more favorable to aggregation than *Osborn*, and some would be less favorable. For a brief discussion, see JAY TIDMARSH & ROGER H. TRANGSRUD, COMPLEX LITI-GATION AND THE ADVERSARY SYSTEM 320-21 (1998).

31. 15 U.S.C. § 77p, Pub. L. No. 105-353, 112 Stat. 3227 (1998). The case must involve at least 150 plain-tiffs and be removable to federal court, if filed in state court.

32. 15 U.S.C. § 6615 note, Pub. L. No. 106-37, 106 Stat. 185 (1999). There are some limitations, including class actions primarily involving citi-zens of one state or class actions with less than $10,000,000 in controversy.

33. *E.g.*, S. 248, 106th Cong., 1st Sess. (1999).

34. *E.g.*, S. 353, 106th Cong., 1st Sess. (1999).

federal jurisdiction require sensitive judgments about congressional intent, judicial power, and the federal system."[35]

Likewise, on the diversity side, the Supreme Court has over the years carved out limited exceptions to its rule of complete diversity in such areas as class actions[36] and intervention.[37] The tools to craft rules of federal subject matter jurisdiction for large-scale cases are in place.

Thus far, however, the federal courts have resisted the temptation to create specialized rules of jurisdiction for large-scale cases. Indeed, *Merrell Dow* itself was a mass tort case in which the federal litigation had been multidistricted, but state litigation remained dispersed. Had *Merrell Dow* taken an expansive view of federal jurisdiction, the federal court system would have been able to claim jurisdiction over many of the cases located in state court.[38] *Merrell Dow* did not. Even worse, in attempting to determine the appropriate weight to give to the federal and state interests in the case, the opinion did not mention the issue of optimal aggregation or suggest that optimal aggregation should enter into the equation used to calculate § 1331 jurisdiction.

Nonetheless, *Merrell Dow* did not reject the argument that the needs of optimal aggregation should influence the glosses on § 1331, so the argument is technically still available. Moreover, *Merrill Dow* can arguably be distinguished. Although efficiency interests may have counseled aggregation, *Merrell Dow* did not involve a case in which non-aggregation threatened to create an inequitable distribution of a remedy among similarly situated tort victims; Merrell Dow had sufficient assets to conduct the litigation and to

35. *Merrell Dow*, 488 U.S. at 808, 810, 814 (quoting Franchise Tax Bd. v. Constr. Laborers Vacation Trust, 463 U.S. 1, 8 (1983)).

36. The Supreme Court has held that the existence of complete diversity in a class action is determined by comparing the citizenship of the class representatives who file the case on behalf of class members and the defendant(s). The citizenship of the class members themselves is neglected, even when class members have the same citizenship as the defendant(s). Supreme Tribe of Ben-Hur v. Cauble, 255 U.S. 356 (1921). We will explore class actions in greater detail *infra* at pp. 103-63.

37. A person who sought to intervene "of right" in a diversity case did

not destroy diversity jurisdiction, even though complete diversity was present. Wichita R. & Light Co. v. Pub. Util. Comm'n of Kansas, 260 U.S. 48 (1922). This rule was subsequently changed as part of Congress's enactment of supplemental jurisdiction. *See* 28 U.S.C. § 1367(b). We will explore intervention in greater detail *infra* at pp. 77-86.

38. Some claims would not have been removable. Not every Bendectin case involved a state-law negligence *per se* claim based on an alleged violation of the federal statute. Even if *Merrell Dow* had come out the other way, future plaintiffs could still have avoided federal jurisdiction with the simple strategic device of declining to assert a violation of federal statute.

make whole all deserving plaintiffs. Suppose, counterfactually, that Merrell Dow was insolvent, that state-law cases filed in state court by some of the tort victims would have depleted Merrell Dow's remaining assets, and that the tort victims in federal court consequently would have been deprived of any meaningful remedy. In this situation, one person's adversarial autonomy to litigate in the court of his or her choice would have a negative impact on another person's autonomy. Moreover, the interest of the federal system in providing effective relief to those who have invoked its jurisdiction is threatened. Might this present a case in which the federal courts should craft federal jurisdictional rules that remove restrictive statutory glosses and expand statutory jurisdiction toward the ample constitutional maximum?

We do not know the answer to this question, which has never been raised as a part of a jurisdictional claim.[39] The question does suggest, consistent with Millsian notions of liberty, that one person's autonomy ends at the point that this autonomy harms the equally autonomous interests of others.[40] It also suggests that this concern for equality of procedural opportunity to achieve a fair outcome — the like procedural treatment of like people — acts as a check on adversarialism and the interests of state courts, and that this concern is a more powerful reason for changing settled rules than "mere" efficiency. Finally, this question helps to define what optimal aggregation is, and suggests a powerful, but limited, reason for federal courts to act to achieve that level of aggregation.

Of course, such a response would not automatically overcome intersystem aggregation problems; the strategic behavior of lawyers who chose to locate cases in state court would still need to be addressed. Nonetheless, whether done by legislation or judicial fiat, wiping away the statutory glosses of the well-pleaded complaint rule, the "arising under" test, the complete diversity rule, and the each-plaintiff aggregation rule in large cases would go a long way toward achieving optimal aggregation in the federal court system.

Such a move, however, has significant consequences for our entire federal system of government. Expansion of federal jurisdiction in the instance of remedial inequity would increase the workload of federal courts, would probably require a significant number of new federal judges, and might create an enormous judicial bureaucracy. More significantly, state courts would be robbed of a fully participatory role in the development of the state and federal law that should

---

39. For development of this argument, see TIDMARSH & TRANGSRUD, *supra* n.30, at 322-23, 331-32, 340.

40. *See* William B. Rubenstein, *Divided We Litigate: Addressing Disputes Among Group Members and Lawyers in Civil Rights Campaigns,* 106 YALE L.J. 1623 (1997).

apply to large-scale cases. The balance between state and federal power, which has always been a delicate matter in our country, would have shifted sharply to the federal side.

This is not the book to explore the reasons for or against American-style federalism. In some people's minds, the needs of optimal aggregation outweigh concerns for federalism; for many others, the opposite is true. In either event, the argument over optimal aggregation must necessarily consider the role that state courts are expected to play in a federal system of government.

2. Dismissals and Stays

In intra-system litigation, we encountered three forms that dismissal and stay doctrines could take: dismissal of the case in an inconvenient forum (followed, presumably, by the plaintiff's refiling of the case in an appropriate forum), self-stay by the judge hearing the case in the inconvenient forum (again followed by a refiling of the case in the appropriate forum), and a stay issued by the judge in the appropriate forum against litigation in any inconvenient forum. In general, the second type of stay was preferable as an aggregation tool, but it also raised more serious questions of judicial power and comity. None of the three forms of dismissal and stay was particularly effective in achieving optimal intra-system aggregation.

Although their names are different, all three devices have their counterparts in intersystem litigation. But the delicate problem of balancing state and federal interests makes the devices even less effective aggregation tools in the intersystem context.

a. Abstention. As a general matter, intersystem dismissal and the self-stay have traveled under the doctrinal name of "abstention." Abstention doctrines, in which courts of one system abstain in favor of the courts of another system, are intricate, and were not designed with intersystem aggregation in mind. They can frustrate the process of intersystem aggregation as often as they can assist it.

Depending on how they are counted, federal courts have developed somewhere between three and six abstention doctrines. The Supreme Court has specifically recognized three: *Pullman* abstention,[41] *Burford* abstention,[42] and *Younger* abstention.[43] Three

---

41. R.R. Comm'n of Texas v. Pullman., 312 U.S. 496 (1941).

42. Burford v. Sun Oil Co., 319 U.S. 315 (1943). The formulation of *Burford* abstention in the text follows its recent recasting in New Orleans Pub. Serv., Inc. v. Council of City of New Orleans, 491 U.S. 350 (1989).

43. Younger v. Harris, 401 U.S. 37 (1971). For a case describing the expansion of *Younger* into the civil arena, see Pennzoil Co. v. Texaco, Inc., 481 U.S. 1 (1987). *See generally* HART & WECHSLER, *supra* n.3, at 1256-1308.

others — *Colorado River* abstention,[44] *Thibodaux* abstention,[45] and certification[46] — have never been recognized as abstention doctrines by the Court, but they operate in the same fashion. Only *Burford* abstention, *Colorado River* abstention, and *Thibodaux* abstention result in dismissal of the federal case; the others contemplate that the federal court will enter a stay, but might eventually lift it to adjudicate any issues not determined in the state proceeding.

The most fundamental problem with federal abstention, from an aggregation viewpoint, is that they tend to push cases into state forums in which intra-system aggregation is a difficult task. None of the doctrines was developed with the problem of complex litigation in mind; instead, each was designed to respect and foster the integrity of an independent state judicial system. *Pullman* abstention is intended to give state courts an ability to construe unclear state law before a federal court decides a federal constitutional issue that arises from one of the possible constructions of state law. *Burford* abstention requires federal courts to defer to state administrative or judicial proceedings when a federal case would involve the determination of a complex and exceptionally important state law issue, or would disrupt efforts by the state to establish a coherent policy in an area of significant state concern. *Younger* abstention requires federal courts to defer to criminal (and some civil enforcement) cases that were commenced in state court before the federal case significantly progressed on the merits. *Colorado River* abstention permits federal courts, as a matter of "wise judicial administration," to abstain in favor of ongoing related state proceedings; the factors used in making an abstention decision include the inconvenience of the federal forum, the desirability of avoiding piecemeal litigation, whether the case is governed by state or federal law, and any possible inadequacies in the state forum.[47] *Thibodaux* abstention requires federal courts to defer to state proceedings in special situations, such as eminent domain proceedings, that are "intimately involved with sovereign prerogative."[48] Certification allows federal courts to certify a question of state law to the state's highest court in order to obtain a definitive ruling.

Of the various abstention doctrines, only two have any significant potential for the aggregation of complex litigation: *Burford* and

44. Colorado River Water Conservation Dist. v. United States, 424 U.S. 800 (1976).

45. Louisiana Power and Light Co. v. City of Thibodaux, 360 U.S. 25 (1959).

46. *See* Lehman Bros. v. Schein, 416 U.S. 386 (1974).

47. 424 U.S. at 817-18. The last two of the *Colorado River* factors were first identified in Moses H. Cone Mem. Hosp. v. Mercury Constr. Co., 460 U.S. 1, 23, 26 (1983).

48. 360 U.S. at 28.

Colorado River. In theory, *Burford* abstention can assist intersystem aggregation when a state proceeding is better positioned to determine the entire controversy. For example, insolvency or receivership proceedings against state-regulated insurers or state-chartered institutions are often better concentrated in state courts, at least when the state has developed mechanisms to resolve the entire case and the federal plaintiffs threaten to create remedial inequity by jumping into federal court, getting a quick judgment, and collecting full value on their claims.[49] But *Burford* abstention suffers from certain difficulties as well. In the Supreme Court, there has not been a successful invocation of *Burford* abstention for forty years. Moreover, in *Quackenbush v. Allstate Insurance Co.,*[50] the Supreme Court held that *Burford* abstention was available only when the federal plaintiff sought equitable or other discretionary relief, not when the plaintiff sought money. Finally, *Burford* abstention requires the party seeking abstention to move for abstention in each federal court; no centralized decisionmaker exists.

Colorado River abstention is the only form of abstention clearly geared to duplicative litigation. It too can lead to the concentration of cases in state court, at least when the state court first obtained jurisdiction, the case involves state law, and the state is a superior forum for adjudicating the case. As an aggregation device, however, it has thus far proven to have limited utility. First, *Colorado River* has been used primarily when the parties in the state and federal cases are identical, or at least closely allied; it does not apply to cases in which the plaintiffs in the two courts are different. Second, the Supreme Court has clear said that *Colorado River* abstention is not to be invoked with frequency; federal courts have a "virtually unflagging obligation . . . to exercise the jurisdiction given them" by Congress,[51] and a strong presumption against abstention exists.[52] Third, as with *Burford* abstention, no centralized decisionmaker can ensure that all the federal courts will abstain. Fourth, *Colorado River* abstention is easily defeated when the plaintiff asserts a federal claim.[53] Finally, *Colorado River* abstention merely ends the federal suit. It does not force the plaintiff to file the suit in any particular state forum; and, as we have seen, states have very limited

---

49. *See* Brandenburg v. Seidel, 859 F.2d 1179 (4th Cir. 1988); Riley v. Simmons, 839 F. Supp. 1113 (D. N.J. 1993).

50. 517 U.S. 706 (1996).

51. *Colorado River,* 424 U.S. at 817.

52. *Moses H. Cone,* 460 U.S. at 16.

53. *Id.* at 26; *see also* Life-Link Int'l, Inc. v. Lalla, 902 F.2d 1493 (10th Cir. 1990). When some of the claims lie within the exclusive jurisdiction of a federal court, abstention is almost never appropriate. *See* 17A CHARLES A. WRIGHT ET AL., FEDERAL PRACTICE & PROCEDURE § 4247, esp. n.57 (1988).

tools to move cases among their courts. The general inferiority of state courts in this respect makes *Colorado River* abstention even less likely to achieve optimal aggregation than *Burford* abstention.

This last point highlights the overarching problem with abstention: It puts the case into the state system, which (except in unusual situations such as receiverships) are worse equipped to achieve optimal aggregation than federal courts. It dumps cases into the state system in an uncoordinated and sporadic way, since the doctrine relies on defendants to raise abstention motions and lacks any central decisionmaker to coordinate the delivery of cases to a single state court.

Closer to the mark would be "reverse abstention," under which state courts abstain in favor of a federal system that can consolidate the cases under its MDL authority. The idea of reverse abstention, however, is trickier than it first sounds, both because federal jurisdiction over certain state-law claims may be lacking and because state courts cannot generally refuse to entertain federal question claims.[54] Nonetheless, some state courts have shown resourcefulness in developing reverse abstention doctrines, which remain among the least explored doctrines in complex litigation.[55] Up to this point, however, state courts have not developed a uniform approach to reverse abstention, in either complex or routine cases. Even if they were to do so, such a doctrine would suffer from the problem of decentralized decisionmakers.

b. Anti-Suit Injunctions. Since the dismissal and self-stay often prove ineffective in achieving intersystem aggregation, the remaining alternative is the second form of stay, in which a court in the optimal aggregation system stays the cases in courts of the non-optimal system. This type of stay is often called an "anti-suit injunction." In theory, such an injunction could be entered by any state or federal court that has jurisdiction over one of the related cases. Although the injunction would not itself force the aggregation of cases, it would prevent related cases from being filed elsewhere, thereby indirectly achieving the same result.

Anti-suit injunctions can be divided into three types: *in rem*, *quasi-in-rem*, and *in personam*. When a court, whether state or federal, obtains jurisdiction over a *res* (a piece of property), it is generally thought to have the necessary power to issue an anti-suit injunction against any subsequently filed cases that seek to affect

---

54. *See* Testa v. Katt, 330 U.S. 386 (1997); Howlett v. Rose, 496 U.S. 356 (1990); *but see* Alden v. Maine, 527 U.S. 706 (1999).

55. For a discussion of these doctrines, which include reverse-*Burford* and reverse-*Colorado River* abstention, see TIDMARSH & TRANGSRUD, *supra* n.30, at 437-42.

the *res*.[56] The rationale is that the *res* itself is before the court, other lawsuits are tampering with the court's ability to adjudicate ownership of the *res*, and the court is therefore empowered to protect its *in rem* jurisdiction. The rule has generally been thought to include *quasi-in-rem* proceedings.[57]

Few complex cases, however, are *in rem* or *quasi-in-rem* proceedings; nearly all are *in personam*. In this context, we see another advantage of the federal system as a forum for aggregation. The Supreme Court has made perfectly clear, even in cases involving sympathetic facts, that state courts have *no* power to issue an anti-suit injunction against an *in personam* federal case.[58] Although the power of federal courts to issue an anti-suit injunction against a state proceeding is limited, the utter inability of state courts to issue injunctions against federal proceedings provides a comparative advantage for the aggregation of cases in federal court.

What, then, is the scope of a federal court's anti-suit injunctive power? The answer develops from the two primary doctrinal concerns about a federal court's issuance of an anti-suit injunction: the source of the court's power to issue the injunction and the Anti-Injunction Act,[59] which prohibits federal courts, except in limited situations, from enjoining ongoing state proceedings. Beginning with the issue of power, Congress has provided federal courts with explicit authority to enjoin state proceedings in some instances. The most notable are statutory interpleader[60] and bankruptcy,[61] which we examine in more detail later in this book. In addition, some courts have held that they have an anti-suit injunctive power under the ubiquitous All Writs Act, which permits federal courts to "issue all writs necessary or appropriate in aid of their respective jurisdictions and agreeable to the usages and principles of law."[62]

The seminal case for a federal anti-suit injunction in complex *in personam* litigation is *In re Corrugated Container Antitrust Litigation*.[63] In *Corrugated Container*, various defendants agreed to settle a multidistrict class action that alleged violations of federal antitrust law. Before the settlement was finalized, however, some disgruntled

---

56. Kline v. Burke Constr. Co., 260 U.S. 226 (1922) (federal injunction against state case); Princess Lida of Thurn & Taxis v. Thompson, 305 U.S. 456 (1939) (state injunction against federal case).

57. *See* Donovan v. City of Dallas, 377 U.S. 408 (1964).

58. *Id.* at 412-13; Gen. Atomic Co. v. Felter, 434 U.S. 12 (1977).

59. 28 U.S.C. § 2283.

60. 28 U.S.C. § 2361.

61. 11 U.S.C. §§ 105, 362.

62. 28 U.S.C. § 1651.

63. 659 F.2d 1332 (5th Cir. 1981), *cert. denied sub nom.* Three J. Farms, Inc. v. Plaintiffs' Steering Comm., 456 U.S. 936 (1982).

members of the class filed a new class action lawsuit in state court in South Carolina, alleging only violations of South Carolina's antitrust laws. Obviously, this new suit threatened to upset the federal settlement, since the defendants had little reason to settle the federal suit if it faced additional liability in state court. The district court enjoined the renegade class members from continuing their South Carolina proceeding. On appeal, the Fifth Circuit assumed that the district court possessed the power to issue the anti-suit injunction; it skipped to the second step of the analysis and focused its attention on whether the injunction was consistent with the Anti-Injunction Act. It is generally thought that the All Writs Act served as the source of the power to issue the injunction.

The scope of the All Writs authority was more clearly presented in a factually similar case, *In re Baldwin-United Corp.*[64] *Baldwin-United* involved twenty-six multidistricted securities class actions. Eventually eighteen of twenty-six defendants agreed to settle. Believing that the proposed settlements were inadequate, various state attorneys general began investigations into the defendants' activity with an eye toward commencing *parens patriae* lawsuits on behalf of their citizens. The district court issued an injunction preventing New York's attorney general and other attorneys general receiving notice of the injunction from commencing a case in any state or federal court concerning the matter. The injunction was thus broader than *Corrugated Container*'s injunction in two respects: It operated against a person who was not a party to the original cases, and it extended the injunction to benefit not only the eighteen defendants that settled but also the eight that did not. The Second Circuit affirmed the injunction. The court of appeals thought that the step was necessary to preserve the court's jurisdiction over a potential settlement that was "so far advanced that it was the virtual equivalent of a *res* over which the district court required full control."[65] Since the attorneys general were merely seeking relief on behalf of citizens who were already class members, the court of appeals was untroubled by the their nonparty status. Extending the injunction to non-settling defendants was a closer question in the court's mind, but it thought the action justified — at least until the situation stabilized — with respect to the settlement involving the eighteen other defendants. The court of appeals located the authority for both halves of the anti-suit injunction in the All Writs Act: "An important feature of the All-Writs Act is its grant of authority to preserve the court's ability to reach or enforce its decision in a case over which it has proper jurisdiction."[66]

64. 770 F.2d 328 (2d Cir. 1985).   66. *Id.* at 338.
65. *Id.* at 337.

Despite its seemingly broad sweep and the presence of a centralized decisionmaker, federal courts' anti-suit injunctive power is significantly constrained in ways that make it less useful for optimal aggregation than it might initially appear. For instance, both *Corrugated Container* and *Baldwin-United* exercised the power only when the federal court had before it something that resembled a *res* — in both cases, a proposed settlement. An effective aggregation power, however, would come into play long before the settlement stage; by the time of settlement, most of the inefficiency of parallel state and federal proceedings has already been suffered. As long as the federal courts are captured by the distinction between *in rem* and *in personam* jurisdiction, however, they would appear to lack a more general power to enjoin parallel state proceedings at an early stage. As the Supreme Court observed in a related context, "[w]e have never viewed parallel *in personam* actions as interfering with the jurisdiction of either court."[67] Put differently, the concern for optimal aggregation is not the concern of the All Writs Act.

Neither the interpleader nor the bankruptcy stay suffers from this late-in-the-day problem; these stays can be entered as soon as the interpleader action or the bankruptcy petition is filed. But each of them is limited as well. Obviously, the bankruptcy stay applies only when a company or its creditors feel the need to seek the protection of the bankruptcy court — a step that is never taken lightly. The problem with the interpleader stay is more complex. The idea of interpleader is that everyone who claims to have a stake in a particular piece of property or asset should be joined in a single proceeding in which the actual ownership interests in that property can be determined conclusively. To see the limits of interpleader in this context, consider *State Farm Fire & Casualty Co. v. Tashire*,[68] in which several dozen people were killed or injured in an accident between a bus and a truck. The owner of the truck had a $20,000 insurance policy, which was clearly insufficient to satisfy all claims. Cases against the truck's owner and driver, as well as against the owner and driver of the bus, sprang up in several state and federal courts. The truck owner's insurance company commenced a statutory interpleader action in federal court. The court initially enjoined only those state and federal proceedings against the truck owner and his insurance company. Eventually, however, the judge expanded the injunction to preclude the prosecution of any cases against any

---

67. Vendo Co. v. Lektro-Vend Corp., 433 U.S. 623, 642 (1977) (plurality opinion). Ortiz v. Fibreboard Corp., 527 U.S. 815 (1999), although deciding a different point, might also counsel hesitation about excessive creativity in attempting to analogize settlement funds to a traditional *res*. *Ortiz* is discussed in detail *infra* ch.5, nn.133-39, 201, 281-85 and accompanying text.

68. 386 U.S. 523 (1967).

defendant in any forum other than his court. Effectively the district court had crafted an injunction that drew all cases into a single forum, thus achieving what appeared to be optimal aggregation.

The Supreme Court overturned the injunction. It ruled that the limits of the court's interpleader stay power was the property or asset at stake; it did not have a more general power to stay proceedings related to, but not directly affecting, the insurance policy. "There is nothing in the statutory scheme . . . which requires that the tail be allowed to wag the dog in this fashion. . . . We recognize, or course, that our view of interpleader means that it cannot be used to solve all the vexing problems of multiparty litigation arising out of a mass tort. But interpleader was never intended to perform such a function, to be an all-purpose 'bill of peace.'"[69]

When one conceives of the bankruptcy estate or the interpleaded property as a *res*, and combines that with the quasi-*res* analysis of *Baldwin-United*, one can see how tightly connected a federal court's anti-suit power and the notion of an *in rem* proceeding are. Despite occasional calls from commentators for a more expansive power,[70] a general anti-suit injunctive power designed to achieve intersystem aggregation remains as elusive as a similar power in intra-system aggregation.

Any putative anti-suit injunction power in the intersystem context is made even more difficult by the strictures of the Anti-Injunction Act. 28 U.S.C. §2283 provides: "A court of the United States may not grant an injunction to stay proceedings in a State court except as expressly authorized by Act of Congress, or where necessary in aid of jurisdiction, or to protect or effectuate its judgments." A cornerstone of our federal system, § 2283 is designed to prevent the friction that might arise from federal interference in ongoing state proceedings. It does not apply to cases that have not yet commenced;[71] hence, the injunction in *Baldwin-United* did not implicate the Act. Once a state case has commenced, as it had in

---

69. *Id.* at 535. For a brief description of the bill of peace, an old equitable device to prevent needless relitigation and its modern fall into desuetude, see TIDMARSH & TRANGS-RUD, *supra* n.30, at 423-25.

70. A recent example is the proposal of the American Law Institute. As part of a series of reforms intended to permit aggregation of multiparty multiforum litigation in one forum, the ALI recommended that the aggregation court be given the power to "enjoin transactionally related proceedings" in other courts when these cases "substantially impair[ ] or interfere[ ] with the consolidated actions" and the injunction "would promote the just, efficient, and fair resolution of the actions before" the court. AMERICAN LAW INSTITUTE, COMPLEX LITIGATION: STATUTORY RECOMMENDATIONS AND ANALYSIS § 5.04 (1994).

71. Dombrowski v. Pfister, 380 U.S. 479 (1965).

in *Corrugated Container*, the Act comes into play and prevents any anti-suit injunction that does not come within one of its three exceptions.

Corrugated Container itself was somewhat unclear about which exception entitled the district court to enter the injunction against the South Carolina case. There was no express authority from Congress to permit the injunction.[72] Arguably, however, both the second exception ("necessary in aid of its jurisdiction") and the third ("to protect or effectuate its judgments") applied. The leading case on the second exception is *Atlantic Coast Line Railroad Co. v. Brotherhood of Locomotive Engineers*,[73] which suggests that the exception should be very narrowly read, and is akin to the third exception: "Both exceptions . . . imply that some federal injunctive relief may be necessary to prevent a state court from so interfering with a federal court's consideration or disposition of a case as to seriously impair the federal court's flexibility and authority to decide that case."[74] The leading case on the third (or "relitigation") exception is *Chick Kam Choo v. Exxon Corp.*,[75] which suggests that the exception does not come into play until a state proceeding threatens to undo the preclusive effect of a federal judgment.

Notably, the second exception to the Anti-Injunction Act tracks the language of the All Writs Act, a fact suggesting that the Anti-Injunction Act serves as no barrier when the All Writs Act authorizes an injunction. Courts have tended to construe the two Acts in this consistent fashion, and have even used *Atlantic Coast Line* to discern the meaning of the All Writs Act.[76] Since *Atlantic Coast Line* is parsimonious in its understanding of the second exception, a federal court's anti-suit power is narrow indeed; the mere existence of related state proceedings is not a sufficient reason to invoke § 2283's second or third exception.[77] The first exception holds the most promise, at least when Congress acts. It has done so with bankruptcy and interpleader stays, but these statutory powers are too limited to serve as the basis for a general anti-suit power. Congress has never considered enacting a general power in complex cases.

---

72. In limited circumstances, an express authorization from Congress may not be required. The leading case is Mitchum v. Foster, 407 U.S. 225 (1972).

73. 398 U.S. 281 (1970).

74. *Id.* at 295. It is generally believed that a federal court's power to enjoin state proceedings when the court first obtains jurisdiction over a *res* is "necessary in aid of its jurisdic-

tion," so that *in rem* injunctions pass muster under the Anti-Injunction Act. *See* Standard Microsystems Corp. v. Texas Instruments, Inc., 916 F. 2d 58 (2d Cir. 1990).

75. 486 U.S. 140 (1988).

76. *See Baldwin-United*, 770 F. 2d at 335.

77. *Standard Microsystems*, 916 F. 2d at 60.

Once again, the scope of our present aggregation doctrines falls short of the needs of optimal aggregation. As the Anti-Injunction Act reminds us, however, optimal aggregation is neither the only relevant value, nor perhaps the most important. Maintaining a proper respect for the dignity and independence of state courts is an essential aspect of any aggregation doctrines in complex litigation.

3. Removal

As we saw in the context of intra-system aggregation, stays and anti-suit injunctions are not the only mechanisms by which aggregation can occur; it is also possible to develop a device that directly transfers a case from one forum to another. At present only one power exists to transfer cases: removal from state to federal court. This power is a one-way ratchet: Cases can be removed from the state to the federal system, but there is no "reverse removal" from the federal to the state system.[78] Once again, the federal system demonstrates an advantage as the system for optimal aggregation.

Although there are dozens of specific removal statutes scattered throughout the United States Code, the basic removal statute is 28 U.S.C. § 1441. Removal must occur within 30 days of the time when the case first becomes removable; thus, if Smith files his case in state court against TUV (a non-diverse defendant), and six months later amends the complaint to include a federal question claim, TUV has thirty days from the amendment to effect removal.[79]

Under § 1441, removal jurisdiction is keyed to the federal courts' original jurisdiction; removal does not create federal jurisdiction over a claim that otherwise lacks it. (Note the parallelism between this rule and *Hoffman v. Blaski*, which did not permit § 1404 transfer to a court unless that court would have been a proper original venue.) To some extent, this is an overstatement; even some cases that could have been properly filed in federal court as an original matter cannot be removed to federal court subsequently. First, a plaintiff who wishes a diversity case to remain in state court need only file the case in a court in a state in which one or more defendants is a citizen; the case then becomes non-removable.[80] Second, also in diversity

---

78. The American Law Institute, as part of its general proposals to effect aggregation of multiparty multi-forum litigation, has proposed reverse removal in some circumstances. *See* ALI, *supra* n.70, § 4.01.

79. 28 U.S.C. § 1446(b). In this hypothetical, the federal court would have supplemental jurisdiction over

the state law claim if it arose from a common nucleus of operative fact. *See* City of Chicago v. Int'l College of Surgeons, 522 U.S. 156 (1997).

80. 28 U.S.C. § 1441(b). In federal question cases, removal is permitted without regard to defendants' citizenship.

cases, a case becomes non-removable one year after the case is filed in state court; thus, if A files a case against XYZ and TUV (recall that XYZ is diverse) in state court, and if TUV is dismissed from the case more than one year after the case commenced, XYZ cannot remove the case.[81] Third, in both federal question and diversity cases, if multiple defendants are sued in state court, most courts have held that the case is not removable unless all the defendants sign the notice of removal; if XYZ or TUV is satisfied with A's choice of a state forum, the other can do very little to effect a transfer of the case to a federal forum.[82]

As an intersystem aggregation device, removal suffers from some significant deficits. First, in those few cases in which a state court is the better forum for aggregation, removal frustrates, rather than advances, optimal aggregation. Second, since removal jurisdiction is keyed to original jurisdiction, a plaintiff who wishes to obtain a state forum can act strategically to thwart a federal forum by refusing to plead any federal claim and then either joining a non-diverse additional party or suing in a state court of the defendant's residence. In this situation, a defendant's only chance at removal is to attempt to convince the federal court that the plaintiff's joinder of the defendant(s) that make the case non-removable is fraudulent. A relatively large body of case law has developed around a defendant's claim that a plaintiff fraudulently joined non-diverse additional parties and the court's ability to ignore the citizenship of fraudulently joined persons. Suffice it to say that proving fraudulent joinder is a difficult matter.

Third, the federal forum is not completely secure even after removal; sometimes a plaintiff can fiddle with his or her claims to remove the basis for federal jurisdiction. When this happens, the federal court in some situations will ignore the plaintiffs' patently strategic behavior. In other cases, however, the federal court will permit the case to be "remanded" to state court.[83]

Fourth, removal usually places the fate of optimal intersystem aggregation in the hands of the defendants, who are more concerned with strategic advantage than with optimal aggregation. If at least

---

81. 28 U.S.C. § 1446(b). Federal question cases have no comparable one-year limitation; the case is removable within 30 days of the first assertion of the federal claim.

82. *See* 28 U.S.C. § 1441(a); 14C CHARLES A. WRIGHT ET AL., FEDERAL PRACTICE & PROCEDURE § 3731 (1998). One option is for defendant on a fed-

eral question claim to argue that the federal question is "separate and independent" within the meaning of 28 U.S.C. §1441(c).

83. For a brief look at the situation in which remand may or may not occur, see TIDMARSH & TRANGSRUD, *supra* n.30, at 385.

some defendants are happy with the state forum, then the case usually cannot be removed. In recent years, however, some courts have claimed to enjoy a *sua sponte* power to remove some cases that the parties either did not or could not remove. These courts typically locate this removal power, which runs counter to adversarial theory, in the All Writs Act.[84] Such a power, if it exists at all, "is not a jurisdictional blank check which district courts may use whenever they deem it advisable"; the state case must interfere in an important way with an ongoing federal case, and this is difficult to demonstrate.[85] Without a strong *sua sponte* power, therefore, removal decisions usually remain decentralized. There is no equivalent to the Judicial Panel on Multidistrict Litigation to ensure optimal aggregation.

Fifth, the lack of a "Judicial Panel for Removal" highlights another problem with the present removal statute: Removal merely brings a case into the federal system; it does not aggregate the cases in a single forum. When a case is removed, its venue is the federal district that encompasses the state court from which it was removed.[86] In widely dispersed litigation in which removal occurred, the cases would still remain dispersed across many federal forums. As we have seen, there exist important limits on the ability of federal courts to aggregate related dispersed litigation in a single federal venue. Thus, bringing the cases into the federal system does not guarantee optimal aggregation.

At the end of the day, therefore, removal is an imperfect solution to the problem of intersystem aggregation. Nothing remotely akin to the Judicial Panel on Multidistrict Litigation, which was useful in dealing with intra-system aggregation, exists to deal with inter-system aggregation. The American Law Institute has proposed the creation of such a panel, called the Complex Litigation Panel, that would have the power both to remove cases from any state court to a single federal court and to aggregate dispersed federal cases in that same federal court.[87] Thus far, however, neither Congress nor the courts have taken up the ALI's invitation to create a truly effective intersystem and intra-system aggregation authority.

---

84. *See* NAACP v. Metro. Council, 144 F.3d 1168 (8th Cir.), *cert. denied*, 525 U.S. 826 (1998).

85. *In re* "Agent Orange" Prod. Liab. Lit., 996 F.2d 1425, 1431 (2d Cir. 1993), *cert. denied sub nom.* Ivy v. Diamond Shamrock Chem. Co., 510 U.S. 1140 (1994). Shortly before this book went to press, the Supreme Court granted certiorari in order to determine whether district courts in fact enjoy an All Writs removal power. Syngenta Crop Prot., Inc. v. Henson, *cert. granted*, 122 S. Ct. 1062 (2002).

86. 28 U.S.C. § 1441(a).

87. ALI, *supra* n.70, §§ 3.01, 5.01.

D. CONCLUSION

The present tools fitfully permit intersystem aggregation. As long as removal is keyed to the original jurisdiction of the federal courts, the only hope for optimal intersystem aggregation is a more expansive view of federal subject matter jurisdiction in large-scale cases. Even this more expansive view, however, is an insufficient response as long as our problems of federal intra-system aggregation remain unresolved.

The difficult question is whether these problems should be resolved. Some of our most cherished procedural assumptions seem hopelessly in conflict. Transactionalism and efficiency push for greater powers of intra-system and intersystem aggregation. Litigant autonomy and federalism caution against them. Uneasily in the mix is our trans-substantive ideal, which is ill-served when the timing of an aggregation decision can have a dramatic effect on the outcome of the aggregated litigation and when such outcomes might vary from the outcomes in routine litigation.

These considerations seem imponderable enough. In fact, they ultimately involve only a segment of the aggregation problems in complex litigation: the problem of how to handle the cases that have already been filed. In many ways, the most difficult aggregation problems involve the potential cases that have not yet been filed. Whether and how these claims might be aggregated is the subject of the next chapter.

Chapter 5

STRUCTURAL COMPLEXITY: NONPARTIES, JOINDER, AND PRECLUSION

Until now, we have examined devices to bring together cases that already have been filed. Unless these cases can be brought together, optimal aggregation is not possible. Bringing already-filed cases together, however, is not a sufficient response to the aggregation question. The other half of the problem is bringing into the litigation the claims of those who have not yet commenced a lawsuit.

The importance of the nonparty problem varies with the type of litigation. On one end of the spectrum is a single-event lawsuit, such as a train wreck or a single instance of securities fraud, in which all of the allegedly harmful conduct and resulting injuries have already occurred. In this circumstance, the operation of the statute of limitations puts a realistic end to the assertion of the plaintiffs' claims; if plaintiffs sit on the sidelines for too long, they will simply lose their rights. Later-filed claims will put no great demands on the legal system. Assuming reasonably good mechanisms of intra-system and intersystem aggregation, inefficient relitigation occurs only when the first-filed cases might realistically be expected to conclude before the statute of limitations runs out — a rare event indeed.

At the other end of the spectrum is a latent injury mass tort, such as DES, asbestos, or tobacco, in which the allegedly harmful conduct may have occurred over a long period of time. People are exposed to the product and suffer injuries over a similarly long period of time. In this circumstance, the early cases likely will be completed long before the injuries of later-injured plaintiffs have even manifested themselves. There is a realistic risk of inefficiency by virtue of the trial of similar issues time and again. In extreme cases, the early cases may even exhaust the resources of the defendant and leave the later plaintiffs with no effective remedy. Also at this end of the spectrum lie various injunctive cases, such as desegregation or discrimination cases, in which groups of students or workers may have varying interests regarding the relief sought. If one group sits out the first litigation, and then files a separate case that results in an order for relief that is inconsistent with the relief obtained in the first litigation, the remedies obtained by the early plaintiffs will be insecure. On the other hand, if the latter group is precluded from obtaining a remedy because of the first litigation, their own day in court has been effectively pretermitted without their consent or participation — a fact that is not consonant with our usual notions of due process.

These situations cry out for some sort of solution to aggregate nonparties, in order either to reduce the burden to the parties and the court of relitigation, or to ensure that both early-filing and late-filing plaintiffs enjoy an equitable share of any remedy. But aggregation of nonparties immediately raises tensions with some of our other procedural ideals, such as the autonomous right to choose when, where, how, and against whom to file suit and the desire to ensure that procedural variations in ordinary and aggregated litigation do not cause outcome-determinative differences.

Assuming that aggregation of nonparties is in fact desirable, the next issue is the best approach. One possibility is a "joinder" solution: All persons with related claims or interests are forced to join as parties in the first litigation. A second possibility is a "preclusion" solution: The persons with related claims or interests are precluded from contesting the factual and legal issues that are determined in the first litigation and that are relevant to the nonparties' cases as well. A compromise solution would extend to nonparties the opportunity to join the early litigation, but would not insist on joinder. Whether they joined the litigation or not, however, the nonparties would be bound by the relevant factual and legal determinations from the first litigation.

In this chapter, we begin by examining our present rules of joinder and preclusion in order to determine whether they can, and should, achieve nonparty aggregation. We focus on joinder and preclusion rules at the federal level, both because these rules have been adopted in many states and because, as we have seen, the federal system has significant advantages in dealing with the aggregation of already-filed cases.

At the end of chapter, we will address the most intractable problem in nonparty aggregation: "future" plaintiffs. Nonparty claimants can be broken down into three types: those that presently have injuries due to defendant's wrongdoing but have not yet asserted them, those that have been exposed to the defendant's wrongdoing but have not yet suffered an injury, and those that have neither been exposed to defendant's wrongdoing nor suffered an injury. The first category presents the standard nonparty aggregation problems on which most of this chapter will focus. The latter two categories are the "future plaintiffs"; sometimes the second category is referred to as the "present futures," and the third category is referred to as the "future futures." Future plaintiffs present a most difficult aggregation problem indeed.

A. JOINDER

It is typical to divide the joinder rules into two types: voluntary (or permissive) joinder rules and involuntary joinder rules. As we shall see, this division is somewhat artificial, but it provides a convenient initial structure for describing how to bring nonparties into a lawsuit.

1. Voluntary Joinder

The basic voluntary joinder rule is Federal Rule of Civil Procedure 20. The first sentence of Rule 20(a) states in part: "All persons may join in one action as plaintiffs if they assert any right to relief . . . in respect of or arising out of the same transaction, occurrence, or series of transactions or occurrences and if any question of law or fact common to all these persons will arise in the action." The second sentence states the obverse proposition: "All persons . . . may be joined in one action as defendants if there is asserted against them . . . any right to relief in respect of or arising out of the same transaction, occurrence, or series of transactions or occurrences and if any question of law or fact common to all defendants will arise in the action."

The first critical matter to notice is the word "may": Rule 20 joinder is permissive, both in the sense that plaintiffs with related claims may, but are not required to, join together; and in the sense that the plaintiff(s) may, but are not required to, join all defendants. Rule 20 does not *require* that plaintiffs join together, or that they join all defendants. Instead, Rule 20 relies on a model of consent: No person can be made a plaintiff against his or her will, and no person can be made a defendant against the will of the plaintiffs.

This permissive approach to joinder is highly consistent with an adversarial system, in which plaintiffs seek to structure the litigation to their best advantage. If joinder of additional plaintiffs or defendants is strategically advantageous, then joinder is available as long as all Rule 20 plaintiffs consent. If joinder is not strategically advantageous, then plaintiffs are not compelled to join additional plaintiffs or defendants. From the viewpoints of efficiency, transactionalism, and optimal aggregation, however, this approach is far from ideal. Moreover, as with other doctrines of aggregation that we have examined, this rule contains structural constraints that both limit its aggregation potential and create opportunities for aggregation-frustrating strategic behavior.

a. *Structural Limitations.* Even when a plaintiff wishes to join the sideline-sitting potential plaintiffs and defendants in an optimal fashion, Rule 20 joinder is not automatic. As already mentioned, the first limitation is that the joinder of additional plaintiffs requires their consent. This limitation is not expressly stated in the text of Rule 20, but it seems a necessary implication of other joinder rules that provide for compulsory joinder. The few cases that bear on the subject suggest that a plaintiff cannot use Rule 20 to force the involuntary joinder of other plaintiffs, a defendant cannot use Rule 20 to force the joinder of additional plaintiffs or defendants, and the court cannot use Rule 20 as a source of *sua sponte* power to force involuntary joinder of either plaintiffs or defendants.[1] Thus, Rule 20 requires the acquiescence of the sideline-sitting plaintiffs — an agreement that, even assuming that the putative plaintiffs can be identified and located, is unlikely to be forthcoming in a significant percentage of cases.

Second, the rule itself contains two restrictions: The joined claims must arise out of the same transaction, occurrence, or series of transactions or occurrences, and at least one common question of law or fact must exist. The "commonality" requirement is not usually difficult to surmount; the harder question is exactly what constitutes a "transaction, occurrence, or series of transactions or occurrences." Perhaps the most famous case interpreting this language is *Mosley v. General Motors Corp.*,[2] a case which involves the consensual joinder of plaintiffs. In *Mosley*, ten employees brought suit against their employer and union, alleging racial and gender discrimination in hiring, promotions, and terms of employment. Since the ten employees did not work together and had been injured in different ways by different conduct at different plants of the defendant, the district court held that the complaint did not satisfy Rule 20. The Eighth Circuit disagreed, stating that the "transaction or occurrence" test is a flexible one in which all "reasonably related claims can be

---

1. Lyne v. Arthur Anderson & Co., 1991 WL 247576 (N.D. Ill.); Pan Am. World Airways, Inc. v. United States District Court for the Central District of California, 523 F.2d 1073 (9th Cir. 1973); *but see* Cle-Ware Ray-co, Inc. v. Perlstein, 401 F. Supp. 1231 (S.D.N.Y. 1975) (on plaintiff's motion, joining additional plaintiff under Rule 20; whether additional plaintiff consented to joinder is not clear from the opinion).

2. 497 F.2d 1330 (8th Cir. 1974). For a recent similar opinion, see Alexander v. Fulton County, 207 F.3d 1303 (11th Cir. 2000).

joined together.[3] The key, according to *Mosley*, was that all the putative plaintiffs alleged that the discrimination arose from the same set of corporate policies that had a common genesis and purpose, albeit with different individual manifestations.

Although *Mosley* suggests a generous attitude toward permissive joinder and Rule 20 sometimes has been used to join thousands of plaintiffs in one case, *Mosley* is better viewed as a case on one end of the Rule 20 spectrum rather than as the ultimate word on its meaning. Other cases appear to require a somewhat tighter connection among the putative plaintiffs' claims in order to satisfy Rule 20.[4] An excellent test of the breadth of Rule 20 is to revert back to Smith's asbestos lawsuit against XYZ and Jones's asbestos lawsuit against QRS. Assuming that there existed a court with jurisdiction over both defendants, could Smith and Jones join their separate cases of asbestos exposure together in a single suit? Would the answer depend on whether Smith and Jones alleged some sort of concerted action or conspiracy on the part of XYZ and QRS? Similarly, suppose that Smith and Green are both injured by XYZ's asbestos, but in different plants at different times while performing different jobs. Could Smith and Green join in one case, or would their only hope be to file their cases in the same court and consolidate them through the mechanisms we examined in Chapter 2?

The cases decided under Rule 20 do not give a great deal of guidance on questions such as these; they tend to be long on reciting the Rule's elements and short on describing which principles should bear on the questions posed in the last paragraph. Some of our procedural system's foundational principles would suggest that joinder by Jones (or Green) would be appropriate. First, Rule 20 does not present one of the standard aggregation concerns: depriving plaintiffs of their right to control the forum for their case. Jones and/or Green have voluntarily chosen to join with Smith. Likewise, as long as XYS and QRS acted in similar ways towards the plaintiffs, the transactional preference supports joinder. Efficiency concerns would dictate joinder whenever the joinder of the cases would be less costly than the adjudication of separate disputes. Other basic principles cut the other way. Plaintiffs will presumably join together only when they see some tactical advantage in doing so: in other words, only when they perceive that the outcome of a joined suit will be more favorable than the outcomes of separate suits. If the reason for the better outcome is greater efficiency and more net gain to the plaintiff, then the court need not be concerned with joinder. But if

---

3. *Id.* at 1333.

4. *See, e.g.,* Bailey v. Northern Trust Co., 196 F.R.D. 513 (N.D. Ill. 2000); Grazione v. Am. Home Prod. Corp., 202 F.R.D. 638 (D. Nev. 2001).

the tactical advantage is that a joined case can impose greater costs on the defendant, or that a joined case will increase the likelihood of a plaintiffs' victory,[5] then concerns for inequitable outcomes for defendants, and the use of procedural rules that treat like cases (i.e., those cases that are joined compared to those that are not joined) in a disparate fashion, become more critical.

Rarely does a court make explicit the policy considerations that should underlie the process of giving content to the vacuous "transaction or occurrence" standard. Nonetheless, to some extent courts seem to intuit these concerns. For example, as we have seen, the rule regarding the joinder of additional plaintiffs is nearly identical to that for the joinder of defendants: It requires a single "transaction or occurrence" and a "common question of law or fact." With defendant joinder, of course, plaintiffs will not join defendants under Rule 20 unless there is some tactical advantage in doing so. In some cases, this advantage is nothing more than the tactical disadvantage that joinder causes to the defendants. Since the defendants have not volunteered to be part of the case, the issue is whether courts should take account of this dynamic and interpret the amorphous "transaction or occurrence" test somewhat more narrowly for defendant joinder than for plaintiff joinder.

Although cases do not often explicitly say that the "transaction or occurrence" test means different things in the plaintiff joinder and the defendant joinder contexts, the results in some cases are perhaps best explained by this proposition. In *Desert Empire Bank v. Insurance Co. of North America*, the court of appeals thought that the critical issue for Rule 20 joinder of defendants is whether it "comport[s] with the principles of fundamental fairness."[6] Other cases, however, seem to suggest that there is no difference in the plaintiff joinder and the defendant joinder contexts, and the determining factors in both contexts are trial convenience, the plaintiff's need for complete relief, and the elimination of multiple lawsuits.[7]

A third set of structural limitations on Rule 20 joinder is implicit in the rule: jurisdiction and venue. Since the Federal Rules of Civil Procedure cannot enlarge federal jurisdiction or venue,[8] the joinder

---

5. *See supra* ch.2, nn.3-4 and accompanying text.

6. 623 F.2d 1371, 1375 (9th Cir. 1980); *see also* Intercom Research Assoc., Ltd. v. Dresser Industries, Inc., 696 F.2d 53 (7th Cir. 1982); Nassau Cty. Assoc. of Ins. Agents, Inc. v. Aetna Life & Cas. Co., 497 F.2d 1151 (2d Cir.), *cert. denied*, 419 U.S. 968 (1974). Since they decided within days of each other, *Nassau* provides and especially stark contrast to *Mosley*.

7. League to Save Lake Tahoe v. Tahoe Reg. Planning Agency, 558 F.2d 914 (9th Cir. 1977).

8. F.R.Civ.P. 82.

of additional parties is still subject to the jurisdiction and venue rules we discussed in the last two chapters. The court must have territorial jurisdiction over all the parties joined under Rule 20, venue must lie in the chosen federal forum, and the joinder of additional parties must not defeat federal subject matter jurisdiction.

The enactment of 28 U.S.C. § 1367 in 1990 has engendered some confusion concerning subject matter jurisdiction over Rule 20 parties. Prior to § 1367, the rules were plain, albeit fairly hostile to large-scale aggregation in federal court. If all plaintiffs asserted well-pleaded federal claims against all defendants, jurisdiction existed over all the additional claims asserted by the plaintiffs joined under Rule 20. If all plaintiffs pleaded only state-law claims against all defendants, federal jurisdiction existed only if complete diversity existed and the separate claim of each plaintiff met the matter-in-controversy limitation.[9] If one plaintiff asserted a federal claim and the others asserted state claims for which complete diversity and the matter-in-controversy existed, federal jurisdiction was also present. But if one plaintiff asserted a federal claim and the others asserted state law claims that destroyed complete diversity or failed to meet the amount in controversy, or if one plaintiff asserted a federal claim against one defendant and a non-federal claim against another defendant, federal jurisdiction hinged on "pendent party jurisdiction" — a concept that the Supreme Court never expressly recognized. The lack of federal jurisdiction was even more plain when one plaintiff properly asserted a diversity claim against one defendant, but the other plaintiffs or defendants either were not diverse or else the additional claims lacked the requisite matter-in-controversy. Here, too, the Court had never explicitly permitted pendent party jurisdiction.

The absence of federal jurisdiction in some of these scenarios is less certain after the passage of § 1367. The scenario in which federal claims by some plaintiffs are mixed with state-law claims by other plaintiffs joined under Rule 20 is addressed in § 1367(a): The federal court has jurisdiction over the state-law claims as long as all claims "are so related . . . that they form part of the same case or controversy under Article III"; this test, presumably but not certainly, is the *Gibbs* "common nucleus of operative fact" test.[10] The scenario in which some plaintiffs with claims under state law meet the complete diversity and matter-in-controversy requirements and co-plaintiffs joined under Rule 20 lack either diversity or the matter-in-controversy requirement is addressed in § 1367(b). Unfortunately, this section of the statute is hardly a model of clarity. On the one

---

9. *See supra* ch.4, nn.11-18 and accompanying text.

10. *See supra* ch.4, n.20 and accompanying text.

hand, § 1367(b) seeks to preserve the complete diversity and matter-in-controversy aggregation rules of § 1332; on the other, the statute applies only to "claims by plaintiffs against persons made parties under Rules 14, 19, 20 or 24 of the Federal Rules of Civil Procedure, or over persons proposed to be joined as plaintiffs under Rule 19 of such rules, or seeking to intervene as plaintiffs under Rule 24 of such rules." Thus, § 1367(b) preserves the rule of complete diversity for plaintiffs' claims asserted against additional *defendants*. Notably absent from the list in § 1367(b) are claims by other *plaintiffs* joined under Rule 20. Apparently, the requirements of complete diversity and per-plaintiff matter-in-controversy have been abandoned, as long as § 1332's requirements are satisfied by at least one plaintiff. If this reading of the text is sound, the only jurisdictional limit on the joinder of such Rule 20 plaintiffs would appear to be § 1367(a)'s "relatedness" test.

It is difficult to believe that Congress intended such an obvious breach of the time-worn complete diversity and matter-in-controversy rules; but, at the same time, it is difficult to escape the plain language of the statute. The question has received considerable academic attention (in part because of the nice "text versus context" debate that it engenders). Some courts have held that the plain text prevails, and § 1367(b) has washed away the complete diversity and per-plaintiff matter-in-controversy limitations on the joinder of additional Rule 20 plaintiffs.[11] This question ultimately awaits review in the Supreme Court. In the meantime, it is difficult to bemoan the possible collapse of two statutory glosses — complete diversity and per-plaintiff matter-in-controversy — that have frustrated the optimal aggregation of complex cases for many years. A fairer criticism of this expansive interpreation of federal jurisdiction is that § 1367(b) has also eliminated these glosses in non-complex cases, in which the interests of federalism might have suggested a different outcome.

b. Strategic Behavior. Until now, we have focused on the statutory and rule-based limitations imposed on a plaintiff who wanted to use Rule 20 to aggregate related claims of potential plaintiffs against potential defendants in an optimal way. In the real world, plaintiffs do not have an incentive to achieve optimal joinder; they have an incentive to structure the litigation in the manner likeliest to produce a favorable outcome. In a significant number of

---

11. *See* Stromberg Metal Works, Inc. v. Press Mech., Inc., 77 F.3d 928 (7th Cir. 1996); Patterson Enterprises, Inc. v. Bridgestone/Firestone, Inc., 812 F. Supp. 1152 (D. Kan. 1993). *Contra,* Casteel v. Sara Lee Corp., 51 F. Supp. 2d 816 (E.D. Mich. 1999). Of course, even if jurisdiction existed, a federal court could in its discretion decline to hear the claims. 28 U.S.C. § 1367(c).

cases, this structure will depart from the optimal aggregation structure. Nor is Rule 20 equipped to respond to such strategic behavior by the plaintiffs. It is a rule of voluntary joinder; neither the court nor the defendants can force the joinder of additional parties.

To overcome strategic behavior by plaintiffs, rules that permit defendants, sideline-sitting plaintiffs, and/or the court to join additional parties are needed. The next section explores the ability of a nonparty who wishes to join in the case to intervene. After that, we turn to rules of involuntary or compulsory joinder of nonparties.

2. Intervention

Intervention is something of a hybrid — a midpoint between voluntary and involuntary joinder. The idea of intervention is that a nonparty that has certain interests in ongoing litigation, but has not been joined by the present parties, can join (or intervene in) the case. If intervention is permitted, the intervenor becomes a party and is bound, at least with regard to matters within the scope of the intervention, by the judgment.

In its way, intervention is a form of voluntary joinder. There is no requirement that a person intervene in the litigation, and no negative legal consequences to that person's right to file a separate case if he or she chooses not to intervene.[12] On the other hand, intervention is a paradigm shift from a pure system of voluntary joinder, because the creation of a right to intervene shifts to putative intervenors some measure of the plaintiff's autonomous right to determine the shape of the litigation. The shift can arguably be justified by transactionalism — our preference for adjudicating all aspects of a set of related events in a single case. Intervention is also supported by our desire for efficiency under the following conditions: when the intervention can dispose of issues or claims that might otherwise be repetitively litigated in separate suits, and when the intervention does not inject so many new parties or issues into the case that any gains from eliminating duplicative litigation are wiped out. Finally, to the extent that intervention can bring into the case persons needed to achieve remedial equity,[13] our preference for the like treatment of similarly situated persons would also support a right of intervention.

In the federal system, the balance among these competing concerns is struck by Rule 24. Rule 24 distinguishes between two types of intervention: intervention of right (Rule 24(a)) and permis-

---

12. *See* Martin v. Wilks, 490 U.S. 755 (1989).

13. For a description of remedial equity, see *supra* p. 11.

sive intervention (Rule 24(b)). As its name implies, intervention of right grants to the putative intervenor a right to intervene; he or she is able to enter the case as a party with full rights of participation, even when the existing parties oppose the request and even when the court thinks that the intervention is undesirable. Permissive intervention, on the other hand, provides a looser standard for intervention, but the putative intervenor must obtain the permission of the trial judge, who can either deny the application to intervene if it appears undesirable or limit the participation of the intervenor to something less than the full rights accorded other parties. Since intervention of right is the form of intervention usually sought by putative intervenors, as well as the one that is more thematically important in terms of the ability of the parties and the court to structure a lawsuit that includes nonparties, we focus here on the structural limitations and the strategic choices involved in intervention of right.[14]

a. *Structural Limitations.* Rule 24(a) provides for intervention of right when either Rule 24(a)(1) or Rule 24(a)(2) has been satisfied. Rule 24(a)(1) authorizes intervention when a "timely" request for intervention has been made and when, in addition, a statute authorizes intervention. Rule 24(a)(2) authorizes intervention when a "timely" request has been made and when, in addition, "the applicant claims an interest relating to the property or transaction which is the subject of the action and the applicant is so situated that the disposition of the action may as a practical matter impair or impede the applicant's ability to protect that interest, unless the applicant's interest is adequately represented by existing parties." Statutes permitting intervention of right are rare, and even when they do exist, they often track the language of Rule 24(a)(2). Rule 24(a)(2) is the critical provision for intervention of right.

To revert to our ongoing hypothetical, suppose that Smith sues XYZ in the United States District Court for the District of Maine. Smith does not join Green, whose case against XYZ arose elsewhere. Nor does he join Jones and QRS. There is no statutory right of intervention. Could Green intervene in the case? Could Jones? Assuming that it wished to, could QRS intervene?

The answers to these questions lie within the murky text of Rule 24(a)(2). Courts usually parse Rule 24(a)(2) into four distinct elements: timeliness, a protectable interest, an impairment of that interest, and a lack of adequate representation. For the most part,

---

14. For a short examination of Rule 24(b) permissive intervention and other doctrines of limited participation such as *amicus curiae*, see JAY TIDMARSH & ROGER H. TRANGSRUD, COMPLEX LITIGATION AND THE ADVERSARY SYSTEM 153-55 (1998).

each of these elements has been read in a flexible way, in order to achieve (in the words of one famous formulation) as much joinder "as is compatible with efficiency and due process."[15] To begin with the bookends, neither timeliness nor adequacy of representation poses a significant hurdle. Timeliness depends on a host of factors, such as the length of the delay before seeking to intervene, the reason for the delay, and the prejudice to the various participants created by the intervention or non-intervention.[16] For nonparties such as Green, Jones, or QRS that wish to intervene, and that presumably will do so at the earliest opportunity, this requirement usually poses an insignificant hurdle.

The same is true of the adequacy requirement. In *Trbovich v. United Mine Workers of America*, the Supreme Court noted that the requirement is fulfilled when the putative intervenor shows that representation of the intervenor's interest "'may be' inadequate; and the burden of making that showing should be treated as minimal."[17] In *Trbovich*, a disgruntled union member sought to intervene in a case brought by the government to obtain a new election of union officers. Even though both the government and the union member had a similar goal, the Court held that representation by the government was inadequate; the government was required by statute to serve the public interest, and not just the union members' private interests. Thus, a nonparty seeking to intervene to represent his or her specific interests in a case brought by others seeking to protect their specific interests generally has little difficulty identifying sufficient differences in strategy or circumstance to pass over the "minimal" inadequacy threshold.[18]

The remaining two issues — interest and impairment — present greater challenges for Green, Jones, QRS, and other putative intervenors. Exactly what should count as an "interest" for the purposes of Rule 24(a)(2) has been the subject of some disagreement, both in the Supreme Court and elsewhere. In one case, the Court took a stringent line, holding that the target of an IRS investigation did not have a "significantly protectable interest" in his corporation's records, which the IRS had subpoenaed as part of its investigation of

---

15. *See* Nuesse v. Camp, 385 F.2d 694, 700 (D.C. Cir. 1967) (speaking specifically of the "protectable interest" element).

16. *See* 7C CHARLES A. WRIGHT ET AL., FEDERAL PRACTICE & PROCEDURE § 1916 (1986).

17. 404 U.S. 528, 538 n.10 (1972).

18. For a case failing to find that the burden had been met in the context of litigation commenced by the government, see United States v. Hooker Chemicals & Plastics Corp., 749 F.2d 968 (2d Cir. 1984). *See also* Edwards v. City of Houston, 78 F.3d 983 (5th Cir. 1996) (describing presumption of adequacy in governmental litigation).

the target.[19] On the other hand, the Court permitted the intervention of California at the remedial phase of an antitrust case brought by the United States; California claimed a desire to protect the interests of its citizens in a competitive marketplace.[20] The same disagreements manifest themselves in the decisions of the lower courts. The generous view appears to be the dominant one; for instance, employees who are alleged victims of racial discrimination have been allowed to intervene as plaintiffs in a case brought by similarly situated employees,[21] and chambers of commerce and municipalities concerned about the deleterious economic consequences of an environmental suit against a major industry have been allowed to intervene as defendants.[22] According to the standard argument, broad joinder best comports with the concerns of efficiency and due process, and Rule 24(a)(2) should be read liberally in the large "atypical cases."[23] But cases to the contrary can also be found.[24]

The "interest" test is not, however, infinitely elastic. If Green (who also has a claim against XYZ) wants to intervene in Smith's case against XYZ, the relevant interest would probably exist. But if Jones, who was injured by QRS's asbestos, wants to intervene in order to aggregate related asbestos cases, it is harder to see how Jones has any "significantly protectable interest" in *Smith v. XYZ*. At best, Jones might have a general interest in the favorable development of substantive and evidentiary law, but in the absence of the court's inability to provide any useful remedy to Jones, that interest is highly attenuated. Jones's only hope for aggregation would be to file a separate suit and attempt to employ one of the aggregation devices we examined in earlier chapters.

The same general orientation toward intervention, with the same cautionary countertrend, exists for the "impairment" element of Rule 24(a)(2). As an initial matter, finding an impairment from non-intervention creates a theoretical challenge. After all, if a nonparty fails to intervene, he or she is not typically bound by the judgment in the case, and is still free to bring a separate lawsuit. In what sense,

19. Donaldson v. United States, 400 U.S. 517 (1971).

20. Cascade Natural Gas Corp. v. El Paso Natural Gas Co., 386 U.S. 129 (1967).

21. Cook v. Boorstin, 763 F.2d 1462 (D.C. Cir. 1985).

22. United States v. Reserve Mining Co., 56 F.R.D. 408 (D. Minn. 1972). In the same case, the judge allowed numerous states and public interest environmental groups to intervene as plaintiffs.

23. *Nuesse v. Camp*, 385 F.2d at 700.

24. *See* Envl. Def. Fund, Inc. v. Costle, 79 F.R.D. 235 (D.D.C. 1978 (distinguishing *Reserve Mining*); Susan Bandes, *The Idea of a Case*, 42 STAN. L. REV. 227, 282-83 (1990) (finding that federal courts employ at least six different tests to determine an "interest").

then, can the putative intervenor's case be regarded as "impaired" or "impeded"? Courts seeking to use Rule 24 to achieve broader joinder have answered this challenge by seizing on the words "as a practical matter"; even if the putative intervenor's interests may not be *legally* affected by the outcome of a case, the interests might be *practically* constrained. The classic constraint, often relied on by parties seeking to intervene, is the *stare decisis* effect of the present litigation: Although the first case does not legally bind a non-intervenor, the court's ruling on questions of law or evidentiary admissibility in the first case *might* establish unfavorable precedents that would guide the court in a subsequent case filed by the non-intervenor.[25] Another recognized constraint exists when the first lawsuit could establish a remedy that would have a negative, subsequently uncorrectable effect on the nonparty's economic or other interests.[26]

How does Green, who has arguably shown the requisite interest to intervene in Smith's suit, fare under the impairment prong? If Smith's case is likely to consume all of XYZ's assets, then Green can make a strong showing of such impairment; but rarely is a defendant so teetering on the edge of insolvency that a single case like Smith's will make this argument viable. Likewise, Green could say that the evidentiary or substantive rulings in the *Smith* case would create *stare decisis* impairment. If Green files his case in New York and Smith's case is in Maine, however, it is not clear that the same substantive law would apply, and the *stare decisis* effects of any evidentiary rulings would not exist (since Maine and New York are in different federal circuits). Since Jones does not have a claim against XYZ, his difficulties in showing a sufficient impairment are self-evidently greater.

There may be, however, one narrow escape route for Green, and perhaps for Jones as well. Starting from the premise that all four of the stated Rule 24 (a)(2) factors are directed toward a single purpose of achieving the broadest joinder consistent with efficiency and due process, some courts have suggested that the four factors should be interpreted with flexibility; as long as efficiency and fairness are served, a weak showing on one factor can be overcome by a strong showing on other factors.[27] Other courts have suggested that a stricter adherence to each of the four factors is required,[28] or else have suggested that efficiency and due process are not the only

---

25. Atlantis Dev. Corp. v. United States, 379 F.2d 818 (5th Cir. 1967); *Cook v. Boorstin*, 763 F.2d at 1470.

26. *Reserve Mining*, 56 F.R.D. at 414; *Edwards*, 78 F.3d at 1005-06.

27. *See, e.g.*, Kleisser v. United States Forest Serv., 157 F.3d 964 (3d Cir. 1998); Daggett v. Comm'n on Gov'tal Ethics & Election Practices, 172 F.3d 104 (1st Cir. 1999).

28. *See Kleisser*, 157 F.3d at 975 (Becker, J., concurring).

relevant considerations in making an intervention determination. Perhaps the best example of this latter line of thinking is *Bethune Plaza, Inc. v. Lumpkin*,[29] in which the court of appeals took a narrower view of *stare decisis* as an impairment factor. *Bethune* held that only the *stare decisis* effect of an appellate decision can constitute an impairment, and even then there can be no impairment if *amicus curiae* participation would be adequate. In reaching this conclusion, the court of appeals rejected the notion that broad representation of various interests and perspectives is an unadulterated good: "Permitting intervention liberally raises the costs of litigation and makes settlement harder, which may well discourage the initial suit and effectively block the real plaintiff from vindicating its own rights. To allow [putative intervenors] to intervene as of right would turn the court into a forum for competing interest groups, submerging the ability of the original parties to settle their own dispute (or have the court resolve it expeditiously)."[30]

Bethune Plaza highlights again the inherent tensions in our modern procedural goals. The transactional assumption favors strongly the resolution of all related interests in a single case, and the failure of the original parties to create a sufficiently broad party structure favors a strong right of intervention. This broad view is particularly appropriate in "public law litigation," which touches on myriad distinct interests whose full representation renders the party structure amorphous.[31] Efficiency underpinnings also favor a broad right of intervention, at least when the benefits of reduced relitigation of common issues outweigh the costs of additional complexity in party structure. But the adversarial preference, which grants the original parties the right to define the party structure and which works far less effectively with a cacophony of competing views,[32] takes a less enthusiastic approach to intervention of right.

How might these competing concerns, whose different directions seem to find reflection in the differing outcomes of cases, best be resolved? One solution requires us to return to the concept of the socially optimal litigation structure first discussed in Chapter 2, and particularly to the distinction between inefficient relitigation and remedial inequity.[33] If the right of intervention is interpreted largely

---

29. 863 F.2d 525 (7th Cir. 1988).

30. *Id.* at 531-33; *see also* FDIC v. Jennings, 816 F.2d 1488 (10th Cir. 1987).

31. For the classic description of public law litigation, see Ahram Chayes, *The Role of the Judge in Public Law Litigation*, 89 HARV. L. REV.

1281 (1976).

32. For the classic argument that the adversarial system functions best in a biopolar, two-sided dispute, see Lon L. Fuller, *The Forms and Limits of Adjudication*, 92 HARV. L. REV. 353 (1978).

33. *See supra* pp. 10-11.

in terms of efficiency, as some courts seem want to do, concerns such as transactionalism and autonomy slip into a subsidiary position — a subjugation that is explicable only if efficiency is (controversially) accorded *primus inter pares* status as a procedural principle. If the right of intervention is interpreted in accordance with concerns for remedial inequity, however, each principle receives some (albeit partial) vindication. Remedial inequity occurs when the first-filed litigation either renders later litigation on the same matter irrelevant or is undercut by later litigation that effectively unravels the rights determined in the first case. In these circumstances, a concern for the fair distribution of a remedy to all those whose interests are implicated in a particular transaction requires the structuring of joinder rules in a way that guarantees the putative intervenor the right to intervene. When inequity is not present, however, intervention *may* occur; but the nonparty seeking to intervene bears a much greater burden of showing either seriously inefficient relitigation or the outright inapplicability of usual autonomy concerns (by, for example, showing that the plaintiffs consented to the new party structure).

This last interpretation of the intervention issue is our own, although it is also highly consistent with the results of the cases. It vindicates each procedural principle partially, and none completely. Autonomy and transactionalism are respected in many, but not all, circumstances, and truly inefficient relitigation is prevented even as some inefficient relitigation is tolerated. Aside from its solomonic quality, can anything good be said about this resolution? We believe so. It starts from a premise of autonomy — the autonomy of the present parties to conduct their litigation as they see fit. It compromises that principle primarily when continued adherence to it would cause a loss of the equally valued autonomy interests of others. Our reconciliation of the clash of two incommensurable claims to free action assures the equal procedural treatment of all, and is therefore a sensible (albeit not the only possible) mediating principle.

To some extent, of course, this argument about the proper scope of intervention of right proves too much, for it argues as well for the involuntary joinder of nonparties. Intervention comes into play only when the nonparty "volunteers" for the case. Put differently, a right of intervention solves only a part of the problem of remedial inequity. A putative intervenor has an incentive to intervene when the first litigation will effectively preclude his or her rights, but usually he or she has little incentive — and more important, no obligation — to intervene when he or she is capable in the second litigation of enforcing his or her rights at the expense of the rights of the first litigant. Nor would there appear to be any "impairment" of the putative intervenor's interests in such a situation, thus making it hard to see how intervention is appropriate in this remedially inequitable situation. This criticism is valid, and we will return to it when we examine compulsory joinder shortly.

For now, however, let us assume that remedial equity provides the correct principle for considering questions of intervention. We now examine two final, significant limitations that prevent the parties and the court from achieving optimal aggregation through intervention. The first is subject matter jurisdiction. Prior to the passage of 28 U.S.C. § 1367,[34] the claim of an intervenor of right needed no independent basis of federal jurisdiction: As long as the district court had jurisdiction over the underlying case in which intervention was sought, the court usually had ancillary jurisdiction over the claim in intervention.[35] Section 1367, however, partially modified this rule: When the underlying claim is based in whole or part on grounds other then diversity, § 1367(a) provides that jurisdiction also exists over a claim in intervention as long as the two claims are "so closely related" as to be part of the same Article III case or controversy. Given the history of ancillary jurisdiction and § 1367, § 1367(a) appears to maintain the traditional scope of jurisdiction for a claim of intervention of right. But when the underlying claim is based solely on diversity of citizenship, § 1367(b) now provides that the claim of intervention of right cannot violate the requirements of 28 U.S.C. § 1332. Therefore, unless courts can "ungloss" the complete diversity and matter-in-controversy limitations of § 1332,[36] some claims made by intervenors of right — those state-law claims that destroy complete diversity or fail to exceed $75,000 — are structurally incapable of being integrated into the federal case.

A second and related limitation is the "standing" doctrine. Standing is partly constitutional and partly prudential in nature. It seeks to ensure that the litigants in a case have a close enough connection to the case or controversy to justify the invocation of federal jurisdiction. The general subject of standing is beyond the scope of this book; in broad terms, however, a party seeking to prove standing must show an "injury in fact," the traceability of the litigant's injury to the conduct of the defendant (i.e., causation, and the likelihood that a favorable decision will remedy the injury (i.e.,

---

34. For a general discussion, see *supra* ch.4, nn.23-26 and accompanying text.

35. *See* Wichita R. & Light Co. v. Pub. Util. Comm'n of Kansas, 260 U.S. 48 (1922). The rule was different for

permissive intervention, for which an independent basis of federal jurisdiction was required.

36. *See supra* ch.4, nn.11-18, 30-40 and accompanying text.

redressibility).[37] In some cases, an intervenor of right may have difficulty meeting these tests. One circumstance involves public interest advocacy groups or other organizations who suffer only indirect and remote harm due to the allegedly unlawful conduct. Another circumstance involves putative intervenors whose claims have not yet ripened — the "future future" plaintiffs. We return to the problem of the standing of "future futures" in the final part of this chapter.

Therefore, with intervention we see repeated a now-familiar story: Structural constraints in rules, statutes, and the Constitution can prevent the aggregation of related claims even when such aggregation would be regarded in some sense as optimal.

b. Strategic Behavior. Until now, we have largely operated on the assumption that the absent party desired intervention. In many situations, however, a nonparty may prefer not to intervene in the ongoing litigation, but instead to bide his or her time and file in a different forum of his or her choosing. If the nonparty files while the first litigation is still going on, then the issue becomes one of intra-district, intra-system, or intersystem aggregation. If the first litigation comes to a close before the nonparty files suit, aggregation is impossible.

Intervention rules are powerless to prevent this type of sideline-sitting. Just as Rule 20 is premised on the voluntary joinder choices of the plaintiff, Rule 24 is premised on the voluntary intervention decision of the nonparty. No court has thus far claimed a *sua sponte* power to order intervention.

This voluntary dimension of intervention is tempered in the real world, as we have seen, by the possibility that the ongoing litigation may as a practical matter determine the nonparty's rights. The ongoing litigation may deplete all of the defendants' available assets, or may result in an injunction that will immutably alter the legal or practical relationships of the nonparty. In these cases self-interest will often drive a nonparty to intervene; the preservation of the autonomous right to be heard in a forum of the nonparty's choice is a Pyrrhic victory when others have previously emptied the defendants' pockets.

In some cases, the tactical decisions run the other way. For instance, in *Martin v. Wilks,*[38] a group of African-American fire-fighters sued the City of Birmingham for racial discrimination. Although the case was widely known, no white firefighters inter-vened in the case to protect their interests in employment and

---

37. Lujan v. Defenders of Wild-   **38.** 490 U.S. 755 (1989).
life, 504 U.S. 555, 60-61 (1992).

promotion. The case resulted in a consent decree that arguably disadvantaged white firefighters. A group of white firefighters then sought to intervene to contest the decree, but their application was denied as untimely. The consent decree was entered. In a subsequent case by a different group of white firefighters challenging the consent decree as discriminatory, the Supreme Court, in a 5-4 decision, held that the plaintiffs were not bound to the prior consent decree and were free to challenge it. The rationale for the court's decision was somewhat unclear; it indicated both that there would be due process problems with seeking to bind a nonparty to a judgment and that the Federal Rules of Civil Procedure, including Rule 24, contemplated joinder as the proper mechanism for binding a person to a judgment.[39]

Martin v. Wilks is not an intervention case. But it does tell a nonparty that wants to see how a prior case turns out before deciding whether or when to file suit that there will be no legal repercussions if he or she does so. Whether to enter the case to affect its shape or to remain poised on the sidelines for an attack in the event that the case goes badly is a strategic choice left to the nonparty.

Given our views about remedial inequity, tools other than intervention therefore must be developed to deal with cases in this category. These tools might also be useful for dealing with cases in which the limits of Rules 20 and 24 create significant and inefficient relitigation. Therefore, intervention responds to, at best, only a small part of the need to achieve optimal aggregation. Nonetheless, as we shall see, it retains an influence over the involuntary joinder and preclusion alternatives that have been developed to address strategic refusals of nonparties to participate in a case.

3. Involuntary Joinder

As we have now seen, voluntary joinder and intervention limit, to some extent, the ability of a willing nonparty to enter a case. More

---

39. In a subsequent case arising from state court, the Supreme Court cited *Martin v. Wilks* in the course of holding that the due process clause prevents, in most circumstances, the attempt to bind a nonparty to a judgment. Richards v. Jefferson County, Alabama, 517 U.S. 793 (1996). *Cf.* S. Cent. Bell Tel. Co. v. Alabama, 526 U.S. 160 (1999) (same; citing *Richards* but not *Martin v. Wilks*).

In 1990, Congress amended Title VII to overrule the result in *Martin v. Wilks*; any person with notice of and an opportunity to object to a Title VII judgment prior to its entry cannot challenge the judgment subsequently. 42 U.S.C. § 2000e-2(n). This statute would appear to reflect Congress's judgment that *Martin v. Wilks* is not a decision of constitutional stature. The Supreme Court has not yet passed judgment on the constitutionality of the statute.

significantly, neither approach to joinder can force an unwilling nonparty into the case. We move, then, to rules of involuntary joinder. The focus here is whether these rules are capable of overcoming the structural limitations and strategic choices that we encountered in Rules 20 and 24.

There are three primary involuntary joinder devices: necessary party joinder (Rule 19), interpleader (Rule 22 and 28 U.S.C. § 1335), and class actions (Rule 23). Before we consider each in detail, however, it is worth pausing a moment to recall what is at stake with involuntary joinder.

As we have seen throughout this book, the fundamental orientation of our procedural system is toward litigant autonomy in matters concerning the commencement and maintenance of a lawsuit. That orientation manifests itself in the context of nonparty aggregation by insisting generally on a system of voluntary joinder — either the plaintiffs or, in the context of intervention, the nonparty must consent to the joinder. Any system of involuntary joinder departs from this fundamental orientation, and must therefore be justified by a principle of at least equivalent value. Unless we completely subvert the autonomy interests underlying Rule 20, any principle needs to be careful not to swallow the principle of voluntariness. Is efficiency an adequate justification? Is remedial equity? Won't any such justification create different systems of rules — one for small voluntarily joined cases and one for large involuntarily joined ones? How might that departure from our trans-substantive ideal be explained?

   a. Rule 19 (Necessary Party) Joinder. Derived from equity practice, the present Rule 19 requires the involuntary joinder of those nonparties whose presence in the lawsuit is "needed for just adjudication," if their joinder is feasible. Equity's term for such nonparties was "necessary parties," and although present Rule 19 does not use this term, the old label persists. Who exactly is a "necessary party" — or put differently, exactly when can we justify the joinder of a nonparty against the will of the plaintiff and/or the nonparty? What happens when it becomes impossible to join a necessary party, whether because the party's presence in the case would destroy the subject matter jurisdiction or venue of the federal court, the court may not be able to exercise territorial jurisdiction over such a nonparty, the nonparty may enjoy an immunity from suit, or there may exist some other barrier to joinder? By definition, the party is necessary. Should the court dismiss the case? Should it muddle along and adjudicate the case on a less than just and complete basis? Or should it attempt to remove the barrier to suit through creative interpretation of jurisdiction, venue, or immunity rules?

(i) Structural Limitations. Rule 19 attempts to answer these questions. Rule 19(a) defines who a necessary party is. Rule 19(b) describes how a court is to respond to a situation in which a necessary party cannot be joined — whether the nonparty is so "indispensable" that the case must be dismissed in the person's absence.

(A) Rule 19(a): Necessary Parties. According to Rule 19(a), there are three different types of necessary parties. The first, listed in Rule 19(a)(1), is the nonparty in whose "absence complete relief cannot be accorded those already parties." The second, under Rule 19(a)(2)(i), is the nonparty who "claims an interest relating to the subject of the action and is so situated that" adjudication of the case without the nonparty "as a practical matter impair[s] or impede[s] the [nonparty's] ability to protect that interest." The third, under Rule 19(a)(2)(ii), is the nonparty who "claims an interest relating to the subject of the action and is so situated that" one of the already joined parties is "subject to a substantial risk of incurring double, multiple, or otherwise inconsistent obligations." At the risk of some simplification, Rule 19(a)(1) protects the interests of existing plaintiffs in achieving a complete remedy by forcing the joinder of nonparties that might undo the remedy in the first case; Rule 19(a)(2)(ii) protects the interests of present defendants by forcing the joinder of nonparties whose separate suits might force the defendant to provide too much remedy; and Rule 19(a)(2)(i) protects the interests of the nonparties by forcing their joinder when the existing case will significantly impair their ability to obtain a remedy in subsequent litigation.

Recast in this light, Rule 19 mandatory joinder seems inconsistent with the view that aggregation should be required whenever it would be efficient to aggregate. On the other hand, Rule 19(a) seems strikingly consistent with the view that socially optimal aggregation should seek to overcome remedial inequity, which occurs whenever the nonparty will be deprived of an equitable share of a remedy by the outcome of the prior case (*cf.* Rule 19(a)(2)(i)) or the nonparty's subsequent suit will effectively undermine the finality of the remedy obtained in the first suit (*cf.* Rules 19(a)(1) and 19(a)(2)(ii)).

The case law has tended to interpret Rule 19(a) in a way that is narrower than the efficiency rationale would suggest is appropriate, but in a way that is consistent with the principle of remedial equity. For instance, in *Temple v. Synthes Corp.*,[40] the plaintiff filed suit in federal court against the manufacturer of a medical device, and in state case against the doctor who performed the operation and the hospital. Had the plaintiff chosen to bring the entire case in federal

40. 498 U.S. 5 (1990).

court, he could have done so; complete diversity of citizenship and the requisite matter in controversy were present. But the plaintiff did not wish to do so, and the doctor and hospital could not remove the state case to federal court since it had been filed in their home state. The manufacturer filed a motion to dismiss, arguing that the doctor and hospital, who had been participating in discovery in the federal case, were necessary parties. Although it did not specify the exact section of Rule 19(a) on which it relied, the district court ordered the plaintiff to join the state court defendants or face dismissal. The court reasoned that it had jurisdiction over the claims, that proceeding with the case would have an unspecified "effect on the absent parties,"[41] and that judicial economy would be served by the joinder. The plaintiff did not comply, so the district court dismissed the case against the manufacturer.

The Supreme Court overturned the dismissal in a *per curiam* opinion. "It has long been the rule," the Court said, "that it is not necessary for all joint tortfeasors to be named as defendants in a single lawsuit"; the various defendants were merely "permissive parties."[42] Although the Court recognized that there existed a "public interest in limiting multiple litigation,"[43] this consideration was not sufficient to carry the Rule 19(a) analysis. To put it in our terms, the separate suits, although inefficient, created no risk to plaintiff, defendant, or nonparties of an inequitably distributed remedy.

Similarly, in *Eldredge v. Carpenters 46 Northern California Counties Joint Apprenticeship and Training Committee*,[44] two plaintiffs brought a sex discrimination case against a joint labor-management committee that ran an apprenticeship and journeyman training program. The program admitted to membership any person first hired by an employer and then placed on the applicant registry for the program. Since employers were required by a labor agreement to hire a certain number of apprentices on each job site, the program has a steady stream of applicants. Women, however, were significantly underrepresented in the program.

Since it merely trained applicants that were independently hired, the defendant claimed that the 4,500 employers and 60 union locals involved in the hiring process were necessary parties. The district court agreed and ordered their joinder. When the plaintiffs found it impossible to effect such widespread joinder, the district court held that complete relief could not be given without the absent employers and unions, and that these nonparties were indispensable. As a result, the court dismissed the case.

---

41. Temple v. Synthes Corp., 130 F.R.D. 68, 69 (E.D. La. 1989).

42. 498 U.S. at 7, 8.

43. *Id.* at 7.

44. 662 F.2d 534 (9th Cir.), *cert. denied*, 459 U.S. 917 (1982).

The court of appeals reversed. Although it recognized that the employers had an interest in the fate of the training program, it did not believe that their absence left the remaining parties with less than complete relief. If the program were itself discriminating, relief against it was appropriate — even if this relief did not eradicate the root cause of the discrimination by employers and union locals.

Arguably, *Eldredge* booted the Rule 19(a) analysis. To a large extent, the training program's purported discrimination merely reflected the discrimination engaged in by the employers. If the employers continued to discriminate in their hiring practices at the end of the *Eldredge* suit, then one of two things would appear to be true. The first possibility is that the training program would still take applicants on the same basis as before the lawsuit, meaning that, under Rule 19(a)(1), the employers would need to be part of the case in order for the plaintiffs to get complete relief. The second possibility is that an injunction against the training program would force it to train apprentices on a non-discriminatory basis, thus meaning that employers either would be forced to alter their hiring patterns or would not be able to obtain for some of their selected employees the available training. Under the second possibility, the nonparty employers' interests in the training program would be practically impaired, thus bringing Rule 19(a)(2)(i) into play. *Eldredge*, however, never analyzed the Rule 19(a)(2)(i) issue.

This apparent failing disappears if Rule 19(a) is understood in accordance with the principle of remedial inequity. On the one hand, the failure to include the employers did not give the plaintiffs more relief than they were entitled to. On the other hand, this does not appear to be a situation like *Martin v. Wilks*; the nonparty employers cannot undermine the remedy obtained by the plaintiffs through subsequent litigation, since they do not enjoy a legal right to discriminate and since their state-law contractual rights with the training program are subsidiary to the federal requirement of non-discrimination.[45]

The third and final section of the rule, Rule 19 (a)(2)(ii), has also received an interpretation that accords with concerns for remedial inequity, but not necessarily with those of efficiency. For instance, in Smith's case against XYZ, might XYZ be able to invoke Rule 19(a)(2)(ii) in order to force Smith to join Green (and all of XYZ's other asbestos victims), upon penalty of dismissal if he cannot? XYZ's argument would be this: If Smith, Green, and the rest all sue

---

45. A different, and more difficult, Rule 19(a)(2)(i) problem would have been presented if, as in *Martin v. Wilks*, prospective male trainees would subsequently have been able to challenge the plaintiffs' injunction in subsequent litigation.

XYZ separately, XYZ will almost certainly win some cases and lose others. XYZ will owe "inconsistent obligations" to similarly situated claimants. Hence, Rule 19(a)(2)(ii) requires their joinder, if feasible.

Such an interpretation of the text of Rule 19(a)(2)(ii) seems straightforward, and would certainly advance the cause of aggregation. But it also runs afoul of the general preference for plaintiff autonomy, since this argument would seem to require the forced joinder of many plaintiffs and defendants in multi-party disputes. Not surprisingly, therefore, this interpretation of Rule 19(a)(2)(ii) has never carried the day.[46] A much stronger showing — that a party cannot simultaneously fulfill the obligations that the two suits might impose — has been required.[47]

Our suggestion about the congruence of Rule 19(a) and remedial equity does not mean that Rule 19(a) has been consciously used to achieve remedial equity; ours is a descriptive observation that simultaneously accounts for the main line of cases and provides a framework for evaluating new situations. Some of the types of cases that might test the validity of our suggestion are lacking; for instance, we know of are no Rule 19 cases in which the rule has been used to achieve the joinder of significant numbers of additional plaintiffs against an insolvent defendant (a Rule 19(a)(2)(i) claim), as might occur if the sum total of potential asbestos claims against XYZ exceeded their assets. One reason for the lack of such cases is that, with mass torts such as this, the joinder of each nonparty would be impractical. (Note that Rule 19(d) exempts class actions from the ambit of Rule 19.[48]) Likewise, in *Martin v. Wilks*, no one invoked Rule 19 to force the joinder of the nonparty white firefighters, even though a consent decree entered in their absence would have, on the dissent's view, limited their rights (a classic Rule 19(a)(2)(i) problem) or, on the majority's view, left the nonparties free to attack the judgment in subsequent litigation (a classic Rule 19(a)(1) problem). One reason may be that neither the plaintiffs nor the defendants wanted the nonparties in the case, and thus they had no reason to call the matter to the court's attention — as they should have done pursuant to Rule 19(c).

---

46. *See generally* 7 CHARLES A. WRIGHT ET AL., FEDERAL PRACTICE & PROCEDURE § 1604 (2001); *cf.* F.R.CIV.P. 23(b)(1)(A), discussed *infra* nn.122-29 and accompanying text.

47. *See, e.g.*, Haas v. Jefferson Nat'l Bank of Miami Beach, 442 F.2d 394 (5th Cir. 1971); O'Leary v. Moyer's Landfill, Inc., 677 F. Supp. 807 (E.D. Pa. 1988).

48. *Cf.* Pan Am. World Airways, Inc. v. United States Dist. Court for the Cent. Dist. of California, 523 F.2d 1073 (9th Cir. 1975) (Rule 19(a)(1) could not serve as basis for district court to provide notice to nonparties in aviation disaster of the pendency of a related lawsuit).

(B) Rule 19(b): Indispensable Parties. There may also be another dynamic at work that prevents Rule 19 from being consistently interpreted in a way that avoids remedial inequity: the effect of Rule 19(b). As Rule 19(b) acknowledges, in a certain number of situations the necessary party cannot be joined. We have examined many of the reasons for nonjoinder — subject matter jurisdiction, territorial jurisdiction, and venue — while some other reasons — such as sovereign immunity — lie beyond the scope of this book. When one of these roadblocks to involuntary joinder exists, Rule 19(b) instructs a court to determine whether "in equity and good conscience" the case can proceed without the absent party. The rule lists four factors — the extent of prejudice to the parties or nonparty if joinder is not effected, the possibility that the prejudice might be lessened by creative shaping of the relief, the adequacy of a judgment rendered in the nonparty's absence, and the availability of an adequate remedy to the plaintiff if the case is dismissed — that help to guide this judgment.[49] When a court makes this judgment, and determines it is better to dismiss the case than to let it proceed without the necessary party, the party is called "indispensable." Although courts may try to avoid dismissal of the case if at all possible, the bottom line is clear enough: Rather than trying to find creative ways around the absence of nonparties, the court must accept their absence, and in at least some situations dismiss cases in which the absence cannot be overcome.

An excellent case demonstrating the workings of Rule 19(b) is *Makah Indian Tribe v. Verity*,[50] in which 24 Indian tribes in the Pacific Northwest enjoyed treaty rights for catching Columbia River salmon. Various other interests, such as commercial fisheries and sport fishermen, also fished the same waters for salmon, resulting in severe declines in the salmon population. In order to preserve the species while still honoring treaty obligations, a complex judicial and administrative regime was developed. As a part of this regime, a regional council determined the allowable salmon harvest in each year and then assigned to various Indian tribes their quota of the overall catch. When the Makah tribe deemed its quota too low, it sued the Secretary of Commerce on two theories: that the Secretary

---

49. In Provident Tradesman Bank & Trust v. Patterson, 390 U.S. 102, 109-11 (1968), the Court recast these four factors into four interests served by the indispensable party rule: the plaintiff's interest in the forum, the defendant's interest in avoiding excessive relief, the nonparty's interest in the outcome of the case, and the interest of the court and public in "complete, consistent, and efficient settlement of controversies." In some ways, this functional analysis seems preferable, but it likely leads to the same outcome as the stated Rule 19(b) factors in most if not all cases.

50. 910 F.2d 555 (9th Cir. 1990).

had violated federal regulations governing the process by which the allocation decision was made, and that the tribe was entitled to a greater share of the allowable catch. It sought a reallocation, an equitable adjustment for lost fish in the past year's harvest, and an injunction requiring the Secretary's future compliance with the regulations. The Secretary argued that the other 23 tribes whose allotment would be shrunk if the Makah's case succeeded were necessary parties; and since their sovereign immunity prevented them from being joined, they were also indispensable parties whose absence required dismissal of the case.

On appeal from the dismissal, the Ninth Circuit held that the other tribes were not necessary parties to the Makah's injunctive claim. All of the other tribes had an equal interest in assuring that the government followed its own procedures in making the quota decision. On the reallocation question, however, the court of appeals agreed that the other tribes were necessary parties. Under Rule 19(a)(2)(i), a decision in their absence might impair their quotas, and under Rule 19(a)(2)(ii), the government could face inconsistent obligations if other tribes in later litigation similarly succeeded in obtaining higher quotas for themselves. The court then came to the difficult Rule 19(b) question. It found that the first three "equity and good conscience" factors militated in favor of dismissal; the other tribes would be prejudiced by the case, there was no way to shape relief to avoid that prejudice, and the remedy in the other tribes' absence was not adequate. The fourth factor — the availability of another forum — cut against dismissal, since there existed no other forum in which all the other tribes were amenable to suit. Despite this fact, the court of appeals upheld the dismissal of the re-allocation part of the case, agreeing with the district court that, on balance, the other tribes were indispensable.

Makah was a classic case of remedial inequity — a finite pie that, however it was re-sliced, left some getting more and some less. If the Makah's case effectively bound the other tribes in their absence, these tribes might have received less than their equitable share; if it did not, other later-suing tribes could re-slice the pie in ways unfair to the early-litigating Makah, to the government, or to both. Yet the court was unable to use Rule 19 to achieve joinder. Thus, the operation of Rule 19(b), in conjunction with the rule of sovereign immunity, left the Makah without any remedy — a stark instance in which the absence of nonparties created remedial inequity.

The Rule 19(b) dismissal thus creates a perverse litigation dynamic that ultimately makes Rule 19 a poor tool for the prevention of remedial inequity. The defendant has an incentive to press the Rule 19 involuntary joinder argument only when the nonparties

cannot be joined and might be regarded by the court as indispensable. Courts are aware that an expansive interpretation of Rule
19(a)'s three categories can result in the dismissal of significant
numbers of lawsuits.

This fact also helps to explain an apparent anomaly in the
Federal Rules: the inconsistent interpretations given to the nearly
identical "interest" and "impairment" language in Rules 24(a)(2) and
19(a)(2)(i). We saw in the prior subsection that, for purposes of Rule
24, interest and impairment were construed consistently with
"efficiency and due process," and even minimal stare decisis effects
counted as sufficient grounds for intervention. But under Rule
19(a)(2)(i), stare decisis effects are insufficient, without more, to force
the joinder of a nonparty; and "efficiency and due process" are no
longer the relevant criteria. The simple reason: If Rule 19(a)(2)(i)
were construed as broadly as Rule 24(a)(2), many nonparties would
need to be involuntarily joined if feasible (a result that grates against
the generally consensual nature of party joinder); in at least a
significant number of those cases, joinder of some nonparties would
not be feasible; and in some percentage of those cases, the case would
need to be dismissed for the lack of indispensable parties (a result
that grates against the desire to use joinder rules to achieve, rather
than to subvert, optimal aggregation).

An obvious solution to this problem is to create new forms of
aggregation-favoring interpretations of subject matter jurisdiction,
territorial jurisdiction, venue, and other impediments to optimal
joinder. In previous chapters, we traced the lines of some of the
arguments that could be made in favor of such interpretations in
complex cases. At this point, we can appreciate that another benefit
of such interpretations would be to assist in the involuntary joinder
of nonparties that optimally should be joined. There is nothing in
Rule 19, however, that aids in this interpretive endeavor. Rule 82
states that the Federal Rules themselves cannot expand jurisdiction
or venue, and 28 U.S.C. § 1367(b) makes plain that in pure diversity
cases Rule 19 necessary parties receive no special jurisdictional
treatment.

A final problem with Rule 19 is the one alluded to in *Eldredge*:
the difficulty of achieving individual joinder of all nonparties. If
Smith and Green are the only asbestos victims of XYZ, then involuntary joinder under a more expansive version of Rule 19 could be
accomplished easily. If there are tens of thousands of asbestos
victims, however, individual joinder of the kind that Rule 19
contemplates is difficult to imagine — especially when some of the
victims of XYZ's asbestos exposure may be unknown or unknowable.
As *Eldredge* shows, the inability to join all necessary parties creates

another reason, like jurisdiction, venue, or immunity, to employ the Rule 19(b) indispensable party analysis and to dismiss the suit.

Simply put, the structural limitations of Rule 19 mandatory joinder make its successful use as an aggregation tool an occasional occurrence at best.

(ii) Strategic Behavior. As the last section described, the Rule 19(b) dismissal creates an incentive for strategic use by parties that wish the case to be dismissed rather than optimally joined. Even when this behavior does not occur, Rule 19 joinder cannot be used to overcome the other hurdles, such as subject matter jurisdiction, territorial jurisdiction, and venue, that aggregation-opposing plaintiffs strategically use to make single-forum aggregation difficult or impossible. As a result, Rule 19 often cannot overcome the non-optimal aggregation decisions of the parties or help the parties and the court to achieve optimal aggregation. At the end of the day, therefore, Rule 19 is a limited tool for the aggregation of nonparties, and a potential cause of some mischief in the pursuit of optimal aggregation.

b. Interpleader. In contrast, interpleader has greater potential as a method of involuntary joinder, but a more limited scope. Like Rule 19, interpleader derives from equity practice. The concept of interpleader is that a person (usually called the stakeholder) has possession of property or a tangible asset to which there are multiple claimants. If each putative claimant could sue the stakeholder seriatim, the following situation might arise: The first claimant sues the stakeholder for the property, the court decides that the claimant is the true owner of the property, the stakeholder gives the property to the claimant, a second claimant then brings a separate action against the stakeholder, the second claimant also succeeds in convincing a court that the second claimant s the true owner, and the stakeholder is then liable to the second claimant for conversion of the property. Since our system does not generally bind nonparties to a judgment in which they did not participate, the stakeholder would not usually be able to raise as a defense the prior judgment that established the first clamant as the true owner. The pattern could be repeated for each additional claimant. Since the first claimant to the courthouse would normally have little incentive to join together with other claimants who might have superior claims, the stakeholder is in an untenable position.

In this factual setting, the stakeholder prevailed on the Chancellor to step in, to enjoin the separate legal actions of the various claimants, and to "interplead" all claimants as defendants in a single equitable proceeding to conclusively determine the parties' rights. In the original (or "true") interpleader action, the stakeholder could not claim any interest in the property. In latter-day equity practice, proceedings "in the nature of interpleader" permitted a stakeholder to claim that he or she also had an interest in the asset.

From this background, the modern system of interpleader developed. Like necessary party joinder, interpleader is a system of forced, or mandatory, joinder. But interpleader inverts the party structure, making the claimants into nominal defendants and giving the stakeholder the right to establish the party structure. Self-interest usually dictates that the stakeholder effect complete joinder of all interested claimants.

(i) Structural Limitations. In the federal system, two distinct forms of interpleader exist: statutory and rule interpleader. Statutory interpleader actions are conducted under the auspices of 28 U.S.C. §§ 1335 and 2361; rule interpleader is provided for in Rule 22. The two forms are different in several significant ways. Since statutory interpleader generally is a more potent mandatory joinder device, we begin our consideration with §§ 1335 and 2361.

(A) Statutory Interpleader. 28 U.S.C. § 1335(a) grants original jurisdiction to the federal district courts to entertain "actions of interpleader or in the nature of interpleader" when a stakeholder has "in his or its custody or possession money or property of the value or amount of $500 or more." 28 U.S.C. § 1335 states two additional jurisdictional requirements: First, "[t]wo or more adverse claimants, of diverse citizenship, . . . are claiming or may claim to be entitled to such money or property"; and second, the plaintiff has either "deposited such money or property . . . into the registry of the court, there to abide the judgment of the court," or has given a satisfactory bond to the court. As we have seen, statutory interpleader extends subject matter jurisdiction to the constitutional maximum of minimal diversity;[51] § 1335 also slashes the matter-in-controversy requirement to an insignificant $500. Except in the rare case in which all adverse claimants are from a single state,[52] § 1335 has effectively overcome one of the great obstacles to single-forum aggregation — federal subject matter jurisdiction.

Statutory interpleader also overcomes various other hurdles to single-forum aggregation. 28 U.S.C. § 2361 provides that a § 1335 court "may issue its process for all claimants," and service may be accomplished in "the respective districts where the claimants reside or may be found"; in other words, the limitations of state-law territorial jurisdiction are wiped away, and nationwide service of

51. *See supra* ch.4, n.11 and accompanying text.

52. In some of these rare cases,

rule interpleader might be available; in others a state court can act as the proper forum.

process is permitted.[53] Likewise, 28 U.S.C. § 1397 authorizes venue in a § 1335 action in "the judicial district in which one or more claimants reside." As a result, there is no difficulty in situating the entire controversy in a single venue.

Statutory interpleader not only has the most generous jurisdictional and venue rules presently available, but it also has a final useful power: 28 U.S.C. § 2361 authorizes a § 1335 court to issue an order that "restrains [all claimants] from instituting or prosecuting any proceeding in any State or United States court affecting the property, instrument or obligation involved in the interpleader action until further order of the court."[54] This anti-suit injunctive power, which comes into play as soon as the interpleader action is filed, prevents the claimant quickest to a courthouse from obtaining a remedy that either deprives remaining claimants of a meaningful remedy or subjects the stakeholder to multiple liabilities.

In short, statutory interpleader is a how-to manual of aggregation: mandatory joinder of nonparties, generous subject matter jurisdiction, territorial jurisdiction, and venue rules, and anti-suit injunctive power. Indeed, the aggregation package for interpleader is so complete that you might have wondered why we waited so long to discuss it.

The simple reason is that statutory interpleader is not the silver bullet for aggregation problems; like every device we have explored, it has limitations. The primary limitations derive from interpleader's requirement that the dispute concern a tangible or intangible thing — a *res*. The requirement of a *res* has two significant effects. First, most complex disputes do not involve skirmishes over a *res*; they involve personal liability of individuals or corporations. The defendant's assets are only indirectly relevant to the suit; they will be called upon to satisfy the judgments of the claimants, but no claimant has a legal claim upon any specific piece of the defendant's property. Such a specific claim has been the traditional touchstone of interpleader.

In order for interpleader to work in most complex cases, therefore, something of the defendant's must be analogized to a *res* in which claimants do have a specific legal interest. If the underlying claims against an interpleader plaintiff seek injunctive relief designed to re-orient the interpleader plaintiff's future conduct, the analogy stretches too thin and breaks; hence, interpleader has never

---

53. Of course, even nationwide service of process is ineffective for resolving controversies in which foreign nonparties cannot be found in the United States.

54. By its terms, this power is not effective against foreign litigation; and is thus limited in its way.

been perceived as a viable joinder option in most cases seeking injunctive relief. For monetary claims that claimants would be asserting against the putative interpleader plaintiff, the analogy to a dispute over a *res* might hold when the value of the claims exceeds the sum of defendant's assets. In this scenario, the defendant is theoretically insolvent, and the award of full claim value to the first-filing claimants jeopardizes the availability of defendant's assets — the "*res*" — to later-filing claimants.

So far, no federal court has accepted this analogy, and only one case has expressed sympathy with the argument.[55] A number of roadblocks ultimately stand in the way of the analogy's victory. First, the use of interpleader in this fashion is historically inapt. The reason that defendants sought, and equity granted, interpleader relief was the risk of multiple liability; here, a defendant that becomes insolvent after the first judgments does not have that concern. Whether interpleader is capable of making the transition from a device preventing remedial inequity to putative defendants to one preventing remedial inequity to late-filing nonparties is still a largely speculative matter — especially given the lack of any mechanism in interpleader to distribute assets equitably. Second, the use of interpleader in this fashion effectively substitutes interpleader for bankruptcy, without providing to creditors the protections of the bankruptcy code; it is difficult to believe that Congress would have intended this inversion, and easy to believe that such a use of interpleader is pre-empted by the Code.[56] A third legal obstacle is the occasional statement found in interpleader cases that interpleader, like equitable devices generally, cannot be employed by those with unclean hands. In the cases with which we are concerned, the putative defendant certainly has unclean hands as that phrase has been interpreted in equity, and, if this doctrine is applicable, cannot invoke interpleader to join the sideline-sitting plaintiffs.[57]

Analogizing a defendant's assets to a *res* also has significant practical effects that make the use of interpleader problematic. One of the jurisdictional prerequisites of § 1335 is the deposit of the *res* into the court (or, in the alternative, the posting of a bond). When the "*res*" amounts to the assets of a defendant, depositing them into the court is, in nearly all cases, impossible. Likewise, a bond (which may cost 10% or more of the face value of the assets) would be so

55. Aetna Cas. & Ins. Co. v. Ahrens, 414 F. Supp. 1235 (S.D. Tex. 1975).

56. For a short examination of some aspects of bankruptcy as an aggregation device, see *infra* pp. 182-89, 194-96.

57. *See* Farmers Irrigating Ditch & Reservoir Co. v. Kane, 845 F.2d 229 (10th Cir. 1988).

expensive that it might cripple many ongoing enterprises. Next, most defendants would have little to no incentive to obtain such a bond, or to use interpleader at all, for a simple reason: At the end of the day, they will have nothing left for themselves. With bankruptcy, a defendant may hope to emerge as a going concern after reorganization; and even if it cannot, at least bankruptcy is more likely to result in greater protection to trade creditors with whom the defendant has a long-term relationship. With a class action, a defendant may hope to achieve a settlement that preserves some of its capital for the equity holders. With interpleader, the defendant is essentially forced to liquidate; and defendants rarely have an incentive to do this voluntarily.

A second significant structural limitation on the use of statutory interpleader also derives from the stubborn demand of a *res*: the limited scope of interpleader. As the Supreme Court made clear in *State Farm Fire & Casualty Co. v. Tashire*, interpleader is not an "all-purpose 'bill of peace' in the context of multiparty litigation arising out of a mass tort."[58]

In *Tashire*, which we also discussed in Chapter 4,[59] a truck-bus collision killed two passengers and injured thirty-three. The owner of the truck held a $20,000 insurance policy, which was grossly inadequate to cover the injuries. Some victims commenced in various state and federal courts suits against the owner of the truck, the bus line, and the two drivers. The truck owner's insurer then paid the $20,000 policy into the United States District Court for the District of Oregon and commenced a § 1335 interpleader action against the victims, the bus line, and both drivers. The federal court then invoked its § 2361 power to enjoin prosecution of all other lawsuits against the truck owner. Seeking to resolve the entire matter in one forum, the bus company asked that the injunction be expanded to prevent the prosecution of suits against the company or its driver in any forum other than the District of Oregon. The district court obliged.

The Supreme Court held that the injunction in favor of the bus company and its driver was broader than necessary to protect and determine the ultimate ownership of the *res* (the insurance proceeds). Interpleader "cannot be used to solve all of the vexing problems of multiparty litigation arising out of a mass tort . . . ."[60] The Court resisted the notion that the fortuity of a limited insurance policy should "sweep[ ] dozens of lawsuits out of the various state and federal courts" at the behest of a single defendant with a limited

58. 386 U.S. 523, 537 (1967). and accompanying text.

59. *See supra* ch.4, nn.11, 68-69   **60.** *Id.* at 535.

interest in the case, or that the interpleader statute might be read in a way that would deprive litigants their "substantial rights" to "choose the forum in which to establish their claims."[61] To allow a $20,000 insurance policy to fundamentally shape the litigation would allow "the tail . . . to wag the dog."[62]

In the context of *Tashire* itself, this result does not seem inappropriate. The bus company, Greyhound, was not rendered insolvent by the accident. While it would certainly have been more economical and convenient to have forced the litigation of all the claims into a single federal forum, we have seen repeatedly in this book that economy and convenience are rarely sufficient reasons, by themselves, to overcome plaintiffs' adversarial right to locate a suit in a forum of their choosing. Something more — something like remedial inequity — is required. Separate lawsuits against Greyhound posed no issues of inequity; each plaintiff was able to receive a full and complete remedy in the forum of his or her choice. The same was not true with regard to plaintiffs' claims that sought their satisfaction in an admittedly inadequate insurance policy. Here, the early successful suits would have left nothing for the later-filing claimants.

Even though *Tashire* can be justified, its outcome creates a new type of aggregation problem: the fracturing of related claims against related parties into separate forums. In *Tashire*, for instance, all claims against one defendant were centralized in a single forum, while the related claims against other defendants remained spread out in various state and federal courts. This splintering of the case might have created an advantage for both sets of defendants, each of whom could now use the "empty chair" to blame the absent defendant.[63] Moreover, such a party-based division of the case might create greater inefficiencies for everyone except the interpleader plaintiff, a result that is certainly not desirable.

Even when these numerous difficulties to interpleader can be overcome, a final hurdle remains: the identification and joinder of the interpleader defendants (i.e., the underlying plaintiffs). In a case such as *Tashire*, the universe of potential plaintiffs was both knowable and confined. In some cases, however, determining the identity of the injured parties and effecting their individual joinder

---

61. *Id.* at 536.

62. *Id.* at 535.

63. It is not clear whether such a tactical disadvantage might induce plaintiffs to refile their suits in the interpleader forum and move for consolidation — a possibility that would reduce the disaggregative potential of *Tashire* at a practical level. But this possibility would also effectively concede to a defendant (the interpleader plaintiff) the venue privilege that plaintiffs are usually thought to enjoy.

are time-consuming and expensive processes that may be less than perfectly successful.[64]

(B) Rule Interpleader. Provided for in Federal Rule 22, rule interpleader is used far less frequently than statutory interpleader. As Rule 22(2) emphasizes, the two forms of interpleader are independent; neither limits the other. Rule interpleader's standard — that the interpleader plaintiff "is or may be exposed to double or multiple liability" as a result of possible claims by the interpleader defendants — suggests that it might provide broader relief than statutory interpleader. In practice, however, this standard has been interpreted exactly as statutory interpleader has: It applies only to situations in which there exist both multiple or inconsistent claims to a *res* or limited fund and an inability to satisfy all claims in full.[65]

In other ways, rule interpleader turns out to be a generally less desirable remedy than statutory interpleader. First, rule interpleader still requires an independent basis of jurisdiction, whether it be federal question or diversity. Since the diversity must be complete (rather than § 1335's minimal diversity) and the matter in controversy must be more than $75,000 (rather than § 1335's $500), rule interpleader almost always presents a worse jurisdictional situation than statutory interpleader. The only situation in which subject matter jurisdiction exists for rule interpleader but not for statutory interpleader is the rare one in which all persons claiming against the *res* or fund have the same citizenship, and the stakeholder either is of diverse citizenship or raises a federal question as the basis of jurisdiction.

In other regards, rule interpleader compares unfavorably to statutory interpleader. There is no nationwide service of process; the ordinary rules of territorial jurisdiction apply. Ordinary venue rules also apply. Rule interpleader contains no express requirement, as exists for statutory interpleader, that a bond be posted by the interpleader plaintiff in the event that the stake is not deposited into court.[66] Finally, Rule 22 contains no authority to issue anti-suit injunctions, as statutory interpleader does. Since equity traditionally issued these injunctions, federal courts do issue them, but such an anti-suit injunction is not expressly authorized by statute and thus raises Anti-Injunction Act problems with respect to ongoing state

---

64. This problem is obviously exacerbated when plaintiffs are injured over time, and some of these injuries have yet to manifest themselves. We take up the problem of the "future" plaintiffs at the end of this chapter.

65. *See* WRIGHT ET AL., *supra* n.46, § 1704.

66. A court does have the discretion to require the posting of a bond.

litigation.[67] A standard method for avoiding the Act has been to conceive of the interpleaded stake as a *res* over which the court has acquired jurisdiction. This conception allows the court to invoke the "necessary in aid of jurisdiction" exception to the Anti-Injunction Act.[68] The Supreme Court has not yet determined that this move is appropriate; and, in any event, this move keeps rule interpleader tightly tied to the limiting concept of a *res*.

If rule interpleader could ever be conceived of as an aggregation device to deal with a situation of limited assets, this might be an important advantage for rule interpleader in relation to statutory interpleader, although even here the problem of rule interpleader superseding bankruptcy would remain an issue.[69] Until rule interpleader is so conceived, the jurisdictional and venue limitations of Rule 22 make it a less desirable rule of mandatory joinder than § 1335.

(ii) Strategic Behavior. Like Rule 19,[70] statutory and rule interpleader put into the hands of a defendant the ability to affect the party structure. The stakeholder will only invoke interpleader when there is some strategic advantage, such as a limitation on liability exposure, a more efficient litigation unit from the stakeholder's perspective, a preemptive strike against lawsuits, a shift to a more favorable venue, an inconvenience to the claimants, or some other advantage. As we have seen, an advantage to the stakeholder can sometimes result in a disadvantage to everyone else, since they must litigate their claim against other defendants in an array of lawsuits. Since the circumstances in which interpleader can be invoked are at present few, however, these strategic issues have little effect on the operation of most complex litigation.

Moreover, although interpleader is a device that forces the joinder of nonparties whom the plaintiff cannot or will not join, it is

---

67. *See supra* ch.4, nn.71-77 and accompanying text.

68. United States v. Major Oil Corp., 583 F.2d 1152 (10th Cir. 1978); Pan Am. Fire & Cas. Co. v. Revere, 188 F. Supp. 474 (W.D. La. 1960).

69. The problem would be especially acute because, as a Federal Rule of Civil Procedure, Rule 22 is subject to the limitations of the Rules Enabling Act that the rule not "abridge, enlarge or modify" the parties' substantive rights in bankruptcy.

70. Rule 19 bears some textual affinity to Rule 22 interpleader. Rule

19(a)(2)(ii) makes a necessary party out of anyone claiming an interest in a case when that person's absence leaves "any of the persons already parties subject to a substantial risk of incurring double, multiple, or inconsistent obligations"; Rule 22(1) allows joinder of persons whose claims may subject the interpleader plaintiff to "double or multiple liability." Rule 22, however, has no indispensable party analysis in the event that one or more claimants against the stake cannot be joined.

important to keep in mind that the device is, in its way, still a permissive joinder device. As the nominal plaintiff, the stakeholder is in charge of deciding the party structure. When the stake is a tangible thing to which there are multiple legitimate claims, there will often be an incentive for the stakeholder to achieve complete joinder through interpleader. When the stake is less tangible — say, a corporation's assets — the motivation to effect complete joinder (assuming interpleader could be so used) is less apparent. Moreover, unless there is an excellent chance that the corporation will be exonerated on all claims, why create a lawsuit that risks the stakeholder's insolvency? Since stakeholders are presumably indifferent (at best) about the equitable distribution of its assets among claimants, what incentive does the stakeholder have to interplead all potential plaintiffs? Putting the power of joinder in the stakeholder's hands does not solve the problem of incomplete joinder.

c. *Class Actions.* Thus far, we have found that the available joinder devices hold some promise for aggregation, but that all lack in important ways. The class action is the last joinder option that might achieve the optimal aggregation of nonparties. As a joinder device, it is without parallel. A creation of equity, the class action was specifically designed to overcome the problem of a multitude of lawsuits filed by or against large numbers of persons with similar interests. The concept of the class action is simple: A single case is brought by (or against) one or more persons that sue (or are sued) on their own behalf and also on behalf of others (the "class") that are similarly situated. Individual members of the class do not present or defend their own cases, but rely on the class representatives to do so on their behalf. The judgment obtained by the representatives binds all members of the class. A class action is broad enough to sweep into the class not only nonparties but also persons who have already filed suit elsewhere. At first blush, therefore, the class action seems the optimal joinder device for the aggregation and efficient resolution of large numbers of related claims.

On further consideration, the picture becomes more muddled. For plaintiff classes, the class action stands a plaintiff's traditional venue privilege and autonomy interests on their head. Not only can a putative plaintiff be made an involuntary party in a forum not of his or her choosing, but the nonparty is also forced to cede to the class representatives the power to conduct the litigation on his or her behalf. Problems of conflicts of interest among class members, self-regarding behavior, and collusion between the class representative and the opponent remain constant risks. Powerful reasons, significant protections, and carefully constructed boundaries must attend this inversion of the traditional American process, lest the class action become the exception that swallows the rule.

On the assumption that the benefits of class actions outweigh their risks in some cases, a class action rule must accomplish two things. First, it must describe and justify the circumstances under which the assumptions of litigant autonomy and control give way. Second, it must ensure vigorous representation by the class representatives and provide adequate protections for class members. Obviously, these two tasks are intertwined; the greater the protections, perhaps, the greater the permissible scope of the class action.

In Federal Rule of Civil Procedure 23, these tasks are accomplished primarily by subsection (a), which states the minimal requirements for adequate representation, and subsection (b), which states four circumstances in which class actions can be employed. In order for a class to be certified, all of the requirements of Rule 23(a) must be met; in addition, one of the four standards of Rule 23(b) must be satisfied. Class actions must also comply with various other structural limitations such as jurisdiction and venue; as we shall see, they generate tensions with other constitutional concerns as well.

Before we examine the details of Rule 23 and its surrounding constraints, two aspects of class actions should be addressed. First, unlike Rule 19 and interpleader, which are true mandatory joinder devices capable of overcoming a plaintiff's non-optimal aggregation choice, Rule 23 is an imperfect mandatory joinder device. In most class actions, the class representative and class counsel usually establish the boundaries of the class; therefore, the scope of the class still depends in important ways on the consent of the original plaintiff. Even more critically, of the four types of Rule 23(b) class actions, only the first three are mandatory, in the sense that the class members cannot generally remove themselves from the class. But each of these class actions — the (b)(1)(A), (b)(1)(B), and (b)(2) class actions — arise in relatively discrete contexts. The final and most common form of class action — the (b)(3) class action — is an "opt-out" class action. This means that class members must be accorded an opportunity to remove themselves from the class. Complete mandatory joinder is not possible.

Second, the assumption underlying our discussion of joinder rules up to this point has been that joinder should be accomplished for the purpose of litigating common claims. Unlike other joinder devices, class actions need not be used as a litigation device. For instance, after litigating its case with Smith, XYZ might wish to settle the controversy. It might be reluctant to do so, however, for fear that one settlement will expose the company to a rash of new lawsuits. Therefore, it might propose to settle with Smith, but only if it can also buy "global peace" and settle all of its asbestos liability in one fell swoop. None of the joinder devices we have previously studied would typically be capable of sweeping all the actual and potential claims together in a single settlement. Class actions might be able to do so. As you read the materials on class actions, it will be useful for you to keep this distinction between "litigation class actions" and "settlement class actions" in mind, and to appreciate the dual uses to which this unique aggregation device can be put. For the most part, this section assumes that the class seeking to be certified intends to litigate its claims. We take up the issue of settlement class actions in greater detail in the final section of this chapter, which concerns plaintiffs with future claims.

(i) *Structural Limitations.* As with all joinder rules, the structural limitations on the use of class actions are a combination of the limits imposed by the language of Rule 23 and a panoply of constitutional, jurisdictional, venue, and common law restraints. In the subsection we examine each of these issues.

(A) *The Elements of Rule 23(a).* We begin by examining the concept of adequate representation contained in Rule 23(a). Rule 23(a) must be understood against the background of the seminal case in modern class action practice: *Hansberry v. Lee.*[71] The Hansberrys were African-Americans who moved into a home that was subject to a racially restrictive covenant. The covenant had been drawn up by the neighborhood's property owners many years before their purchase. According to its terms, the covenant became effective once it had been signed by 95% of the property owners in the neighborhood. Long before the Hanberrys bought their property, another property owner leased a home to an African-American family. Some of the other property owners then sued, both on their own and "on behalf of" all property owners subject to the covenant, to enforce the covenant. In that case, which was filed in Illinois state court, the parties stipulated that 95% of the property owners had signed the covenant, and therefore that the covenant was in effect. Based on the stipulation, the state court found as a matter of fact that the covenant had come into effect, and granted the relief requested.

When the Hansberrys bought their property, other property owners went into state court to rescind the sale because it violated the covenant. The Hansberrys sought to defend by showing that the covenant had never become effective — it had been signed by only 54%, and not the requisite 95%, of the property owners. In response, the property owners claimed that the Hansberrys were bound by the determination in the prior case that the covenant was effective. Their reasoning, which the Illinois courts accepted, was that the Hansberrys' grantor was a member of the class in the prior proceed-

71. 311 U.S. 32 (1940).

ing, and that the court's determination about the covenant bound the grantor (and thus the Hansberrys).

The Supreme Court of the United States reversed the Illinois Supreme Court. The Court held that the state court's attempt to bind the Hansberrys to the prior stipulation violated the due process clause of the Fourteenth Amendment. The Court's reasoning, unfortunately, was less than pellucid, and the exact constitutional defect in the state court's action is not entirely clear. The Court began with "a principle of general application in Anglo-American jurisprudence that one is not bound by a judgment *in personam* in a litigation in which he is not designated as a party or to which he has been made a party by service of process."[72] Taken to its limit, of course, that principle would effectively eliminate class actions; the Court therefore acknowledged, without elaboration or justification, the "recognized exception" to the rule in class action cases.[73] The Court then observed that the due process clause did not require states to enact any specific form of a class action rule; rather, the clause came into play

> "only in those cases where it cannot be said that the procedure adopted, fairly insures the protection of the interests of absent parties who are to be bound by it. . . . It is familiar doctrine of the federal courts that members of a class not present as parties to the litigation may be bound by the judgment where they are in fact adequately represented by parties who are present, or where they actually participate in the conduct of the litigation in which members of the class are present as parties, or where the interests of the members of the class, some of whom are present as parties, is joint, or where for any other reason the relationship between the parties present and those who are absent is such as to legally entitle the former to stand in judgment for the latter."[74]

Applying this general principle to the Hansberrys' situation, the Court stated that no single property owner could have represented the interests of all the home owners in the previous class. The interests of property owners diverged; some wanted the covenant enforced, and others did not. To the extent that the class representatives sought to represent only the interests of those who wished the covenant enforced, those who wished to contest it were not in the class and not bound by the judgment concerning the covenant's validity. To the extent that the class representatives sought to represent both sets of interests, the "dual and potentially conflicting interests"[75] of those who did not wish the covenant enforced made it

---

72. 311 U.S. at 40.

73. *Id.* at 41.

74. *Id.* at 42-43 (citations omitted).

75. *Id.* at 44.

impossible to accomplish that end. "[A] selection of representatives for purposes of litigation, whose substantial interests are not necessarily or even probably the same as those whom they are deemed to represent, does not afford that protection to absent parties which due process requires."[76]

Hansberry raises more questions than it resolves. For instance, what if it could be shown that the prior owner of the Hansberrys' property did in fact support the covenant, but had a change of heart later in life? Years after litigation is over, it is easy enough to claim that a person's interests, as they ultimately develop, diverged from the class representatives' position. More significantly, how much divergence in interest becomes constitutionally too much? Except in cases of a joint interest, the interests of parties rarely match exactly. *Hansberry* does not say how much divergence in interest can be tolerated; obviously, more latitude for divergence creates more room for the class action to operate, but it also creates more concerns for the fair representation of absent class members. Finally, are there any due process constraints on class representatives other than the avoidance of obvious and acute conflicts? The Court seemed to believe so, but it never specifically identified them.

First adopted in 1966, Rule 23(a) attempts to work through these concerns by specifying a series of necessary elements — four numbered elements[77] and two elements implicit in the introductory language of the rule. Each element must be satisfied in order for a class action to be maintained, and the person seeking class certification bears the burden of proving them. The implicit elements are that a definable class must exist, and that the class representative must be a member of that class. The four numbered elements are that the class must be so numerous that individual joinder is impracticable (the "numerosity" requirement of (a)(1)), there must be questions of law or fact common to the class (the "commonality" requirement of (a)(2)), the claims or defenses of the representative parties must be typical of those of the class (the "typicality" requirement of (a)(3)), and the representative parties must fairly and adequately represent the interests of the class (the "adequacy" requirement of (a)(4)).

Each element interlocks and builds cumulatively to ensure that a class will be adequately represented. The requirement that a definable class exists ensures that it can be known who is and who is not in the class, so that potential conflicts can be unearthed and the preclusive effect of a judgment can be determined. The requirement that a class be so numerous that other methods of joinder are

---

76. *Id.* at 45.　　　　　　　　**77.** F.R.CIV.P. 23(a)(1)-(a)(4).

impracticable helps to limit class actions to situations in which the limits of the more autonomy-centered joinder rules are apparent. The commonality requirement begins the process of ensuring that the class has sufficient internal cohesion and absence of inconsistent interests to justify the use of representative litigation. The membership, typicality, and adequacy requirements train their attention more specifically on the class representative and his or her relationship to the remainder of the class. When a class representative is not a member of the class he or she purports to represent, there is good reason to worry about the vigor of his or her representation. The typicality requirement seeks to ensure that the case of the representative will raise the common issues in a typical way; if the representative's claims are atypical, then there is reason to worry that the representative will represent only his or her own interests. Finally, the adequacy requirement examines whether there are specific reasons that *this* representative will not be a good representative — perhaps the representative has a more specific conflict of interest, suffers from bouts of insanity, is colluding with the defendant, or has chosen an attorney without the skills or resources to conduct the litigation with vigor.

It is generally believed that the requirements of Rule 23(a) satisfy the constitutional requirements of *Hansberry*, although it is not clear which defect — commonality, typicality, or adequacy — the class action in *Hansberry* would have suffered from if it had been brought under the modern Rule 23(a). It is also not clear how close to the constitutional line Rule 23(a) is, and whether a class action rule in either state or federal court could insist on fewer and less stringent requirements to ensure adequacy. At present, this latter question is largely moot, for there is little movement afoot to change Rule 23(a), and the rule has had a significant influence on state class action practice as well.

Numerosity. Each of the four numbered elements of Rule 23(a) has spawned an interpretive body of case law that imposes significant constraints on the use of class actions.[78] Of the four, numerosity usually presents the least serious obstacle. Below a certain point — around 15 to 20 potential plaintiffs — the number is small enough that joinder through other devices is practicable.[79] Above a certain point — 100 or more potential plaintiffs — the number seems to

---

78. In order to focus on the four numbered requirements, we leave aside the implicit requirements of a class and membership in that class. For more detailed treatments of these elements, see RICHARD L. MARCUS & EDWARD F. SHERMAN, COMPLEX LITI- GATION 220-31 (3d ed. 1998) and TID-MARSH & TRANSGRUD, *supra* n.14, at 556-59.

79. *See* Gen. Tel. Co. of the Northwest v. EEOC, 446 U.S. 318, 330 (1980).

satisfy the numerosity requirement almost automatically.[80] In the middle lies uncertain ground. Courts often try to decide which way to go in this middle area by resort to the policies underlying class actions (such as the prevention of litigation hardship or inconvenience[81]) or by use of multi-factor tests (such as consideration of judicial economy, geographic dispersion of class members, resources of class members and their ability to commence individual suits, and requests for injunction relief[82]). Although these policies or factors might be extended to analyze either larger or smaller classes, they rarely are; and, except in close cases, the numerosity issue is usually conceded.

Commonality. Likewise, commonality is rarely a stumbling block to class certification. The purpose of the commonality inquiry is to ensure that the claims of the class's members (including the class's representatives) present common questions of law or fact; if not, it is difficult to imagine how some members of the class could represent all others, or how any significant gains in efficiency would occur.[83] That much seems evident. The hard question is how much commonality is required: Must the class member have most questions in common, or only a few? Rule 23(a)(2) is silent on the matter. The only textual hint is in Rule 23(b)(3), which permits an opt-out class action to be maintained when common questions "predominate" over individual ones. This language implies that the (a)(2) requirement can be satisfied even when common questions do not predominate.

The standard account is that "[t]he threshold of 'commonality' is not high. . . . [T]he rule requires only that resolution of the common questions affect all or a substantial number of the class members."[84] It is often said that "a single" or "at least one" question of law or fact is all that is required,[85] though some cases suggest that two or more are needed.[86] This minimalist approach to commonality has led some commentators to wonder whether the requirement of commonality should simply be abandoned, on the theory that any case that would satisfy one of the four standards of Rule 23(b) would automatically

---

80. *In re* Am. Med. Sys., Inc., 75 F.3d 1069, 1079 (6th Cir. 1996).

81. *In re* Drexel Burnham Lambert Group, Inc., 960 F.2d 285, 290 (2d Cir. 1992), *cert. denied sub nom.* Hart Holding Co. v. Drexel Burnham Lambert Group, Inc., 506 U.S. 1088 (1993); Boggs v. Divested Atomic Corp., 141 F.R.D. 59, 63 (S.D. Ohio 1991).

82. Robidoux v. Celani, 987 F.2d 931, 936 (2d Cir. 1993).

83. *See* Gen. Tel. Co. of the Southwest v. Falcon, 457 U.S. 147, 157 n.13 (1982).

84. Jenkins v. Raymark Indus., Inc., 782 F.2d 468, 472 (5th Cir. 1986).

85. J. B. *ex rel.* Hart v. Valdez, 186 F.3d 1280, 1288 (10th Cir. 1999); Baby Neal *ex rel.* Kanter v. Casey, 43 F.3d 48, 56 (3d Cir. 1994).

86. Forbush v. J.C. Penney Co., 994 F.2d 1101, 1106 (5th Cir. 1993); Applewhite v. Reichhall Chem., Inc., 67 F.3d 571, 573 (5th Cir. 1995).

satisfy Rule 23(a)(2) as well.   A reply, which is only partially satisfactory, is that the objects of Rules 23(a) and 23(b) are different, and it is important to consider the adequacy issue from as many perspectives as possible.

Although a weak filter for adequacy concerns, commonality does occasionally sound the death knell to a class action. For instance, in *J.B. ex rel. Hart v. Valdez*,[87] the plaintiffs sought to certify a class of developmentally disabled children who were in state custody and who allegedly were denied the protections and services they were due under five different federal statutes and the due process clause. Although the class representatives addressed the full range of alleged violations, each child came into state custody in a different way, and none could claim that each alleged violation had occurred in his or her case.   Despite the plaintiffs' contention that their commonality lay in the systematic failures of the state's child welfare system, the court thought that "no common factual link joins these plaintiffs," and therefore upheld the district court's refusal to certify a class. Similarly, in *In re American Medical Systems*,[88] four patients whose penile implants allegedly had failed sued on behalf of a class of patients with defective implants.   The manufacturer, however, made ten different implants.   The court of appeals held that each representative's claim of product defect lacked sufficient commonality with the claim of other representatives or with the claims of the users of the other six types of implants to permit class certification.

J.B. ex rel. Hart and *American Medical Systems* can fairly be said to represent a strong view on commonality. Indeed, the result in *J.B. ex rel. Hart* appears to conflict with cases in two other circuits holding that a similar battery of individual claims constitutes a systemic challenge to the child welfare system and therefore possesses sufficient commonality.[89] Commonality has become a word of flexible meaning, more useful as a means of surfacing the classes' exact claims in order to hold them up to the searching light of typicality and adequacy than as a principle of exclusion. Nor, in any event, is the commonality problem an insurmountable one. Plaintiffs can remove any lingering commonality problems by creating a series of separate classes, subclasses, or issue-specific classes — although such divisions might affect the financial incentives for attorneys to bring the case and thus indirectly have an effect on the viability of the class's claims.[90]

---

87. 186 F.3d 1280 (10th Cir. 1999).

88. 75 F.3d 1069 (6th Cir. 1996).

89. *See Baby Neal*, 43 F.3d 48; Marisol A. v. Giuliani, 126 F.3d 372 (2d Cir. 1997).

90. Courts can permit the creation of subclasses and issue classes, although they rarely are used in practice by plaintiffs. F.R.CIV.P. 23(c)(4).

Typicality. Commonality bleeds over into the typicality requirement of Rule 23(a)(3). Typicality examines the way in which the class representatives will litigate the common claims — the evidence they will seek, the arguments they will make, and so on — in order to make sure that the common claims will be fairly presented. If the circumstances will lead the representatives to press common claims in an odd or unusual way, then there is good reason to worry about the adequacy of the representation the class members are receiving; if the claims will be presented in the way that the class members would likely have presented them, then it becomes easier to justify allowing the representatives to stand in for the class members.

The leading case on Rule 23(a)(3) is *General Telephone Co. of the Southwest v. Falcon.*[91] Falcon, a Mexican-American, alleged that his employer had discriminated against him by failing to give him a promotion. He then filed a class action on behalf of all Mexican-Americans who had been the victims of the company's discriminatory behavior — whether in initial hiring or in promotion decisions. The district court ruled that the company had not discriminated against Falcon in hiring him, but it had intentionally discriminated in failing to promote him. With regard to the class, the converse was true: The company did not generally discriminate in its promotion practices, but did discriminate in its hiring practices. The district court therefore awarded Falcon and disappointed the Mexican-American job applicants who could be located a backpay remedy.

The difficult issue was whether Falcon, whose claim of individual discrimination varied from the claims of other class members, could serve as a representative for the class. The court of appeals held that Falcon could serve, on an "across-the-board" theory that any victim of employment discrimination could represent any other victim discriminated against on the same racial or ethnic basis. The Supreme Court reversed, holding that Falcon was not an adequate representative for either the "failure to hire" or the "failure to promote" claimants. In order to be a class representative, Falcon needed to "'possess the same interest and suffer the same injury' as the class members."[92] The Court focused on the fact that the evidence of intentional discrimination necessary to prove Falcon's case of individual discrimination in promotion was significantly different than the statistical evidence used by Falcon to prove the class's claim of discrimination in hiring and promotion. As a result, Falcon's claim did not have questions of law and fact in common with those of class members, and was atypical of the claims that these class members possessed.

---

91. 457 U.S. 147 (1982).

92. *Id.* at 156 (quoting E. Tex.

Motor Freight Sys., Inc. v. Rodriguez, 431 U.S. 395, 403 (1977)).

Falcon was not entirely clear about whether it was ultimately an (a)(2) commonality case, an (a)(3) typicality case, or an (a)(4) adequacy case; indeed, it rather studiously straddled the issue. In a well-known footnote, the Court observed:

> "The commonality and typicality requirements of Rule 23(a) tend to merge. Both serve as guideposts for determining whether . . . maintenance of a class action is economical and whether the named plaintiff's claim and the class claims are so interrelated that the interests of the class members will be fairly and adequately protected in their absence. Those requirements therefore also tend to merge with the adequacy-of-representation requirement, although the latter requirement also raises concerns about the competency of class counsel and conflicts of interest."[93]

Falcon is probably best understood as a typicality case. It is difficult to believe that Falcon's claim failed to clear the modest commonality hurdle usually ascribed to Rule 23(a)(2). More credibly, the different remedial goals of Falcon and the "failure to hire" claimants could be seen as generating a conflict of interest of the kind that Rule 23(a)(4) was designed to prevent. The reason for this arguable conflict of interest, however, was the atypicality of Falcon's claims in relation to the claims of class members. Falcon's claim of intentional discrimination was not typical of the "pattern and practice" claims of others who were not promoted, and it was not remotely like the claims of those discriminated against in the hiring process. Falcon simply did not possess the financial incentive to press the members' cases as vigorously as the class members would have pressed their own cases in a traditional adversarial setting. That lack of incentive does not mean that Falcon did not in fact press the class members' cases vigorously; indeed, it appears that he did do so. But Rule 23(a)(3) is concerned with risks; and the risk that a class representative will use the class for bargaining leverage on an individual claim rather then for the benefit of the class gets proportionally greater as the atypicality of the representative's claim increases.

At the same time, *Falcon* correctly perceived the interrelationship among the elements of Rule 23(a). Each element of the analysis is a piece of an interlocking inquiry into the class representative's adequacy for the task. In a certain sense, the focus must remain on that ultimate inquiry of *Hansberry* rather than on the more specialized inquiries of the Rule 23(a) subparts. Indeed, read strongly, footnote 13 suggests that one or more of the Rule 23(a) factors need

---

93. *Id.* at 157 n.13.

only be minimally established, as long as the adequacy of representation is clear overall.

Whatever the fate of that suggestion, *Falcon* should not be read to make an insurmountable hurdle out of typicality. In some areas, such as a price-fixing conspiracy or a fraud perpetrated on the securities market, typicality is usually established easily: The class's injuries arise from a single event or course of conduct, involve the same legal theories, and present few factual divergences among class members. Left to their own devices, class members would presumably prosecute their cases in a substantially similar fashion, using the same evidence and arguments that the class representative proposes. Efficiency is advanced by having one such presentation rather than one hundred, and the class members' day in court, while compromised, is indirectly vindicated by the surrogate presentation.

Given the central role of typicality in ensuring that the representatives will adequately handle the class's claims, some courts have questioned whether Rule 23(a)(4), which requires that the representative be adequate, has any independent meaning.[94] The answer is that it is does, but only if you adopt the view that Rules 23(a)(3) and (a)(4) split the adequacy inquiry between them: Rule 23(a)(3) examines the general congruence between the representative's and the class's claims, and Rule 23(a)(4) checks for specific deficiencies in the representative's ability to vigorously advocate for the class.

For the most part, courts have construed the rule by dividing responsibility in exactly this way. The first parts of Rule 23(a) have shown that a class exists and that the class representatives will assert the class's common claims in a typical way. Rule 23(a)(4) then trains a more searching eye on the class representatives to see if any specific obstacles will prevent the representatives from fulfilling their obligation of vigorous representation. At the same time, Rule 23(a)(4) has been utilized to perform a second, absolutely critical function that has no textual support in Rule 23: to ensure that the lawyer who represents the class will also be an adequate counsel.[95]

Adequacy of the Class Representative. As a general matter, the inadequacies of class representatives fall into four categories. First,

---

94. *See* Taylor v. Safeway Stores, Inc., 524 F.2d 263 (10th Cir. 1975).

95. The use of Rule 23(a)(4) to check the adequacy of counsel is long-standing. *See* Dolgow v. Anderson, 43 F.R.D. 472 (E.D.N.Y. 1968). Despite its lack of textual support, this use is deeply entrenched in class action practice. *See, e.g.,* Senter v. Gen. Motors Corp., 532 F.2d 511, 525 n.31 (6th Cir.), *cert. denied,* 429 U.S. 870 (1976). As of this writing, proposed amendments to the Federal Rules of Civil Procedure would create a new Rule 23(g), which would, among other things, make explicit the court's obligation to assure adequacy of counsel.

regardless of how typical their claims might be, the court must be satisfied that the class representatives have no physical or mental impairments that will render them inadequate to manage the case. Findings of such infirmities are relatively rare, since plaintiffs' lawyers try to choose representatives with care; but occasional cases do exist, and a serious physical or mental deficiency can factor into the court's decision not to certify the class.[96]

Second, the court will examine whether the class representatives lack appropriate resources and incentives to litigate the case. A common argument in the early years of the modern class action rule was that the representatives' financial incentive in the litigation was often too slight to believe that they would press the case with appropriate vigor. For instance, the shareholder with only a few shares of stock in a multi-million dollar securities fraud action, or the antitrust victim with only a few dollars in damage, might not appear to have a sufficient stake in the case to watch over the class's interests; similarly, many such victims are relatively impecunious, and expecting them to fund litigation expenses that might run into the millions of dollars just to recover a few pennies seems unlikely.

Despite the apparent sense of these concerns, courts have not generally looked deeply into the issue of financial incentives. A large financial stake is sometimes cited as a positive feature, but a small stake is rarely disabling. One reason is that, at least in small-stakes litigation, any requirement that the class representatives have a large financial stake in the outcome might doom the class to failure at the outset; since individual claims are by definition not worth pursuing, the defendant therefore might avoid any liability. Another reason, rarely stated openly in the opinions, is that the critical player with respect to financial issues is the class's attorney, who is expected to have the financial wherewithal to sustain the litigation and whose own financial incentives to recover these expenses and to earn a fee ensure vigorous advocacy. Therefore, financial issues concerning the class representative are infrequently raised,[97] except in one important situation. In an attempt to cut back on what it perceived to be frivolous securities class actions brought by "professional" class representatives with minuscule financial holdings in the target companies, Congress passed the Private Securities Litigation

---

96. *See, e.g., Am. Med. Sys.,* 75 F.3d at 1083.

97. For an early case rejecting the financial argument, see *Dolgow,* 43 F.R.D. 472. For a more recent case finding the representative inadequate when the counsel shouldered all costs and expenses and the representative refused to accept responsibility for even a *pro rata* share of these costs and expenses, see Weber v. Goodman, 9 F. Supp. 2d 163 (E.D.N.Y. 1998). In *Weber,* a redrafted attorney-client arrangement ultimately resulted in class certification. Weber v. Goodman, 1998 WL 1807355 (E.D.N.Y.).

Reform Act of 1995,[98] which required, among other things, that the shareholder with the largest financial stake in the outcome of the litigation should be the presumptive class representative.

Third, class representatives' personal characteristics can be significant in determining adequacy. A lack of conscientiousness, usually manifested in a lack of knowledge about the underlying litigation, is sometimes claimed as a reason to find the representation inadequate. As with financial issues, the point has theoretical merit: Representatives who have done little to educate themselves about the facts or the legal theories of the case would seem ill-suited to protect the interests of class members. The extent of the representatives' knowledge is frequently probed at their depositions, which are usually taken prior to class certification. For the most part, though, courts adopt a middle-ground approach to the problem; perfect knowledge or legal comprehension is not required, especially when the class's counsel is a strong, experienced attorney.[99] On the other hand, courts cast a jaundiced eye on a representative's prior record of dishonesty or demonstrated neglect of others' interests.

Fourth, conflicts of interest between the class representatives and the class members are treated strictly. Such strictness is almost inevitable in the wake of *Hansberry*, which, on one reading at least, located the constitutional deficiency in the conflict between the interests of the class representative and those of some of the class members. The entire class does not need to have a conflict with the representatives; as long as at least some class members have interests that conflict with those of the representatives or other class members, the representatives cannot be regarded as adequate for all. Leaving aside a nagging fact in *Hansberry* that the Court did not address — whether the conflict of interest existed at the time that the original class action was filed or arose only afterwards as the interests of some class members evolved — *Hansberry*'s irreconcilable differences among covenant-enforcing and covenant-breaking class members present a paradigmatic conflict of interest. Similarly, a class representative who either is a potential defendant or is closely associated with the defendants cannot be trusted to maintain the requisite loyalty to the interests of the plaintiff class.

Another type of conflict that everyone agrees is unacceptable is collusion between the representative and the opposing party. A defendant cannot bribe the representative with, say, a million dollars in return for the representative's neglect of the class's claims. That

98. 15 U.S.C. §§ 77z-1(a)(3)(8)(iii), 78u-4(a)(3)(B)(iii).

99. *See, e.g.*, Peil v. Nat'l Semiconductor Corp., 86 F.R.D. 357 (E.D. Pa. 1980); Kirkpatrick v. J.C. Bradford & Co., 827 F.2d 718 (11th Cir. 1987), *cert. denied*, 485 U.S. 959 (1988).

much is obvious. The difficulty lies in ferreting out collusion on often ambiguous facts. For instance, is a defendant's offer to settle the representative's claim on terms somewhat more favorable than those extended to class members a bribe, a recognition of the relative strength of the representative's case, or a well-deserved reward for having assumed the sometimes difficult job of class representative?

The Supreme Court's most detailed exploration of the relationship between Rule 23(a)(4)'s adequacy requirement and conflicts within a class is *Amchem Products, Inc. v. Windsor*.[100] *Amchem* involved a settlement class action that sought to resolve the claims of thousands of asbestos claimants who had not yet filed suit. Some of those claimants were already suffering an asbestos-related injury; others had not yet suffered an injury. Of this latter group, some were likely to suffer injury in the near future, others would suffer injury in the more distant future, and still others would escape any injury. It was impossible to tell which individuals fell into which category. Some of *Amchem*'s class representatives had existing asbestos injuries, and some did not. The settlement terms scheduled a payment within a specified range for each specific type of asbestos injury. With the exception of a limited number of exceptional cases each year, all the presently injured and those that manifested injuries in the future were to receive a settlement within this range.

After some class members challenged the certification and settlement, the Supreme Court held that the settlement structure created irreconcilable conflicts of interest among class members. Those claimants who were already injured had an interest in large immediate awards; those yet to be injured had an interest in preserving the bulk of settlement funds for later. Relatedly, the present claimants had no need to be concerned with the effects of inflation on the scheduled damages; in contrast, the future claimants would want to account for inflationary effects and increase awards over time to retain real-dollar consistency among temporally dispersed awards. On both matters (and on some other minor matters as well), the settlement tended to favor the presently injured over those that would be injured in the future, thus creating sufficient conflicts to doom the class under Rule 23(a)(4).[101]

One of the challenges posed by *Hansberry* and *Amchem* is to determine the point at which conflicts among class members are so significant that the class stumbles on the Rule 23(a)(4) hurdle. Rarely are the interests of all class members so perfectly aligned that each member has precisely the same incentives and interests in the

---

100. 521 U.S. 591 (1997). We examine other aspects of *Amchem* *infra* nn.172-76, 280-86 and accompanying text.

101. 521 U.S. at 625-29.

litigation. In *Amchem*, class members had important interests that were highly consonant, including an interest in an inexpensive and expeditious alternative to the nightmare of asbestos litigation and an interest in preserving the settling defendants from bankruptcies that would jeopardize recoveries by all class members. Nonetheless, the Court found that the remaining conflicts in *Amchem* precluded class certification. *Amchem* itself suggested one possible solution to avoid these conflicts — to bring separate class actions on behalf of each set of interests, or at least to form separate subclasses out of each set of interests[102] — but it gave no guidance about when this solution, which certainly makes class action aggregation more cumbersome and less efficient, would need to be applied.

One way to understand *Amchem* and *Hansberry* — and to extract from them a more general conflict of interest principle — is to place them within the traditional adversarial universe. In this universe, each plaintiff is master of his or her own interests and is free to assert them as aggressively and selfishly as he or she wishes. Wrongs are done to individuals, not to the collective; remedies are given to individuals, not to the group.[103] The representative's goal must be to maximize each member's utility, not to maximize the utility of the group as a whole. In this universe, the class action is the aberration, heavily policed to ensure that the individual's interests are not swallowed up in the collective's goods. Any significant divergence in litigation strategy, especially one that might affect the outcome that the individual would have striven to achieve in individual litigation, amounts to a "conflict."

On this account, autonomy trumps efficiency. It may even trump general welfare. Only a truly monolithic large-scale case — perhaps an airplane crash in which each plaintiff's liability claim is essentially identical — will readily pass through the conflict filter; here, autonomous individual and collective group interests become indistinguishable.

Whether this strong account of autonomy has the same persuasive force in small-stakes cases, in which the alternative to class action litigation is often no litigation at all, is uncertain. In these cases, a pragmatic attitude might suggest that any positive outcome for the individual is better than the lack of redress that is likely in a non-aggregated setting, so conflicts of interest would need to be more acute to justify a finding of inadequacy.[104] Such an analysis grates

---

102. *Id.* at 627.

103. For an interesting discussion of the two models for class actions — as the aggregation of individuals or as a distinct collective entity — see David L. Shapiro, *Class Actions: The Class as Party and Client*, 73 NOTRE DAME L. REV. 913 (1998).

104. *Cf.* Phillips Petroleum Co. v. Shutts, 472 U.S. 797, 809 (1985) (not-

against the trans-substantive nature of the Federal Rules, because it makes certification in small-stakes class actions, such as securities fraud or antitrust, more likely than in cases in which individual cases are economically viable, such as dispersed mass torts. Nor does this analysis generate a full and coherent theory of the nature of permissible conflicts and of the boundary between the permissible and the impermissible.

A different starting point for analyzing conflicts of interest would be a collectivist perspective that sees the class action as an entity separate from the interests of the members that comprise it. From this perspective, the goal of a class action is to achieve the greatest good for the class that is consistent with social interests in optimal deterrence. Only those conflicts that frustrate achievement of the class's welfare or blunt the deterrent force of the class action should defeat class certification.[105] Indeed, some commentators have even suggested that the class representative is little more than a "decorative figurehead" that should no longer be required.[106] On this view, the only critical inquiries are the cohesiveness of the class and the adequacy of the class counsel. This move would make a class action behave more like a true collective action, and would eliminate one of the ways in which the class action, at least formally, is made to appear more like the bipolar litigation of traditional adversarial theory. Such a move, however, has thus far gained no momentum in the courts or the rule-making process.

Whatever the theoretical merits of either view, cases such as *Falcon* and *Amchem* seem to signal the Supreme Court's present commitment to viewing class actions as a vehicle for aggregation of individual claims. As such, the class action is a device approached with some suspicion, and the "inherent tension between representative suits and the day-in-court ideal"[107] must be closely monitored and carefully managed.

Adequacy of Class Counsel. The final adequacy inquiry is the adequacy of class counsel. At present, the requirement for an

ing that, in a case with damages of approximately $100 per plaintiff, "most of the plaintiffs would have no realistic day in court if a class action were not available").

105. For a recent defense of the collectivist approach to class actions, see David Rosenberg, *Mandatory-Litigation Class Action: The Only Option for Mass Tort Cases,* 115 HARV. L. REV. 831 (2002).

106. *See* Jean W. Burns, *Decora-* *tive Figureheads: Eliminating Class Representatives in Class Actions,* 42 HASTINGS L.J. 165 (1990); *cf.* Jonathan R. Macey & Geoffrey P. Miller, *The Plaintiffs' Attorney's Role in Class Action and Derivative Litigation: Economic Analysis and Recommendations for Reform,* 58 U. CHI. L. REV. 1 (1991) (proposing to abandon inquiry into representatives' knowledge of case).

107. Ortiz v. Fibreboard Corp., 527 U.S. 815, 846 (1999).

adequate class counsel is implicit in Rule 23.[108] The case law on the adequacy of class counsel parallels in many ways the expectations that have been imposed on class representatives. Counsel must be legally competent, financially and logistically capable of sustaining a large case, honest and ethical, and free of any conflicts of interest or collusive behavior.

Competence of counsel entails no more than that — competence. Class counsel does not need to be the "best" attorney. Counsel does not need to possess either an extensive prior class action practice,[109] or extensive experience in litigating the specific type of claim the class is asserting.[110] Of course, experience is a desirable trait; and especially with the rise of a sophisticated class action bar in recent years, it can usually be expected.

Financial and logistical capability enters into the competence equation. Although the class representatives and class members theoretically remain responsible for reimbursing counsel for the costs and expenses of the litigation, in most class actions this money is "fronted" by the attorney and then deducted from the recovery, if any. Since a recovery is often years off, the attorney must be capable of absorbing thousands, and sometimes millions, of dollars in costs, expenses, and overhead. In addition, counsel must have a demonstrated ability to handle the case. Counsel must have a sufficient numbers of partners, associates, and paralegals to staff the case, access to the technology necessary to manage vast quantities of documents and other information, and resources for communicating with class members, the media, and others.

The need for an attorney's honesty and ethical behavior is self-evident. Class counsel cannot possess impermissible conflicts of interest and cannot collude with an opposing party. To some extent, this requirement obliges class counsel to obey the ordinary rules of professional responsibility and ethical behavior. Counsel cannot normally represent both the class and one or more potential defendants. Counsel cannot have a claim as a class member (although sometimes a close relative can). Counsel cannot use the class action primarily as a tool to leverage a better outcome for other, individually represented clients.[111]

The rules of professional responsibility and the ordinary expectations of ethical behavior, however, were developed against the

108. On the proposal to make this requirement explicit in a new Rule 23(g), see *supra* n.95.

109. *See Dolgow*, 43 F.R.D. 472.

110. Bowling v. Pfizer, Inc., 143 F.R.D. 141 (S.D. Ohio 1992).

111. For a general examination of the ethical responsibilities of lawyers in large-scale litigation, see TIDMARSH & TRANGSRUD, *supra* n.14, at 898-925.

backdrop of the standard two-party lawsuit. In some regards, the class action presents conflicts of interests that are different than those presented in a standard two-party dispute, and here the present ethical standards have not caught up with the realities of class action practice. For instance, even though the class representative must have a common and typical claim, Rule 23(a) does not demand a perfect congruence of interests among the class's members. Some disagreements — perhaps concerning litigation strategy, preferred remedies, or the desirability of trial or settlement — are almost inevitable with a class. The quandary of class counsel is how to represent all these interests with the loyalty and vigor that adversarial theory and our present ethical rules demand.

One example of this problem was presented in *In re "Agent Orange" Product Liability Litigation*.[112] The plaintiff class had been represented by a consortium of several law firms, which ultimately negotiated a settlement on the class's behalf. Although most class members supported the settlement, some did not. The district court approved the settlement over their objections. On appeal, two of the law firms that had worked as part of the consortium sought to represent the objectors. Members of the consortium still representing the class then moved to disqualify the two firms, claiming that they had a classic conflict of interest: Their present representation against the class's interests was inconsistent with their prior representation in favor of those interests.

Under traditional ethical standards, disqualification should have been automatic: A lawyer cannot represent a client for half the case, and then turn around to work against that client for the remainder. As the Second Circuit realized, however, such standards cannot apply without modification in the class action context. Class actions blur the lines of decision-making authority between the lawyer and the client. Divergence of interest among class members is the usual and expected course of events, especially in the remedial phase of a class action. To require a lawyer's withdrawal when clients' interests split apart would have drastically negative consequences for class actions, and would often deprive objecting clients of their best representation. Therefore, the Second Circuit proposed a balancing test that factored in the amount of confidential client information the lawyers had obtained, the prejudice that might result from possession of the information, and the costs of and ease with which new counsel could be retained to represent the objectors.

Agent Orange does not suggest a new ethical structure for class counsel, and it does not abandon the concern for attorney conflicts of

---

112. 800 F.2d 14 (2d Cir. 1986).

interest. It does recognize, however, the need to temper traditional ethical rules in light of the demands of class action practice and the unique facts of the case. These ethical dilemmas and the blurring of traditional principles are common in complex litigation.[113] The next logical step, which neither *Agent Orange* nor other conflict of interest cases have taken thus far, is to develop a coherent and general ethical theory of class representation.[114] Until then, the exact boundary between permissible and impermissible conflicts for class counsel remains unclear — just as they are unclear for class representatives and class members.

Under no ethical theory, however, would an attorney's collusion with the opponent or an attorney's "selling-out" of the class's interests be defensible. The problem, once again, is not with the theoretical principle, but with the practical application. As we have noted, class counsel often fronts thousands of dollars to cover the costs of the class action. Consequently, counsel is typically the largest stakeholder in the outcome of the litigation. The financial pressures on counsel can become enormous. When the defendant proposes a settlement that provides a modicum of relief to the class, covers the counsel's expenses, and provides a significant attorneys' fee, the counsel's incentive to continue to prosecute the case to an uncertain conclusion can understandably diminish. Similarly, a defendant sometimes faces multiple overlapping class actions concerning the same behavior. It would be rational for a defendant to "shop" among the various class counsel to see which one might give the best "deal." This dynamic can set up a reverse auction in which various counsel might try to underbid each other to get the settlement and recover their own fees and expenses. In the process, of course, the class's recovery spirals downward.

In the literature and lore of class actions, there are a few famous anecdotal examples of counsel "selling out" a class. Indeed, the notion that class actions exist primarily to profit lawyers while doing little for clients has reached the status of urban legend. The available data do not suggest that collusion or "selling out" is a common occurrence in class actions; in fact, attorneys tend to receive

---

113. Another recurring dilemma is whether a lawyer may represent individual clients as well as a class with similar claims; and if so, whether the lawyer may settle the individual claims on different, and arguably more favorable, terms than the terms given to the class? *See* Susan P. Koniak, *Feasting While the Widow Weeps*: Georgine v. Amchem Products, Inc., 80 CORNELL L. REV. 1045 (1995); Carrie Menkel-Meadow, *Ethics and the Settlement of Mass Torts: When the Rules Meet the Road*, 80 CORNELL L. REV. 1159 (1995).

114. For an important effort to do so, see JACK B. WEINSTEIN, INDIVIDUAL JUSTICE IN MASS TORTS LITIGATION (1995).

fees in class actions that are slightly lower than those in individual litigation, and the phenomenon of large fees in relation to small class recoveries is rarely observed.[115] Nonetheless, this is a matter on which the court must be ever vigilant, in order to ensure the adequacy of the class's representation.

Summary: Contesting the Adequacy of the Representation. Having worked through the intricacies of each element of Rule 23(a), we risk losing focus on the larger picture of Rule 23. Rule 23(a) does not provide any reasons to join groups of people together in a class action. That work is left to Rule 23(b). Rule 23(a)'s work is to set the foundational minimum for any class action. This *sine qua non* is adequacy of representation, and Rule 23(a)'s specific factors attempt, each in its way, to guarantee that adequacy — the substitute for the litigant's autonomy to bring suit — exists.

We are now in a better position to evaluate whether the sacrifice of autonomy that the class action entails is sufficiently compensated for through the vigor and loyalty of the class representative and class counsel acting on the individual's behalf. It is possible that there is no single answer to this question. Some areas, such as mass torts with valuable individual claims or property disputes with significant racial implications, may raise different issues of adequacy than penny-stakes consumer or securities cases. Litigation that is still relatively immature raises different adequacy issues than litigation that is fully developed. Achieving deterrence and the common good may have greater importance in some types of cases, while vindicating individual interests may have greater salience in others. Therefore, the need for a strong interpretation of adequacy may vary.

Whatever the "correct" understanding of adequacy, a final issue remains: When a class member believes that he or she was not adequately represented, how can that member try to establish his or her claim? One way, obviously, is to contest the motion for class certification. But what happens when the inadequacy of the representation does not become apparent before class certification? Suppose, for instance, that Smith is successful in certifying a nationwide class action against XYZ for its improper manufacture of asbestos. The district court finds that Smith and his chosen counsel are adequate, and that the other requirements of Rule 23(a) are met. The case goes to trial, and the class loses. Alternatively, you can assume that the case is settled, but class members get only a few hundred dollars apiece for their serious injuries. Green, a member of the class, does not believe that Smith and/or the class counsel adequately represented the class's interests during pretrial and at

---

115. THOMAS E. WILLGING ET AL.,   FOUR FEDERAL DISTRICT COURTS 68-
EMPIRICAL STUDY OF CLASS ACTIONS IN   69, 77 (1996).

trial. Is Green bound by the judgment or settlement? Or can he challenge the representation in new litigation, cite *Hansberry*, avoid the negative consequences of the class judgment, and continue his own litigation?

This question is presently one of the hot button issues of class action practice. On the one hand, individuals sacrificed their autonomy on the assurance of adequate representation; it seems a violation of reasonable expectations, if not of due process, to bind someone to an outcome that does not live up to this assurance. On the other hand, the district court made findings of adequacy that should be binding on Green in any subsequent case. In addition, no judgment that is unfavorable to a class will ever be safe from subsequent attack if class members can easily make successful claims of inadequacy. Then one of the benefits promised by the class action — the final determination of the claims of similarly situated parties and nonparties — will have vanished, and the utility of the class action as an aggregation tool will have been seriously compromised.

Thus far, courts have split on the issues of whether and when a challenge to adequacy can be made. The most famous (or infamous) case is *Epstein v. MCA, Inc.*[116] *Epstein* involved claims of federal securities fraud, over which the federal courts had exclusive jurisdiction, and state-law fraud. Originally, an opt-out class action alleging only the state-law violations was filed in Delaware state court. Epstein, a class member in the Delaware case who did not opt out, then filed a federal class action alleging the federal securities claims. The federal district court held that Epstein did not state a claim for violation of federal law, and that the case should not be certified as a class action. While this judgment was on appeal, the class representative and class counsel in the Delaware case entered into a settlement with MCA. The settlement specifically released the federal securities claims, even though the state court had no jurisdiction to entertain them. The Delaware trial court found that the class representatives and counsel were adequate, and entered an order approving the settlement and discharging the federal claims. This order was ultimately affirmed by the Delaware Supreme Court. Meanwhile, the federal court of appeals reversed the district court, holding that the federal plaintiffs did have a viable federal securities claim and that the case could be maintained as a class action. It also held that the Delaware state courts had no power to discharge the federal claims.

The United States Supreme Court reversed the court of appeals on this last holding; as part of a settlement, state courts were indeed

116. 126 F.3d 1235 (9th Cir. 1997), *withdrawn and superceded by* 179 F.3d 641 (9th Cir.), *cert. denied,* 528 U.S. 1004 (1999).

able to discharge federal claims over which they had no jurisdiction.[117] On remand, Epstein then argued vehemently that he and other class members had been inadequately represented in the state case and were therefore not bound by its judgment. As a factual matter, this argument was not entirely baseless. There was ample evidence that MCA had shopped a settlement around, and had found that the lawyers in the state case, who would have received nothing for their efforts if they had not accepted a settlement, were willing to take a lower deal than the lawyers in the federal case. There was also evidence that the state-law claims were rather weak, and the federal claims were relatively strong — a fact which gave the state-court lawyers very little leverage. The substance of the state-court settlement was also favorable to MCA. In short, whatever the reality, the settlement had the appearance of a reverse auction in which the members of the class might have received less than they otherwise could have.

In a 2-1 decision, the court of appeals held that the Delaware class action had failed to adequately represent the interests of class members. As a result, the class members in *Epstein* were not bound by the outcome of the Delaware case, and were free to pursue their federal claims in federal court. The dissent argued that the *Epstein* plaintiffs' attempt to attack the Delaware judgment collaterally was impermissible because the Delaware court had entered a finding that the representation was adequate, the plaintiffs had never attempted to object the representation in the Delaware courts, and the United States Supreme Court had arguably operated under the assumption that the representation in state court had been adequate. The dissent claimed that the majority's ruling permitted disappointed class members to have two bites at the apple — a result that was a particular affront to sound notions of federalism and respect for state courts.

After the judge who wrote the majority retired and the other member of the majority changed his mind, the court of appeals reversed itself on rehearing. In another 2-1 decision, the original dissent's view thus prevailed: A class member cannot collaterally attack a judgment by claiming inadequacy of representation. Any known difficulties with adequacy must be raised in the case itself.

The final word on this controversy has yet to be written. Recently, another court of appeals aligned itself closely with the original decision of the *Epstein* court, and held that the adequacy of class representation could be challenged in a subsequent proceeding. That case, *Stephenson v. Dow Chemical Co.*,[118] arose out of the

---

117. Matsushita Elec. Indus. Co. v. Epstein, 516 U.S. 367 (1996).

118. 273 F.3d 249 (2d Cir. 2001).

settlement of the *Agent Orange* litigation. *Agent Orange* had been certified as a class action in federal court. The class members included all military personnel who fought in the Vietnam War. The class settlement, which was approved in 1984, called for payments due to certain disabilities arguably related to exposure to Agent Orange. Because the available literature suggested that all injuries would manifest themselves within twenty-five years of exposure, the settlement fund terminated in 1994 — twenty-five years after the last significant use of Agent Orange. All claims of class members against the defendants were discharged in the settlement.

The *Stephenson* plaintiffs alleged that their injuries from Agent Orange did not manifest themselves until after 1994. Relying on *Amchem*, they argued that post-1994 victims of Agent Orange had an irreconcilable conflict with pre-1994 victims, so that Rule 23(a)(4) was violated when both groups were placed in a single class. The defendants contended that the plaintiffs' claims were barred; all Agent Orange claims had been discharged by the settlement, and as class members, the plaintiffs were bound to that settlement.

The court of appeals agreed with the plaintiffs. The plaintiffs in *Stephenson*, as well as other plaintiffs whose injuries did not manifest themselves until after 1994, had been effectively unrepresented in the original class action due to the internal conflict within the class. The court of appeals distinguished *Epstein* with the observation that, unlike the Delaware judgment in *Epstein*, the prior judgment in *Agent Orange* had never specifically considered the adequacy of representation with respect to post-1994 plaintiffs. The court of appeals also stated that there are two distinct adequacy inquiries. The first is whether the district court made an initially correct determination that the class representatives would adequately represent the class; the second is whether, after the fact, the class representative did adequately represent the class. The second inquiry necessarily invokes collateral review.[119]

Although the two cases can be distinguished because *Epstein*'s federalism concern is not present in *Stephenson*, they are fundamentally inconsistent. The same divergence of opinion can be found in the academic commentary on the cases.[120] It does seem difficult to

---

119 *Id.* at 258-59 (citing Gonzales v. Cassidy, 474 F.2d 67, 72 (5th Cir. 1973)).

120. *See, e.g,* Marcel Kahan & Linda Silberman, *The Inadequate Search for "Adequacy" in Class Actions: A Critique of* Epstein v. MCA, Inc., 73 N.Y.U. L. REV. 765 (1998); Henry P. Monaghan, *Antisuit Injunctions and Preclusion against Absent Nonresident Class Members*, 98 Colum. L. Rev. 1148 (1998); Geoffrey C. Hazard, Jr. et al., *An Historical Analysis of the Binding Effect of Class Suits*, 146 U. PA. L. REV. 1849 (1998).

maintain *Epstein*'s strong view of class members' inability to challenge the adequacy of representation collaterally; otherwise, the judgment in *Hansberry*, on which the entire law of adequacy has been built, cannot be defended. But allowing a plaintiff like Epstein, who was armed with knowledge of the adequacy problems, to sit idly by seems equally unattractive. The matter seems destined for ultimate resolution in the Supreme Court. We will then have another opportunity to see whether the model of the class action as an aggregation of individual interests (a model that seems to be more supportive of *Stephenson*) or the model of the class action as a collective force (a model that seems to be more supportive of *Epstein*) is more compelling.

(B) The Elements of Rule 23(b). Rule 23(a) establishes the necessary foundation for all class actions; it does not provide any standards for when or justifications for why a class action should be brought. That task belongs to Rule 23(b), which was drafted and expanded as part of Rule 23's 1966 revision.

Rule 23(b) provides four distinct circumstances in which class actions might be used. First, Rule 23(b)(1)(A) permits class certification when separate actions by or against individual class members would create a risk of inconsistent or varying adjudications that might lead to incompatible standards of conduct for the party opposing the class. Second, Rule 23(b)(1)(B) authorizes the use of a class action when separate lawsuits would as a practical matter be dispositive of, or at least substantially impair or impede the ability to protect, the interests of class members not party to the lawsuits. Third, Rule 23(b)(2) class certification may be granted when injunctive relief for the class as a whole is appropriate because the person opposing the class has acted on grounds generally applicable to the class. Finally, Rule 23(b)(3) states that a class action can exist when common questions of law or fact predominate and when a class action is a superior means of resolving the controversy. It is typical for practitioners to refer to class actions by the provision of Rule 23(b) under which they were certified; thus, you might hear a lawyer referring to a case as a "(b)(3) class action."

Unlike Rule 23(a), Rule 23(b) does not require the class to meet each standard; the four standards operate disjunctively, so that a class action meeting one standard can be certified even if it cannot meet any of the others. It is possible, however, for a class action to meet more than one of the standards. It is also possible that some parts or claims of the class action might satisfy one standard, and other parts a different standard; it is not necessary that the entire class and all its claims fit within a single Rule 23(b) provision. A single class action might satisfy more than one standard, or some parts of a class action might satisfy one standard and another part another standard. Certification of all or part of a class action under different provisions sometimes occurs.

In a certain sense, the most critical architectural principle of Rule 23(b) is the division between the "mandatory" and the "opt-out" class action. The first three types of class action — the (b)(1)(A), (b)(1)(B), and (b)(2) class actions — are "mandatory," in the sense that class members cannot remove themselves from the class.[121] The (b)(3) class action is an "opt out" class action, which means that class members have the right to remove themselves from the class. According to Rule 23(c)(2), this opt-out right can be meaningfully exercised only after the class has received the (often expensive) "best practicable" notice of this right. Therefore, the opt-out class action provides a nod in the direction of litigant autonomy — albeit not as strongly as the "opt-in" approach of Rule 20, the basic permissive joinder rule. Those who opt out are free to pursue litigation on their own, which creates the concern that complete single-forum aggregation is impossible even with the class action. In terms of comprehensive aggregation, therefore, mandatory class actions come closer to the mark than opt-out class actions.

We now examine in detail each of the four class actions.

The "Inconsistent Standards" Class Action: Rule 23(b)(1)(A). Rule 23 (b)(1)(A) permits a class action when independent suits by class plaintiffs would create a risk of "inconsistent or varying adjudications" that "would establish inconsistent standards of conduct" for the defendant. It is settled law that the risk of separate suits by class members seeking injunctive relief fits within this provision. In such a situation, different injunctions might order the defendant to do different things, and the defendant might be unable to comply with all the orders; hence, bringing the plaintiffs together in a single suit makes sense. It is equally settled law that the risk of inconsistent damage awards — in which some plaintiffs might lose, some might win a modest amount, and some might win large judgments — is not covered by the Rule. In this situation, the inconsistency in ordering a defendant to pay differing amounts of damages to similarly situated plaintiffs does not subject the defendant to incompatible standards of conduct; it is perfectly feasible for the defendant to pay one claimant and not pay another.[122] Although

---

121. Some courts have held that a district judge has the power to permit a member of a mandatory class to opt out in extraordinary circumstances. *See, e.g.,* County of Suffolk v. Long Island Lighting Co., 907 F.2d 1295 (2d Cir. 1990). Whether this power in fact exists is unclear; in any event, it rarely has been exercised.

122. *See e.g., In re* Dennis Greenman Sec. Litig.,* 829 F.2d 1539 (11th Cir. 1987).

the necessity of this linguistic interpretation might be questioned,[123] Rule 23(b)(1)(A) has, as a practical matter, been used almost exclusively in cases seeking injunctive or declaratory relief.[124]

Plaintiffs' attorneys have shown some creativity in avoiding this limitation. In the mass tort area, for instance, some states have recognized that a defendant owes an obligation of medical monitoring to those persons exposed to the defendant's product but not yet injured by it. Although medical monitoring could be handled by awarding a sum of money so that exposed persons could seek private medical attention, some class plaintiffs have convinced the court that the defendant can be forced to create a monitoring program — a form of relief that the district court would establish through an injunction. In *In re Teletronics Pacing Systems, Inc. Accufix Atrial "J" Leads Products Liability Litigation,*[125] the plaintiffs then convinced the court to take the next analytical step: Since individual cases might force the defendant to establish monitoring programs that would clash with each other, it was necessary to certify a Rule 23(b)(1)(A) class comprised of all victims entitled to medical monitoring. Because an award of money to seek private medical attention would appear to be an adequate remedy at law, and because the evidence of conflicting monitoring programs was speculative, it is not obvious that *Telectronics* was correct.[126] If it is, however, *Telectronics* achieves something rather extraordinary: It finds a theory under which those with no present injuries (i.e., "future claimants") can be joined in a single class on a non-opt-out basis. Once joined, the hope would be, the plaintiffs would settle with defendants, and thus obviate the need for further proceedings.[127]

---

123. *See* Note, *Class Certification in Mass Accident Cases under Rule 23(b)(1)(A),* 96 HARV. L. REV. 1143 (1983).

124. For two contrary cases that certify class actions in cases seeking monetary claims, see *In re* Ikon Office Solutions, Inc. Sec. Litig., 191 F.R.D. 457 (E.D. Pa. 2000) (also certifying class under (b)(1)(B) for purposes of settlement); *In re* Fed. Skywalk Cases, 93 F.R.D. 415 (W.D. Mo.), *vacated on other grounds,* 680 F.2d 1175 (8th Cir.), *cert. denied,* 459 U.S. 988 (1982).

125. 172 F.R.D. 271 (S.D. Ohio 1997).

126. For a case disagreeing with *Telectronics,* see O'Connor v. Boeing N. Am., Inc., 180 F.R.D. 359 (C.D. Cal. 1997). *See also* Zinser v. Accufix Research Inst., Inc., 253 F.3d 1180 (9th Cir.), *amended by* 273 F.3d 1266 (9th Cir. 2001) (use of Rule 23(b)(1)(A) inappropriate when plaintiffs sought creation of monitoring fund, rather than monitoring program).

127. For a fuller exploration of whether it is possible to settle the cases of future claimants, see Section D *infra.* The plaintiffs in *Telectronics* ultimately did achieve a settlement by means of a (b)(1)(B) class action. The settlement was overturned when the class was ordered decertified on appeal. *In re* Telectronics Pacing Liab. Litig., 221 F.3d 870 (6th Cir. 2000).

The fundamental point of the (b)(1)(A) class action is to protect a defendant from the injustice of trying to comply with class members' demands for inconsistent remedies. The analogy is to Rule 19 (a)(2)(ii) joinder, for which the necessity of protecting a defendant from the risk of "double, multiple, or *otherwise inconsistent* obligations" is a sufficient ground to require the involuntary joinder of absent parties.[128] The rationale behind Rule 23(b)(1)(A) is the same, but here the interested parties are so numerous that individual joinder is impracticable. In the attempt to ensure fairness to the defendant, a greater breach of adversarial protocol is tolerated under Rule 23(b)(1)(A) than was tolerated under Rule 19(a)(2)(ii). Unlike Rule 19(a)(2)(ii), each party joined under Rule 23(b)(1)(A) cannot participate individually to protect his or her own interests. That work is done by the class representatives.

The Rule 23(b)(1)(A) class has other internal difficulties that require justification. The defendant would not be exposed to inconsistent standards of conduct unless the members of the class have either different legal rights or different legal interests that lead them to contend for the imposition of different relief. When such differences exist within the class, however, it can become difficult for the class to pass Rule 23(a) muster: When different legal rights are involved, commonality and typicality become strained; when different legal interests are involved, internal class conflicts emerge to threaten adequacy. Does the (b)(1)(A) class action tilt too far in favor of avoiding unfairness to defendants, and thus tolerate inherent conflicts that should be fatal to class certification?

This question is not easy to answer — and certainly not as easy as the standard hornbook statement that Rule 23(b)(1)(A) can be used whenever class members seek injunctive relief. As we have already seen, complete convergence of interest among class members is usually impossible, and divergences often emerge on the issue of remedy.[129] To some extent, the demands of fairness to the defendant and simple efficiency require us to tolerate some tensions within the class. The degree of tension that can exist within a (b)(1)(A) class without breaching the adequacy requirement of Rule 23(a), and whether this tension can be alleviated through the use of subclasses, are issues rarely explored with the necessary depth in the case law.

The "Impaired Interest" Class Action: Rule 23(b)(1)(B). Like Rule 23(b)(1)(A), Rule 23(b)(1)(B) concerns itself with the untoward

---

128. Rule 19(a)(2)(ii)'s concern for "double or multiple" obligations finds its parallel in Rule 22 interpleader, which permits mandatory joinder when a defendant faces "double or multiple liability."

129. *See, e.g., Agent Orange,* 800 F.2d 14, discussed *supra* nn.112-14 and accompanying text.

effects that separate lawsuits by class members create. Unlike the (b)(1)(A) class, the focus of the (b)(1)(B) class is not on the untoward consequences to the defendant, but rather on the untoward consequences that individual suits by putative class members would have on the rights of other putative class members. Thus, the (b)(1)(B) mandatory class action seeks to prevent the risk of individual actions that "would as a practical matter be dispositive of the interests of the other [putative class] members not parties to the adjudications or substantially impair or impede [the putative class members'] ability to protect their interests." In this situation, the idea is first to gather all the interested plaintiffs into a class, and then to find an appropriate, complete, and equitable solution to the controversy.

Just as the counterpart of Rule 23(b)(1)(A) is Rule 19(a)(2)(ii), the counterpart of Rule 23(b)(1)(B) is Rule 19(a)(2)(i). Both seek to achieve mandatory joinder of those who might otherwise find that prior individual adjudication has fundamentally compromised the interests that they wish to pursue. Both are designed to protect the interests of absent claimants. With Rule 23(b)(1)(B), however, the number of absent interested claimants is so great that their individual joinder and participation is impracticable.

Parallels also exist between Rule 23(b)(1)(B) and Rule 24(a)(2), which permits a person with potentially impaired interests to intervene in a case. As we saw earlier, however, impairment for Rule 19(a)(2)(i) purposes and impairment for Rule 24(a)(2) purposes are not the same thing.[130] The same is true for Rules 23(b)(1)(B) and 24(a)(2): The impairment language gets a different, more restrictive meaning when people are involuntarily joined in a class action. In particular, the *stare decisis* impairment that is often regarded as sufficient when intervention is sought under Rule 24(a)(2) is not regarded as a sufficient reason to invoke Rule 23(b)(1)(B);[131] forcing the involuntary joinder of a party requires greater justification than acquiescing in that party's decision to intervene to protect an interest — especially because, under Rule 23, the party's interests will be represented by another individual.

The necessary justification exists in a variety of situations. For instance, injunctive claims that seek the restructuring of an institution might have the practical effect of impairing the interests of others that have relationships with the institution. Rule 23(b)(1)(B) is similarly appropriate when a suit that seeks to require a company to pay a particular shareholder a dividend would, as a practical

130. *See supra* p. 94.
131. 7A CHARLES ALAN WRIGHT ET

AL., FEDERAL PRACTICE & PROCEDURE
§ 1774 (1986).

matter, establish similar shareholders' right to a dividend. Claims concerning the management or distribution of trust funds, or other forms of property in which numerous claimants have beneficial or joint ownership interests, also fit within the language of the rule.

The most frequently discussed use of Rule 23(b)(1)(B) has been in the context of a limited fund — in other words, a fund that is insufficient to pay fully all of the claims against that fund. Like interpleader, where we also encountered the limited fund concept,[132] individual litigation would result in the full satisfaction of the early-filed claims, and modest or no satisfaction of the later-filed claims. With interpleader, the defendant remained responsible for satisfying later claimants — an inequity that gave the defendant a reason to desire complete joinder. When the claimants are too numerous for joinder through interpleader, the defendant caught in this whipsaw would have a reason to seek Rule 23(b)(1)(B) certification. In other limited fund cases, however, the defendant will not be responsible for paying claims beyond the scope of the fund. Thus, the early exhaustion of the fund works to the disadvantage of later-filing claimants rather than the defendant. The defendant has a reduced incentive to seek complete joinder, since he or she is likely to be indifferent about the fund's distribution among claimants. Therefore, when the claimants against the fund are numerous enough, the claimants, rather than the defendant, might wish to seek class certification under Rule 23(b)(1)(B).

A classic situation involving this issue occurs when the legitimate claims against the defendant exceed its assets: Early-filing claimants would receive full value on their claims, and later-filing claimants would receive pennies on the dollar or nothing. In cases in which the only difference between early and late claimants is the fortuity of the claim's timing, this creates an inequitable situation. The question is whether Rule 23(b)(1)(B) may be used to avoid the inequity.

The present answer from the Supreme Court is "sometimes." In *Ortiz v. Fibreboard Corp.*,[133] an asbestos manufacturer and two of its insurers struck a deal designed to resolve all future claims. All asbestos plaintiffs that had not yet asserted a claim against the manufacturer were joined in a Rule 23(b)(1)(B) class. The facts of *Ortiz* and the settlement's terms are complicated.[134] In essence, two of Fibreboard's insurance carriers were allegedly responsible to indemnify Fibreboard in unlimited amounts for all of Fibreboard's asbestos claims that were based on asbestos exposure before 1959; only Fibreboard itself, however, was responsible for paying those

---

132. *See supra* n.55 and accompanying text.

133. 527 U.S. 815 (1999).

134. We look at additional aspects of *Ortiz infra* nn.201, 281-85 and accompanying text.

based on post-1959 exposure. While the pre-1959 insurance coverage dispute was being litigated between Fibreboard and the insurers, Fibreboard, the insurers, and plaintiffs' lawyers who represented many of Fibreboard's past and present victims entered into settlement negotiations. A settlement was struck for $1.535 billion, to which the insurers contributed $1.525 billion and Fibreboard contributed $10 million. The settlement left untouched Fibreboard's remaining assets of $235 million, as well as the insurance companies' remaining assets, which totaled in the billions of dollars. Since the insurers would settle only if the settlement ended all of their obligations and brought them total peace, the settlement had to be accomplished by means of mandatory joinder of the future claimants. The theory of the settling parties was that the $1.535 billion settlement kitty was a limited fund, which might be depleted by early-filing claimants unless all claimants were joined. Certification of a mandatory class action was sought under Rule 23(b)(1)(B).

The Supreme Court held that Rule 23(b)(1)(B) could not be used as the joinder vehicle for the settlement. The Court recognized that a limited fund presents a situation in which Rule 23(b)(1)(B) can be employed, but stated that the modern rule should hew closely to equity's traditional understanding of a limited fund. In particular, a Rule 23(b)(1)(B) limited fund must satisfy three criteria: The maximum amount of the fund must be inadequate to satisfy the maximum amount of the "aggregated liquidated claims,"[135] the whole of the fund must be devoted to the payment of the claims, and the claimants with common theories of recovery must be treated equitably among themselves.

Leaving open the question whether Rule 23(b)(1)(B) could ever be used to aggregate individual tort claims,[136] the Court held that the *Ortiz* settlement failed to fulfill these criteria in two ways. First, the fund from which compensation was to be provided was not set at its maximum, but was instead established at an amount agreed upon by the parties.[137] The Court suggested two different ways of conceiving the maximum amount of the *Fibreboard* fund: either the amount that would render the insurers and Fibreboard insolvent or the

---

135. 527 U.S. at 838-41. A separate matter, which the Court did not resolve, is the exact burden of proof that must be satisfied in a (b)(1)(B) context. Some courts have held that the existence of a limited fund must be proven to a high degree of certainty, while others have held that a reasonable possibility of a limited fund is enough. *Id.* at 849 n.26.

136. *Id.* at 842.

137. The Court also noted that the tort claims were unliquidated, which made Fibreboard's future liability uncertain. *Id.* at 850. But it did not base its holding on this fact.

amount that was equivalent to the size of the insurance company's assets discounted by the risk that Fibreboard would lose the insurance coverage litigation. Since both of these methods for establishing a limited fund would have stretched somewhat the usual notion of a limited fund, the Court did not necessarily approve either method. The *Fibreboard* settlement did not purport to use either approach, so the Court had little difficulty in finding the settlement fatally flawed.

The other stumbling block in *Ortiz* was the third element of a (b)(1)(B) limited fund: the equitable treatment of those with a claim against the fund. On this element two deficiencies emerged. First, the class definition included within the class only those with no pending claims against Fibreboard. All those who had previously settled with Fibreboard but had not yet been fully paid, as well as all those who had a pending claim against Fibreboard, had their cases settled separately with a somewhat different mechanism and under somewhat different terms. Second, the class members who had been exposed to Fibreboard's asbestos during the time that the insurance policies were in effect (up to 1957 for one policy and up to 1959 for the other) had claims that were far more valuable than those with post-1959 claims. Post-1959 claimants could look only to Fibreboard and its modest assets for satisfaction. Within the class, therefore, were people with inconsistent interests; the pre-1959 claimants and their differing legal position required separate representation and perhaps even separate classes or subclasses. The settlement, however, made no distinctions among class members in terms of representation, and it provided no greater settlement amounts to those exposed in or before 1959. The Court noted explicitly that this (b)(1)(B) concern overlapped with the (a)(4) adequacy problem detected in *Amchem*,[138] and it implied that it would have reversed the case on (a)(4) grounds had it been necessary to reach the issue.[139]

Ortiz does not make the use of the limited fund theory impossible, but the square corners that must be turned reduce the utility of (b)(1)(B) as an aggregation device in many situations. We turn, therefore, to the third form of class action — the (b)(2) class.

The Injunctive Class Action: Rule 23(b)(2). Also a mandatory class action, Rule 23(b)(2) requires class certification when the party opposing the class "has acted or refused to act on grounds generally applicable to the class, thereby making appropriate final injunctive relief or corresponding declaratory relief with respect to the class as a whole." The (b)(2) class action is therefore usually described as the injunctive class action, and has been used to certify class actions in

---

138. *See supra* nn.100-01 and accompanying text.

139. 527 U.S. at 856-57.

a host of circumstances requiring injunctive relief, such as civil rights, government benefits, and employment discrimination litigation. It has also seen occasional use in areas such as medical monitoring claims.[140] Its two essential elements — "generally applicable" conduct and a request for final injunctive or declaratory relief—have posed only a few interpretive difficulties on the margin.

Given Rule 23(b)(1)(A), which also appears to cover claims for injunctive relief, perhaps the most interesting question under Rule 23(b)(2) is whether it needs to exist at all. There are a number of possible historical, practical, and theoretical answers. An historical answer is that Rule 23(b)(2) is a studied redundancy. The 1966 Advisory Committee Note for the newly drafted Rule 23(b)(2) suggest that the drafters were aware of the rule's overlap with Rule 23(b)(1)(A), but wanted to make crystal-clear that the class action rule was intended to apply to then-emerging civil rights litigation, in which litigants usually sought injunctive relief.[141]

A second, practical answer also emerges from the Advisory Committee Note. Not infrequently, litigants seeking prospective injunctive relief also have damage claims demanding compensation for the past consequences of the defendant's behavior. Nothing in the text of Rule 23(b)(2) suggests that it can be used to handle related damages claims. But the Advisory Committee Note implies that Rule 23(b)(2) can be so used, stating that the (b)(2) class action "does not extend to cases in which the appropriate final relief relates exclusively or predominantly to money damages."[142] Although the converse proposition — that Rule 23(b)(2) can be used to aggregate claims for damages as long as they do not predominate over the injunctive claims — is never affirmatively expressed, it seems to follow from the quoted language.

The battle over Rule 23(b)(2) has largely been waged on the question of predominance ever since. At a practical level, having a mechanism to join damage claims on a non-opt-out basis could be an important advance in terms of aggregation. As we have seen, neither of the mandatory classes under Rule 23(b)(1) has widespread applicability to actions for money. Moreover, since no notice or right to opt out needs to be afforded to class members, the (b)(2) class promises greater preclusive effect with less expense and delay. On

---

140. The medical monitoring experience is a checkered one. *Compare* Cook v. Rockwell Int'l Corp., 151 F.R.D. 378 (D. Colo. 1993) (certifying medical monitoring class) *with* Cook v. Rockwell Int'l Corp., 181 F.R.D. 473 (D. Colo. 1998) (decertifying same class).

141. *See* WRIGHT ET AL., *supra* n.131, §§ 1775-76.

142. F.R.CIV.P. 23 advisory committee note (1966), *reprinted in* 28 U.S.C.A., FEDERAL RULES OF CIVIL PROCEDURE RULES 17 TO 25, at 385 (1992).

the other hand, a broad use of Rule 23(b)(2) renders Rule 23(b)(3) superfluous, overlooks the autonomy interests of individuals in controlling the prosecution of economically significant damages claims, and expands the scope of the litigation.

The seminal "predominance" case is *Wetzel v. Liberty Mutual Insurance Co.*,[143] in which plaintiffs who were victims of workplace discrimination sought both injunctive relief and individual awards of equitable back pay. Believing the back pay awards to be merely incidental to the injunctive relief sought, *Wetzel* included the back pay claims within the (b)(2) class, thus eliminating the ability of class members to opt out of the class to pursue their own back pay awards. Subsequent cases accepted *Wetzel's* basic analysis, and a significant body of case law has developed to distinguish between cases in which the damage claims "prodominated" (thus, no (b)(2) class for damages), and cases in which the damages claim was merely "incidental" to the injunctive claim (thus, a (b)(2) class for both injunction and damages). Courts generally address the "predominant/incidental" question by looking at whether the injunctive relief is substantial and important, in order to ensure that the injunctive tail is not wagging the monetary dog. Evincing an even more generous attitude, one set of influential commentators has observed that any serious inquiry into predominance is neither helpful to the disposition of the case on the merits nor a "useful expenditure of energy. . . . If the Rule 23(a) prerequisites have been met and injunctive or declaratory relief has been requested, the action should be allowed to proceed under subdivision (b)(2)."[144] This latter attitude allows a (b)(2) class action to have the broadest binding effect without the difficulties and expense of notice and opt-out, though it also forces individuals' monetary claims into the (b)(2) class.

Until recently, the debate about Rule 23(b)(2) tended to vacillate between a generous and a very generous attitude toward its use. *Allison v. Citgo Petroleum Corp.*,[145] however, has now reversed the debate's flow. Like *Wetzel*, *Allison* involved claims of a group of employees allegedly discriminated against in the workplace. After *Wetzel* and before *Allison*, however, the relevant employment discrimination statute had changed, so that employees could recover full compensatory damages rather than more modest equitable back pay, so that a jury rather than a judge determined the appropriate amount of damages. Seizing on these differences to distinguish the cases in the *Wetzel* line, *Allison* struck out in a very different direction.

143. 508 F.2d 239 (3d Cir.), *cert. denied*, 421 U.S. 1011 (1975).

144. WRIGHT ET AL., *supra* n.131, § 1775, at 470.

145. 151 F.3d 402 (5th Cir. 1998) (2-1 decision).

Allison began from the same premise as other cases: Rule 23(b)(2) permits the award of damages that are incidental to the injunctive relief. Its definition of "incidental," however, is quite different and much narrower. According to *Allison*, damages are incidental only when they flow directly from the injunctive relief and are awarded to the group as a whole. Moreover, such damages must be easy to calculate using objective standards. An example of such incidental relief is a statutorily mandated penalty for a violation of a consumer statute. Compensatory damages to victims of employment discrimination, on the other hand, are individualized and subjective, and are therefore not incidental.

Allison's recasting of incidental damages claims has become the focal point of subsequent legal development on (b)(2) classes. The Seventh Circuit has shifted toward *Allison's* interpretation of Rule 23(b)(2), but is more open to using Rule 23(b)(3) to aggregate the damages aspects of these cases.[146] The Second Circuit has rejected *Allison* in favor of an *ad hoc* balancing approach that focuses on (1) the likelihood that the injunctive claim would have been brought even in the absence of the monetary claim, and (2) the necessity of the injunction.[147]

Whether *Wetzel* or *Allison* represents a better view of Rule 23(b)(2) depends in part on whether the plain text of Rule 23(b)(2) should be enforced, and in part on the relative value of class members' right to assert adversarial control over their damages claims. It might also depend on the answer to the theoretical question of why (b)(2) needs to exist at all. Presumably courts could engraft a comparable "predominant/incidental" analysis onto Rule 23(b)(1)(A). What, then, is the *raison d'etre* of Rule 23(b)(2)?

We will turn to a fuller consideration of how Rule 23(b)(2) might be understood and justified in the near future, when we summarize some lessons that we could draw from Rule 23(b).[148] Before we can do that, however, we must first understand the fourth and final form of class action, the Rule 23(b)(3) class.

The Opt-Out Class Action: Rule 23(b)(3). As we have previously observed, Rule 23(b)(3) is different from the other forms of class action because class members have a right to opt out of the class. In order for that right to be exercised in a meaningful way, class members must be notified that they are members of the class and

---

146. Jefferson v. Ingersoll Int'l Inc., 195 F.3d 894 (7th Cir. 1999). In *Allison*, the court of appeals also refused to permit aggregation of the damage claims under Rule 23(b)(3).

147. Robinson v. Metro-North Commuter R.R. Co., 267 F.3d 147 (2d Cir. 2001), *cert. denied*, 122 S. Ct. 1349 (2002).

148. *See infra* pp. 146-51.

advised of their right to exclude themselves from the class.[149] The Supreme Court has held that the notice provision requires that individual notice — through first-class mail or an equivalent — be given to every class member who can be identified. For those that cannot be identified, substituted notice — such as newspaper, television, and radio advertisements — is appropriate, as long as the substituted notice is reasonably calculated to reach class members.[150] Notice can be expensive in large-scale class actions, and the cost must be borne by the plaintiffs.

Rule 23(b)(3) has two specific elements that must be satisfied. The two elements are that the "questions of law or fact common to the class predominate over any questions affecting only individual members," and that "a class action is superior to other available methods for the fair and efficient adjudication of the controversy." As with Rule 19(b), a list of four additional factors helps to provide meaning and context to the original two. These four factors are "(A) the interest of individual members of the class in individually controlling" their own cases, "(B) the extent and nature of any litigation already commenced" in the matter, "(C) the desirability or undesirability of concentrating the litigation" in the forum, and "(D) the difficulties likely to be encountered in the management of a class action." Most of the (b)(3)(A)-(D) factors appear to address aspects of the superiority question. Only (A) and (B) have any arguable bearing on the predominance issue.

Rule 23(b)(3) was an entirely new concept when it was added in 1966. It was a product of the movement, also seen in the contemporaneous changes in Rules 19 and 24, to create joinder rules that were consonant with the goal of making the transaction the appropriate unit for litigation. The driving forces behind Rule 23(b)(3) were efficiency and uniformity of result. When a sufficient number of common questions exist, the court and the parties can realize significant savings through a single resolution. No other joinder method — permissive joinder, intervention, interpleader, or mandatory joinder of necessary parties — can as easily accomplish this task of assembling a numerous group of common, related claims. Against these gains in efficiency, however, stand weighty concerns for individual autonomy and control. The opt-out mechanism attempts a solomonic compromise. Those who are willing to cede control to the class representative in return for this efficiency can stay put; those who wish to assert adversarial control over their claims can opt out. Rule 23(b)(3) thus seeks to balance efficiency and autonomy, but it serves neither master perfectly well.

---

149. F.R.CIV.P. 23 (c)(2).

150. Eisen v. Carlyle & Jacquelin, 417 U.S. 156 (1974).

The case law interpreting the elements and factors listed in Rule 23(b)(3) reflects this split personality. Rule 23(b)(3) is by far the most commonly used form of class action, and (b)(3) certification has been sought thousands upon countless thousands of times since 1966. For nearly every case finding that predominance or superiority has been established, there exists a comparable case finding that the elements have not been established. For every case finding that a proposed class conglomeration is too confusing, unruly, and unmananageable, another case believes that the class's management problems can be solved. At best, therefore, we can speak only of general tendencies, trends, and commonly encountered issues.

For the most part, courts tend to analyze the (b)(3) issue by resort either to the two "predominance" and "superiority" prongs or to the four (A)-(D) factors. We start by examining the predominance and superiority elements. For predominance, courts do not require that all questions of law and fact be common in order to meet the predominance test.[151] Nor do they apply a mathematical formula, counting up disputed issues to ensure that 50.1% are common. Instead, the analysis tends to be qualitative, with an eye toward satisfying the fundamental goal of the (b)(3) class. When efficiencies can be achieved by resolving a non-trivial common question, courts tend to find the predominance test satisfied — even though important and perhaps even dispositive issues that depend on non-common circumstances, such as the statute of limitations or contributory negligence, still remain open. The real question is whether a decision on the common issues will advance significantly the termination of the case.

For instance, in *Jenkins v. Raymark Industries, Inc.*,[152] the plaintiffs sought class treatment of an asbestos case comprising approximately 900 claimants. The predominance criterion was met, the plaintiffs argued, because the issue of the "state of the art" in the asbestos industry was a defense common to all of the cases. The defendants argued the opposite; important individual questions such as exposure, causation, damages, the statute of limitations, and contributory negligence overwhelmed the common issues in both quantity and amount of time that would be devoted to them. The court of appeals sided with the plaintiffs, holding that the "state of the art" defense constituted a "significant part" of each class member's case.[153] A single resolution of this important, and potentially dispositive, issue would save the time and expense of hundreds of trials using the same evidence. Therefore, *Jenkins* found that predominance had been established.

---

151. *See* WRIGHT ET AL., *supra* n.131, § 1778.

152. 782 F.2d 468 (5th Cir. 1986).

153. *Id.* at 472.

On the other hand, in *Castano v. American Tobacco Co.*,[154] the same court of appeals subsequently refused to certify a nationwide class of millions of injured cigarette smokers who became addicted due to defendants' actions. Although common factual questions about nicotine addiction and defendants' alleged enhancement of smoking products with nicotine existed, the court stated that multiple state laws would be involved in the case, and the "variations in state law may swamp any common issues and defeat predominance."[155] The court distinguished *Jenkins* as a case involving fewer than 1,000 claimants, all of whom sought recovery under the law of one state. The number of plaintiffs, number of defendants, number of legal theories, number of years of wrongful behavior, and number of state laws were all greater in *Castano* than in *Jenkins*. In addition, the court emphasized that, unlike the asbestos claims in *Jenkins*, the smoking claims were novel and untried when class certification was sought. That immaturity made it difficult for the court to know how the cases should be tried, and thus made it impossible "to know whether the common issues would be a 'significant' portion of the individual trials."[156]

Although these distinctions have force, at a fundamental level *Jenkins* and *Castano* evince very different attitudes about the appropriateness of using Rule 23(b)(3) to handle mass tort litigation. The cases seemed to assign different weights to the values of efficiency and individual control in mass tort cases, and to hold different views on the role of class actions in holding corporations accountable for their actions. In neither case could the "predominance" inquiry be divorced from the policy debate about the value of class actions.

A comparable debate existed for some time in the securities arena. Securities cases typically require proof of fraud, and fraud requires proof of reliance — that an individual received the fraudulent misrepresentation and acted on it. For some time, defendants argued, á la *Castano*, that the individual question of reliance predominated over any common questions of defendant's behavior, so that class certification under Rule 23(b)(3) was inappropriate. The success of this argument varied, but its use eventually led to a significant change in securities law. Plaintiffs began to urge courts to accept a theory of "fraud on the market": If a misrepresentation regarding a security was made generally to the public, then individual reliance could be presumed and proof of individual reliance could

---

154. 84 F.3d 734 (5th Cir. 1996).

155. *Id.* at 741. *Accord, In re* Rhone-Poulenc Rorer Inc., 51 F.3d 1293 (7th Cir.), *cert. denied*, 516 U.S. 867 (1995) (Posner, C.J.); Stirman v. Exxon Corp., 280 F.3d 554 (5th Cir. 2002).

156. 84 F.3d at 745.

usually be dispensed with. The "fraud on the market" theory became widely accepted,[157] and was eventually adopted by the Supreme Court.[158] The motivating force behind, and the ultimate consequence of, this theory was to make it easier for plaintiffs to meet the predominance test. Today, securities fraud cases rarely stumble on the question of predominance.

Even when common questions predominate, however, a class action is not necessarily the best way to resolve a controversy. The second half of the (b)(3) analysis — superiority — seeks to ensure that no other mechanisms will dispose of the case as efficiently as the class action. In considering this question, the court needs to balance the costs and benefits of class treatment against those of other mechanisms, and to certify a (b)(3) class only when the overall balance tips in favor of class treatment.[159] To some extent, therefore, the superiority analysis is internal; if the costs of class certification are greater than its benefits, it cannot be superior. To some extent, the superiority analysis is external, or comparative; if other aggregation devices such as multidistricting on balance have fewer costs and greater benefits than the class action, the class action is not superior to these other devices. If either the internal or the external calculus fails, certification under Rule 23(b)(3) must be denied.

This need to justify its superiority is unique to the (b)(3) class action. The superiority of the (b)(1) or the (b)(2) class to other aggregation mechanisms inheres in their very nature; if class certification doe not occur, the defendant faces an unacceptable risk of being subjected to inconsistent standards, or nonparties face an unacceptable risk that their interests will be significantly impaired. The (b)(3) class contains no similar measuring stick of superiority, and requires the court to consider a host of circumstances.[160] Some of the most frequently mentioned include whether the small size of individual members' relief makes consolidated handling essential; whether the plaintiffs have adequate resources to sustain individual litigation; whether the statute of limitations for filing individual claims has run out after filing the class complaint; whether individual litigation would result in a judgment that would have preclusive effect in future cases; whether the litigation is sufficiently mature to have a sense of whether class treatment might prevent many separate filings, and of how the class action might be tried; whether aggregation in a single distant forum represents a serious hardship

157. See Blackie v. Barrack, 524 F.2d 891 (9th Cir. 1975), cert. denied, 429 U.S. 816 (1976).

158. Basic, Inc. v. Levinson, 485 U.S. 224 (1988) (plurality opinion).

159. See WRIGHT ET AL., supra n.131, § 1779.

160. For a general discussion of factors, see id.

for class members; whether multidistricting can accomplish the necessary coordinated handling; whether a single course of discovery and trial on common issues will expedite the ultimate resolution of the litigation or prolong it; whether one law or multiple state laws govern the dispute; and whether the class action presents complications that make it difficult for the court to shepherd the case through the pretrial and trial phases.

Many of these circumstances can also be shoehorned into the factors listed in Rule 23(b)(3)(A)-(D). Because these factors provide somewhat more definite standards for analysis than the "predominance" and "superiority" tests, they are frequently used by courts. Indeed, although Rule 23(b)(3)(A)-(D) is intended to be only "a non-exhaustive list of factors pertinent to a court's 'close look' at the predominance and superiority criteria,"[161] they become, in many judicial opinions, the universe of relevant variables. But the factors are hardly self-applying. The weight to be given to each factor is unclear, and they seem to overlap both with each other and with some of the factors of Rule 23(a).

As we have observed, none of the four factors is designed primarily to address the question of predominance; all are geared principally to the superiority prong. The first — the class members' interest in individual adjudication — both examines the strength of the autonomy interest and compares the advantages and disadvantages of individual adjudication to class adjudication. The large or small size of the class members' recovery is relevant to this inquiry, as are the likelihood that a significant number of people may opt out and the preclusive effect that individual litigation would or would not create.

The second factor — the amount of existing litigation — is a two-edged sword. A significant amount of litigation demonstrates both a strong interest in individual control and the economic viability of separate litigation; it also portends a large number of opt-outs. But a large number of individual cases heightens the need for a single resolution of common claims and issues. Conversely, a lack of other litigation can signal either the inappropriateness of class treatment, because there is little reason to create a massive case upon such a limited showing of interest, or the necessity of class treatment, because individual actions are not viable. Indeed, Rule 23(b)(3)(B) can often be twisted to support whichever result the court otherwise wishes to achieve.

---

161. *Amchem*, 521 U.S. at 615 (quoting Benjamin Kaplan, *Continuing Work of the Civil Committee: 1966* *Amendments to the Federal Rules of Civil Procedure (I)*, 81 HARV. L. REV. 356, 390 (1967).

The third factor — the desirability of concentrating the litigation in one forum — is more one-directional in its application. The problem is that the factor is more of a conclusion than a method of analysis. Included within this factor are often considerations such as the elimination of duplicative litigation, the forum's fairness and convenience for witnesses and parties,[162] and the law or laws that would apply to class members' cases.

The fourth factor — the difficulties that the management of the class action would present during pretrial or trial — is the 800-pound gorilla of the four factors. It is nearly impossible to imagine a court certifying a class action after determining that the class cannot be managed.[163] Often called the "manageability" inquiry, Rule 23(b)(3)(D) usually receives the most sophisticated and detailed analysis in judicial opinions. It is closely aligned with the superiority analysis, and many of the factors that we have already identified as relevant to the superiority analysis are equally pertinent here.

One issue that manageability specifically invites the court to consider is how the class action will be moved through the pretrial and trial process. We will turn to particular management devices in Chapters Six and Seven, but you should realize now their bearing on the (b)(3) certification issue. At the time of class certification, it is not unusual for lawyers to present — and for judges to demand — a brief outlining the pretrial and trial plan for the certified class action. If the plan appears unrealistic or requires the use of a confusing array of subclasses to narrow the case for trial, the court is likely to find the case unmanageable as a class action. If the plan appears to streamline discovery and shape the trial in a way that promises a more efficient resolution than other methods of individual or aggregated litigation, the class is well along the way to certification.

Regardless of whether the "predominance/superiority" approach or the four-factor analysis of Rule 23(b)(3) is used, certain types of cases fit more readily into the (b)(3) mold than others. Small-stakes cases, which are sometimes called "negative value suits,"[164] are prime

---

162. *Cf.* 28 U.S.C. §§ 1404(a), 1407(a) (permitting transfer from one federal district to another when fair and convenient for the witnesses and the parties). These transfer provisions are discussed *supra* ch. 3, nn.52-72 and accompanying text.

163. On rare occasion, a court will admit that a (b)(3) class presents major management challenges, find that individual litigation presents greater challenges, and certify the class de-

spite its misgivings. *See, e.g.,* Brennan v. Midwestern United Life Ins. Co., 259 F. Supp. 673 (N.D. Ind. 1966).

164. A negative value suit is one in which it would cost a plaintiff more to prosecute a case (in terms of costs, expenses, and attorneys fees) than the plaintiff could expect to recover in a judgment. The only way to make these small-stakes cases viable is to pool them together to achieve economies of scale.

candidates for class treatment. Large-stakes cases, in which individuals have an incentive to prosecute the cases separately, are problematic. Similarly, cases in which liability issues vary little from case to case are better candidates for (b)(3) treatment than those in which some elements of the claims or defenses hinge on individual circumstances. Combining these two sets, small-stakes cases presenting few individual variations are considerably better candidates for (b)(3) treatment than large-stakes cases with important individual issues. Small-stakes cases with individual variations and monolithic large-scale cases present mixed pictures for certification. As a general rule, therefore, small-stakes, low-variability claims such as securities, antitrust, and consumer fraud receive class certification with the greatest regularity and ease. Large-stakes, high-variability claims such as mass torts are the most likely to stumble on Rule 23(b)(3).

Indeed, for mass torts, the drafters of Rule 23(b)(3) stated specifically that the opt-out class action was "ordinarily not appropriate."[165] For quite some time, courts adhered to this admonition, even in mass torts, such as airplane crashes, in which the variability on liability issues was very low.[166] With the rise of mass product liability claims in 1970's, pressure grew for a collective responses. By the 1980's some chinks had appeared in the drafters' armor, as class actions in mass torts involving Agent Orange, asbestos, and DES were certified.

Among the cutting-edge cases in this era was *Jenkins*, which thought that a single resolution on the question of the "state of the art" of asbestos manufacture made class treatment superior. If the plaintiffs prevailed on the "state of the art" issue, the mind-numbing task of presenting identical evidence in nine hundred trials would be avoided, and thousands of trial days would be saved; if the defendants prevailed, nine hundred cases would be terminated in an instant. An added advantage of class treatment was that the court could control the class counsel's attorneys fees, and thus reduce the costs to class members. Although significant individual issues of exposure, causation, and damages remained, these did not deter the court of appeals. It recognized that the volume and frequency of mass disasters forced it to reconsider its alternatives and priorities. "Necessity," it said, "moves us to change and invent."[167]

A different attitude toward the superiority of mass tort (b)(3) classes developed in some cases in the 1990's. A classic example is *Castano*, which held that a nationwide nicotine-dependent smokers'

---

165. *See* advisory committee note, *supra* n.142, at 386.

166. *See e.g.,* Hobbs v. Northeast

Airlines, Inc., 50 F.R.D. 76 (E.D. Pa. 1970).

167. *Jenkins*, 782 F.2d at 473.

class action could not establish superiority. The class had severe manageability problems: "different choice of law determinations, subclassing of eight claims with variations in state law, *Erie* guesses, notice to millions of class members, . . . and the difficult procedure for determining who is nicotine-dependent."[168] Moreover, the "most compelling rationale for finding superiority — the existence of a negative value suit — is missing in this case."[169] The court of appeals stated that the class action skewed trial outcomes, and created inappropriate pressure on the defendants to settle. Moreover, the smoking litigation was immature, making it difficult for the court to evaluate the plaintiffs' proposed trial plan, or to discern whether the merits of the case would lead to repetitive litigation in the absence of class certification. A better alternative, the court thought, was to leave the matter to individual litigation, in which the relevant issues and trial strategies could be honed and a record could be built for how a single resolution would be more efficient.[170]

It is tempting to use the maturity of the asbestos litigation to distinguish *Jenkin's* superiority analysis from that of *Castano*, but other courts either have certified immature torts for class treatment or have failed to certify asbestos cases under Rule 23(b)(3).[171] In the past decade, the flat rule that mass torts cannot be certified under (b)(3) has essentially vanished. Actually obtaining class certification of a mass tort, however, is still a tricky matter.

Nowhere is this ambivalence better shown than in *Amchem*, an asbestos settlement class action that purported to resolve the claims of many thousands of future asbestos victims with claims against twenty asbestos defendants. As we have already discussed, the Supreme Court believed that the class suffered from fatal (a)(4) adequacy of representation problems.[172] The Court also held that the class had equally fatal (b)(3) problems. To begin with, the Court dispensed with the notion that mass torts were generally inappropriate candidates for class treatment. It thought that "mass tort cases arising from a common cause or disaster may, depending upon the circumstances, satisfy the predominance requirement . . . . [T]he text of the rule does not categorically exclude mass tort cases from class certification."[173]

---

168. *Castano*, 84 F.3d at 747.

169. *Id.* at 748.

170. The court of appeals also foresaw Seventh Amendment problems with class certification. *Id.* at 750-51. We consider that issue *infra* nn.205-13 and accompanying text.

171. *See generally* 7B CHARLES A. WRIGHT ET AL., FEDERAL PRACTICE & PROCEDURE § 1783 (1986).

172. *See supra* nn.100-02 and accompanying text.

173. *Amchem*, 521 U.S. at 625.

Nonetheless, when a mass tort combined large stakes with significant disparities among individual cases, the Court "call[ed] for caution" in using Rule 23(b)(3).[174] *Amchem's* specific holding was that the plaintiffs could not prove predominance. The future asbestos victims had certain common issues, including their exposure to defendants' asbestos, the overarching dispute about the health consequences of asbestos' exposure, and their interest in receiving fair and speed compensation. Although the Court suggested that these shared issues might have been enough to satisfy the (a)(2) commonality hurdle, the (b)(3) predominance hurdle required more. How much more is not, unfortunately, clear from the opinion. The Court immediately shifted to a description of the dissimilarities among the plaintiffs' cases — the differences in exposure amounts, in exposure duration, in workplaces, in injuries, in medical histories, in damages, and in relevant state law — without providing any test to distinguish the mass tort with predominant questions from the mass tort without such questions. The Court did observe that no similar class action was "as sprawling as this one."[175] But such a conclusory adjective ends analysis rather than commences it.

Amchem also demonstrates the overlapping, and arguably incoherent, nature of the predominance and superiority analysis; many of the facts that *Amchem* cited as predominance-defeating could also be cited to defeat superiority. Moreover, *Amchem's* outcome foretells a limited future for class action aggregation. Prior to *Amchem*, asbestos litigation, which was the most mature and predictable litigation of all time, had resisted every effort at significant aggregation. After being handed an aggregation mechanism on a platter, the Court refused to accept it. Its refusal should not necessarily be regarded as a death knell for aggregation; *Amchem's* effort to settle future claims presented unique and perhaps insurmountable challenges, and there were several aspects of the *Amchem* settlement that were unappealing.[176] But little in the Court's analysis on the (b)(3) issue hinged on those challenges or deficiencies in the settlement. The maturity of asbestos litigation was never viewed as a positive factor, as it had been in *Jenkins* and in *Castano*. Simply put, *Amchem* built a brick wall at exactly the point in the road where traffic was most congested, and most in need of unclogging.

---

174. *Id.*

175. *Id.* at 624.

176. For an examination of the challenges that the settlement of future claims present, see *infra* pp. 192-

99. For a review of the settlement's terms and some of its difficulties, see JAY TIDMARSH, FIVE MASS TORT SETTLEMENT CLASS ACTIONS 51-54, 57-58 (1998).

Therefore, the (b)(3) class action presents a muddied picture. Rule 23(b)(3) is deeply committed to efficiency and uniformity, but deeply troubled about the loss of individual control that it entails. A Janus-faced rule wielding so much power and outcome-determinative potential is likely to be unstable, controversial, and loathed and loved in equal measure.

Summary: Final Reflections on the Architecture of Rule 23(b). Each of the four Rule 23(b) class actions that we have now examined permits joinder in a specific situation in order to accomplish a specific purpose. The reasons why joinder is appropriate for these situations and purposes, and not for others arguably deserving aggregated treatment, is not apparent on the face of Rule 23. An historical answer — that these were simply the classic forms of class action in equity — is inaccurate; neither the (b)(2) nor the (b)(3) class has exact analogues in prior class action rules, and the Court in *Ortiz* was seemingly willing to consider at least modest departures from historical practice for Rule 23(b)(1)(B) classes. Is there any conceptual theme that accounts for the circumstances in which our system does, and does not, permit representative litigation? Why are some class actions mandatory, and some opt-out? Is the architecture of Rule 23(b) a mere matter of historical accident and pragmatic invention?

One way to search for an answer to these questions is to return to the fundamental nature and tensions that underlie all of our joinder rules. These rules are the product of competing tendencies. Given our modern procedural assumption that the appropriate litigation unit is the transaction, our joinder rules wish to be expansive enough to permit the joinder of all transactionally related claims and defenses. Our procedural system also cherishes efficiency in adjudication. Oftentimes transactionalism and efficiency run in the same direction, but not always; sometimes the transaction is too large and messy. Here efficiency acts as a brake on transactionalism. So too does the assumption of individual, autonomous, adversarial control, which looms over the entire joinder field. Different joinder rules work out the balance among these assumptions in different ways. Although it is nowhere to be found in the text or the language of cases such as *Mosley*, the concern for autonomy dominates Rule 20, with transactionalism and efficiency more lightly in the mix. In Rule 19 and interpleader, autonomy is more muted, but neither transactionalism nor efficiency adequately explains the shift. As we have suggested, the concern for remedial equity — a fair distribution of a remedy from the multiple viewpoints of the plaintiff, the defendant, and the litigation's outsiders — seems to be the most powerful influence.

The same tussle for supremacy reflects itself in Rule 23(b). The first two mandatory classes — (b)(1)(A) and (b)(1)(B) — respond to the roughly the same concerns for remedial equity that drove mandatory joinder in the Rule 19 and interpleader contexts. Of course, important differences among these rules exist. Most obviously, Rule 23(b)(1)(A) and (b)(1)(B) classes involve a greater number of affected parties and, due to their representative nature, an even greater sacrifice of litigant autonomy. Moreover, Rule 23 does not have the constraining influence of Rule 19(b), and can achieve joinder even when interpleader is not appropriate. But all the rules are willing to sacrifice litigant autonomy when the counterbalancing interests are strong enough. That interest is not mere efficiency, nor even transactionalism — though both can be advanced by Rule 23(b)(1) classes. Rather, the interest is remedial equity; and, as *Ortiz* shows, creative attempts to expand mandatory class joinder, without ensuring an equitable distribution of the remedy among all those affected, cannot succeed.

If remedial equity acts as the justificatory force behind the (b)(1) classes, then two questions remain. First, what is the justification for the (b)(2) class? Second, what is the justification for the (b)(3) class?

One answer to the first question is simply to see the (b)(2) class as redundant of the (b)(1)(A) class.[177] A different answer, which we admit is entirely our own, is that Rules 23(b)(1)(A) and (b)(2) are designed to deal with quite different aspects of remedial inequity. In some situations, various parties have differing, and to some extent mutually exclusive, legal rights in a dispute that is brought by one of the parties. A classic example is a case of racial discrimination in the workplace. After the Supreme Court's development of a theory of "reverse discrimination," both minority and majority workers have a legal right not to have their race counted against them in employment decisions. When the employer has discriminated against minority workers, however, the court might need to take race-conscious remedial actions that favor the minority employees. Since employment decisions can be seen as a zero-sum game, favoring the minority race means disfavoring the majority race — a result that clashes with the majority race's legal right not to be discriminated against. Therefore, any remedy for minority workers must achieve a nice adjustment among competing legal rights.

A different situation is presented when other parties have legal *interests*, but no legal *rights*, that vary from the interests presented by the dispute between the plaintiff and the defendant. A classic

177. *See supra* n.141 and accompanying text.

example is prison reform litigation, in which no one has a legal right to insist that prisoners be maintained in unconstitutional conditions. Although prisoners may disagree amongst themselves about the scope of their rights and the appropriate remedy, the appropriate right and remedy are in theory knowable. Therefore, there exists a fundamental consonance among the prisoners in terms of their entitlement. When Rule 23 (b)(2) was enacted, before the development of the theory of reverse discrimination, this consonance also described most civil rights litigation.

Our suggestion is that Rule 23(b)(2) should be understood as applying only to this latter situation of consonance of legal rights among a class. When there exists dissonance in legal rights among the entire group or class affected by an injunction, the proper rule to use is Rule 23(b)(1)(A). When a class representative attempts to use Rule 23(b)(2) to handle a "dissonance" case, he or she creates remedial inequity by excluding those with affected legal rights from the litigation. This result should not be countenanced.

You might wonder what difference it makes whether the class is certified under one rule or the other. In one sense, it does not. In another sense, however, keeping the two scenarios distinct forces courts to focus on a matter often overlooked in class action practice: the under-inclusiveness of class actions. When certain employees believe that they are the victims of discrimination, it seems natural to include only similarly situated employees in the case. But in a zero-sum or conflicting-rights situation, awarding just one group its injunction creates exactly the type of remedial inequity that other joinder rules, such as Rule 19, labor against. Any injunction obtained by the minority employees would either effectively determine the rights of the majority employees, or be subject to collateral attack and dismantling in a later suit brought by the majority employees. The only solution — though one fraught with problems of conflicting interests and potential inadequacy of representation — is to create a class large enough to resolve all claims once and for all. The use of subclasses or separate classes may be necessary. An under-inclusive class should be dismissed for lack of the joinder of necessary class members.

In other situations, the dangers of under-inclusion are not present. When Rule 23(b)(2) was drafted in 1966, this was thought to be the situation in civil rights litigation; only subsequent developments made (b)(2) classes such as those in *Allison* under-inclusive. Of course, even here the conflicts within the class may be a significant management concern. But at least the focus of the court can be on these issues rather than on questions of inclusiveness.

There is no necessary reason that Rule 23(b)(1)(A) would need to be the rule for "dissonance claims" and Rule 23(b)(2) would need to be the rule for "consonance claims." But the language of each — with Rule 23(b)(1)(A) focusing on the risk of "inconsistent adjudications" and Rule 23(b)(2) focusing on "generally applicable" behavior — lends itself to such a division.

On this theory, *Allison's* holding that the case could not be certified as a (b)(2) class was right for the wrong reasons. *Allison* was not a (b)(2) case, but rather a (b)(1)(A) case in which the class representatives attempted to define an under-inclusive class comprised only of minority employees, rather than an inclusive class of all employees with rights in a fair and appropriate remedy. The critical failure was not the inclusion of individual claims for damages, as *Allison* held; rather, it was the exclusion from the class of persons with significant legal rights. Since the only leverage available to encourage the joinder necessary to prevent remedial inequity was to deny the (b)(2) certification request, *Allison* was correctly decided.

This account of Rules 23(b)(1)(A) and (b)(2) still leaves important questions unanswered. The first is how to assemble a (b)(1)(A) class. For instance, in *Allison*, the class representatives, who were minority workers, were clearly unable to represent the interests of majority workers. Must the court then create two classes and involuntarily join one or more majority workers as class representatives of a majority workers' class? Who will serve as counsel for this class, and how will counsel be compensated?

A second question is whether the (b)(2) "consonance" class action is even necessary. If all class members have essentially comparable interests, a suit by a single individual should in theory result in a remedy identical to the remedy that the class would achieve. The problem with that thinking, or course, is that the judgment in a single individual's case would not bind other similarly situated claimants, and the remedy that was achieved in that case would simply become the baseline upon which other claimants would attempt to improve. Concerns for efficiency and equitable treatment of the defendant make the (b)(2) class desirable.

A third set of questions concerns class members' individual claims for incidental damages. Damages are often an individualized matter; when they are substantial, they threaten to break down or minimize the consonance of a (b)(2) class or of a separate (b)(1)(A) class or subclass of similarly situated people.[178] The test should be whether the damages aspects of the case significantly affect the

---

178. In a (b)(1)(A) "dissonance" class, it is likely that only a limited number of the separate classes or subclasses will have monetary claims.

consonance of the relevant class or subclass by making individual class members focus more on their distinct damages claims than on their unifying injunctive claims. This is not a precise, bright-line rule. When the test suggests significant dissonance, the only option is to seek certification of the damage claims under (b)(3).

This account of the (b)(1) and (b)(2) classes emphasizes the prevention of remedial inequity and thereby provides a justification for mandatory class treatment. It also leaves scant room for the more general use of mandatory classes in cases involving primarily monetary claims. As we have just suggested, a bit of wiggle room exists to handle incidental monetary claims. Arguably, more wiggle room exists in the instance of a limited fund. When the fund is truly limited (for instance, a trust account with numerous beneficiaries whose *in rem* claims exceed the account's assets), inequity to some beneficiaries can be avoided only by the joinder of all. Such *in rem* claims are, however, infrequent. When the claims are *in personam* and the defendant is a for-profit concern with insufficient assets, *Ortiz* cautions against the use of Rule 23(b)(1)(B) unless all available assets are placed into the kitty and a process that gives each claimant his or her fair due is created. These are the simple demands of remedial equity as well, but they make the use of mandatory classes for damage claims generally unavailable.

That leaves the (b)(3) class action. The (b)(3) class cannot be justified on the grounds of remedial equity, nor can be justified under a strong view of litigant autonomy (both because of its representational natures and because of its opt-out, as opposed to opt-in, approach to joinder). Efficiency and transactionalism are Rule 23(b)(3)'s mainsprings — even more so than its closest cousin, Rule 20(a). But to ground Rule 23(b)(3) only in these concerns would be misleading. As Rule 23(b)(3)(A) says, autonomy is relevant to the (b)(3) calculus, and the opt-out right of the (b)(3) class cannot be explained simply in efficiency or transactional terms. It is also tempting to explain Rule 23(b)(3) as a delicate and pragmatic balance among autonomy, efficiency, and transactional concerns, but the same can be said of each of our joinder rules. The question is whether there is some fundamental norm that leads ineluctably to the particular balance that Rule 23(b)(3) has struck.

Serious reflection might lead us to think that there is not. On this view, Rule 23(b)(3) is simply a pragmatic compromise, standing a bit outside of the normal boundaries for joinder. Without firm footing, it is an unstable rule, wobbling among judicial opinions with different predilections about aggregation. Lending some credence to this view is the fact that the pitched political and legal battles over class actions usually concern classes brought under Rule 23(b)(3).

An alternate view is that Rule 23(b)(3) can be justified on a rationale quite different than those of other joinder rules. What Rule 23(b)(3) promises to deliver, in a way that other joinder rules simply cannot, is deterrence. In small-stakes cases, individual lawsuits are unlikely. In the absence of an effective joinder mechanism, certain forms of small-stakes wrongdoing would simply go unpunished. The class action is therefore necessary to gain an appropriate level of deterrence. In large-scale cases, parties have the economic incentive to pursue the litigation on their own, and the need for (b)(3) deterrence diminishes. Deterrence, of course, is not the only relevant variable; the class action would, for instance, still need to present an efficient package for resolving the dispute. But deterrence can explain the additional step that (b)(3) takes beyond the usual boundaries of joinder. It can also explain why, in general, Rule 23(b)(3) is more leery about joinder in large-stakes securities, antitrust, and consumer cases.

If deterrence justifies Rule 23(b)(3), then other problems arise. Unlike adversarial autonomy, procedural efficiency, transactionalism, and the like, deterrence is more a *substantive* than a *procedural* value. The line between procedural and substantive values is not absolute; autonomy and efficiency can justify substantive rules as easily as they can justify procedural rules. But deterrence has only a substantive component. Thus, the deterrence rationale makes the (b)(3) class action behave more like a substantive rule and less like a procedural rule. As a result, the (b)(3) class action inevitably raises concerns about its legitimacy under the Rules Enabling Act,[179] and can be expected to be legally and politically controversial in a way that the (b)(1) and (b)(2) class actions usually are not.

(C) Other Structural Limitations on Class Actions. Up to now we have focused on the language of Rule 23 and the limitations that it places on the use of class actions. As with all joinder rules, however, a panoply of other doctrines also limit the rule's use. We examine four of the most significant: subject matter jurisdiction, territorial jurisdiction, Anti-Injunction Act, and jury trial issues.

Subject matter jurisdiction is a classic "good news/bad news" scenario for class actions. When the well-pleaded class complaint

---

179. The Rules Enabling Act. 28 U.S.C. § 2072, requires that no Federal Rule of Civil Procedure "abridge, enlarge or modify any substantive right." In Burlington Northern R. Co. v. Woods, 480 U.S. 1, 9 (1987), the Court held that "[r]ules which *incidentally* affect litigants' substantive rights do not violate [§ 2072] if reason- ably necessary to maintain the integrity of that system of rules." (Emphasis added.) Even with this limitation, the Supreme Court has noted the Rules Enabling Act problem of (b)(3) class actions, and of expansive, non-traditional readings of Rule 23 in general. *See Amchem*, 521 U.S. at 613; *Ortiz*, 527 U.S. at 845.

raises a federal question applicable to all members, federal jurisdiction exists under § 1331; and under ordinary removal principles, the class action can be removed to federal court if it is filed in state court. If the case is brought under state law, the matter is somewhat more complicated. All diversity cases must satisfy both the complete diversity and matter-in-controversy requirements. Recall that, for individual joinder, complete diversity meant that no plaintiff could have the same citizenship as any defendant.[180] For class actions, the complete diversity requirement has received a modification that is friendly to federal jurisdiction: No class *representative* can have the same citizenship as any defendant, but the citizenship of the class *members* is ignored.[181] Therefore, if the defendant is a citizen of Maine, federal jurisdiction can be obtained simply by choosing class representatives who are not citizens of Maine. Conversely, of course, if a plaintiff class wishes to defeat federal jurisdiction, he or she need only make sure that at least one class representative comes from Maine.[182]

Now for the bad news: the matter-in-controversy rule. In *Snyder v. Harris*,[183] the Supreme Court held that class members, none of whom individually met the statutory matter-in-controversy, could not aggregate their claims to satisfy the matter-in-controversy. Thus, a class of 100,000 members, each of whom has a $10 state-law claim, could not invoke federal jurisdiction. The Court expanded the *Snyder* rule in *Zahn v. International Paper Co.*,[184] in which each class representative had a claim meeting the matter-in-controversy, but some of the class members did not. The Court held that each *member* of a class must satisfy the matter-in-controversy requirement — a holding that seems hard to reconcile with the Court's prior holding that each class member did not need to satisfy the complete diversity requirement.

Although courts try to indulge in as liberal a calculation of the class members' matter-in-controversy amount as possible in order to avoid *Zahn's* bite,[185] *Zahn* does prevent some class actions from reaching aggregation-friendlier federal courts. As a result, some

---

180. *See supra* ch.3, nn.10-13 and accompanying text.

181. Supreme Tribe of Ben-Hur v. Cauble, 255 U.S. 356 (1921).

182. There is a small but important exception to this rule. The Securities Litigation Uniform Standards Act of 1998 provides that certain state-law class actions arising out of the purchase or sale of securities can be removed to federal court without regard to the lack of diversity. Pub. L. No. 105-353, 112 Stat. 3227.

183. 394 U.S. 332 (1969).

184. 414 U.S. 291 (1973).

185. *See In re* Joint E. and S. Dists. Asbestos Litig., 982 F.2d 721 (2d Cir. 1992), *modified on other grounds*, 993 F.3d 7 (2d Cir. 1993); Carlough v. Amchem Prod., Inc., 834 F. Supp. 1437 (E.D. Pa. 1993).

commentators have called for the overruling of *Zahn* — a result that Congress may have inadvertently accomplished when it enacted the supplemental jurisdiction statute, 28 U.S.C. § 1367, in 1990.

According to the terms of § 1367(a), federal jurisdiction exists state-law claims not otherwise within federal jurisdiction as long as the state-law claims form part of the same constitutional case as claims within federal jurisdiction. Section 1367(a), however, is subject to the terms of § 1367(b), which tried to preserve in cases based entirely on state law the complete diversity and matter-in-controversy glosses that the Supreme Court had attached to § 1332. This fact suggests that state-law class actions are still subject to the holding in *Zahn*. But § 1367(b) contains a significant ambiguity akin to the ambiguity we encountered with Rule 20.[186] The language of § 1367(b) states that the § 1332 glosses apply only to claims brought by plaintiffs against parties joined under Rules 14, 19, 20, or 24, to those joined as plaintiffs under Rule 19, and to those intervening under Rule 24. Conspicuously absent from the list of joinder rules to which the glosses of § 1332 apply is Rule 23. Therefore, as long as one class representative satisfies the diversity and matter-in-controversy requirements of § 1332, jurisdiction over class members' state-law claims appears to be determined not under § 1367(b), but under § 1367(a). If this is true, the matter-in-controversy gloss of *Zahn* is no longer operative against class members' claims; the only jurisdictional requirements imposed on state-law class actions are the modest Article III requirement of minimal diversity and, arguably, a common nucleus of operative facts among class members' claims. Federal jurisdiction over state-law class actions has apparently become a much less onerous barrier to federal aggregation.

Unfortunately, the matter is not quite so simple. In the legislative history accompanying the supplemental jurisdiction statute, the House Report is quite explicit in stating that § 1367 "is not intended to affect the jurisdictional requirements of 28 U.S.C. § 1332 in diversity-only class actions"; the Report specifically cites *Zahn* as a case whose outcome was not intended to be changed by § 1367.[187] The issue posed, therefore, is whether to credit unambiguous statutory language or equally unambiguous, but precisely contrary, legislative history.

Not surprisingly, the courts of appeal have split on the question. Several courts have found that the plain text of § 1367 overrules *Zahn*;[188] other courts have accepted the legislative history and

---

186. *See supra* n.11 and accompanying text.

187. H. R. Rep. No. 101-734, at 29 & n.13, *reprinted in* 1990 U.S.C.C.A.N. 6860, 6875.

188. *See, e.g., In re* Abbott Labs., 51 F.3d 524 (5th Cir. 1995); Gibson v. Chrysler Corp., 261 F.3d. 927 (9th Cir.

statutory context to find that *Zahn's* restrictive rule survives.[189] The Supreme Court granted certiorari to resolve the question in *Free v. Abbott Laboratories*, but affirmed the judgment by an equally divided 4-4 vote, with Justice O'Connor not participating.[190] The issue therefore remains a live, important, and close one.

An issue of even greater import concerns territorial jurisdiction in class actions. This question is different than the territorial jurisdiction question that we encountered in Chapter 3.[191] At that point we were focusing on territorial jurisdiction over *defendants*. The territorial jurisdiction rules for class action defendants are no different than those in most other forms of aggregated litigation; for, unlike statutory interpleader, federal class actions cannot employ nationwide service of process unless the underlying theory of liability permits it. The unique territorial jurisdiction question created by class actions is the scope of the court's territorial jurisdiction over *plaintiffs* — i.e., over absent class members that may have no minimum contacts with the forum in which the class action has been filed. A judgment entered against an inadvertently joined defendant over whom the court has no jurisdiction is invalid; it therefore is not illogical to believe that a judgment entered against an involuntarily joined class member over whom the court had no jurisdiction should be invalid. On the other hand, a stringent requirement of territorial jurisdiction over plaintiffs would seriously restrict the binding effect — and the aggregative potential — of the class action device.

The question of jurisdiction over plaintiffs is unique to class actions. With permissive joinder rules such as Rule 20 or Rule 24, the voluntary action of the additional plaintiffs in entering the case waives any arguable lack of forum contact. With class actions, however, only a blithe lover of legal fictions could conclude that absent class members have consented to the forum's jurisdiction over them. They are brought into a forum on a basis as involuntary as any defendant, and will find their rights determined by that forum. It does not seem unreasonable to expect some connection between the class member and the forum.

In some cases, the connection will be so apparent as to pass without objection. If a class of California consumers, raising claims under California state law, is certified by a California state court, the connection between the class members and the forum is patent. But

2001), *cert. denied*, 122 S. Ct. 903 (2002); Rosmer v. Pfizer, 263 F.3d 110 (4th Cir. 2001), *cert. pending*, No. 01-1390 (filed Mar. 14, 2002).

189. *See, e.g.*, Meritcare Inc. v. St. Paul Mercury Ins. Co., 166 F.3d 214 (3d Cir. 1999); Leonhardt v. Western Sugar Co., 160 F.3d 631 (10th Cir. 1998).

190. 529 U.S. 333 (2000).

191. *See supra* pp. 18-20, 25-27.

many modern class actions — including those with the greatest aggregative potential — are regional or nationwide in scope. For instance, if Smith wishes to bring a class action against XYZ, more aggregation is achieved by a nationwide class action than by a class only of Maine asbestos victims. If the territorial jurisdiction rules require separate class actions for XYZ's victims in New Hampshire, North Carolina, and each other state, then the effectiveness of one of our best aggregative devices will have been diminished. Indeed, this jurisdictional question provides yet another context in which two incommensurable forces — the need for optimal aggregation and the demand of fairness to the individual — are pitted against each other.

The Supreme Court finally entered the debate in *Phillips Petroleum Co. v. Shutts.*[192] *Shutts* involved a Kansas state-court class that was certified under an opt-out rule equivalent to Rule 23(b)(3). Allegedly the defendant had failed to make appropriate royalty payments to 33,000 owners of natural gas leases. Approximately 5,000 class members either opted out of the class or were otherwise excluded from it. The class was nationwide in scope, and only about 1,000 of the class members were residents of Kansas. The remaining 27,000 class members were residents of Oklahoma, Texas, and Louisiana. Most class members had no minimum contacts with Kansas. The defendant therefore contended that the Kansas state court could not constitutionally exercise jurisdiction over the non-resident class members unless, like Rule 20 plaintiffs, they affirmatively consented to the court's jurisdiction by opting into the case.

Although it did find that due process concerns were implicated by class actions, the Supreme Court rejected the defendant's argument that distant class members must opt in. Instead, the Court held that territorial jurisdiction concerns could be satisfied if class members received an opt-out right (accompanied, of course, by constitutionally adequate notice advising them of this right). The Court thought that the contexts of territorial jurisdiction over defendants and territorial jurisdiction over plaintiffs were sufficiently distinct to justify an opt-out rule for class members. Unlike a defendant, who faces the power of a state's judicial system alone, class members were constitutionally entitled to adequate representation at all times. The class members had no obligation to defend or prosecute the case with their own resources, or to incur any expenses in a distant forum. The district court was obliged to watch over the class members' interests, and not to approve unreasonable settlements. Therefore, the Court stated that provision of an opt-out right for class members who wished to have their claims adjudicated in another forum was constitutionally sufficient process. Since the

192.   472 U.S. 797 (1986).

Kansas court accorded class members adequate notice and a right to opt out, the Supreme Court held, it properly exercised jurisdiction over all absent class members that remained.

At the present time, *Shutts* is the 800-pound gorilla of class action practice. The reason is not so much what *Shutts* holds on the facts of the case, but what it portends for class action aggregation more generally. Holding that an opt-out right is constitutionally required in a class action that already has an opt-out right is no great matter. As we have seen, however, not all class actions have opt-out rights; (b)(1)(A), (b)(1)(B), and (b)(2) class actions are mandatory. If *Shutts* means that *all* class actions must afford an opt-out right to absent class members that have no minimum contacts with the forum, then there can be no truly mandatory nationwide class actions. Aside from the expense that the requisite notice would entail, an opt-out right would almost certainly mean that some class members will opt out and commence litigation in other forums. In order to avoid this problem, plaintiffs would need to commence a series of similar class actions in every state, and attempt some coordinated MDL pretrial handling of the class actions brought in federal court. The single-forum aggregation potential of the class action would be destroyed.

Shutts recognized the concern, but avoided its answer. In footnote 3, the Court stated that its "holding today is limited to those class actions which seek to bind known plaintiffs concerning claims wholly or predominantly for money judgments. We intimate no view concerning other types of class actions, such as those seeking equitable relief."[193] Lower courts have made a number of different stabs at dealing with the *Shutts* problem. The usual reading of footnote 3 has been that *Shutts* requires no opt-out right in mandatory class actions seeking injunctive relief. When monetary relief is also requested, a number of responses to *Shutts* have been assayed. One approach has been to find that the objecting parties waived the jurisdictional issue by contesting the class action on the merits.[194] Echoing the Rule 23(b) debate, another approach has been to hold that *Shutts* is inapplicable when injunctive relief predominates over monetary relief.[195] Yet another escape hatch has been to contend that the *Shutts* opt-out right does not apply as long as the class action has adequate alternative procedural protections for class members.[196] Another argument has been that the *Shutts* rule applies

---

193. *Id.* at 811 n.3.

194. White v. Nat'l Football League, 41 F.3d 402 (8th Cir. 1994), *cert. denied*, 515 U.S. 1137 (1995).

195. White v. Nat'l Football

League, 822 F. Supp. 1389 (D. Minn. 1993), *aff'd*, 41 F.3d 402 (8th Cir. 1994), *cert. denied*, 515 U.S. 1137 (1995).

196. *Id.*

only in state courts; in federal court, the relevant *Shutts* question is whether the class members have minimum contacts with the nation as a whole.[197] Finally, one court has argued that, because the (b)(1) classes have their ancestry in equity, any mandatory (b)(1) class — even a limited fund class disbursing money — is an equitable class action within the contemplation of footnote 3 and therefore not subject to the opt-out requirement.[198] One set of commentators has proposed a four-factor test — efficiency, equity, prevention of the abusive use of a distant forum, and members' interest in individual control of their litigation — to determine if *Shutts* applies.[199]

The Supreme Court has on several occasions granted certiorari in cases that might have clarified the question. In the first two,[200] the Court found itself unable to reach the question because it had not been properly presented for Supreme Court review. The third case was *Ortiz*, a mandatory class action that the Court reversed on (b)(1)(B) grounds. The Court nonetheless devoted significant attention to the *Shutts* issue, noting in dicta that it was one of the concerns that an expansive reading of Rule 23(b)(1)(B) would raise. Beyond that, the Court's discussion of *Shutts* was cryptic, but readers of tea leaves might conclude that the Court was signaling its willingness to have required an opt-out right in *Ortiz* had it been necessary to do so.[201]

After *Ortiz* restricted the use of (b)(1)(B) class actions to deal with monetary claims, the *Shutts* question has had somewhat less urgency. Nonetheless, it remains a live question, and Supreme Court resolution of the "efficient aggregation versus individual control" tension inherent in *Shutts* can ultimately be expected.

A third potential jurisdictional limitation on federal class actions is the Anti-Injunction Act, 28 U.S.C. § 2283. This statute, which we previously encountered in Chapter 4,[202] prevents federal courts from enjoining ongoing state proceedings. It contains only three exceptions: when Congress authorizes an injunction, when an injunction is necessary in aid of the federal court's jurisdiction, and when an

---

197. Ahearn v. Fibreboard Co., 1995 U.S. Dist. LEXIS 11523 (E.D. Tex.).

198. *In re* Asbestos Litig., 90 F.3d 963 (5th Cir. 1996), *vacated and remanded*, 521 U.S. 1114 (1997), *aff'd on remand*, 134 F.3d 668 (5th Cir. 1998), *rev'd on other grounds sub nom.* Ortiz v. Fibreboard Corp., 527 U.S. 815 (1999).

199. Arthur R. Miller & David Crump, *Jurisdiction and Choice of Law in Multistate Class Actions after Phillips Petroleum Co. v. Shutts*, 96 YALE L.J. 1 (1986).

200. Ticor Title Ins. Co. v. Brown, 511 U.S. 117 (1994); Adams v. Robertson, 520 U.S. 83 (1997).

201. *Ortiz*, 527 U.S. at 847-48.

202. *See supra* ch.4, nn.71-77 and accompanying text.

injunction is needed to protect or effectuate a federal court's judgment. Unlike statutory interpleader, class actions contain no statutory authorization to issue an anti-suit injunction against related proceedings.

The applicability of this statute in the class action context might not be immediately apparent. The argument for § 2283's applicability runs as follows: In many class actions filed in federal court, members of the class will also have filed individual suits or else competing and overlapping class actions in state court. When a federal court certifies a mandatory class action, all of these state-court plaintiffs become involuntary members of the federal case. At that point, their maintenance of a separate state case is inconsistent with their membership in the federal class. In effect, the mandatory federal class action forces them to abandon their state claims, and the class certification therefore acts as a *de facto* injunction against the state proceeding. The certification fits none of the exceptions to the Anti-Injunction Act: Rule 23 is not an express authorization of Congress, the federal "injunction" is not necessary in aid of jurisdiction over the federal class action, and the "injunction" is not necessary to protect or effectuate a federal court's judgment.

This logic has been accepted in a few cases. The most notable is *In re Federal Skywalk Cases*,[203] a mass tort that represented one of the earliest (albeit failed) efforts to harness the mass tort to the (b)(1)(B) class action. If *Federal Skywalk*'s argument is correct, then the Anti-Injunction Act limitation applies to all mandatory class actions in which related state actions have already been filed. Along with *Shutts*, this Anti-Injunction Act argument portends a one-two punch that severely limits the utility of mandatory classes.

Unlike *Shutts*, however, the *Federal Skywalk* reasoning has never been sanctioned by the Supreme Court. There is good reason to believe that its holding is based on a faulty assumption, and therefore is simply wrong. The arguably faulty assumption is that certification of a mandatory class actions requires class members to abandon their state claims. To the contrary, our dual court system regularly tolerates plaintiffs that file and simultaneously litigate identical cases in state and federal court.[204] Barring exceptional circumstances, the federal court cannot enjoin the related state proceeding. It is not obvious that the rule should be different when the plaintiff is a class member in the federal case and a named plaintiff in the state case. Nothing in Rule 23 expressly requires this

---

203. 680 F.2d 1175 (8th Cir.), *cert. denied*, 459 U.S. 988 (1982).

204. *See* Kline v. Burke Constr.

Co., 260 U.S. 226 (1922); Rhonda Wasserman, *Dueling Class Actions*, 80 B.U. L. REV. 461 (2000).

inversion of the normal (albeit inefficient) rules of state-federal practice. Without such an inversion, the result in *Federal Skywalk* cannot be sustained. On the other hand, *Federal Skywalk* has a point; it is difficult for the federal class action to proceed in a workable manner if the state cases are not enjoined.

A fourth limitation on class actions is the Seventh Amendment, the federal jury trial right.[205] The Seventh Amendment has two critical guarantees. The first clause of the Seventh Amendment guarantees a right to jury trial in "Suits at law" with a dollar value exceeding twenty dollars. This right has long been understood not to apply to claims sounding in equity, and has more recently been understood to require that, when facts are relevant to both jury-tried and a judge-tried aspects of a single case, the jury must decide the disputed factual issues first.[206] The second half of the Seventh Amendment forbids the re-examination by another jury or court of any fact found by the jury.

We will have occasion to explore the more detailed workings of the Seventh Amendment in Chapter Seven,[207] but these basic principles are sufficient for present purposes. At first blush, neither of the Seventh Amendment's guarantees seems to be implicated by class certification. Recent decisions have, however, suggested that the connection is stronger than it appears.

The first concerns relate to mixed injunction-damages class actions. In *Allison v. Citgo Petroleum Corp.*,[208] employees alleging racial discrimination sought both injunctive and monetary relief under (b)(2). After the court of appeals held that the monetary claims could not be certified under (b)(2) or (b)(3), it then found that the Seventh Amendment barred the injunctive claims as well. Its reasoning was that certain factual issues, such as the existence of discriminatory employment policies, were relevant to both the (b)(2) injunctive claims and the non-class monetary claims. The Seventh Amendment required the jury to determine the overlapping factual issues, so that the (b)(2) injunctive claims could not be severed and tried first. Since these issues could not be tried first, the court of appeals held that the (b)(2) class should not be certified.

Allison seems to overread very strongly the jury trial right. Granting that common factual issues would need to be tried to a jury,

---

205. For the text of the Seventh Amendment, see *infra* ch. 6, n.1.

206. Beacon Theatres, Inc. v. Westover, 359 U.S. 500 (1948). *Beacon Theatres* did not base this holding explicitly on the Seventh Amendment, though the Amendment's influence permeated the decision.

207. *See infra* ch. 7, nn.7-22, 39 and accompanying text.

208. 151 F.3d 402 (5th Cir. 1998). For an analysis of other aspects of *Allison*, see *supra* pp. 135-36, 148-49.

there was no reason that the (b)(2) claims needed to be severed and tried first. *Allison* jeopardizes the use of (b)(1)(A) or (b)(2) classes whenever some class members might also have related damage claims. A better approach would be to treat the non-class damages claims as sufficiently distinct from the class injunctive claims that the judgment on the injunctive claims would not bar later actions of individual class members on their damages claims,[209] thus eliminating the need for the class's case to hear any damages claims. This solution should also avoid any constitutional difficulties. The Seventh Amendment requires only that the jury decide overlapping factual issues brought in the same case; it does not require, as *Allison* implies, that the jury hear overlapping issues when the injunctive and monetary claims are brought in separate cases. Indeed, using a strained reading of the Seventh Amendment to supercede clear language in Rule 23(b)(2) that permits the use of injunctive class actions is highly debatable.

A second set concerns involves the latter clause of the Seventh Amendment — the prohibition against re-examination of a jury's findings of fact. The argument runs as follows: In some class actions containing many individual issues, the only sensible way to litigate the case is to try common issues first, and individual issues in subsequent trials. In some cases, however, the common issues are so intertwined with the individual issues that it is impossible for the second jury not to determine again the facts found by the first jury. For instance, in a (b)(3) mass tort class action, a common issue is often the defendant's negligence. Some or all of the plaintiffs may have contributed to the injury as well, thus allowing the defendant to raise a comparative negligence defense. Comparative negligence, however, is usually an individual issue that would not be tried for all of the plaintiffs in one proceeding. Therefore, it would make sense to try the issue of negligence first, and to reserve the issue of comparative negligence to later proceedings. This solution, however, requires the second jury in the individual trial to examine again the question of defendant's negligence, in order to compare it against the plaintiff's negligence. Several courts have held that such a re-examination would violate the Seventh Amendment.[210]

For reasons that we discuss in Chapter Seven,[211] it is not apparent that this argument is correct, or that the second jury would need to re-examine the exact facts found by the first jury. Nonetheless, this concern looms over any class action with significant

---

209. *See* Cooper v. Federal Reserve Bank of Richmond, 467 U.S. 867 (1984); *infra* n.231 and accompanying text.

210. *See, e.g., Castano,* 84 F.3d 486; *Rhone-Poulenc,* 51 F.3d 1293.

211. *See infra* ch. 7, n.39 and accompanying text.

individual issues. It is easy enough to make the objection disappear by using another plan for trying the case, but in many of the cases with significant individual issues, other plans are often difficult to come by. The lack of a desirable alternate plan, in turn, makes the class action less manageable and makes it harder to argue that the class action is a superior method for resolving the dispute. If the case involves a (b)(3) certification, the Seventh Amendment concern can therefore unravel the class action and lead a court to decide not to certify the class.

A final jury trial concern was raised in *Ortiz*. *Oritz* involved a settlement by asbestos victims who had not yet filed suit. As we have seen, the Supreme Court decided the case on (b)(1)(B) grounds. The Court hewed close to the traditional (b)(1)(B) line and refused to interpret the rule expansively for a number of reasons, including, as we have seen, concerns about *Shutts* and the Rules Enabling Act.[212] Another reason that the Court mentioned was the Seventh Amendment. It thought that a mandatory class action that settled monetary claims of class members "obviously implicates the Seventh Amendment jury trial rights of absent class members" and "compromises their Seventh Amendment rights without their consent."[213]

Whether this statement is better regarded as dicta or as essential to the Court's (b)(1)(B) holding is uncertain. Its scope is limited: It applies only to mandatory class actions seeking monetary relief, and only when these class actions settle rather than are tried. *Ortiz* was brought for the purpose of settling the members' claims, so it is not clear whether the Court's concern would extend to mandatory monetary class actions in which the class members' were litigated before the settlement occurred. It is also unclear whether the Court's jury trial concern would extend even to those mandatory monetary class actions that fulfilled *Ortiz's* three criteria — in other words, to those cases in which the class action was necessary to prevent remedial inequity.

Whatever the answers to these questions, it should be obvious that class actions face significant constitutional and statutory hurdles. Some of the hurdles are placed in the path of mandatory class actions, and some are place in the path of class actions seeking monetary relief. Class actions that both seek monetary relief and attempt mandatory joinder are in an especially troubled position.

(ii) Strategic Behavior. The structural limitations on class actions are daunting indeed, and present significant challenges to the plaintiff that wishes to use Rule 23 to achieve optimal aggregation.

---

212. *See supra* nn.179, 201 and accompanying text.

213. 527 U.S. at 846.

As we have seen throughout this book, however, not all parties are interested in achieving optimal aggregation. Some wish to use the rules for strategic purposes, and no rule is more subject to the charge of strategic use and misuse than the class action.

The reason is simple. Class actions have all of the usual aggregation-evading jurisdictional stratagems. For instance, a plaintiff who wishes to avoid federal jurisdiction on a state-law claim need only name non-diverse class representatives or (assuming that *Zahn* has not been overruled) define the class to include some claimants with matter-in-controversy amounts of $75,000 or less.[214] A federal-question class action can be filed in state court, and it will remain there unless the defendant(s) take steps to remove it. Plaintiffs can file overlapping class actions in state and federal courts, or in different federal courts, and race each other to judgment;[215] there are no particular class action devices that prevent this tactic,[215] and courts must rely on inadequate anti-suit injunctive powers and MDL procedures to wrestle with the problem.

Class actions also present unique strategic opportunities to frustrate aggregation. In a (b)(3) class, for instance, the opt-out right can lead to a significant amount of satellite litigation. Similarly, the definition of a class can be expanded or contracted in ways that can lead to excessive or insufficient aggregation.

Most significantly, parties often request or oppose class certification based not on the optimality of aggregation but rather on the potential to advance private litigation agendas. As we have already noted, aggregation has a strong potential to change litigation dynamics: The claims of class members may be worth less than in successful individual litigation, but the chances for success rise as more cases are aggregated.[216] Relatedly, in many class actions, the number of aggregated claims is so great that a successful class action, even with reduced individual recoveries, can threaten the viability of the defendant. The possibility of bankruptcy can make defendants very skittish about taking class actions to trial, even when the plaintiffs' claims appear to have little merit. Therefore, a standard complaint about class actions is that they amount to legalized extortion or blackmail in the hands of unscrupulous attorneys, and their unjustified social costs outweigh their benefit.[217] A standard

---

214. These strategies would not work with some state-law securities cases. *See supra* n.182.

215. We exclude the arguable anti-suit injunction that accompanies a mandatory class certification. *See supra* nn.202-04 and accompanying

text.

216. *See supra* ch.2, n.4 & ch.3, n.65 and accompanying text.

217. *See, e.g.*, Milton Handler, *The Shift from Substantive to Procedural Innovations in Antitrust Suits — The Twenty-Third Annual Antitrust Re-*

response is that the collective power of the class action simply eliminates the imbalance between individual victims and powerful wrongdoers.

Measuring the strength of this argument and its counterargument is difficult to do in an objective fashion. Anecdotes and theoretical models of behavior can be marshaled on each side, but determining the actual merits of a class's claims — the fact upon which both arguments ultimately hinge — may well be an impossible matter. It seems likely that the outcome-affecting potential of class actions induces some class actions to be filed for reasons that are not socially optimal, but whether that strategic behavior is counterbalanced by other cases in which optimal deterrence would be unattainable without the class action is unclear.

Class actions can also induce strategic behavior by the person opposing the class. The most obvious behavior is collusion, in which the defendant rewards the class representatives or their counsel handsomely in return for their acceptance of a class settlement that is far below the value of the claims. Likewise, as we have also discussed, the defendant can sometimes induce a reverse auction among overlapping class actions, again with the goal of achieving a below-value settlement.[218] An early class certification in immature litigation can also favor the defendant.[219] Finally, one of the great benefits of a class action to a defendant is that the class action can bring global (with mandatory class actions) or near-global (with opt-out class actions) peace. As *Amchem* and *Ortiz* show, it is extremely important in such cases to ensure that the interests of some class members are not neglected in the rush to achieve this peace. The protections of Rule 23(a) and (b) are designed to prevent this result, but constant vigilance is required to ensure class members' protection. When the class representatives, the class counsel, and the defendant have all agreed on a deal to procure global or near-global peace, the necessary vigilance can be a commodity in short supply.

4. Summary

Rule 23 is our most promising, despised, intricate, and ultimately inadequate joinder rule. In examining its branches and twigs, we

---

view, 71 COLUM. L. REV. 1, 9 (1971) ("Any device which is workable only because it utilizes the threat of unmanageable and expensive litigation to compel settlement is not a rule of procedure — it is a form of legalized blackmail."). The classic modern statement of the "bet-the-company" black-

mail concern is found in *Rhone-Poulenc*, 51 F.3d at 1299-1300.

218. *See supra* p. 121.

219. On the issue of maturity, see *supra* ch. 2, n.3 & ch.3, n.64 and accompanying text.

risk losing sight of the forest in which the class action is but one tree. The point of this chapter has been to determine whether and how the cases of nonparties can be aggregated with those cases already filed. The method of aggregation that this section has explored is joinder: The nonparties are joined to the case as additional parties, and thus are bound to the judgment.

In this section, we have seen four models of joinder of nonparty claimants: (1) joinder with the consent of the party and the nonparty ("opt-in" joinder, as in Rule 20(a)); (2) joinder with the consent of the nonparty (intervention, as in Rule 24); (3) joinder without the consent of the nonparty (mandatory joinder, as in Rule 19, interpleader, and Rules 23(b)(1) and (b)(2)); and (4) joinder without consent of the nonparty, but with a nonparty right of exclusion ("opt-out" joinder, as in Rule 23(b)(3)). These various approaches reflect the different weights that our system places on autonomy, efficiency, transactionalism, trans-substantivity, and deterrence in different contests. Without a single approach to the weight of these variables, and therefore to joinder itself, it is perhaps inevitable that the joinder rules leave gaps in any efforts to achieve optimal aggregation.

The joinder rules themselves are not the only limitations on optimal aggregation. Rules of subject matter and territorial jurisdiction create additional barriers, as do other federalism concerns and even constitutional guarantees such as the right to jury trial.

As with other forms of aggregation — intra-district, intra-system, and intersystem — nonparty aggregation by means of joinder presents opportunities for aggregation in the right circumstances, but does not guarantee optimal aggregation in all circumstances. Joinder seems to work best to aggregate claims that, if left unjoined, would create remedial inequity. If the prevention of remedial inequity is optimal aggregation, then the joinder rules do a decent but not perfect job of achieving optimal aggregation; even here, however, jurisdictional and other structural limitations may frustrate optimal aggregation. On other understandings of optimal aggregation — for instance, the prevention of all inefficient multiparty, multiforum litigation — the present joinder rules generally perform even less well.

As it has throughout this book, concerns for litigant autonomy that undergird our adversarial system remain the primary theoretical roadblock to wider aggregation. It should be apparent by now that it may be impossible to make choices about how much aggregation is appropriate without first having some sense of how much litigant autonomy is appropriate.

B. PRECLUSION

The focus of the last section in this chapter was the joinder of those persons that sit on the sidelines rather than commence a lawsuit. The effect of joinder is to make the sideline-sitters into parties, and then to bind them to the judgment as parties. An alternative to joinder is to bind nonparties to a judgment without joining them. In this section, we explore this alternative of precluding nonparties in order to see if it either fares better than joinder as a method for dealing with nonparty disaggregation, or is at least a device capable of plugging some of the holes that we have uncovered in our present joinder law.

You were probably exposed to the law of preclusion in a basic class in Civil Procedure. The two main forms of preclusion are claim preclusion ("res judicata") and issue preclusion ("collateral estoppel"); there are a few other forms as well, such as the preclusion of compulsory counterclaims. For the most part, preclusion has developed through the common law rather than through statutes or procedural rules. The various forms of preclusion use a final judgment on the merits in one case and then bar, or preclude, parties in a second case from raising certain claims or issues.[220] With claim preclusion, a party may not bring certain claims that either were, or should have been, brought in the first case. With issue preclusion, a party may not contest certain factual issues that were actually decided and necessary to the outcome of the first case.

Stated at this level of abstraction, preclusion would appear to have some potential to achieve indirectly the goal of nonparty aggregation. If claim preclusion could be used in such a way that nonparties risked the loss of their claims when they failed to file a lawsuit related to an ongoing case, then claim preclusion would act as a powerful inducement to the filing of all related claims. (This would not, of course, secure the aggregation of such claims; tools we have studied in other chapters, such as multidistricting, would need to be used to accomplish aggregation of the filed claims.) To return to our hypothetical, if Smith were to file an asbestos suit against XYZ that would have the effect of precluding Jones's suit against ABC, Jones would have a strong incentive to file suit immediately,

---

220. Each jurisdiction (state and federal) can create its own rules of preclusion, although federal creation of preclusion law may be limited for state-law claims to which the *Erie* doctrine applies. A most useful review of the general law of preclusion, the *Erie* issues in the law of preclusion, and the circumstances in which a court must give preclusive effect to a judgment rendered in another jurisdiction is DAVID L. SHAPIRO, CIVIL PROCEDURE: PRECLUSION IN CIVIL ACTIONS (2001).

preferably joining Smith's suit in order to have some control over the outcome of the litigation and the judgment.

Less powerful would be the use of issue preclusion. If there existed the possibility that the jury in Smith's case against XYZ would find asbestos to not be a defective product, and if this finding could then be used by ABC against Jones in his case, Jones would have an incentive to participate in Smith's case. But issue preclusion can also create the opposite incentive. The jury in Smith's case might find asbestos to be defective; and if Jones could use that finding preclusively against ABC without having to participate in Smith's case, Jones would probably prefer to stay on the sidelines. ABC might have the incentive to intervene in Smith's case; but as we have seen, defendants such as ABC have very little power to force the joinder of nonparties such as Jones.)

For aggregation purposes, the issue is whether claim or issue preclusion can be used by or against nonparties in ways that create important incentives toward aggregation. Once again, however, the fundamental "day-in-court" principle upon which our party joinder system is built stands in the way. "It is," the Supreme Court said in *Hansberry*, "a principle of general application in Anglo-American jurisprudence that one is not bound by a judgment *in personam* in a litigation in which he is not designated as a party or to which he has not been made a party by service of process."[221] The Court has continued to hew to this principle. In *Martin v. Wilks*, the Court explained that "[t]his rule is part of our 'deep-rooted historic tradition that everyone should have his own day in court.' A judgment or decree among parties to a lawsuit resolves issues as among them, but it does not conclude the rights of strangers to those proceedings."[222]

To sort out these concerns, the following material is broken into two sections: first, a section on the use of claim preclusion and its limitations; second, a section on the use of issue preclusion and its limitations.

1. Claim Preclusion

The hornbook statement of claim preclusion is this: A valid final judgment on the merits bars, in a subsequent action between the same parties, any claim that was or should have been brought in the

---

221. 311 U.S. at 40.

222. 490 U.S. 755, 762 (1989) (quoting 18 CHARLES A. WRIGHT ET AL., FEDERAL PRACTICE AND PROCEDURE § 4449, p. 417 (1981)). *Accord,* Richards v. Jefferson County, Ala-

bama, 517 U.S. 793 (1996). *Richards* indicates that this is a principle of constitutional statute, and inheres in the due process clause. *See supra* n.39.

first case.[223] Most American jurisdictions give a broad transactional definition to the word "claim," so that any legal theories that are related in time, space, or motivation are regarded as part of the same transaction and hence part of the same claim.[224] At some point, of course, the elasticity in the concept of the transaction ends; it is not likely, for instance, that Smith's case of asbestos exposure against XYZ would be part of the same transaction as Jones's case against ABC (at least barring some joint venture or conspiracy theory that links ABC's actions to those of XYZ). But the modern concept of a "claim" might be capacious enough to include both Smith's and Green's cases against XYZ.

The real bite of the broader transactional definition of a claim comes from the fact that not only are the claims that were originally brought precluded in a second action, but the claims that "should have been brought" are also precluded. Modern claim preclusion therefore does more than merely prevent a litigant from obtaining a second bite of the apple on the exact same theory on which the case was previously filed. The phrase "should have been brought" has generally been understood to be "might have been filed." In a world of liberal, transactional claim joinder, this understanding means that any related claims that might have been filed at the same time but were not are also barred. Smith cannot sue XYZ on a negligence theory, lose, and then bring a second case on a strict products liability theory. The products liability claim should have been brought in the first case, and is therefore precluded.

However broadly "claim" is understood, neither Jones's nor Green's claim is likely to be precluded by a judgment against Smith. As a doctrinal matter, claim preclusion requires, in addition to an identity of claims, a "valid and final judgment on the merits" and the "same parties." The "judgment" requirement dramatically limits the effectiveness of claim preclusion. Most cases, including most high-stakes cases, settle; and in most of these cases, the case is dismissed and no final judgment on the merits is ever entered.[225] Even when a final judgment is entered, it may not be "on the merits." The judge may have dismissed the case for lack of subject matter or territorial jurisdiction; the case may have been dismissed on statute of limitations grounds; or in a class action settlement, the judge may have

---

223. *See, e.g.*, Federated Dept. Stores, Inc. v. Moitie, 452 U.S. 394 (1981).

224. RESTATEMENT (SECOND) OF JUDGMENTS § 24 (1982). Some jurisdictions still use other, usually more restrictive definitions of claim.

225. An exception to this statement is the consent decree, in which the court incorporates the parties' settlement into a final judgment. These consent decrees have long been used in institutional reform and environmental litigation.

decided only that the settlement was fair, adequate, and reasonable.[226] To the extent that claim preclusion hinges on a judgment on the merits, few cases supply the needed judgment.

The validity of a judgment can also limit the scope of claim preclusion. A prior judgment cannot be used to preclude the claims of a person over whom the prior court had no territorial jurisdiction, claims over which the court had no subject matter jurisdiction, or claims for which the party had no notice of the prior proceeding.[227] Some jurisdictions will not give claim-preclusive effect to a judgment if the rendering court did not have subject matter jurisdiction over the claims that are allegedly precluded. Likewise, *Shutts* would prevent a court from giving claim-preclusive effect to class action judgments that seek to bind absent class members over whom the original court had no territorial jurisdiction, at least in the absence of giving the class members an opt-out right.[228] More generally, the *Shutts* principle would make it impossible to bind nonparty plaintiffs over whom the court had no territorial jurisdiction to a judgment issued by that court.[229] Thus, even if other claim preclusion hurdles could be overcome, it might be impossible for a victorious XYZ to bind Green to the judgment in Smith's case if Smith files the case in a court that lacks minimum contacts with Green.

By far the most substantial limitation on the broader use of claim preclusion, however, is the "same parties" requirement. With a few exceptions, "same parties" means what it says: Claim preclusion can be used only in later litigation between the exact parties that were involved in the original litigation. Complex litigation, however, rarely involves repetitive litigation by the same parties; it involves repetitive litigation by one or more new parties. If claim preclusion

---

226. *Cf.* Semtek Int'l Inc. v. Lockheed Martin Corp., 531 U.S. 497 (2001) (discussing preclusive effect to be given in federal court when state court dismissed case on statute of limitations grounds). The term "on the merits" is somewhat misleading, and has been abandoned by the *Restatement (Second) of Judgments*. The reason is that certain judgments that do not determine the actual merits of a dispute — for instance, judgments dismissing a case for failure to state a claim or as a sanction for willful discovery violations — are nonetheless entitled to claim preclusive effect. The phrase "on the merits" remains in general usage in the case law.

227. There is a recent shift, not yet fully accomplished, toward removal of subject matter jurisdiction from the list of grounds that can be used to contest validity. *See, e.g.,* Gargallo v. Merrill, Lynch, Pierce, Fenner & Smith, 918 F.2d 658 (6th Cir. 1990).

228. For a fuller discussion of *Shutts*, including some important potential qualifications on the statement in the text, see *supra* nn.192-201 and accompanying text.

229. *See In re:* Gen. Motors Corp. Pick-Up Truck Fuel Tank Prod. Liab. Litig., 134 F.3d 133 (3d Cir. 1998).

can stop Smith from suing XYZ a second time, but cannot be used by the victorious XYZ to stop Green's suit, claim preclusion is a doctrine of very limited utility.

The critical question, therefore, is the scope of the exceptions to the "same party" requirement. In general, the exceptions break into several categories. The first category is the rare set of cases in which a nonparty has controlled the party's prosecution or defense of a claim; subsequent claims by or against the nonparty may also be precluded. Another unusual category involves a nonparty who contractually agrees to be bound to the outcome of the prior litigation. A third, somewhat more common exception to the "same party" requirement involves a nonparty that has a legal relationship with a party. For example, a property owner that litigates a claim regarding the property binds all future owners of that property to the judgment. (Indeed, had this not been true, the lawsuit in *Hansberry* would never have arisen.) These legal relationships, which include survivorship and vicarious liability claims in tort law, assignor and assignee claims in contract law, and certain claims involving partnerships, fail to capture most situations of concern to complex litigation;[230] for example, neither Smith and Green, nor XYZ and ABC, are likely to have a legal relationship of the kind that would render one the "same party" as the other for preclusion purposes.

The final category in which nonparties are treated as parties is the representative action. In some cases, a party acts as a fiduciary to represent the interests of others; in these cases, the beneficiary is bound to the outcome that the fiduciary obtained. The most common form of representative action, or course, is the class action. In the last section, we learned that the class action joins the absent class members to the case and thus binds them to the judgment. To some extent, this joinder rationale is a legal fiction; the absent class members do not actually join the case in any traditional sense. Another, less fictionalized lens through which to view the class action is as a preclusion device, in which nonparties are bound to an outcome achieved by the class representative as long as the representative performs his or her task adequately. In this view, the class representative is (still fictionally) deemed to be the "same party" as the class members for purposes of claim preclusion.

As we have seen, however, adequacy of the representation acts as the limit on this preclusive power. Inadequate representatives cannot bind class members to a judgment purportedly achieved for their benefit. Nor can claim preclusion bar class members from asserting related claims beyond the scope of the representation. For

---

230. For a complete list of these relationships, see RESTATEMENT, *su-*   *pra* n. 224, §§ 43-61.

instance, in *Cooper v. Federal Reserve Bank of Richmond*,[231] alleged victims of employment discrimination brought a class action on behalf of all similarly situated employees. The district court found a pattern and practice of discrimination in pay grades 4 and 5, but not in others. In addition, some class members who intervened also brought claims of individual, intentional discrimination; two prevailed and two did not.

Some class members then brought another suit alleging that they too had been intentionally discriminated against. All were employed above level 5, and were not entitled to the relief on the "pattern or practice" claim. The defendant argued that, under standard claim preclusion principles, the prior class action precluded the individual discrimination claims: Since it arose out of the same transaction as the "pattern or practice" theory, the intentional discrimination theory should have been brought in the class action, as some other class members had done. The defendant's argument has some force. Had an individual litigant received a judgment in a "pattern or practice" case, standard claim preclusion analysis would have block his or her subsequent efforts to file an intentional discrimination claim arising from the same employment. The reason the rule should be different for class members than for individual litigants is not manifest or irrefutable; some class members intervened to assert their intentional discrimination theory of recovery, and it is not illogical to preclude the claims of other class members that did not.

The Supreme Court, however, refused to accord preclusive effect to the prior class judgment. The scope of the class representation had been the classwide "pattern or practice" claim; the representatives had not purported to represent class members on individual theories of recovery they might have. Moreover, the Court worried that a preclusion requirement would inundate the class action with the related individual claims of class members, thereby failing to achieve the economy and efficiency that the class action promises.

Aside from class actions, two other claim preclusion mechanisms have some utility in complex litigation. The first is the concept of "virtual representation," which stretches the "same party" element to include those that are "virtually" represented by a party to the case. The second is bankruptcy, a special remedial scheme that hinges on the notion of discharging the debts of the debtor (i.e., precluding actions against the debtor for pre-discharge actions). Bankruptcy does not depend on the notion of representative litigation at all, while virtual representation pushes the notion to —

231. 467 U.S. 867 (1984).

and perhaps beyond — its limits. Because both concepts raise unique issues and concerns, we consider them in future sections.[232]

Expansions of traditional claim preclusion principles should be approached with caution. If claim preclusion principles are to operate as an inducement to optimal aggregation, both the meaning of optimal aggregation and the strengths and weaknesses of joinder law must be clearly understood. So must the relationship between the law of preclusion and the law of joinder. As the nonparty preclusive effects of a case expand, the impairment of nonparty interests expand. This expansion would then serve as a reason to force more mandatory joinder under Rules 19(a)(2)(i) and 23(b)(1)(B), and more intervention under Rule 24(a)(2). But once joinder occurred, preclusion would no longer be necessary — creating a classic bootstrap argument that seems more flimsy and less honest than simply expanding joinder rules directly. Finally it is also important to keep in mind that class actions have several built-in safeguards to protect the interests of class members. Presumably, an expansion of claim preclusion principles to address the claims of nonparties would require comparable protections.

2. Issue Preclusion

As its name implies, issue preclusion seeks not to preclude entire claims in future litigation, but only to preclude the re-litigation of certain factual or legal issues.[233] In complex cases, this preclusion may be enough. If a judgment in one case determines factual issues that are relevant to a host of related cases, and if the judgment can conclusively establish these common issues for other cases, then the related cases can focus on the remaining non-common issues. The judgment can thus have the binding effect on common questions that we desired, but could never quite obtain, with the various forms of party joinder.

The question is whether issue preclusion can deliver on this promise. The hornbook statement of issue preclusion is this: A valid judgment on the merits bars the re-litigation, in a subsequent case between the same parties, of identical legal or factual issues that were actually determined and necessary to the final judgment of the

---

232. For virtual representation, see *infra* pp. 181-82; for bankruptcy, see *infra* pp. 182-89, 194-96.

233. Since claim and issue preclusion are distinct concepts, one may apply even if the other does not. In particular, issue preclusion principles may bar re-litigation of certain factual issues in subsequent litigation even though claim preclusion principles would not bar litigation of the entire claim.

first case.[234] Some of the requirements of issue preclusion — such as validity of the judgment, the meaning of "final judgment," and a disposition "on the merits" — present problems identical to those that we encountered with the same elements of claim preclusion.[235] Some of the elements — especially the identity of the issues, their actual determination, and their necessity to the judgment — are new, and require more extended analysis. Finally, the "same parties" requirement has been given a rather different spin in issue preclusion — a spin that holds some promise for complex litigation but ultimately falls short as a complete response to the re-litigation problem.

Issue preclusion usually requires that there be an "identity of issues" between the first case and the case seeking to use its judgment. In a number of situations, the requisite identity is lacking. For instance, the legal standard is not the same in the first and second case. Maine might use a different definition of negligence than North Carolina. Therefore, the finding of negligence in Maine is not generally entitled to preclusive effect in North Carolina. Similarly, differences in the burdens of proof may keep a fact found in one case from translating over to a second case. Finally, the issue may be so fact-intensive that preclusion is not possible. A finding that asbestos exposure caused Smith's lung cancer cannot be preclusive on the question of whether asbestos exposure caused Green's lung cancer.

The requirement of actual determination can also create difficulties. Unlike claim preclusion, which extends preclusive effect both to claims that were litigated and to claims that should have been litigated, issue preclusion applies only to issues that were litigated and decided. In many complex cases, different lawyers will emphasize and try different issues. If the first asbestos case proceeds only on a strict products liability theory and the second case proceeds on negligence and warranty theories, the ultimate facts of negligence and warranty were neither litigated nor decided in the first case. The first judgment, therefore, cannot preclude their litigation in the second case.

The converse strategy of bringing and trying multiple theories in the first litigation can create difficulties for the next requirement: necessity. In order for an issue to be precluded in the second case, it must have been necessary (or essential) to the judgment — in other words, the judgment could not be supported if this fact had not been determined. Many cases are jury-tried, and may of those jury trials result only in a general verdict that declares the jury's decision but not its rationale. Suppose that Smith sues XYZ on product liability,

---

234. See RESTATEMENT, *supra* n.224, § 27.

235. See *supra* nn.225-26 and accompanying text.

negligence, and warranty theories. The jury returns a general verdict for Smith, and judgment is entered against XYZ. In a second case by Green, can XYZ be precluded from contesting the issue of negligence? Product defect? Applicability of the warranty? The answer to each question is "No." In smith's case, the jury may have found XYZ negligent, but not liable on the other theories, or it may have found XYZ strictly liable, but not liable for negligence or breach of warranty. The problem is that we do not know exactly what the jury decided. Therefore, it is usually thought to be unfair to preclude XYZ from contesting them in another case, and none of the facts can be deemed essential to the judgment. The same problem arises in the obverse situation in which XYZ wins. It might appear that the jury necessarily decided that negligence, product defect, and breach of warranty did not exist. But the jury might simply have decided that Smith's injuries were not related to asbestos, or that Smith was never exposed to XYZ's asbestos. In a multiple theory case in which each theory has multiple elements that were actually litigated, proving that a particular finding was essential to the judgment is a tricky business.[236]

Assuming that all of these shoals of issue preclusion can be navigated, a final requirement looms on the horizon: Preclusion must involve the "same parties." Until rather recently, this requirement meant much the same as it does with claim preclusion.[237] The usual way used to describe this element was "mutuality of preclusion": A person could not take advantage of a previously found issue unless that person would have been bound by the opposite finding. Since parties are the only persons usually bound by the adverse findings of a judgment, the only persons that typically could take advantage of issue preclusion were either the parties to the prior judgment or those with some legal or representative relationship to these parties. As we have seen with claim preclusion, this understanding of "same parties" severely limits the utility of preclusion in complex litigation.

Unlike claim preclusion, however, the wall of mutuality has now been breached in most jurisdictions. The destruction of mutuality occurred in two steps. First, some courts and commentators recognized that mutuality led to a particularly undesirable result in one scenario. For instance, assume that Smith sues XYZ or asbestos injuries; the jury returns a verdict clearly indicating that Smith has

---

236. For an asbestos case showing the difficulty of using a general jury verdict to preclude the manufacturer from contesting liability in future cases, see Hardy v. Johns-Manville Sales Corp., 681 F.2d 334 (5th Cir. 1982).

237. *See supra* nn.230-32 and accompanying text.

suffered no injuries related to asbestos; the judgment is entered in accordance with the verdict; and Smith then commences an action against ABC, claiming that exposure to ABC's asbestos caused his injuries. Under the mutuality rule, ABC would not be able to use the prior judgment to bar Smith's suit, for ABC would not have been bound to accept the obverse ruling that Smith had suffered asbestos-related injuries. Nonetheless, allowing Smith two bites at the apple is unseemly; not only might inconsistent verdicts result, but Smith has an incentive not to effect the broadest joinder possible in the first case. Smith can keep suing asbestos manufacturers whose products were at his worksite until one of the juries believes that his injuries were asbestos-related. This result serves neither fairness nor efficiency.

Therefore, in this context, the requirement of mutuality has been largely abandoned. It has been replaced with a notion of "defensive collateral estoppel": A nonparty to the first case can defend himself or herself with the actually determined facts necessary to the first judgment.[238] In effect, defensive collateral estoppel allows a new defendant to use findings from a prior judgment as a shield against the unrelenting plaintiff. Defensive collateral estoppel, however, is only occasionally useful in complex litigation. Repeated litigation of common issues by one plaintiff against multiple defendants can sometimes occur, and defensive collateral estoppel is useful to prevent this behavior. But the real challenge in most complex cases is repeated litigation of common issues by multiple plaintiffs against a defendant (or defendants). Here, defensive collateral estoppel is not helpful.

More helpful would be the ability of a new plaintiff to use findings from a prior judgment as a sword against the losing defendant. For instance, suppose that Smith brings only a negligence claim against XYZ, and wins his case. The issue of negligence was both actually determined and necessary to the judgment. If Green could now use this finding as a sword against XYZ, Green would not have to prove negligence, and an issue common to many claims against XYZ will have been resolved once and for all — without the necessity of having to join Green or XYZ's other victims in Smith's case.

Although this solution sounds tidy, the use of "offensive collateral estoppel" is considerably more controversial than the use of defensive collateral estoppel. A principal reason is that offensive collateral estoppel, unlike its defensive cousin, can create unfortunate

238. The federal case accepting defensive collateral estoppel is Blonder-Tongue Labs., Inc. v. University of Illinois Foundation, 402 U.S. 313 (1971).

litigation incentives. Green, who may have the opportunity to join Smith's litigation, has little reason to do so. Since he is not bound by an unfavorable judgment, but would receive the benefit of a favorable judgment with offensive collateral estoppel, Green might rationally prefer not to participate in Smith's case. The whole point of our inquiry into joinder and preclusion law has been to find ways to eliminate sideline-sitting. Offensive collateral estoppel can actually foment sideline-sitting. Moreover, Green's sideline-sitting can be especially unfair to XYZ. XYZ may have won ten asbestos verdicts in a row before stumbling over Smith's claim. To allow Green and every other victim of XYZ's asbestos henceforth to take advantage of the verdict distorts the aberrational nature of Smith's success.

Like many state counts, federal courts have cautiously accepted the use of offensive collateral estoppel. The seminal case is *Parklane Hosiery, Inc. v. Shore*,[239] in which a defendant had been found liable for securities violations in an enforcement action by the Securities and Exchange Commission. Subsequently, disappointed stockholders brought a class action, and proposed to use the judgment in the SEC case to estop the defendant from contending that it had not violated the securities laws. If successful, this use of preclusion would have streamlined the second litigation enormously. But the defendant objected, claiming that the procedure was unfair.

The Supreme Court permitted the use of offensive collateral estoppel in federal-law cases brought in federal court. Recognizing the potential dangers of the doctrine, the Court made application of the doctrine discretionary, and identified four circumstances in which that discretion should generally disfavor use of the doctrine: when the plaintiff seeking to preclude the defendant had the opportunity to join the prior case but did not; when the defendant did not have the same incentive in the first case to contest the issue; when there have been prior inconsistent judgments, with some favoring the defendant; and when the defendant did not have procedural opportunities or safeguards available in the first case that were available in the second. Applying those factors in the case before it, the Court found that the stockholders could not have joined the SEC enforcement action, the defendant had every incentive in the SEC action to contest vigorously the issue of securities violation, no prior inconsistent judgments existed, and no procedural opportunities were available in the section action not available in the first.[240] It

239. 439 U.S. 322 (1979).

240. This last holding is remarkable because the SEC action had been bench-tried, but the stockholders' case was to be tried to a jury. The court thought that "the presence or absence of a jury as factfinder is basically neutral." *Id.* at 332, n.19. It also rejected the defendant's claim that the application of offensive collateral estoppel in

therefore approved of the use of offensive collateral estoppel on the facts.

In many complex cases, however, one or more of these four circumstances will prevent the use of offensive collateral estoppel. For instance, in *Hardy v. Johns-Manville Sales Corp.*,[241] an asbestos defendant lost a judgment for $68,000. As is typical with immature litigation,[242] approximately half of the 70-odd asbestos cases that had been tried after this judgment had resulted in judgment for the defendant. At the time of the first judgment, the defendant was facing no other asbestos litigation; by the time of *Hardy*, the defendant was facing thousands of asbestos claims, many seeking millions of dollars apiece. The district court in *Hardy* allowed the fifty-eight plaintiffs sought to use the prior $68,000 judgment offensively against the defendant. The court of appeals reversed. The prior inconsistent verdicts, as well as the defendant's relatively weak incentive to litigate liability because of the unforeseeability of the catastrophic crush of litigation that ultimately followed from this single loss, led the court to believe that offensive collateral estoppel ought not to be employed.

Parklane Hosiery's two other limitations — lack of procedural opportunities in the first case and refusal to join the first case — can also derail offensive collateral estoppel in complex litigation. Lack of procedural opportunities is relatively rare, but some cases do exist.[243] The "refusal to join" circumstance is perhaps the least well-developed of the *Parklane Hosiery* doctrines. The cases that invoke the limitation tend to involve multidistrict litigation in which certain plaintiffs were clearly sitting out and taking a "wait-and-see" attitude, but even here preclusion is sometimes permitted.[244] Presumably, this limitation on the use of offensive collateral estoppel would not apply to plaintiffs that were not injured at the time of the first case, that were unaware of the case, or that were unable, for jurisdictional or other reasons, to join the first case. If the limitation is ever interpreted to prevent the use of estoppel by nonparties that could have either intervened or commenced a lawsuit and consolidated it with the first case, very different joinder incentives might be created. Of course, to note again the circularity often inherent in joinder-preclusion arguments, preclusion-based incentives for joinder diminish the need for preclusion in the first place.

this context violated the Seventh Amendment.

241. 681 F.2d 334 (5th Cir. 1982).

242. For a description of the life cycle of litigation on its way to full maturity, see *supra* ch.2, n.3 and ac-

companying text.

243. For a fuller discussion, see TIDMARSH & TRANSGRUD, *supra* n.14, at 202-03.

244. For cases, see *id.* at 203.

Both defensive and offensive collateral estoppel, however, are limited in an important way. Both can be applied only *against* a person that was party to prior litigation *by* a nonparty to that litigation. A complete preclusion response for complex litigation would also require a doctrine that can be applied *against* a nonparty *by* a party to the prior litigation. For instance, if XYZ won its case against Smith because the jury found that XYZ was not negligent, present notions of issue preclusion would not allow XYZ to preclude Green from contesting the negligence issue anew. Thus far, the law of preclusion has been unwilling to cross this frontier and abolish this limitation on the use of issue preclusion against nonparties.[245]

This limit on preclusion is consistent with the principle that a person cannot be bound by an adverse judgment unless that person is a party to the case. More deeply, this limit is consistent with the principles of autonomy and individual control on which our party joinder and preclusion systems are constructed. Issue preclusion can fitfully help complex litigation run more efficiently, and at the margins it can provide modest incentives to encourage the joinder of transactionally related cases. But it cannot help to achieve the single resolution of all claims unless we are willing to sacrifice the adversarial notion that it is unfair to bind people to outcomes in which they did not participate.

3. Summary

The use of preclusion principles to help accomplish optimal aggregation requires, as a first step, that we understand what we are attempting to achieve. If aggregation is understood in terms of the need to prevent remedial inequity, then present joinder law already does a modestly good job, although there remains a lack of any clear mechanism to deal with the problem of insufficient assets. The preclusion principles that we have studied do little to deal with cases involving insufficient assets. On the other hand, if optimal aggregation is understood as the prevention of inefficient relitigation, then present joinder law does far less well, and there is more room for preclusion doctrines to influence aggregation in a positive fashion.

Beyond the question of goals is the question of means. Although the difficulties of using aggregation are many, the principal failing of both claim and issue preclusion as aggregation mechanisms is that the doctrines cannot generally be applied against nonparties. Presumably, if we were to change preclusion and apply it more generally to nonparties, procedural protections akin to those that

---

245. For the discussion of some cases that have tried to cross this line, see *infra* nn.248-50 and accompanying text.

attend class actions would need to be developed. It is not clear what such mechanisms would look like — although some form of reasonably effective notice would be constitutionally required — or how these protections would lead to anything markedly different than the present class action device. On balance, it seems easier, and more direct, to focus efforts on joining nonparties rather than creating an entirely new system of preclusion protections for nonparties.

Finally, use of preclusion as an indirect means of aggregation does not avoid the policy battles of joinder, but only redraws the battlelines. The fundamental questions remain: When is it appropriate to deprive an individual of his or her day in court, or of the right to control the presentation of his or her case? When should concerns for efficiency lead us to apply preclusion principles as means to achieve aggregation? Should more expansive preclusion rules apply only to complex cases? If so, to what extent do novel rules of preclusion threaten to change the outcomes of complex cases in comparison to ordinary cases? Historically, these have not been the questions with which preclusion, with its primary emphasis on the tension between finality and a full and fair opportunity to litigate all relevant issues, has struggled. Joinder has confronted these central aggregation questions in a more direct fashion. Perhaps it is best to wage these battle as a matter of joinder law — at least unless Congress directs otherwise, as it has done with bankruptcy.

These are some of the points to ponder as we examine bankruptcy and other non-traditional joinder and preclusion responses to the nonparty problem.

C. RESPONSES

So far in this chapter we have dealt with the two ways presently available to address the aggregation of nonparties: joinder and preclusion. As we have seen, our system strongly prefers the joinder approach; preclusion of claims or issues usually occurs only when a person has been joined as a party to the litigation. In prior chapters, we saw courts develop either a creative interpretation of existing doctrines or entirely new doctrines to respond to the need for the aggregation of related cases. A fair question is whether any similar responses might present more satisfactory solutions to the nonparty problem. As we examine potential responses, you will see that some are in daily use, but most remain on the drawing board.

1. Changing Settled Rules

In prior chapters we have seen a willingness to change settled rules or expand settled powers to help achieve optimal aggregation.

With joinder and preclusion, however, such changes and expansion have been relatively rare.

a. Joinder. With joinder, one reason for this reluctance has undoubtedly been that the rules of joinder are fixed by code or statute, and often have lengthy precedential pedigrees that pre-date the rise of the complex litigation phenomenon. Another reason is that the standards contained in most joinder rules are already flexible and provide significant discretion to judges to achieve aggregation. As we have seen, however, flexibility and discretion have not led invariably to aggregation-friendly interpretations of the rules, but rather to a frustratingly broad range of approaches.

A different type of response to the settled rules of joinder would be to give judges a *sua sponte* power to invoke the joinder rules in order to achieve optimal joinder. The idea of *sua sponte* power is hardly new to us. In the last two chapters, we frequently saw judges claiming to enjoy *sua sponte* powers to help achieve intra-system or intersystem aggregation; and as we shall see in future chapters, judges also claim *sua sponte* powers to overcome pretrial and trial obstacles in complex cases. Should the judge enjoy a similar power in joinder matters? If, for instance, Smith brings an action against XYZ, should the court be able to expand the lawsuit to include all other plaintiffs that could have been, but were not, joined by Smith under Rule 20? If Smith and Green file a case against XYZ, can the court on its own volition order the matter certified as a class action?

Granting this power to the judge is a delicate matter. On the one hand, we have seen that the rules of party joinder provide great flexibility to judges in joinder matters, so the next step of allowing judges to exercise that power on their own initiative does not seem that large. There exists textual support for such a *sua sponte* power in Rule 21, which states that "[p]arties may be dropped *or added* by order of the court on motion of any party *or of its own initiative* . . . on such terms as are just."[246] Rule 17, concerning joinder of real parties in interest, and Rule 19 contemplate comparable judicial initiative. Neither statutory interpleader nor Rule 23 is quite so explicit, but both joinder devices grant the judge equitable powers out of which a *sua sponte* joinder authority could be fashioned.

On the other hand, if judges can simply override the joinder decisions of the parties, the Federal Rules' carefully constructed system of part-voluntary, part-mandatory joinder will collapse, and with it the premise of litigant autonomy on which the system is founded. If the power is limited just to complex cases, difficult questions of defining complexity and justifying the limited applica-

---

246. F.R.Civ.P. 21 (italics added).

tion of the power arise. Such a power also poses practical problems and raises concerns for fairness, including the propriety of judicial action that forces nonparties to obtain legal representation and contest a case in a potentially distant forum. Subject matter jurisdiction, territorial jurisdiction, and venue are still stumbling blocks that often cannot be removed by judicial action. In class actions, other difficulties are presented. Those who do not wish to be joined by judicial fiat can opt out of a (b)(3) class; moreover, recalcitrant class members can create significant issues concerning adequacy of representation.

One of the best-known instances of a judicial attempt to craft the party structure occurred in *Pan American World Airways, Inc. v. United States District Court.*[247] After several relatives of victims of an airplane crash began to file suit in his court, the judge ordered the airline to hand over its passenger lists. Once he had the names of other passengers, the judge intended to send out a notice to all nonparties that were potential plaintiffs and advise them of the pendency of the case. Such a notice was not the same as enforced joinder, but the court hoped that the notice would induce others to file suit in the judge's court. The airline refused to comply with the district judge's order.

On mandamus, the court of appeals held that the judge's order was a clear abuse of discretion. Since no Federal Rule of Civil Procedure or other power specifically authorized this notice, the court of appeals believed that such notice was tantamount to the creation of a *de facto* class action that failed to follow the protections of Rule 23.

Although *Pan Am* is not squarely on point, it does suggest that judges should be cautious in their efforts to amend the parties' chosen structure. Judges have tended to heed this advice. *Sua sponte* judicial power to achieve optimal joinder is rarely discussed, and never used. Therefore, it has not proven to be the panacea to the nonparty aggregation problem.

b. Preclusion. As we have seen, a principal difficulty of preclusion law is its inapplicability to nonparties. A few cases have ventured beyond this standard limitation in order to achieve broader nonparty preclusion. For instance, in *Lynch v. Merrell-National Laboratories,*[248] a judge held that a plaintiff was collaterally estopped from proving causation in a Bendectin case. The district court sought to bind the *Lynch* plaintiffs to the jury's finding in a related multi-

---

247. 523 F.2d 1073 (9th Cir. 1975).

248. 646 F.Supp. 856 (D. Mass. 1986), *aff'd on other grounds,* 830 F.2d 1190 (1st Cir. 1987).

district case that Bendectin did not cause birth defects of the type that the plaintiffs alleged. The plaintiffs in *Lynch* could have participated in that trial, but chose not to do so as a matter of litigation strategy. The judge believed that the procedures used and the outcome of the MDL trial were fair, and determined that the *Lynch* plaintiffs would present no evidence in support of causation different than evidence that had been presented in the MDL trial. Thus, the court found that preclusion against the plaintiffs was appropriate.

Lynch is among a very small handful of cases that has bound a person to a judgment or factual finding rendered in a case in which the person was not a party. This move, which is a step beyond offensive collateral estoppel, promotes efficiency and the finality of the earlier judgment, and avoids the problem of inconsistent judgments. But it also flaunts the notion that individuals enjoy an autonomous right to control their own litigation. Moreover, after *Richards v. Jefferson County*, the preservation of each person's day in court would seem to call *Lynch's* approach into question. Indeed, even in *Lynch*, the court of appeals expressed grave doubts about the district court's preclusion approach, and found another ground on which to affirm the judgment.

A modestly more promising expansion of preclusion law has been "virtual representation." The idea of virtual representation is that a nonparty's claims or factual issues can be precluded by a prior judgment in which the nonparty was virtually represented by someone with essentially identical interests. This concept also underlies class actions, but virtual representation has been used to achieve preclusion in non-class settings. For example, in *Tyus v. Schoemehl*,[249] a group of African-American aldermen challenged a redistricting plan for St. Louis's aldermanic districts. After waging an anemic legal fight, the aldermen lost the suit on summary judgment. While the first suit was pending, a second suit was commenced. Some of the parties in the second suit were that same as those in the first suit, but at least two plaintiffs (African-American state legislators) were new. The claims presented in both cases were essentially identical.

Obviously, the plaintiffs who were parties to the first case suffered the claim preclusive effects of its prior judgment, and their claims were properly dismissed in the second case. But the court of appeals thought that preclusion also ran to the state legislators, who were new parties in the second case. Its theory was that the legislators had precisely the same interests as the aldermen.

---

249. 93 F.3d 449 (8th Cir. 1996), *cert. denied*, 520 U.S. 1166 (1997).

Therefore, the aldermen "virtually represented" the legislators, and the judgment against the aldermen in the first case could fairly be applied to the legislators.

Tyus acknowledged a difference among the courts of appeal about the breadth of the virtual representation doctrine. It opted for a broad interpretation. It did not attempt to state a bright-line test for when the doctrine would come into play, but instead thought that preclusion was appropriate as long as the balance of the equities favored its use. A substantial special relationship between the parties in the first case and the new parties in the second case was the fulcrum on the balance. The relevant factors in determining whether this relationship existed were an identity of interests, a similar incentive to litigate (which the court of appeals called "adequacy of representation"), and the public law nature of the issue subject to preclusion. The weakness of the representation in the aldermen's case — in other words, the inadequacy of the representation in fact — did not deter the court from using preclusion.

Tyus represents one of the strongest uses of the virtual representation doctrine, whose fate remains clouded. The Supreme Court has never accepted the theory. Some courts have recently rejected virtual representation as inconsistent with *Richards* and *Martin v. Wilks*. Others have accepted the theory, but on terms far more limited than those suggested in *Tyus*.[250] Even the most generous theories still require a special relationship between the party and nonparty — a fact that is unlikely to obtain in most private law litigation such as the Smith-Jones-Green asbestos hypothetical. And the more generous theories must ultimately answer this critical question: How can virtual representation be reconciled with the carefully constructed and constrained Rule 23, whose guarantees of adequate representation are better delineated than those generally employed in virtual representation cases?

2. Bankruptcy

To the extent that the prevention of remedial inequity is the goal of aggregation, the weakness of our present joinder and preclusion system is the problem of insufficient assets. To the extent that the prevention of repetitive litigation is the purpose of aggregation, cases involving insufficient assets can trigger a race to the courthouse and inefficient gamesmanship designed to obtain the first shot at the assets. On this view as well, a stronger aggregation power is desirable. Interpleader addresses a modest corner of the issue, and

---

250.   For a general description of the different positions, see TID-   MARSH & TRANGSRUD, *supra* n.14, at 229-32.

Rule 23(b)(1)(B) can help in limited circumstances as well. But a general aggregation power has thus far eluded us.

Congress has created a specialized statutory scheme to deal with the rehabilitation of debtors and the equitable distribution of the debtor's insufficient assets to creditors — the bankruptcy system. Bankruptcy was not designed with the problems of structural complexity in mind, but it contains the most powerful and complete set of aggregation tools available in any single device. It was therefore inevitable that this system would eventually be harnessed to the task of aggregation in complex litigation. The first use of bankruptcy in this fashion occurred in 1982, when Johns-Manville — at the time a solvent and powerful corporation — turned to bankruptcy in order to manage its burgeoning asbestos liability. Hundreds of companies have followed suit in the decades since.

Bankruptcy operates essentially within a preclusion framework. At the end of a successful bankruptcy case, the creditors receive the share of the debtor's estate that the statute permits, and the debtor receives a discharge from virtually all existing debts.[251] This discharge precludes any individual with a pre-discharge claim (i.e., a creditor) from subsequently asserting the claim in any state or federal court. The preclusive effect of a discharge applies whether or not the creditor chooses to assert a claim in the bankruptcy case. Obviously, the discharge serves as a powerful incentive for all claimants to enter the bankruptcy case.

Preclusion against nonparties is just the start of bankruptcy's aggregation powers. Throughout this book, we have seen structurally complex cases stymied by a variety of roadblocks to complete aggregation: subject matter jurisdiction, territorial jurisdiction, venue, lack of transfer mechanisms, lack of removal authority, lack of power to stay related litigation, lack of an ability to reach the cases of nonparties, inequitable treatment of related cases, and so on. Bankruptcy has an answer for each of these problems, but the answers are often complex and nuanced. Here we can hit only a few, somewhat simplified highlights.[252]

Federal courts have exclusive jurisdiction over a bankruptcy case.[253] They also have concurrent jurisdiction over "proceedings . . . arising in or related to" bankruptcy "cases."[254] The bankruptcy "case" is the lawsuit in which creditors' claims are allowed or disallowed,

251. *See* 11 U.S.C. §§ 727, 1141. For claims that are not discharged in bankruptcy, see 11 U.S.C. § 523.

252. More extended treatments of bankruptcy can be found in TIDMARSH & TRANSGRUD, *supra* n.14, at 702-88;

MARCUS & SHERMAN, *supra* n.78, at 199-208.

253. 28 U.S.C. § 1334(a).

254. 28 U.S.C. § 1334(b).

the debtor's estate is distributed among creditors, and the debtor's discharge is granted. Bankruptcy "proceedings," on the other hand, often involve litigation to determine the underlying merits of the creditors' claims and to bring into the estate the debtor's assets. Within this framework, the masses of complex cases that drive the defendant to seek bankruptcy protection are regarded as "proceedings," and not as part of the bankruptcy case itself. Therefore, federal jurisdiction over cases filed subsequent to the filing of the bankruptcy case is possible, but the victims of the debtor's wrongdoing need not file their cases in federal court. Cases commenced against the debtor before the filing of the bankruptcy case also remain spread out among all the courts in which they are pending.

To aggregate these and other related cases, bankruptcy has three separate powers. The first is the power of removal. 28 U.S.C. § 1452(a) gives a "party" the right to remove to the district in which the case is pending any case over which the federal court has original jurisdiction. The removal authority, however, can be declined "on any equitable ground,"[255] and removal to the federal district still does not accomplish consolidation with the bankruptcy case, which may well be pending in another federal district.

The second power is the power to transfer. Under the basic venue provision, 28 U.S.C. § 1408, a number of federal districts can serve as the venue of a bankruptcy case. "Related to" proceedings "may" be filed in the district in which the bankruptcy case is pending. In order to accomplish the transfer of removed cases and "related to" cases filed elsewhere, 28 U.S.C. § 1412 permits a district court to transfer a case to another district "in the interest of justice or for the convenience of the parties." In addition, 28 U.S.C. § 157(b)(5) permits the transfer of tort claims either to the district in which the bankruptcy case is pending or to the district "in which the claim arose." Like § 1404 but unlike § 1407, these cases are transferred to all purposes, including trial.

The final useful power is the bankruptcy stay. Under 11 U.S.C. § 362, the filing of a bankruptcy petition automatically stays, in both state and federal court, all proceedings previously commenced against the debtor, and continues to stay all further cases filed against the debtor during the pendency of the bankruptcy. This stay can be lifted in some situations, but in general terms it forces those with cases against a debtor, including claimants in complex litigation, to work within the bankruptcy proceeding; it prevents claimants from racing their cases to conclusion in order to get the full value of their claims. Bankruptcy also has a second, broader stay provision

255. 28 U.S.C. § 1452(b).

in 11 U.S.C. § 105, which grants the bankruptcy court the power to "issue any order, process, or judgment that is necessary or appropriate to carry out the provisions of this title."

Finally, the Bankruptcy Rules provide for nationwide service of process in a bankruptcy case.[256]

In the bankruptcy case, creditors file claims against the debtor. The bankruptcy court then determines whether to allow the claim. At the same time, the court (often acting through a trustee) collects the assets of the debtor. Once claims are allowed and assets are collected, the process of distribution begins.

The nature of the distribution varies with the nature of the bankruptcy. The most common forms are Chapter 7 liquidation and Chapter 11 corporate reorganization. As its name implies, a liquidation distributes all available assets to the creditors. Certain priorities for payment are established by statute; and all claims within a certain priority must be satisfied before anyone with a lower priority receives money. If there is insufficient money to pay everyone within a particular priority, then all creditors within that priority receive a *pro rata* share of the remaining assets, and those with a lower priority receive nothing. Once the distribution plan is established, the discharge occurs, and all those with claims against the debtor — even those who received only pennies or nothing on the dollar in the distribution — are precluded from asserting the remainder of the claim against the debtor in future litigation.

Corporate reorganization has a somewhat different goal. Unlike a Chapter 7 liquidation, which effectively ends a corporation's existence, a Chapter 11 proceeding attempts to keep the corporation alive as a going concern after the discharge. In order to accomplish this, the debtor must propose a plan under which the various creditors are paid. The bankruptcy court organizes the creditors into various classes,[257] and each class of creditors then has an opportunity to vote on the plan. A class of creditors with claims against the estate does not accept the plan unless two-thirds of the class's claims in dollar amount and one-half in numerical amount vote to accept the plan. If a class of creditors rejects the plan, the court can still "cram down" the plan on the creditors; but it must be shown, among other

---

256. BANKR.R. 7004(d); *cf.* 28 U.S.C. § 1334(e) (granting bankruptcy court exclusive jurisdiction over all property of the debtor and bankruptcy estate.

257. These classes should not be confuses with classes under Rule 23. Typically the trustee will pick a com-

mittee of creditors, often with one or more representative from each class of creditors, to assist in the negotiations and management decisions of the debtor. But neither the individual representatives nor the committee as a whole is representative within the meaning of Rule 23(a).

things, that the creditors in the class will receive at least as much through the plan as they would have received in a liquidation and, with unsecured creditors, that no one in a class with a junior priority will receive any distribution at all. Numerous other requirements must also be met in order for a court to approve a plan; among them are the likelihood of the plan's success and, with a cramdown, the fair and equitable distribution of the estate among classes.[258]

Typically, plaintiffs with claims against the debtor have unsecured claims and comprise one or more of the classes with the lowest priority. Even below them, however, are the stockholders, who have "interests" rather than "claims." The effect of the reorganization requirements is that stockholders can receive no value unless (1) all creditors receive full value, or (2) all classes that do not receive full value and that have priority over the stockholders accept the plan.

As with a liquidation, a successful reorganization ends with the discharge of the claims against the debtor. Even though the debtor emerges with assets and, hopefully, soon earns profits, the claimants with pre-discharge claims cannot sue the debtor for the difference between the full value of the claim and the amount received in bankruptcy. This is true regardless of whether the claimant chooses to file a claim in bankruptcy or to sit on the sidelines;[259] the claim is precluded regardless of whether the claimant ever receives anything for the claim.

The law and practice of bankruptcy and corporate reorganization are complicated and intricate, and we have highlighted only some of their essential features. Our purpose is to determine whether bankruptcy can be useful as an aggregation mechanism. At first blush, it appears so. Bankruptcy has all the bells and whistles of aggregation that we have examined for the past several chapters: removal power, broad anti-suit powers, transfer authority, federal jurisdiction, nationwide service of process, and a powerful preclusive device that forces nonparties to either assert their cases in a single venue or lose them forever. It is difficult to imagine a more complete set of aggregation powers in one device.

In reality, however, bankruptcy suffers from a number of deficiencies that limit its utility in many complex cases. The first is the problem of determining claim values. If XYZ declares bankruptcy and ten thousand plaintiffs present valid claims, it is impossible to know how much each claimant should receive in a *pro*

---

258. *See* 11 U.S.C. § 1129.

259. Bankruptcy law requires that notice be given of the pending of the bankruptcy proceeding, and of the "bar date" beyond which no claims may be presented for payment, in order to ensure that claimants have a full and fair opportunity to present claims. *See* BANKR. R. 2002.

rata distribution until each case is adjudicated. Adjudicating ten thousand cases could take dozens of years, result in repetitive litigation of common issues, and cost enormous amounts of money that otherwise could have gone to creditors. For personal injury claims, this problem is exacerbated; 28 U.S.C. § 157(b)(2)(B) states that the bankruptcy court has no authority to liquidate or estimate tort claims "for purposes of distribution." This means that the determination of the amount of each tort claim must be handled by the court in which it was filed. Indeed, § 157(b)(2)(B) amounts to a statutorily required form of disaggregation. Some courts have noted that § 157(b)(2)(B) does not preclude aggregation of tort claims for purposes other than distribution; for instance, the bankruptcy court can aggregate the cases in order to estimate liability as a part of an inquiry into the feasibility of a reorganization plan.[260] In any event, these requirements virtually guarantee that in a case of thousands of related claims, some form of claims resolution process will be part of the final plan. And in order for that process to work, it will need to be structured in such a way that some significant portion of the claimants will be induced to abandon their right to their day in court.

A second, related problem concerns voting issues in reorganization cases. In one sense, extending voting rights to claimants is to be applauded; direct democracy obviates some of the need for representatives, and presents an intriguing potential reform for class actions. In other ways, however, voting is a logistical nightmare. Determining whether one-half of the class in number support the reorganization plan is easy. Determining whether two-thirds of the class in value support the plan is extraordinarily difficult; in order to make the necessary calculation, each of the claims would need to be liquidated to an exact amount. As we have just discussed, however, liquidating thousands of claims is likely to be an extensive and expensive practice. In past cases, claimants have tended to support reorganization plans overwhelmingly (with many votes approaching 95% approval), allowing the court the luxury of either assigning a fictional $1 value to each claim, presuming that the 5% who dissent do not hold two-third of all claims in dollar value, or using sampling techniques and empirical data to determine the value of the claims held by those who oppose the class.[261] This last method works best with mature litigation.

Even more serious aggregation problems arise in special contexts. Suppose that Smith has been exposed to asbestos from both XYZ and another asbestos company. When Smith sues, he is

---

260. A.H. Robins Co. v. Piccinin, 788 F.2d 994 (4th Cir.), *cert. denied,* 479 U.S. 876 (1986).

261. *See In re* A.H. Robins Co., 880 F.2d 694 (4th Cir.), *cert. denied,* 493 U.S. 959 (1989).

likely to sue both defendants in one case. When XYZ files for bankruptcy, however, Smith must now litigate a single claim in two separate forums that use different procedural protections. Leaving aside § 157(b)(2)(B) issues, bankruptcy may do a good job of aggregating all claims against one defendant in one forum, but its single-minded focus on the debtor leads to the disaggregation of claims against related defendants.

Some bankruptcy cases have dealt with the issue by extending the automatic stay to prevent litigation against co-defendants while the bankruptcy case is proceeding. In theory, such a stay will force the claimants to resolve the entire controversy in one forum. As might be expected, however, issuance of a stay is unusual, and requires a tight legal connection between the debtor and the other defendants. When the other defendants are officers of the debtor, insurers of the debtor, or the corporate parent of the debtor, some courts have shown a willingness to expand the stay.[262] But a stay collapses upon discharge, so the truly patient plaintiff can wait out the stay and continue the case against other defendants at a later time. The response to this problem, of course, would be to expand the bankruptcy discharge to include claims against defendants subject to the stay. Not surprisingly, however, many courts are hostile to the expansion of the discharge (or its equivalent, a permanent injunction against pursuing the claims) to include non-debtor defendants.[263]

Finally, the basic model of bankruptcy presumes that each claimant will present his or her own claim in bankruptcy. When thousands of individuals have claims, however, this scenario is unrealistic, and many claimants are often represented by a few lawyers. Moreover, in a Chapter 11 case, a bankruptcy court will typically organize all of the claimants into a single class of creditors, and appoint one or more members to the committee of creditors to assist in negotiations. But there is no requirement about how classes of claimants are to be constituted, or who may serve as a part of the creditors' committee. If it chooses, a court can lump the claimants together with other trade creditors, or it can divide the claimants into multiple classes. Nor is there any requirement that the representative(s) for a class of creditors satisfy the rigorous Rule 23(a) adequacy of representation standards that a representative of a class must meet. To some extent this problem is cured by direct democracy; each claimant has the opportunity to vote down an unfavorable plan.

---

262. *Robins*, 788 F.2d 994; *In re Dow Corning Corp.*, 86 F.3d 482 (6th Cir. 1996), *cert. denied*, 519 U.S. 1071 (1997).

263. *See, e.g., In re* Am. Hard-woods, 885 F.2d 621 (9th Cir. 1989) (bankruptcy court stayed cases against non-debtor defendants during reorganization period, but refused to issue a permanent injunction).

Unlike a class action, however, a claimant can be outvoted, and minority claimants can find themselves bound to a plan that ill serves their interests. Indeed, unlike Rule 23(a), which seeks to protect minority interests from majority overreaching, the bankruptcy system fosters negotiating behavior that favors the desires of the majority of claimants.

In the final analysis, therefore, bankruptcy presents a unique opportunity to achieve aggregation, albeit in limited circumstances. It helps to plug the hole created by the joinder rules' inability to deal adequately with the remedial inequity of insufficient assets. And it serves as a useful model for the types of aggregation powers that might be employed beyond the confines of bankruptcy. Some of bankruptcy's other features, such as direct democratic voting rights for each claimant, might also be beneficial additions for other joinder and preclusion doctrines that are developed for complex litigation.

But as an aggregation device, bankruptcy is still flawed. Its rules can lead to the disaggregation of some claims, and it has difficulty extending its important stay and discharge powers to non-debtors. Lumped into classes that may have little regard for conflicts of interest and that are often deprived as a practical matter of any opportunity to present the merits of their controversy in open court, claimants in bankruptcy have some important participatory rights but lack other procedural protections. Most important, bankruptcy is a system not built to achieve optimal aggregation. Its fundamental policy concerns are rehabilitation and equitable distribution. The aggregative potential of its rules for complex litigation is merely a byproduct of its basic substantive goals. Understandably, therefore, bankruptcy has not yet achieved, much less fully regarded, the perfect balance among autonomy, efficiency, transactionalism, and trans-substantivity.

3. Preclusion after Notice and an Opportunity to Intervene

A final potential solution derives from a 1994 proposal from the American Law Institute. In response to the perceived pressures of multiparty, multiforum litigation, the ALI suggested the development of a wide array of changes to aggregation rules, many of which we have already considered.[264] The ALI recognized that any aggregation system that failed to address the nonparty problem was incomplete. Therefore, the ALI developed a hybrid mechanism that borrowed elements from both joinder and issue preclusion: All nonparties would be bound to the factual or legal findings of a transac-

---

264. *See supra* ch.3, nn.17 & 25   & 87and accompanying text.
and accompanying text; ch.4, nn.70, 78

tionally related case if (1) the nonparties received notice that they would be bound and (2) the nonparties were extended the right to intervene in the case.[265]   If the nonparties chose to intervene, ordinary principles of preclusion applied; as parties, they were bound to the judgment. If they chose not to intervene, the ALI's proposal worked a significant change in preclusion law, not unlike that suggested by *Lynch* and the doctrine of virtual representation; the nonparties were bound to the relevant findings, whether positive or negative, despite the fact that they had never joined the case.

The linchpin of the ALI's entire aggregation system, this proposal consciously set itself in opposition to *Martin v. Wilks*. In *Martin v. Wilks*, which we have described in greater detail above,[266] the Supreme Court held that neither knowledge of ongoing litigation potentially affecting a nonparty's rights nor an opportunity to intervene in that litigation was a sufficient basis on which to preclude a nonparty's claims. Joinder was required. For the ALI, notice and an opportunity to intervene are a sufficient ground for preclusion; joinder is not required.

The proposal is an important one. It blends aspects of preclusion and joinder, and builds the system on the constitutional cornerstone of actual notice. To some extent, the proposal is simply an expansion of Congress's own response to *Martin v. Wilks*, in which Congress created a similar "preclusion after notice and opportunity to intervene" rule.[267] Passed to overrule the result of *Martin v. Wilks*, this statute was limited just to civil rights cases of the type involved in *Martin v. Wilks*. The *Martin v. Wilks* rule was left standing for other types of litigation. The statute also did not make clear whether precluded parties might be permitted to intervene.[268]   The ALI's proposal expands the preclusion after notice concept to all types of cases, and guarantees the nonparty the right to intervene.

The policy arguments surrounding the ALI's proposal — litigant autonomy, prevention of inefficient relitigation, final resolution of an entire transaction, outcome-affecting determinations in immature litigation, and so on — have been discussed throughout this chapter and book. But the ALI's proposal also faces two other hurdles. The first is the practical problem of reconciling the ALI's proposal with Rule 19(a)(2)(i). If nonparties might find their rights precluded by

---

265. AMERICAN LAW INSTITUTE, COMPLEX LITIGATION: STATUTORY RECOMMENDATIONS AND ANALYSIS § 5.05 (1994).

266. *See supra* nn.38-39 and accompanying text.

267. 42 U.S.C. § 2000e-2(n).

268. Section 2000e-2(n) states only that, in order for preclusion to be effective, persons with actual notice must be afforded an opportunity "to present objections" to a proposed judgment; it does not guarantee a right to intervene.

another case, they seem to fit classically within the definition of parties that must be joined if feasible. Some plaintiffs might not be able to be joined, and as a result some cases might be dismissed for failure to join an indispensable party. That untoward outcome can be avoided only by suspending the operation of Rule 19 in this circumstance, a possibility that leads to the larger question of whether the indispensability analysis of Rule 19(b) should simply be abandoned in complex (or even in all) cases.

The second hurdle is the ALI proposal's uncertain constitutionality. As we have noted, *Martin v. Wilks* was unclear about whether its holding was grounded in due process concerns or an interpretation of the joinder provisions of the Federal Rules. Two later cases that began in state court, in which the Supreme Court's holding was based on due process concerns, suggest that *Martin v. Wilks*'s requirement of joinder before preclusion has a constitutional foundation. In at least one and possibly both of these state cases, the nonparty was aware of the related state litigation, but did not intervene in it — and this knowledge and failure to intervene, to which the ALI would attach the penalty of preclusion, made no constitutional difference in either case.[269] On the other hand, *Martin v. Wilks* recognized that in certain representative suits and "specialized remedial scheme[s]" — the opinion specifically mentioned class actions and bankruptcy — preclusion without individual joinder was constitutionally permissible.[270] Whether the ALI's system to prevent multiparty, multiforum litigation might be considered another such scheme is debatable.

Indeed, the constitutional fate of the ALI's proposal may hinge on the breadth of the proposal's scope. The ALI's basic goal was to reduce multiparty, multiforum litigation. Consequently, the ALI proposed that preclusion after notice be available in any potential cases arising out of the same transaction or occurrence, as long as there was a common question of law or fact between the present and the potential cases. Consequently, the ALI's proposal operates as a strong incursion on the right of parties to structure and control their own litigation in a wide array of cases — even in those in which the need for a single definitive resolution is less compelling. A more narrowly tailored scheme — perhaps preclusion after notice and an opportunity to intervene only in situations of remedial inequity, in which the need for a single resolution presents its most compelling case — seems to stand a greater chance of negotiating the constitutional challenges.

---

269. For a brief discussion of the cases, see *supra* n.39.

270. 490 U.S. at 762 n.2.

In any event, the utility and constitutionality of the ALI's proposal remain for now an academic point. There has been no effort to implement the proposal, either by legislation or through case law.

D. THE PROBLEM OF FUTURE CLAIMANTS

Throughout this book we have dealt almost entirely with the problem of aggregating existing claims. In the last three chapters, the claims that we wished to aggregate had already been filed — whether in the same district, in another court of the same system, or in different court systems. In this chapter, we have dealt with ways to handle cases that had not yet been filed. As we have gone through the chapter, however, we have assumed that the nonparties' claims were ripe for adjudication. The nonparties had present claims, even though their lawsuits were not going to be filed until some time in the future.

There is, however, another group of nonparties: "future" plaintiffs. Like present nonparties, the future nonparties have not yet filed suit; unlike the present nonparties, however they do not yet have a ripe claim. Put differently, although the future plaintiffs might have been exposed to the defendant's wrongful conduct, they have not yet suffered any injury from that conduct. A classic example is a mass tort claim such as asbestos, in which the latency period before injury can be several decades. Smith might have been exposed to XYZ's asbestos and already contracted an illness from it. Green, on the other hand, might have been exposed to XYZ's asbestos a generation later, and is still relatively healthy. Indeed, it is not even certain that Green will ever suffer from an asbestos-related illness.

Some types of litigation rarely involve the future plaintiff problem. With most antitrust and securities cases, for instance, the wrongful behavior causes injury to all within a relatively short time frame. The same is true of some mass torts, such as an airplane crash. In these circumstances, the difficult problem is overcoming the geographical dispersion of the cases and yet-to-be-filed claims.

The future plaintiff problem adds the element of temporal dispersion. This element makes aggregation even more difficult. One problem is simply identifying who the plaintiffs might be. Another is determining which members of this group will in fact suffer injury (and are therefore legitimate plaintiffs) and which will not. Another is attempting to set up a mechanism to resolve or adjudicate the claims or entitlements of people whose injuries are unknown. To some extent, these problems are simply difficult questions of practice. But to some extent, they are also problems of constitutional significance. In particular, difficult questions of Article III ripeness, mootness, and standing and of constitutionally adequate notice to unidentified future claimants loom over any attempts to aggregate.[271] The Seventh Amendment might also be implicated by settlement mechanisms that deny future claimants their day in court before a jury.[272]

Given all these difficulties, it is tempting simply to ignore future plaintiffs, and adjudicate their cases as they ripen. But this is an imperfect solution. Ignoring future claims means the inefficient relitigation of related issues, and the creation of potentially outcome-determinative differences between aggregated present claims and individually handled future claims. Moreover, in some cases, ignoring future claims will create remedial inequity, since the aggregated present claimants will obtain all the assets available to satisfy plaintiffs' claims.

Thus far, however, the appropriate response to the problem has been one of the — if not the — most elusive and frustrating puzzles in all of complex litigation. Books have been written, studies have been undertaken, and high-level conferences and commissions have been convened — all with an eye toward resolving the problem of the future plaintiff. Three approaches are possible: joinder, preclusion, and settlement. Each proposed approach has its failings, and we may be no closer to an answer about the future plaintiff conundrum than we were when we began to consider the problem.

1. Joinder

Of the three approaches, joinder has the least potential. As we have already seen, our joinder rules — class actions arguably excepted — are not set up to achieve the joinder of temporally dispersed claims. For the most part, joinder (whether permissive or mandatory) contemplates individual joinder, and it is often difficult to determine the identity of future plaintiffs. That difficulty can be offset through the representational nature of the class action, in which known future claimants represent others that are similarly situated. But here a second stumbling block occurs: How can putative claims that by definition have not yet ripened be litigated to conclusion? The answer is that they cannot.

---

271. *Cf.* Amchem Prod., Inc. v. Windsor, 521 U.S. 591, 612-13, 628 (1997) (noting without deciding ripeness, standing, and notice problems in class action that tried to resolve future claims). On the requirements of standing, see *supra* n.37 and accom-panying text.

272. *See* Ortiz v. Fibreboard Corp., 527 U.S. 815, 845-46 (1999) (noting without deciding Seventh Amendment issue).

2. Preclusion through Bankruptcy Discharge

Preclusion is arguably a more fruitful approach. Preclusion binds the future claimants to the outcome of the present litigation; it does not require that the claims yet be ripe. But preclusion too has its limits. To begin with, preclusion is rarely possible in the absence of joinder. If precluding a nonparty from asserting a present claim violates due process, as *Richards v. Jefferson County* says, then binding a nonparty with no present claim faces an even greater constitutional challenge. Not only must the *Richards* hurdle be overcome, but the problem of giving constitutionally effective notice to the future claimants must also be solved.

As *Richards* recognized, however, preclusion without joinder may be possible within a specialized scheme such as bankruptcy. If bankruptcy was able to preclude future claims, whether through a discharge or some comparable device, then it might become a preferred method for dealing with the problem. Since 1982, when a then-solvent Johns-Manville took the unprecedented step of filing for bankruptcy in order to find an answer to the burden of future claims, considerable intellectual energy has gone into this project.

One of the first difficulties encountered in bankruptcy is the language of the statute. A bankruptcy court can only discharge a claim.[273] "Claim" is defined as a "right to payment, whether or not such right is reduced to judgment, liquidated, unliquidated, fixed, contingent, matured, unmatured, disputed, undisputed, legal, equitable, secured or unsecured."[274] Such a capacious definition could certainly be read to include future claims, but it would not need to be read so broadly. Unless future claims can be discharged, however, corporate defendants would emerge at the other end of reorganization with another crushing queue of claims, and would have no incentive to seek bankruptcy protection.

In dealing with the future plaintiff problem, different courts have developed different tests for a "claim."[275] The first is the accrued state action test, which requires that a claim be ripe under the applicable law; on this definition, no future claims could be discharged. A second is the wrongful conduct test, which expands "claim" to include any injuries that result from the debtor's pre-bankruptcy conduct; here, as long as the debtor has ceased its wrongful behavior before the bankruptcy, future claims will be

---

273. *See* 11 U.S.C. §§ 523, 727, 1141.

274. 11 U.S.C. § 101(5)(A).

275. For a description of these tests, see Epstein v. Official Comm. of Unsecured Creditors of the Estate of Piper Aircraft Corp., 58 F.3d 1573 (11th Cir. 1995).

discharged. A third, intermediate test is the "pre-petition relation-ship" test, which requires that the victim have had some contact with or exposure to the defendant's wrongful behavior before the discharge, even if that contact or exposure has not yet resulted in injury. This test sweeps many future claims within the preclusive discharge, but not all. A distinction needs to be made between "present futures" — those with present exposure to the wrongful conduct but no present injury — and "future futures" — those who have neither been exposed to the defendant's product or other wrongful behavior nor suffered any injury. The pre-petition relationship test can lead to the discharge of "present future" claims, but not to the discharge of "future future" claims.

Assuming that the definition of claim brings the future claims within the scope of the bankruptcy discharge, other problems arise. First, there are practical problems with fitting future claims into the bankruptcy process. As we have seen, it is important to estimate and value claims accurately for a number of purposes, including making a judgment about the feasibility of the reorganization plan, determining whether two-thirds of a class's votes in value support the plan, and ensuring a fair and equitable distribution of assets. But estimation and valuation of future claims is an imprecise science at best. Similarly, a class's approval vote on a reorganization plan is complicated the presence of future claims. Since the future members do not hold present claims, they are probably not entitled to vote on the reorganization plan. Assuming that they could, communicating with them about their right to vote would be difficult. Moreover, only those claimants that will in fact develop injuries should be able to vote on the plan, but determining who the true voting members are is impossible.

Second, in order for the discharge to be consistent with due process requirements, some notice and opportunity to be heard must be accorded the future claimants. Notifying people who are not injured, and securing representation of their diverse interests, has proven to be a great challenge. The vehicle used in the Manville bankruptcy and in bankruptcies that have been patterned on it has been the appointment of a "Legal Representative." This representative is usually a lawyer, not a future claimant. The representative's responsibility is to participate in negotiations among the debtor, the trade creditors, the equity holders, and the already-injured victims in order to make sure that the interests of future victims are not overlooked in the reorganization plan.

The role of the legal representative is not the same as that of a class representative, and the lack of a constituency to whom the representative is accountable has led to frequent criticisms of the role.[276] Without a portfolio of claims for which he or she is directly responsible, the representative is ineffective as a litigation force. Almost inevitably, therefore, the representative becomes involved in negotiations to settle the future claims. The usual template, created in the Manville reorganization and followed thereafter, is to create a trust for the benefit of the future claimants. The debtor commits a certain amount of cash or stock to fund the trust, which then becomes the exclusive entity from whom future claimants may seek compensation. The administration of the trust, the terms of payment, and the opportunities for a jury trial vary with each trust, whose fundamental terms are negotiated by the legal representative and the other bankruptcy participants.

Typically, victims with present filed claims, victims with present but unfiled claims, and future victims must all look to the trust for compensation. The debtor is discharged (to the extent that the debtor can be discharged); to the extent that a discharge cannot be accomplished, the court issues a "channeling injunction" that orders future victims to seek compensation from the trust. Obviously, the legality of the channeling injunction, which effectively operates as a discharge, is a critical question; if such an injunction is not legal, then future victims with non-dischargeable claims can simply sue the debtor as their claims accrue. Thus far, the propriety of channeling injunctions has not been definitively determined. Congress took a small step in this direction when it passed in 1994 a new provision providing for the discharge of all future asbestos claims that met the type of "legal representative/trust mechanism" criteria present in Manville, and for the recognition of all previously entered channeling injunctions consistent with this structure.[277] But Congress did not authorize the discharge of non-asbestos future claims, a fact which leaves the more general question of the preclusion of future claims through bankruptcy in some doubt.[278]

On balance, therefore, the use of bankruptcy presents serious questions that have not yet been fully worked out under the law.

3. The Settlement Class Action

The third and final method of handling future claims is settlement. As we have seen, settlement of these claims can occur in bankruptcy, but in many cases a defendant would prefer not to go

---

276. *See, e.g.,* Thomas A. Smith, *A Capital Markets Approach to Mass Tort Bankruptcy,* 104 YALE L.J. 367 (1994).

277. 11 U.S.C. §§ 524(g),(h).

278. On the general question of using bankruptcy to handle future claims, see TIDMARSH & TRANGSRUD, *supra* n.14, at 752-69.

through bankruptcy in order to settle the claims. In most cases, it would be impossible for a defendant to identify and then individually settle with each future claimant. The issue is whether there is any way other than bankruptcy to collect the future claimants and settle their cases *en masse*.

Enter again the settlement class action, but now with its focus the settlement of future rather than present claims. If some of the future victims could negotiate a settlement on behalf of all, then perhaps they could file a class action designed to settle, rather than to litigate, future claims; they could serve as class representatives for the class, thus avoiding the need to find and settle with each future class member individually. If the court were to approve the settlement as fair, adequate, and reasonable under Rule 23(e), then all the future claimants (in the context of a (b)(1) or (b)(2) mandatory class) or at least those future claimants who do not opt out (in the context of a (b)(3) class) could have their claims disposed of without the need for repetitive future litigation. If the present claims can also be aggregated and settled at the same time, a defendant can purchase true global peace.

Along with this promise, however, come a number of concerns. The first is simply that a (b)(3) settlement class action cannot buy global peace; a sufficient number of future members may opt out, thus eliminating the hope for an end to repetitive litigation. A more serious concern is collusion, or at least inadequacy of representation. By definition, none of the class members is yet hurt, nor can they yet carry through on the threat of litigation. Particularly when the claims are immature, appropriate settlement values may be hard to determine. Even with mature claims, evaluating a settlement in advance of an actual injury is difficult; compensable losses and judgment values of cases change over time. A defendant can engage in a reverse auction and shop a low-ball settlement proposal among various claimants and law firms; a firm that stands to gain a large fee if it accepts the offer and acts as counsel for the class, but nothing if another firm accepts the offer, has a powerful private incentive to acquiesce. The settlement must be careful to treat future claimants equitably.

These are not the only obstacles of settlement class actions for future claims. Constitutional questions such as standing, the effectiveness of notice to class members who may have no knowledge of their exposure or potential injury, and the scope of territorial jurisdiction over absent future claimants cannot be avoided with settlement class actions. When the state laws, the injuries, the plaintiffs' lifestyles, and the nature of the wrongful behavior vary among class members, the ability of the class representatives to satisfy the typicality and adequacy requirements of Rule 23 emerges as a central issue. Finally, there exists the possibility that such a settlement class action might impermissibly deprive future plaintiffs of their right to a jury trial, circumvent the statutory protections of the bankruptcy law, or otherwise effectively alter the parties' substantive rights in violation of the Rules Enabling Act.[279]

Twice in the last few years, the Supreme Court has evaluated against these concerns settlement class actions that involved future claimants. In both cases — *Amchem Products, Inc. v. Windsor*[280] and *Ortiz v. Fibreboard Corp.*[281] — the Supreme Court reversed the class certification on which a settlement had been based. As we have already discussed, both cases found defects under Rule 23: *Amchem's* class could not be supported due to (a)(4) and (b)(3) problems, and *Ortiz* could not be supported due to (b)(1)(B) problems (which also reverberated into (a)(4) problems that the Court did not examine in detail).[282] The Court also noted, without needing to decide, the collusion, standing, notice, territorial jurisdiction, bankruptcy preemption, jury trial, and Rules Enabling Act concerns in one or both cases.

Neither *Amchem* nor *Oritz* categorically ruled out settlement class actions for future claims, but both set a high bar. *Amchem* particularly cautioned about the need for vigilance in ensuring that the class action met the requirements of Rule 23(a) and (b); it was not enough for a class action merely to satisfy the implicit, "chancellor's foot" requirement of Rule 23(e) that the settlement be fair, adequate, and reasonable.[283] This vigilance is especially necessary because settlement class actions of future claims do not carry the usual threat (and leverage) of litigation, or the ability to adjust the class as the case unfolds. Some of the criteria of Rules 23(a) and (b) might receive less attention in the settlement context; for instance, the Court stated that the manageability criterion of Rule 23(b)(3)(D) would have little influence because the class action would not be tried.[284] "But other specifications of the Rule — those designed to protect absentees by blocking unwarranted or overbroad class definitions — demand undiluted, even heightened, attention in the settlement context."[285]

Both *Amchem* and *Ortiz* also demanded that the structure of the settlement class action account for variations in the future claimants'

---

279. *See supra* n.179 and accompanying text.

280. 521 U.S. 591 (1997).

281. 527 U.S. 815 (1999).

282. *See supra* nn.100-02, 133-39

and accompanying text.

283. *Amchem*, 521 U.S. at 621.

284. *Id.* at 620.

285. *Id.*

individual legal positions. The class cannot be treated as a monolith, with everyone getting the same remedy, when some claimants may have a stronger legal posture or a need to receive inflation-protected dollars. But accounting for such variations may require multiple classes and class representatives, and these new interest groups may make the successful negotiation of a global settlement impossible. Nor can the problem be solved by providing future claimants a "back-end opt-out right," which allows class members to exclude themselves at the time their injuries accrue. Although this tactic helps to reduce the unfairness to far-future claimants, the defendant has limited incentive to offer this arrangement. In any event, both *Amchem* and *Ortiz* contained back-end opt-out rights; *Amchem*'s right was modest, while *Ortiz*'s right had far fewer strings attached to it. Neither back-end opt-out right prevented the Court from rejecting the class action.

None of this means that the settlement of future claims through Rule 23 is impossible. In *Amchem*, the Court went out of its way to affirm the use of settlement class actions in appropriate circumstances. But the circumstances are certainly limited, and even then constitutional and other hurdles must be cleared. The place in which the settlement class for future victims is least likely to be successful is the situation in which the future claimant problem most demands a solution: the temporally dispersed mass tort.[286]

E. CONCLUSION

This chapter brings to a close the first critical task in most complex cases: addressing the problem of structural complexity by achieving the optimal level of aggregation for related claims. Prior chapters already revealed difficulties in the aggregation of related cases that have been separately filed; many of these difficulties defied easy solution. In this chapter we encountered another central aggregation problem that many complex cases pose: finding a way to aggregate or otherwise jointly handle cases that have not yet been filed with those that have been filed. Not surprisingly, no easy solutions emerge here either.

It is fair to say that the principle of litigant autonomy still holds considerable sway in the nonparty context — far more sway that autonomy holds with intrasystem or intersystem aggregation. Perhaps this is as it should be. Removing a case filed in one system to another system constitutes a certain intrusion on litigants'

[286.] For a look at some post-*Amchem* and post-*Ortiz* cases either upholding or rejecting settlement class actions, see JAY TIDMARSH & ROGER H. TRANGSRUD, COMPLEX LITIGATION AND THE ADVERSARY SYSTEM, 64-65 (Supp. 2000).

autonomy, but forcing someone who has never filed suit into someone else's case is an entirely different matter.

Whether appropriately or not, our system lacks fully effective mandatory joinder and preclusion devices. Complex cases often involve hundreds or thousands of people still sitting on the sidelines. With the exception of bankruptcy, preclusion doctrines are simply not a major force in this area; and bankruptcy is highly specialized. Mandatory joinder devices such as Rule 19 or interpleader, or a device such as Rule 24 intervention, are simply too limited in scope to sweep all claimants into a single case. The class action can do so, but it operates as a truly mandatory joinder device only in the relatively restricted circumstances of the (b)(1) and (b)(2) classes. Moreover, the class action, which substitutes the vigor of the representative for the will of the individual, constitutes a very grave inroad on litigant autonomy and a great tax on the limited resources of defendants and the court; understandably, therefore, the class action is hedged in by important limitations that reduce its effectiveness as an aggregation tool. Future claimants, when they exist, create further joinder and preclusion conundrums.

This is the unsatisfying note on which we leave the problem of structural complexity. No magic bullet of aggregation presently exists; no Holy Grail awaits us in the following chapters. Our solutions are imperfect and incomplete. The conflicting pulls of our system's aspirations run deep, and perhaps have no ultimate reconciliation.

Chapter 6

PRETRIAL COMPLEXITY

In addition to structuring the case, the pretrial phase of litigation develops the legal and factual issues for trial. At this point, one of the assumptions of American procedure that we have until now largely ignored — jury trial — becomes important. The existence of a lay jury, as well as the language of the Seventh Amendment's right to a civil jury trial,[1] largely dictate a single trial event in which all legal and factual issues are resolved. This may seem self-evident to Americans, who have grown up with this system. Much of the world, however, employs a very different mode of trial: the continuous trial, in which the development of the legal and factual issues is interspersed with their resolution at a series of "trial" hearings.

We will return to jury trial and its exact limits in the next chapter. For now, we take the jury trial as a given. In terms of procedural design, this means that the full development of legal and factual issues must occur before trial. "Development" of these issues consists first of identifying them, then of exploring their merits, then of winnowing out the issues that lack merit, and finally of preparing the meritorious issues for final disposition at trial.

It may be impossible to develop a pretrial system that perfectly accomplishes each of these goals and is not prohibitively expensive. Trade-offs are inevitable. At common law, the writ system, first

---

1. The Seventh Amendment reads in full:

> In suits at common law, where the value of the controversy shall exceed twenty dollars, the right of trial by jury shall be preserved, and no fact tried by jury shall be otherwise re-examined in any Court of the United States, than according to the rules of the common law.

The Seventh Amendment has never been held applicable to state courts, though virtually every state has a comparable, if not stronger, jury trial guarantee. In federal court, the first clause requires the presence of juries in certain cases (*see infra* pp. 248-53), and the second (or "re-examination") clause makes it difficult to convene different juries to hear different aspects of the same case (*see infra* pp. 261-62).

developed in the Middle Ages, attempted to winnow the entire case to a single legal or factual issue through the exchange of a series of pleadings. Unfortunately, the system neglected entirely the factual and legal exposition of the case, was poorly adapted to multi-issue or multi-party disputes, was unmerciful toward procedural missteps, and often resulted in decisions based on grounds other than the case's true merits. The code pleading system, which replaced the writ system in many American jurisdictions in the nineteenth century, still relied almost entirely on pleadings for pretrial development. It did a somewhat better job than the writ system in terms of developing factual issues, but it too relied on draconian and prolix rules that led to many decisions on pleading technicalities rather than on the merits of the dispute.

Standing in stark contrast to these pleadings-based pretrial systems was the parallel system that applied to suits in equity. Equity was oriented toward achieving complete justice on the merits of the case. Pleading was intended to be (though it was not always so in fact) less rigid and technical, and there were opportunities to discover the facts of the dispute. Unlike the common law system, equity did not usually employ juries, and the evidence (whether documentary or testimonial) was reduced to writing before being submitted to the chancellor. Hence, the chancellor was able to use the continuous trial method. But equity was marred by tardiness, expense, and the inevitable bureaucracy and occasional corruption of concentrated power.

When our Federal Rules of Civil Procedure were adopted in 1938, the drafters married what they perceived to be the best of the common law (a culminating trial with live testimony) with the best of equity (generous pleading rules and opportunities to discover the disputed facts). Then they radicalized the pretrial system. The result for the pretrial process was notice pleading and full-fledged discovery — sort of the equity system on steroids. Taken together, these changes were designed to ensure that decisions were made on the merits rather than on procedural technicalities and miscues. Notice pleading drained the pleading process of the adversarial gamesmanship of writ and code pleading; as long as a pleading gave short and plain notice of a claim or defense to the other side, the case would proceed to a decision on the merits. Discovery, on a scale and with a panoply of device never before harnessed in one procedural system, was intended to lay bare the true state of the facts in advance of trial, thus narrowing the dispute only to those truly in contest and eliminating the common law's trial by surprise. Lacking in the Federal Rules' design, however, were any significant issue-narrowing devices; motions to dismiss or for summary judgment were useful to decide some case-dispositive legal issues and some very lopsided factual disputes, but their utility was limited by high threshold standards. Instead, the drafters believed that unmeritorious legal and factual issues would melt away in the full sunlight of the facts that discovery would uncover.

The drafters' faith that such a hybrid system would work, their belief in objective facts, and their choice to leave adversaries largely in charge of the pretrial process seem rather idealistic in retrospect. It was complex litigation that first exposed the system's fundamental defects. In many complex cases, myriad potential legal theories, millions of potentially relevant pages of documents, thousands of persons with potentially useful information, and lawyers seeking private advantage at every turn threatened to turn a pretrial process committed to development of each and every dispute on its individual merits into a morass that was unlikely within a reasonable time frame to see the light of trial; and if a trial occurred, it was even more unlikely that the trial could proceed in the short and orderly fashion demanded by the common law system of lay juries. This problem was exacerbated by the synergy between voluminous information and often amorphous principles of law. On the one hand, ambiguous or broad legal standards (like negligence, fraud, or monopoly) created a demand for any information that might make proof of the standard more or less likely. On the other hand, the quantity of available information seemed to spawn even more legal issues, which created new demands for information and then spun out new possible legal theories. When the parties were left in charge of the pretrial process and the stakes were high, it was difficult to break this cycle of factual and legal expansion. Complex cases appeared to take on the appearance of equity's worst-case scenario.

An obvious response to this problem was to create a separate pretrial track for complex disputes. But this alternative challenged some of the critical assumptions on which our procedural system was built: trans-substantivity (broadly understood to mean that cases should receive comparable procedures so that outcomes are not markedly different across different categories of cases), a single all-issues trial, and adversary-driven pleading and pretrial. Another response was to effect smaller changes in pretrial procedure that tried to maintain the general procedural template used in other cases, with some tinkering at the margins. But the success of this alternative in the face of intractable massive litigation was uncertain.

As we shall see, judges largely chose the second, incremental approach to complex cases. To see how and where these changes occurred, we divide this chapter into three sections: first, a section on creating the structure for the lawyers and judicial officers that provides the best opportunity for the pretrial process in complex cases to be successful; second, a section on techniques that might be employed to narrow issues during the pretrial stage; and third, a section on techniques that might be employed to discover, in a cost-effective manner, the voluminous information present in many complex cases.

As we examine these issues, two matters bear emphasis. First, recall that the starting point of this book was simply to understand and catalogue the multiple ways in which cases can be "complex." Therefore, no necessary connection exists between complexity in the pretrial phase and the structural complexity that we have just finished examining. Indeed, cases that present no structural issues at all may present enormous issues of pretrial complexity; think, for instance, of two-party suits such as *United States v. AT&T* or *United States v. Microsoft*. The converse can also be true; cases that present great structural challenges may not be especially difficult to shepherd through the pretrial process once they are aggregated. Nonetheless, there is a significant overlap between the two forms of complexity; large aggregated cases often present a serious challenge at the pretrial stage as well. For now, however, we will not attempt to suggest what the connections between these two forms of complexity might be; we return to that question in the Epilogue.

Second, as we describe some of the techniques used to move a large case through the pretrial phase, you may notice that similar techniques are now being employed in routine cases. This is not coincidental. When the procedural template of the Federal Rules failed to meet the needs of complex cases, courts and parties began to freelance away from the standard model. Some (though not all) of those innovations have proven successful enough to be incorporated into the standard model, a fact that has both moved the Federal Rules away from their original design and has reduced the distance (and the trans-substantive tension) between the routine and the complex. Whether this movement is a warranted or positive development for ordinary cases is a legitimate question to consider as we explore the material on pretrial complexity.

Nowhere is this question more evident than in one of the great debates in modern American procedure: the merits of "case management." Case management refers to the more active involvement of judges in the pretrial process — especially in the narrowing of issues but also in the streamlining of discovery. Case management began as a response to the intractable problems of several large post-World War II antitrust cases. A 1951 report (usually called the Prettyman Report) urged judges in these types of cases to abandon the passivity of the standard adversarial model, and to exercise "rigid control from the time the complaint is filed."[2] Once case management appeared to enjoy some success in complex cases, its proponents began to advocate for adoption of stronger judicial controls to curb the perceived excesses in more routine matters.

To the extent that pretrial powers accrete to the managerial judge, they reduce the traditional prerogatives of the lawyers. As the judge obtains greater powers, of course, he or she has more tasks to accomplish, and more need of assistance in performing these tasks. Hence, case management forces a re-invention of the relationships between lawyer and client, and among the judge, the judicial adjunct, the lawyer, and the body politic. In the next section, we explore those relationships in broad context; the subsequent sections provide much of the rich detail of various case management devices and their effect on the traditional form of pretrial litigation.

A. RESTRUCTURING THE LAWYERS AND THE JUDICIARY IN COMPLEX CASES

Party control of the pretrial process is no minor matter. Party control during pretrial is an integral — and arguably a defining — characteristic of a well-functioning adversarial system. It strongly advances the notions of personal freedom and individual autonomy on which the system is based. Thus, in an adversarial pretrial process, the parties' lawyers bear primary responsibility for the specific tasks involved in developing and narrowing factual and legal issues. Any move away from the lawyers' control over these tasks is also a movement away from the adversarial assumption of our procedural system and its deeper philosophical underpinnings.

Such a move also raises an obvious question: If the lawyers are not to control the process, then who is to control it? When we look at the other players in the litigation enterprise (the judge, the jury, or the parties themselves), the only realistic possibility is the judge. Is the shift in power from private lawyers to a public functionary a wise idea? Or a necessary evil? If the judge is given more power in complex cases, must he or she also be given the power in more routine cases, in which party control works tolerably well, in order to maintain a trans-substantive system of rules?

1. Restructuring Lawyers

In a classic adversarial system, each party is entitled to be

---

2. Report of the Judicial Conference of the United States on Procedure in Anti-Trust and Other Protracted Cases (1951), *reprinted in* 13 F.R.D. 62, 66 (1953).

represented by his or her own lawyer, who is ethically bound to represent the client's interests with vigor. In a large two-party suit, such as *United States v. Microsoft,* this basic model can continue to operate. As we have seen, however, many complex matters involve the aggregation of hundreds of cases. When those cases have already been filed, the adversarial model suggests that each party should still be entitled to representation by a lawyer attending to that party's interests. When a nonparty is forced to join existing litigation, adversarial theory would suggest that this person is also entitled to select his or her own lawyer.

At a practical level, however, individual representation of each aggregated party's interests is unrealistic, unworkable, and inefficient. To begin with, in most large-scale cases, a few law firms represent the bulk of the plaintiffs; various well-established systems of referral and the high start-up costs for any individual lawyer combine to funnel cases to a few firms with expertise in that type of case. These referrals are, to some extent, inconsistent with the adversarial model. Counsel may be located in a remote city, may never actually meet the client, and may not be knowledgeable about the particular interests of an individual client. Such a remote lawyer's "client" is, in a sense, an amalgam of the interests of all the clients. It is even possible that, in order to achieve the greatest good for the greatest number, counsel might be forced to take positions that are antithetical to a particular client's position. Of course, these difficulties are offset, and the client's theoretical autonomy is preserved, by the client's consent to a referral — though it might be questioned in practice whether a client truly understands the consequences of having a case referred to distant counsel.[3]

To the extent that the private referral system does not function to limit representation significantly, the logistical problems of coordinating the schedules of hundreds of lawyers threaten to slow discovery and other pretrial matters to a crawl. The court would be inundated with briefs on every motion of importance. The costs in terms of lawyer time for pretrial issues would be staggering. What judicial response is possible, then, when consensual referrals fail to cure the problem of a cacophony of lawyers?

In traditional adversarial theory, the answer is "nothing"; each person is entitled to be represented by a lawyer of his or her

---

3. The difficulties might also be partially offset by the reality that even in litigation conducted in accordance with the traditional adversarial model, contact between lawyer and client and vigorous representation of the client's interests may be less than the model presumes. *See* Deborah R. Hensler, *Resolving Mass Toxic Torts: Myths and Realities,* 1989 U. ILL. L. REV. 89.

choosing.[4] Until the mid-1970's that answer also appeared to be the prevailing attitude of the courts. Although some courts encouraged the plaintiffs to select a "lead counsel" or a steering committee of counsel,[5] only one case — *MacAlister v. Guterma*[6] — clearly gave the trial judge the discretion to appoint a lead counsel for an entire group of claimants. In *MacAlister*, however, the district court had refused to do so, and its decision was upheld on appeal. Thus, *MacAlister*'s arguable appointment power was dicta. During the mid-1970's, however, a sudden spate of appellate decisions began to rely on *MacAlister*'s dicta and affirm the decision of district courts to appoint lead counsel or committees of counsel in complex cases.[7] Within very short order, a sea change in traditional adversarial theory had been effected. District courts routinely began, without the clients' consent, to restructure the attorney-client relationship to meet the needs of the big case.[8]

No statute expressly gives such authority to the district courts.[9] Neither does any Federal Rule of Civil Procedure (except, arguably, Rule 23[10]). But *MacAlister* had opined that the authority for restructuring the parties' relationship to their lawyers was the court's "inherent powers" to control litigation, and later courts have accepted that judgment.

Courts have exercised this power (assuming, for the moment, its existence) to establish a variety of counsel relationships. The least intrusive restructuring is to create a liaison counsel relationship. In this arrangement, each party is still represented by counsel of his or

4. *Cf.* Richardson-Merrell, Inc. v. Koller, 472 U.S. 424, 441 (1985) (Brennan, J., concurring) ("A fundamental premise of the adversary system is that individuals have the right to retain the attorney of their choice to represent their interests in judicial proceedings."); *id.* at 442 (Stevens, J., concurring) ("Everyone must agree that the litigant's freedom to choose his own lawyer in a civil case is a fundamental right.").

5. *See* MANUAL FOR COMPLEX LITIGATION § 1.92 (1972).

6. 263 F.2d 65 (2d Cir. 1958).

7. *See, e.g.*, Katz v. Realty Equities Corp., 521 F.2d 1354 (2d Cir. 1975); Vincent v. Hughes Air West, Inc., 557 F.2d 759 (9th Cir. 1977).

8. *See, e.g.*, MANUAL FOR COMPLEX LITIGATION (THIRD) § 20.22

(1995).

9. The Private Securities Litigation Reform Act of 1995 discusses certain qualifications for class counsel, and authorizes the lead plaintiff(s) to choose such counsel. 15 U.S.C. § 78u-4. But the statute does not allow federal courts to appoint lead counsel.

10. As we have seen, a court has long been thought to be able to determine the adequacy of counsel by implication from Rule 23(a)(4). *See supra* pp. 118-22. Rule 23 does not, however, explicitly give the court the power to select that counsel. As of this writing, however, there is a proposal to amend Rule 23 to add a new Rule 23(g), which would give a district court explicit power to appoint counsel not necessarily of the class representatives' choosing.

her choice, and the court designates one counsel to act as the liaison between the court and all other lawyers with similar interests. The liaison counsel provides notice to other counsel of actions taken by the court or the opposing side, and possibly coordinates the filing of co-counsel's papers with the court. This arrangement is not a marked departure from the adversarial system — and one that may be increasingly unnecessary in a world of e-mail, fax, docketing software, and Internet postings.

Somewhat more intrusive on the standard adversarial relationship is a court's creation of a committee of counsel to handle the pretrial process on behalf of an entire group. The court will often select as members of the committee those lawyers who have the most individual clients, but sometimes other considerations enter the picture. Committee members may have been especially adept in handling pretrial aspects of similar prior litigation, may be in a position to help finance the litigation, or may represent particular points of view about how the litigation should be handled. Committees may be constituted by function, with some members handling depositions, others covering motions, others conducting settlement negotiations, and so on. Although the existence of a committee creates a risk that the interests of some individuals in the represented group will not receive adequate attention, a well-selected committee ensures that diverse views are likely to be represented.

From the viewpoint of the adversarial ideal, the most intrusive counsel structure is the appointment of a lead counsel: a single lawyer or firm that represents all of the interests of a selected group during the pretrial process.[11] Obviously the use of a single lead counsel creates the greatest risk that individual interests will be neglected in favor of the greatest good, and also puts the greatest ethical pressures on the lawyer who must find and speak with a corporate voice for all those whom he or she represents.

A court is not required to adopt any of these structures, nor is it bound to adopt only one model if it restructures the counsel relationship. It may, for instance, appoint a lead counsel to handle discovery, and a committee to conduct settlement negotiations. Nor does the use of one attorney structure during pretrial require that the court adopt the same structure at trial — although that is often the case.

For many years, courts essentially accepted the counsel structure upon which the lawyers themselves agreed. This acquiescence, however, led to allegations that groups of lawyers were engaged in

---

11. As we will see *infra* ch.7, nn.3-7 and accompanying text. Courts can also appoint a lead counsel (often called trial counsel) to try a case on behalf of a group of litigants. Our present focus, however, is on the courts' powers to appoint counsel for pretrial proceedings.

closed-door horsetrading — perhaps guaranteeing favors to some firms in return for their support on the proposed counsel structure — that neglected the best interests of their clients but garnered greater fees for themselves.[12] As a result, more recent cases and authorities have urged judges to become actively engaged in the selection of an appropriate counsel structure.[13] Some courts have put the counsel position up for bid, hoping to find the most competitive arrangement for the represented parties.[14] Even more radical proposals, such as allowing a single entity to buy an entire group's claim and then control the litigation through its chosen counsel, have been made but not yet adopted by any court.[15]

Perhaps lost in the widespread acceptance of, and proposals for more radical reform to, restructured counsel arrangements is the wisdom of allowing the court to become involved in structuring these arrangements. In the first place, the restructuring of counsel is an almost entirely one-sided affair. Courts have not imposed lead counsel or committee of counsel arrangements on defendants; at most, defendants operate with a liaison counsel arrangement, and are left to form consensual counsel groupings. Perhaps the differences in circumstance among defendants and the potential for cross-claims between them justifies the courts' reluctance to restructure defense interests, but the restructuring of plaintiffs' relationships creates a similar potential for conflicts of interest.

Relatedly, the use of lead counsel seeks to make a case behave like a two-party lawsuit. A single counsel cannot effectively represent inconsistent positions; inevitably, counsel will need to determine the "best" position in terms of the overall good of the represented group. But the advocacy of the best position obliterates nuances among similar cases, and neglects potentially promising factual and legal theories that multiple representations would have uncovered.

---

12. For one exploration of these potential problems, see *In re* Fine Paper Antitrust Litig., 98 F.R.D. 48 (E.D. Pa. 1983), *rev'd in part*, 751 F.2d 562 (3d Cir. 1989). A good general discussion is John C. Coffee, Jr., *The Regulation of Entrepreneurial Litigation: Balancing Fairness and Efficiency in the Large Class Action*, 54 U. CHI. L. REV. 877 (1987).

13. *See* MANUAL, *supra* n.8, § 20.22.

14. The seminal case is *In re* Oracle Sec. Litig., 132 F.R.D. 538

(N.D. Cal. 1990). Bids often vary significantly, meaning that a court can indirectly influence the outcome of a case by choosing one counsel arrangement over another. *See* JAY TIDMARSH & ROGER H. TRANGSRUD, COMPLEX LITIGATION AND THE ADVERSARY SYSTEM 888-89 (1998).

15. *See* Jonathon R. Macey & Geoffrey P. Miller, *The Plaintiffs' Attorney's Role in Class Action and Derivative Litigation: Economic Analysis and Recommendations for Reform*, 58 U. CHI. L. REV. 1 (1991).

A committee of counsel arrangement that includes an array of cases reduces, but does not eliminate, these risks.

Indeed, arrangements such as lead counsel and committee of counsel create unique ethical pressures for the lawyers representing an aggregated group. The ethical norm of the adversarial system is zealous representation of the individual client. When a single counsel or committee of counsel represents an entire group, it becomes impossible to represent each *individual* zealously; instead, the lawyers must seek to represent the *group* zealously. But our present ethical theory does not easily allow the lawyer to make the translation from individual to group; until it does, practice inevitably grates against theory.[16] As one set of commentators has observed, "[e]thical questions lie at the very heart of complex litigation, and no proposed solution for complex litigation can be deemed adequate unless the solution works out its ethical implications."[17]

Counsel's establishment of a single litigative position for the group once again raises issues of trans-substantive equity. The substitution of group arguments for individualized arguments may well result in a different outcome for some of the clients represented by a single set of lawyers in comparison to clients represented by a lawyer of their choosing. Such outcome-determinative potential requires justification, as does the departure from the standard adversarial ideal.

Court opinions, however, provide little in the way of justification. One of the judge's most significant case management powers is the creation of new counsel structures, but the decision to exercise these powers is subject to review only for an abuse of discretion. Should a court be able to exercise this discretion whenever it believes that a case might be more efficiently handled on a group basis? Or only when there is a breakdown in the ability of adversarial, individualized representation to develop the factual and legal issues during pretrial? Answers to these questions are never overtly forthcoming in the courts' opinions, but these answers may go a long way toward determining the legitimate boundaries of case management.

---

16. The most complete and thoughtful attempt to craft a set of ethical norms to govern large-scale litigation is JACK B. WEINSTEIN, INDIVIDUAL JUSTICE IN MASS TORT LITIGATION (1995) (calling for use of communitarian or communicitarian ethics). The general issue of ethical norms, conflicts of interest, and disqualification of counsel in complex cases is considered in TIDMARSH & TRANGSRUD, *supra* n.14, at 899-925. *See also supra* ch.5, nn.111-14 and accompanying text.

17. TIDMARSH & TRANGSRUD, *supra* n.14, at 914.

2. Restructuring the Judiciary

In the standard adversarial model, the judge remains neutral and passive. Since the judge must be capable of entering the trial with no predispositions about the case, it is especially crucial that this distance be maintained during the pretrial phase; therefore, pretrial development must be left to the lawyers. Case management stands this concept on its head, and demands the early, active, and ongoing involvement of the judge in pretrial affairs. But case management can take significant amounts of judicial time, especially in complex cases. Hence, if case management is to be successful, a judicial structure that creates the necessary time must be established.

In complex cases, three different judicial structures have been attempted. First, the district judge can bring in additional judges to handle certain aspects of the pretrial process. Second, magistrate judges — who are appointed for a term of years to perform a range of judicial tasks delegated by the district court — can be harnessed to the task of managing a complex case. Third, special masters — who are usually appointed on an *ad hoc* basis to help out in a specific matter — can be used. To the extent that an additional judge, a magistrate judge, or a special master replaces the district judge as case manager, all of these options preserve the district judge's neutrality for trial. Beyond that common advantage, however, these various potential solutions present different advantages and drawbacks.

In the case of using another Article III judge, the drawbacks are usually disabling. If the point of employing judicial adjuncts is to free up judicial time to engage in managerial oversight of the case, the substitution of one judge for another results in no overall savings of judicial resources. Therefore, although other judges have been successfully employed for very discrete tasks (such as mediating a settlement conference or ruling on a time-intensive motion), the use of a second judge to assist in case management is a relatively rare phenomenon.

The use of a magistrate judge is more common. Like district judges, magistrate judges are usually fully engaged by a range of other matters, such as arraignments, misdemeanor trials, referrals from the district judge, and handling their own docket of civil cases in which the parties have consented to a trial by magistrate. Like district judges, magistrate judges do not necessarily bring expertise in the subject area into the courtroom. Moreover, in many districts a magistrate judge does not work exclusively for a single judge, so it is difficult for a magistrate judge, who depends on the district judges' good graces for re-appointment every seven years, to focus single-mindedly on one judge's big case. Hence, magistrate judges have not proven to be a complete solution to increased judicial involvement in pretrial proceedings.

That leaves *ad hoc* judicial officers. Long before the phenomenon of complex litigation, the Chancellor had used court functionaries called "masters" to assist in the many tasks involved in a suit in equity. Though somewhat changed, this tradition has survived in this country, where suits in equity often have used "special masters" — usually private lawyers with specialized knowledge in the relevant field — to handle the trial or determine the remedy in some particularly difficult cases. In a more limited fashion, masters were also used in common law actions.

Acknowledging this tradition, Rule 53 of the Federal Rules of Civil Procedure authorizes the appointment of special masters in both jury-tried and bench-tried cases. The precise standard under which a Rule 53 reference is permitted is less than crystalline. According to Rule 53(b), "[a] reference to a master shall be the exception and not the rule." In cases tried to a jury, "a reference shall be made only when the issues are complicated." In cases tried to the bench, "a reference shall be made only upon a showing that some exceptional condition requires it."[18]

Whatever this language means in general, it might seem that Rule 53 is tailor-made for the case management needs of large-scale litigation. But a number of doctrinal, practical, and theoretical problems stand in the way. To begin with, it is not entirely clear that Rule 53 provides federal courts with the power to appoint masters to handle pretrial tasks. A fair reading of Rule 53 as a whole, as well as its placement in the "Trials" section of the Federal Rules, would suggest that the drafters only contemplated the use of masters at or after trial. On the other hand, nothing in the text of Rule 53 specifically excludes a pretrial master.

Courts and commentators are split on the issue. Most believe that Rule 53 authorizes the appointment of pretrial masters. Others do not, but nonetheless believe that courts possess the inherent power (once again!) to appoint a pretrial master.[19]

---

18. There are two exceptions to the "exceptional condition" standard: "matters of account and of difficult computation of damages."

19. The debate and representative positions are summarized in TID-MARSH & TRANGSRUD, *supra* n.14, at 948-49. As of this writing, the Advi-sory Committee for the Federal Rules of Civil Procedure is considering amendments to Rule 53 that would make the authority for pretrial refer-ences explicit and also clarify the standards under which the reference can occur.

The source of authority, if any, is a significant matter partly because it may make a difference in the standard to be applied in appointing a master. Rule 53 uses language intended to ward off routine references to masters; no comparable restriction would necessarily affect an "inherent power" reference. But, you might object, this concern over standards is all much ado about nothing. Even if the "exception" language of Rule 53 prevails, complex cases surely present the exceptional circumstances required.

The stumbling block to this argument is *La Buy v. Howes Leather Co.*,[20] a case whose dicta has exercised an enormous influence in this area. In *La Buy*, a judge confronted with a six-week antitrust trial and a crowded docket referred the trial to a master, who was a local practitioner. The Supreme Court held that this reference so exceeded the district judge's authority under Rule 53 that a writ of mandamus should issue against the reference. The reference constituted "an abdication of the judicial function depriving the parties of a trial before the court on the basic issues involved in the litigation."[21] The "unusual complexity" that the case presented was not a reason to refer the case; on the contrary, it was "an impelling reason for trial before a regular, experienced trial judge rather than before a temporary substitute appointed on an *ad hoc* basis . . . ."[22]

Obviously *La Buy* can be distinguished, for it dealt with a trial reference rather than a pretrial reference. But its basic point that complexity alone is not an adequate reason for a reference makes this distinction less than persuasive. Indeed, *La Buy*'s reasoning suggests that pretrial references in complex cases should be regarded with the same suspicion as trial references. If case management is such a critical function, foisting the task onto someone who enjoys neither the authority, the stature, the experience, nor the life tenure of an Article III judge is problematic. This abdication of judicial authority in important cases may be especially dubious if the master is appointed because of his or her expertise in the type of litigation that the case involves. With expertise can come bias: The master may have other clients that have an interest in the outcome of this type of litigation. Moreover, a master's "job approval" depends on keeping the court and the parties reasonably satisfied with his or her work; the master does not enjoy the life tenure that helps to ameliorate such external pressures for federal judges.

The use of a master may create additional costs in the pretrial process. As private individuals, masters must be compensated for their work. They are often compensated at rates commensurate with

20. 352 U.S. 249 (1957).   22. *Id.* at 259.
21. *Id.* at 256.

their status as law partners or leading academicians. The costs are typically borne not by the court, but by the parties (in accordance with an allocation formula that the court establishes). Aside from the unseemly aspect of parties paying for their justice, the cost of a master can impose pressures on less well-financed litigants; and, if the allocation formula requires one party to bear most of the cost, there also exists the fear that the master will consciously or unconsciously favor the party paying the lion's share of the bill. Of course, if a master's attention to a case creates overall savings to the parties, cost concerns dissipate; but often the use of a master does not create any savings in comparison to active judicial management of the case. The true beneficiaries of a master are the litigants in other cases, who can now count on more of the judge's time. It seems unfair to require the litigants in the big case in essence to subsidize others' justice at the expense of their own.

Similarly, masters may create additional delay. While a master may be able to handle minor decisions without judicial oversight, significant decisions by the master will remain subject to appeal to the district judge. If the parties routinely take advantage of this avenue of review, many matters will need to be argued twice — a prospect that increases both cost and delay.

Finally, as we have seen and will continue to see in this chapter, the manner in which a case is shaped during pretrial often can have a significant effect on the outcome of a case. If the master shapes the case differently than the judge would have, then we find a procedural device in complex cases with the potential to create different outcomes. Once again, we need to find a sufficient reason — aside from mere convenience to the court — to justify differential treatment that flies in the face of our trans-substantive ideal.

These reservations do not mean that references should to masters never occur. Masters can often serve a valuable function. Since they are dedicated to a single case, they can react speedily and save the parties the expense involved in waiting for a judge's ruling. They are almost always knowledgeable about the relevant field of law, which can streamline decisionmaking. When they are delegated routine or ministerial tasks (such as examining documents to determine if they should be disclosed under guidelines established by the judge), masters can help the judge stay focused on the larger picture of shaping the factual and legal development of the case. They can design and implement time-intensive, creative programs to narrow issues, as the special masters did in the *United States v. AT&T* litigation.[23] They can insulate the judge from excessive

---

23. *See infra* n.68 and accompanying text.

pretrial contacts that might threaten the judge's neutrality. They can operate with a degree of informality with which a judge cannot, perhaps having *ex parte* conversations with one side in order to get a process moving forward. As might be expected, this informality, when it is exercised, is controversial, and is sometimes cited as a reason to oppose masters who step beyond the limits of the adversarial judge.

The cases themselves reflect the same ambivalence about masters that these policy arguments do. In big cases, district courts appoint masters, not routinely perhaps, but with some frequency.[24] As a general rule, the courts of appeal take a more jaundiced view of masters, especially when there is a blanket reference of all pretrial matters.[25] Concerns for efficiency alone seem an inadequate basis for a reference. What is an adequate showing is less clearly stated in the cases.

3. Summary

Restructuring the lawyers and the judicial officers does not directly narrow the legal and factual issues for trial. Nonetheless, this narrowing is likely to be a collateral consequence of choosing a lead counsel for one side. The same is true of expanding the judicial staffing. Creating a larger judicial structure — "Judge and Company" — allows the judge to be more active and creative in employing the issue-narrowing case management tools that we now examine in greater detail.

B. NARROWING ISSUES

The two main activities of a pretrial period are narrowing the factual and legal issues and discovering the facts relevant to the issues that remain. Narrowing issues and discovering facts have something of a chicken-and-egg quality: It is very hard to know which one should come first. In a system such as ours, which is committed to decisions on the merits, it is difficult to narrow issues until there has been a full development of the facts. On the other hand, in a complex dispute presenting endless permutations of facts, it is difficult to know the factual issues on which to concentrate without first knowing what the meritorious issues are.

---

24. For a case giving a master virtually plenary authority in pretrial matters, see *In re* "Agent Orange" Prod. Liab. Litig., 94 F.R.D. 173 (E.D.N.Y. 1982).

25. *See, e.g.,* Prudential Ins. Co. of Am. v. United States Gypsum Co., 991 F.2d 1080 (3d Cir. 1993); *In re* Bituminous Coal Operators' Assn., Inc., 949 F.2d 1165 (D.C. Cir. 1991); *In re* United States, 816 F.2d 1083 (6th Cir. 1987).

To some extent, the two tasks of narrowing the issues and discovering the facts must proceed hand-in-hand. Breaking these tasks into two separate inquiries, as we do in this chapter, has an artificial quality to it. During the course of most large cases, a judge will enter a series of pretrial orders, called "case management orders" (or "CMOs") to guide the case through the pretrial process. Many CMOs will contain both issue-narrowing and discovery aspects. As we separately examine the present pretrial rules for issue narrowing and discovery, the strategic actions these rules foment, and the possible managerial responses to them, you should keep this relationship between issue narrowing and discovery constantly in mind.

1. Structural Limitations on Narrowing Issues

The Federal Rules of Civil Procedure inverted the basic philosophy of the writ system that it replaced, creating both a non-detailed (and hence non-informative) set of pleadings liberally construed to ensure that the case would be determined on its full merits (as opposed to on the single issue to which the writ system had narrowed the case) and an arsenal of tools to uncover the facts. The great advantage of the new "notice pleading" system was its commitment to develop the facts on their merits. The great weakness was its inability to narrow issues.

The Federal Rules did not entirely abandon issue narrowing as a pretrial goal. Three issue-narrowing devices are built into the Federal Rules. The first is the Rule 12(b) motion to dismiss. Dismissal can be requested for any of a number of reasons, among them lack of subject matter jurisdiction (Rule 12(b)(1)), lack of territorial jurisdiction (Rule 12(b)(2)), lack of venue (Rule 12(b)(3)), insufficiency of process or service of process (Rules 12(b)(4) and (b)(5)), and failure to join an indispensable party (Rule 12(b)(7)). Most of these motions involve gatekeeping matters, do not require much discovery, and are unrelated to the merits of the dispute.[26] They are not designed to assist in the issue-narrowing process.

Only one motion to dismiss — the Rule 12(b)(6) motion to dismiss for failure to state a claim — is trained on the merits of the case. But its standard — that "a complaint should not be dismissed for failure to state a claim unless it appears beyond doubt that the

---

26. With several important exceptions including subject matter jurisdiction, failure to state a claim, and failure to join indispensable parties, Rule 12(b) motions are waived if not carefully preserved. *See* F.R.CIV.P. 12(g)-(h). This waiver approach is consistent with a system that prefers adjudications on the merits rather than on gatekeeping technicalities.

plaintiff can prove no set of facts in support of his claim which would entitle him to relief"[27] — is set sufficiently high to make it very difficult to determine the issues before discovery of the factual merits of the dispute. "The Federal Rules reject the approach that pleading is a game of skill in which one misstep by counsel may be decisive to the outcome and accept the principle that the purpose of pleading is to facilitate a proper decision on the merits."[28] All the pleadings need do is provide the opposing party "fair notice of what the . . . claim is and the grounds upon which it rests"[29]; under the Federal Rules, "the liberal opportunity for discovery and other pretrial procedures," not early pretrial motions, are designed "to define more narrowly the disputed facts and issues."[30] To reduce the issue-narrowing capacity of the motion to dismiss even more, the motion to dismiss can be used only against an entire claim or defense; it cannot excise certain issues from the case unless an entire claim or defense would collapse without the presence of that issue.

A second issue-narrowing device is the Rule 36 request for admission. Rule 36 allows a party to ask any other party to admit or deny any matter of consequence to the litigation. If admitted, the matter is conclusively determined for the litigation; if denied, the requesting party can often engage in follow-up discovery to determine the precise facts on which the denial was based. But the responding party is also entitled to respond with an answer of insufficient information.[31] The sole sanction for a responding party that refuses to admit a matter is payment of the requesting party's costs of proving the matter at trial, and there are exceptions — such as the lack of importance of the requested admission or the responding party's reasonable belief that he or she might prevail on the merits — that weaken the sanctioning power.[32]

Not surprisingly, the Rule 36 request for admission has not been an especially effective issue-narrowing tool. Early in the pretrial process, when such admissions would be most effective, a responding party can almost always plead insufficient knowledge. Moreover, the big issues in the case — "Was the asbestos defective?" or "Did the defendant monopolize?" — are usually so hotly contested that a party can deny them without fear of sanctions. Furthermore, a truly determined adversary can deny even truthful assertions if he or she is willing to pay for the recalcitrance. To make Rule 36 even less

---

27. Conley v. Gibson, 355 U.S. 41, 45-46 (1957).

28. Id at 48.

29. Id at 47. Accord, Leatherman v. Tarrant County Narcotics Intelligence and Coordination Unit,

507 U.S. 163 (1993).

30. *Conley*, 355 U.S. 163 at 47-48.

31. F.R.CIV.P. 36(a).

32. F.R.CIV.P. 37(c)(2).

less useful, many districts have local rules that presumptively limit the number of requests that a party can propound.[33]

The third issue-narrowing device is the Rule 56 motion for summary judgment. Rule 56's standard — "that there is no genuine issue as to any material fact and that the moving party is entitled to judgment as a matter of law"[34] — contains both positive and less-than-positive issue-narrowing features. Like the Rule 12(b)(6) motion to dismiss, a motion for summary judgment is, as its name and the second half of the standard both state, available only when its granting will result in the entry of judgment on a claim or defense. Thus, when the only significant dispute is a dispositive legal one, summary judgment seems an ideal judgment-rendering vehicle.

When the parties also dispute the factual issues, however, summary judgment's usefulness as an issue-narrowing device diminishes. First, since the motion is brought to obtain a judgment, Rule 56 lacks the surgical issue-narrowing capacity of Rule 36.[35] Second, unlike Rule 12 (b)(6), Rule 56 is a determination on the merits rather than on the pleadings. This means that the parties must be able to present evidence concerning these factual issues, which by definition are in dispute. As long as the factual dispute is "genuine," Rule 56 says that summary judgment is inappropriate, and the issues cannot be successfully narrowed.

"Genuine" sounds like (and is) an easier standard to meet than Rule 12(b)(6)'s "beyond doubt" standard. But where, exactly, is the line between a genuine and a non-genuine factual issue? Any answer to this question requires us to consider the right to jury trial. It seems a simple matter of constitutional logic that a judge could not decide factual issues during pretrial that are contested hotly enough to be decided by a jury at trial; otherwise, the Seventh Amendment's guarantee would be hollow indeed. (Of course, this does not mean that a judge need go as far as the constitutional line during pretrial, only that the judge cannot go farther.) This sensible proposition has prevailed in the cases.[36] Hence, the critical issue in determining the

---

33. *See* F.R.CIV.P. 26(b)(2) (authorizing such limitations).

34. F.R.CIV.P. 56(c).

35. A modest exception to this statement is contained in Rule 56(d), which allows a court to determine non-disputed factual issues when "judgment is not rendered upon the whole case or for all the relief asked and a trial is necessary." Some courts and commentators have urged a lib-eral reading of Rule 56(a) in order to make Rule 56 into a more general tool for rendering partial summary judgment, but thus far efforts to redraft Rule 56 along these lines have failed. For a discussion, see TIDMARSH & TRANGSRUD, *supra* n.14, at 1064-66.

36. The case most clearly equating the Rule 50 and Rule 56 standards is Anderson v. Liberty Lobby, Inc., 477 U. S. 242 (1986).

"genuineness" standard for purposes of a Rule 56 pretrial motion is the scope of a judge's power to take factual issues away from the jury at trial. That power is stated in Rule 50: A judge may enter judgment as a matter of law against a party when "there is no legally sufficient evidentiary basis for a reasonable jury to find for that party on that issue [and] a claim or defense . . . cannot under the controlling law be maintained or defeated without a favorable finding on that issue." The unspoken obverse of Rule 50 is that, as long as there is credible evidence on both sides of a factual issue, a judge may not take the issue away from the jury under Rule 50. *A priori*, a court may not determine such a factual issue under Rule 56. Rule 56's power to narrow factual issues is therefore a narrow one, immovably constrained by the Seventh Amendment.[37]

A third disadvantage of summary judgment as a device to narrow issues is timing. Ideally issue-narrowing comes before lots of (ultimately needless) discovery, not after. But courts, including the Supreme Court, have demonstrated an unwillingness to consider a Rule 56 motion when the opposing party has not had an opportunity to explore the case's factual merits.[38] Therefore, as a mechanism to narrow issues and avoid their full factual development, summary judgment falls short.

Finally, summary judgment, at least according to Rule 56's terms, requires a motion from a party.[39] By now, it should come as no surprise that parties often have private incentives at variance with socially optimal behavior. A fully functional fact-narrowing authority also requires *sua sponte* judicial power.

The only other arguable issue-narrowing device — and the one on which the Federal Rules put primary reliance — is discovery itself. As we have observed, the drafters' faith that full disclosure would narrow, rather than expand, issues seems pollyannaish in retrospect, and it is a faith largely misplaced in complex litigation. Here the governing legal standards are vague, the available information is vast, the consequent permutations on the facts are never-ending, and the stakes are sufficiently high to justify extraordinary steps during discovery. As an issue-narrowing device in complex litigation, discovery is a failure.

---

37. In theory, factual issues that were not to be tried to a jury (such as factual issues relevant only to an equitable claim) could operate under a looser standard of genuineness, equivalent to the judge's factfinding authority at trial described in Rule 52(c). Thus far, the Supreme Court has not suggested that the standard of genu-

ineness should vary with whether the judge or jury is the ultimate fact-finder.

38. Celotex Corp. v. Catrett, 477 U. S. 317, 322 (1986) (summary judgment appropriate "after adequate time for discovery").

39. *See* F.R.CIV.P. 56(a)-(b).

2. Strategic Behavior

Not only are there certain structural limitations built into the issue-narrowing schemes of the American adversarial process, but the issue-narrowing schemes that do exist can also be subject to strategic manipulation by adversaries seeking private gain. The main issues, for which any system of issue-narrowing devices must account, are avoidance of decisions on the merits, cost imposition, and unilateral information exchange.

Avoidance of decisions on the merits is difficult with our present pretrial system. Nonetheless, parties sometimes use motions to dismiss, requests for admission, and motions for summary judgment in the hopeful attempt to obtain admissions or a ruling that will prevent the other side from inquiring into the merits of certain unfavorable aspects of the case; and, if they succeed, a potentially meritorious avenue of recovery will be foreclosed. As we have seen, however, the pleading rules are generous, summary judgment is difficult to obtain until there has been discovery on the merits, and the Federal Rules discourage the filing meritless motions.[40] Generally speaking, the risk of a motion successfully avoiding the merits is slight with competent opposing counsel, but it increases as competence declines.

The next strategic use of issue-narrowing devices — to impose costs on the opposing side — is a more realistic one. Responding to a motion to dismiss or to a motion for summary judgment is hardly a costless affair, and a well-financed party can make such motions as a way of pricing their opponent out of the litigation (or at least forcing the opponent to expend their time and resources on tasks other than the development of factual issues that might be unfavorable to the richer party). Moreover, the potential of issue-narrowing devices to shift the litigation dynamic — usually in favor of defense interests who can use the possibility of such motions to drive down the settlement value of a case[41] — makes their strategic use almost unavoidable.

A third strategic use of issue-narrowing devices, especially summary judgment, is to effect a unilateral transfer of information from the opposing party (usually a plaintiff) to the moving party (usually a defendant). Motions to dismiss and for summary judgment are premised on the belief that the opponent's present position contains a fatal defect. The motion forces the opponent to

---

40. F.R.CIV.P. 11.

41. For an excellent economic account of the outcome-affecting incentives created by summary judg ment, see Samuel Issacharoff & George Loewenstein, *Second Thoughts about Summary Judgment*, 100 YALE L.J. 73 (1990).

justify the continued maintenance of certain legal and factual theories. This justification process can require the opposing side to abandon certain theories, to make factual concessions, to provide information that discovery may not yet have uncovered, and to give a preview of the opponent's case at trial. Even if the motion is unsuccessful, the value of this information to the moving party can be enormous. "Given the value of this information, strategic misuse of summary judgment must be considered a real possibility."[42]

If stronger issue-narrowing techniques are to be created in complex litigation, these three strategic effects will be magnified. One of the challenges of designing issue-narrowing devices in complex cases is to keep these effects within a tolerable range.

3. Responses

The traditional adversarial method leaves the parties in control of issue narrowing. The court's only job is to rule on the motions and other matters brought before it by the parties. In this section we explore various ways in which that model has been (or might be) amended in complex litigation, and how some of these changes have now moved into more routine litigation as well.

   a. *Changing Settled Rules.* One response to the inadequacy of ordinary issue-narrowing techniques is to change the pretrial rules that make issue-narrowing ineffective. Leaving aside the possibility of redrafting the Federal Rules, the only way to change the issue-narrowing rules — pleadings, motions to dismiss, requests for admission, and motions for summary judgment — is to interpret the rules in light of the needs of complex litigation.

In the case of Rule 36, reinterpretation would be hard to do; the rule is fairly clear and specific. But the other issue-narrowing rules are spongy enough to engage in some differential interpretations. For instance, the "fair notice" requirement of pleading and the "genuineness" requirement of Rule 56 could in theory be interpreted against the backdrop of the size of the case and the need to narrow the issues. Nonetheless, such creative interpretations run into certain obstacles. One is the Supreme Court's steadfast refusal to depart from the Rules' commitment to notice pleading, even in cases where greater specificity in pleading might be socially desirable.[43] A second obstacle is our trans-substantive ideal: our desire to escape a system of different rules for different cases that burdened common law pleading. A third is our desire to determine cases on the merits. The final obstacle, affecting motions for summary judgment and

---

42. Id at 111.   43. *See Conley,* 355 U.S. 41; *Leatherman,* 507 U.S. 163.

indirectly Rule 12(b)(6) motions to dismiss, is the immutable demand of the Seventh Amendment that the jury decide substantially controverted factual disputes.

Despite these roadblocks, some courts indicate a willingness to bend the ordinary rules in big cases. With respect to pleading, the Supreme Court has never squarely addressed a heightened pleading standard — under which parties would be required to provide more detail and would be held to the precise pleadings in deciding the validity of their claims — in complex litigation. Its pronouncements on heightened pleading in other contexts are icy, and no less an authority on pleading than the Federal Rules' primary drafter, Charles Clark, specifically rejected the notion of heightened pleading in a complex antitrust case.[44]

Nonetheless, some courts have begun to sneak the idea of heightened pleading through the back door. Most notably in RICO cases, many district courts now require the plaintiff to file a "case statement" shortly after the complaint. This case statement is often very detailed, and requires the party to state with great particularity the exact events and the individuals responsible for a RICO violation. Courts have then used these statements to dismiss cases in which the proffered statement failed to show a legal violation — even before the parties conducted discovery to determine the actual facts underlying the alleged violation. It is difficult to reconcile the RICO case statement with the notice pleading requirements of the Federal Rules. The courts that have done so have not invoked Rule 8(a) (the basic notice pleading rule), but instead recent legislation under which Congress has given courts freer rein to hold down expense and delay,[45] the inherent authority of courts to establish local rules of practice,[46] or Rule 16 of the Federal Rules.

Rule 16, which we will explore throughout this section, is the linchpin of the modern case management movement. It requires only a couple of modest things: an initial pretrial order establishing a schedule for completing various tasks and a final pretrial order entered shortly in advance of the trial. But Rule 16 is also hortatory, and strongly encourages greater judicial involvement throughout the pretrial phase of a case. Judges can hold as many pretrial conferences as they think advisable, and can consider at these conferences

---

44. Nagler v. Admiral Corp., 248 F.2d 319 (2d Cir. 1957). Subsequent to his drafting of the Federal Rules, Professor Clark was appointed to the federal bench.

45. *See* Civil Justice Reform Act of 1990, codified at 28 U.S.C. §§ 471-82.

46. *See* Northland Ins. Co. v. Shell Oil Co., 930 F. Supp. 1069 (D. N.J. 1996). *But see* F.R.CIV.P. 83(a) (requiring local rules to be "consistent with" Federal Rules).

a host of different techniques designed to make the issue-narrowing and fact-discovering functions run more smoothly. For present purposes, the critical grants of authority are Rules 16(c)(1) and 16(c)(10), which authorize judges at pretrial conferences to consider and "take appropriate action, with respect to . . . the formulation and simplification of the issues, including the elimination of frivolous claims or defenses," and "the need for adopting special procedures for managing potentially difficult or protracted actions that may involve complex issues [or] parties."

Nothing in Rule 16(c) squarely addresses departures from notice pleading, but it is easy enough to see how a judge in an issue-narrowing mindset might use Rule 16 to do just that.[47] By insisting on heightened pleading in order to narrow the issues, the judge is merely taking "appropriate action" regarding the simplification of the issues through the adoption of a special procedure for the big case. Of course, such insistence begs the critical question: Is heightened pleading "appropriate" when it flies in the face of the notice pleading philosophy of Rule 8 and the trans-substantive structure of the Federal Rules?

The same aggressive attitude could spill over from Rule 16 to the other rules we have studied. If the judge is now licensed to take "appropriate action" to eliminate frivolous issues, should he or she be able to *sua sponte* dismiss for failure to state a claim or enter summary judgment? Even more aggressively, might the judge be able to dismiss a claim upon a weaker showing than *Conley*'s "beyond doubt" standard? Might the judge be able to take into account the complexity of a case in deciding whether a "genuine" factual issue exists for summary judgment?

On the first question, courts today are generally regarded as having the authority to raise the question of dismissal or summary judgment *sua sponte*.[48] It is difficult to work this power out under the text of either Rule 12, which talks about motions brought by the parties, or Rule 56, which again speaks only of parties moving for summary judgment. Some courts have nonetheless found the power between the lines of these rules; others have located the source of the power in the capacious language of Rule 16(c).[49] The latter reading

---

47. *See Northland*, 930 F. Supp. 1069 (relying in part on Rule 16(c) to justify use of RICO case statement).

48. *Celotex*, 477 U.S. at 326 ("district courts are widely acknowledged to possess the power to enter summary judgments *sua sponte*").

49. *Compare* B.F. Goodrich v. Betkowski, 99 F.3d 505 (2d Cir. 1996) (Rule 56) *with* Portsmouth Square, Inc. v. Shareholders Protective Comm., 770 F.2d 866 (9th Cir. 1985) (Rule 16). Whether a court finds the power to lie under Rule 16 or Rule 56, the court must apply the procedural protections of Rule 56 — such as 10-day notice before dismissal — to the

probably does less violence to the plain language of the Rules, but still leaves unanswered a fundamental question about why such a marked shift away from adversarial theory is "appropriate." Might a judge with such a power be too quick to judgment? Too biased to sit dispassionately at trial? Too invested in a particular pretrial structure to appreciate the best interests of the case as a whole? These rhetorical questions can, of course, be leveled generally at the concept of case management, of which *sua sponte* dismissal powers are but one part.

On the question of whether case management powers include the ability to alter the standard for a Rule 12(b)(6) dismissal or a Rule 56 summary judgment, there seems to be some divergence of opinion. At a doctrinal level, no case squarely says that *Conley's* "beyond doubt" standard should be loosened in complex litigation. Some cases, however, claim that the complexity of a case makes a difference in determining the "genuineness" of facts for summary judgment purposes. In *Poller v. Columbia Broadcasting System*,[50] the Supreme Court reversed a summary judgment in an antitrust case that appeared to present no extraordinarily difficult factual issues. In the course of its ruling, however, the Court made the following observation: "[S]ummary procedures should be used sparingly in complex antitrust litigation where motive and intent play leading roles, the proof is largely in the hands of the alleged conspirators, and hostile witnesses thicken the plot."[51]

For many years, this comment was read to mean that summary judgment was a disfavored device in complex cases. Without overruling *Poller*, however, the Court seemed to reverse its course in two cases: *Celotex Corp. v. Catrett*, in which it observed that summary judgment "is properly regarded not as a disfavored procedural shortcut, but rather as an integral part of the Federal Rules as a whole"[52]; and more specifically in *Matsushita Electric Industrial Co. v. Zenith Radio Corp.*,[53] one of the most massive antitrust cases ever commenced. The factual theory at the heart of *Matsushita* was that Japanese manufacturers of electronic equipment had engaged in predatory pricing over several decades. The district court had granted summary judgment after years of pretrial activity, but the court of appeals reversed, believing that sufficient indirect evidence existed for a jury to infer such a conspiracy. The

claims. *See, e.g., B.F. Goodrich*, 99 F.3d at 522; Berkowitz v. Home Box Office, Inc., 89 F.3d 24, 29-30 (1st Cir. 1996). *See generally* TIDMARSH & TRANGSRUD, *supra* n.14, at 1076-77.

50. 368 U.S. 464 (1962).

51. *Id.* at 473. *See also* Kennedy v. Silas Mason Co., 334 U.S. 249 (1948).

52. 477 U.S. at 327.

53. 475 U.S. 574 (1986).

Supreme Court upheld the district court's grant of summary judgment because no direct evidence of predation existed and such predatory behavior defied economic common sense. The Court seemed to treat the defendants' conduct objectively, and determined the case on that basis — a move that seems analytically inconsistent with the dicta in *Poller*.

After *Celotex* and *Matsushita*, some courts began to suggest that the "genuineness" standard for summary judgment was easier to satisfy in complex cases than in ordinary ones.[54] Most courts, however, have nominally rejected this view. They have recognized that *Celotex* and *Matsushita* have made summary judgments easier to obtain, but they say that the standard of "genuineness" is the same in the ordinary case and the complex.[55]

Whether the standard is the same in both types of case is less certain. The real issue is not the stated doctrinal standards for motions to dismiss and for summary judgment; instead, it is the application of those standards in practice. There is some evidence that motions to dismiss are granted, in whole or in part, with surprising frequency in antitrust cases.[56] The same may be true of summary judgment motions.[57] This movement toward greater use of dispositive motions in large cases began before *Celotex* and *Matsushita*, and has apparently continued ever since.

The pendulum swing from *Poller* to *Celotex* and *Matsushita* has not been an overly dramatic one; nonetheless, the outcome in at least some cases on the margin has likely been altered by the changing standards. There are some ultimate constraints on how far the Federal Rules can be shifted by judicial reinterpretation — among them the Seventh Amendment, our notice pleading philosophy, the commitments to adversarial and trans-substantive process, the still regnant preference for decisions on the merits, and the potential for the parties' strategic misuse of strengthened issue-narrowing devices. If issue narrowing is to occur on a larger scale, other weapons must be added to the case management arsenal.

---

54. Collins v. Associated Pathologists, Ltd., 844 F.2d 473 (7th Cir.), *cert. denied*, 488 U.S. 852 (1988). For a case rejecting a trial judge's effort to apply a standard more generous than the Rule 50-56 standard, see Fid. & Deposit Co. of Maryland v. S. Utilities, Inc., 726 F.2d 692 (11th Cir. 1984).

55. For cases, see TIDMARSH & TRANGSRUD, *supra* n.14, at 1069-70; *id.* Supp. 2000, at 88.

56. *See* Stephen Calkins, *Summary Judgment, Motions to Dismiss, and Other Examples of Equilibrating Tendencies in the Antitrust System*, 74 GEO. L.J. 1065 (1986).

57. *Id.*; Issacharoff & Loewenstein, *supra* n.41. For a general summary of empirical data, see TIDMARSH & TRANGSRUD, *supra* n.14, at 1068.

b. Establishing Early, Firm Dates. In traditional adversarial theory, the lawyers develop the case for trial largely out of view of the court, and according to their own timetable. While a court may establish target dates for completing pretrial tasks and starting the trial, the lawyers should in theory be able to obtain extensions of these dates upon a showing that their pretrial work is not yet complete. This attitude, however, can create problems in large-scale cases in which the lawyers, left to their own devices, may have difficulty completing their pretrial tasks in a timely enough way to ensure reasonably swift and accurate justice.

Having the court establish dates for the accomplishment of various pretrial tasks and the commencement of trial seems a very modest intrusion on traditional theory. A somewhat greater intrusion on the ability of the lawyers to handle cases according to their views of their clients' best interests occurs when the deadlines are relatively short and rigidly enforced. This technique of early, firm deadlines is designed to focus the lawyers' attention on the crux of their cases; there is little time to be distracted by the periphery. As an indirect method of issue narrowing, these deadlines force the lawyers to strip the case to its essentials.

Early, firm deadlines have been used in complex litigation for some time. The seminal case upholding their use is *In re Fine Paper Antitrust Litigation.*[58] In *Fine Paper*, the district court imposed a discovery deadline and also set a trial date just ten months into the future. That date was ultimately moved back an additional nine months, with one set of plaintiffs scheduled for trial in September and another in October. The latter set of plaintiffs apparently had relied on the first set to do much of the work, or at least expected the first trial to continue past their own trial setting; in any event, they did very little pretrial preparation. When the first set of plaintiffs settled shortly before the scheduled September trial, the second set was woefully unprepared to begin trial in October. The district judge refused to relent on the October trial date, so the second set of plaintiffs was forced to try the case. The trial went so poorly that the district court entered judgment against them during the trial. On appeal, the Third Circuit upheld the trial judge's discretion to establish and then firmly adhere to the trial deadline.

Fine Paper itself says virtually nothing about narrowing pretrial issues. But its affirmance of rigidly enforced deadlines sent lawyers a message about the risk of treating such deadlines cavalierly. And the hoped-for effect of these deadlines, when they are set early and enforced firmly, is to achieve issue narrowing indirectly.

---

58. 685 F.2d 810 (3d Cir. 1982),   Cascade, 459 U.S. 1156 (1983).
cert. denied sub nom. Alaska v. Boise

One of the criticisms of *Fine Paper* that could have been made in its own day was that the authority for the district court's actions was uncertain.[59] After 1983, however, that criticism is no longer possible. As part of the case management revisions to Rule 16 that were made in 1983, courts are now required under Rule 16(b) to impose deadlines for joining parties, making motions, and completing discovery. Rule 16(b) suggests that the court also establish a deadline for the trial. The firmness of these deadlines is guaranteed by Rule 16(b)'s requirement that the deadlines can be modified only upon a showing of good cause. Rule 16(b) says nothing about setting deadlines "early" (i.e., with only enough time to develop the crux of the case); the length of the deadlines remains in the judge's control.

The empirical and ancedotal data on early, firm deadlines initially appear impressive. During the early 1990's, the RAND Corporation performed a study of the efficacy of various case management measures in reducing cost and delay. With respect to early, firm deadlines, RAND found that an early trial date was the most significant case management tool in terms of reducing the time to disposition. The entry of discovery deadlines also reduced the time to disposition. Both deadlines reduced attorney hours spent on a case, though only the discovery cutoff led to a statistically significant reduction. Lawyer satisfaction and litigants' perception of fairness showed little effect from the imposition of deadlines.[60]

These statistics suggest that there is nothing to fear in the use of early, firm deadlines. But the RAND study data must be approached with caution. In the first place, the study did not focus specifically on complex cases, in which greater problems with the firm enforcement of deadlines might be anticipated. Second, the RAND study attempted to measure primarily the variables of cost and delay, and secondarily the satisfaction of litigants, lawyers, and judges with the process. The issue that concerns us is a somewhat different one: Can early, firm deadlines help to narrow issues in a way that avoids needless extensive factual development? Indirectly, short deadlines can avoid factual development, but whether that development was *needless* (as opposed to valuable in determining the case on its actual merits) cannot be determined from the RAND data.

More generally, short deadlines have the potential to favor better-financed parties and those parties with greater access to information. In most big cases, shorter deadlines do not necessarily

---

59. The then-extant Rule 16 authorized courts only to "consider" the "simplification of the issues" and "other matters as may aid in the disposition of the action."

60. JAMES S. KAKALIK ET AL., AN EVALUATION OF JUDICIAL CASE MANAGEMENT UNDER THE CIVIL JUSTICE REFORM ACT (1996).

mean less discovery; they merely mean bigger litigation teams on each side of a case. A well-financed party is better able to assemble a large team and to endure the inefficiencies they entail. Likewise, to the extent that shorter deadlines limit the number of issues that can be explored, the party with greater access to information (and thus less need of discovery) will stand in better stead.

Finally, setting deadlines that are short but not too short (i.e., giving the lawyers adequate time to develop the hearts of their cases but inadequate time to dally on the fine points) requires the judge to have a strong intuitive feel for the litigation. How the judge obtains this feel, and how often the judge will make errors, remain open issues.

We do not know how serious these drawbacks are in complex litigation, for, thus far, no studies have been done to test these concerns. Indeed, it may be impossible to design a study that determines whether the concerns are, or are not, justified. Since cost and delay can be measured, those data are now driving the debate over case management generally and the use of early, firm deadlines particularly. Since even these data do not relate specifically to complex cases, the argument for early, firm deadlines — and for their departure from an ideal in which lawyers handle the allocation of time to pretrial tasks — still needs to be convincingly made.

Despite these possible misgivings, early, firm deadlines, which first were used in complex litigation, have now become a basic case management tool in cases both large and small.

c. Bifurcation. A more direct method of attempting to narrow the issues is to split the pretrial into discrete parts, in order to focus on a small number of issues at a time. This strategy of pretrial issue separation is often referred to as "bifurcation." Technically, bifurcation concerns only the division of a case into two parts. The pretrial may be split into three parts (trifurcation) or more (polyfurcation), but the term bifurcation can be used loosely to describe them all.

Pretrial bifurcation should be distinguished from trial bifurcation, which we consider in the next chapter.[61] Splitting a case into distinct issues at trial is not the same thing as splitting them into distinct issues during pretrial, and there is no necessary relationship between the decision to bifurcate the pretrial and the decision to bifurcate the trial. Nonetheless, it is not unlikely that, once a court has split a case in a particular fashion during pretrial, the same or a similar division will occur at trial.

---

61. *See infra* pp. 259-62.

The brass ring of pretrial bifurcation is finding a discrete issue for which the relevant information is readily available, which will ultimately dispose of the case if the issue turns out one way, and which will not require a lot of retraced steps in the event that the issue turns out the other way. A classic example of such an issue is the statute of limitations. Unfortunately, such an issue rarely presents itself in complex cases. Usually the easy issues are not case-dispositive; and the case-dispositive issues are not easy.

Types of bifurcation other than the single-issue, full-discovery-by-all-parties model are also possible. An increasingly popular form in mass tort litigation is to force each plaintiff in a case to provide factual information concerning his or her individual illness, exposure history to the defendants' products, and basis for believing that a linkage exists between exposure and injury. The failure to provide particularized information to substantiate a plaintiff's claim risks the dismissal of the lawsuit.[62] Known as a *"Lone Pine* order" after the case that first employed the device, this form of bifurcation seeks to determine whether plaintiffs have enough evidence to make a *prima facia* case on causation before consuming the court's time with the massive discovery that a full-blown inquiry into liability and causation entails. In this regard, the *Lone Pine* order acts much like the heightened pleading of a RICO case statement.

Aside from the problem of finding the "right" way to bifurcate a case, it might initially seem that the concept is entirely sensible. But there are hidden difficulties, some of which relate to the pretrial process itself and others to the bifurcated trial that may follow a bifurcated pretrial. Three of the pretrial concerns are the cost, delay, and duplication that result in the event that the selected issue does not end the case. Fourth, there exists a fear of judicial bias. When the judge selects an issue, he or she is making a determination — on little information — that a particular issue is critical to the case. The possibility exists that the determination will become a subconsciously self-fulfilling prophecy, and that the judge will be especially predisposed on an eventual motion for summary judgment to terminate the case at that point.

A fifth issue is the source of the judge's power to bifurcate a case during pretrial. Courts often assume that the authority derives from Rule 42(b), but the express terms of the rule authorize only *trials* on separate issues "in furtherance of convenience or to avoid prejudice." Arguably the *pretrial* bifurcation power lies in one or more of the

---

62. *See* Acuna v. Brown & Root, Inc., 200 F.3d 335 (5th Cir. 2000). For another case using a *Lone Pine* order, see *In re* Love Canal Actions, 145 Misc.2d 1076, 547 N.Y.S.2d 174 N.Y. Sup. Ct. 1989), *modified*, 161 A.D. 1169, 555 N.Y.S.2d 519 (App. Div. 1990).

clauses of the ubiquitous Rule 16(c),[63] but no clear and express language to that effect exists. A likelier source is Rule 26(f)(2), read in conjunction with Rule 26(c)(2),[64] but once again the source of judicial power, as opposed to mutual party consent for bifurcation, is not clearly stated. The authority for less traditional bifurcation, such as a *Lone Pine* order, is even less clear. In a recent case upholding a *Lone Pine* order, the court of appeals located the authority in "the wide discretion afforded district judges over the management of discovery under [Rule] 16,"[65] but it never cited an exact provision of Rule 16 on which to hinge pretrial bifurcation — perhaps because none exists.

A concern that ties in with trial bifurcation is the potentially outcome-determinative effect of bifurcation. Although no studies have yet been done on the effect of pretrial bifurcation, studies on trial bifurcation suggest a rather marked pro-defendant effect.[66] The conventional wisdom to explain this effect is that bifurcation on liability issues eliminates sympathy for the plaintiffs' suffering from the factfinder's calculus; the horror of Smith's injuries does not have the opportunity to influence the determination of XYZ's culpability for its conduct. Whether that fact is a good or bad development is to some extent beside the point; the issue is that a particular choice of procedure creates a significant possibility of a different outcome. To the extent that pretrial bifurcation leads to a dispositive motion or a similar trial bifurcation, there exist issues of trans-substantive equity and fairness for bifurcated plaintiffs in relation to plaintiffs whose cases are not bifurcated. To be sure, we do not know that these effects are present. But that uncertainty is hardly reassuring. To unleash such a potentially significant device without a full apprecia-tion of its consequences is troublesome indeed.

The final concern is one of procedural design. The division of cases into a series of discrete parts is a procedural method associated most often with the continuous trial method of continental or inquisitorial systems of justice, and with our own equity tradition. Pretrial bifurcation does not move us entirely in that direction,[67] but

---

63. *See* F.R.CIV.P. 16 (c)(1) ("for-mulation and simplification of the issues"); (c)(12) ("special procedures for managing difficult or protracted actions"); (c)(13) ("order for a separate trial pursuant to Rule 42(b)"); F.R.CIV.P. 16(c)(14) ("order directing a party or parties to present evidence early in the trial").

64. *See* F.R.CIV.P. 26 (f)(2) (or-dering parties to consider in discovery planning "whether discovery should be . . . limited or focused upon particular issues"); (c)(2) (allowing court to issue protective order that "discovery may be had only on specified terms and conditions").

65. *Acuna*, 200 F.3d at 340.

66. We examine the effect of trial bifurcation *infra* pp. 259-62.

67. As we shall see in the next

it shortens the distance to those processes. Does increased use of bifurcation portend the ultimate demise of the common law trial? The same question should be kept in mind as we evaluate the efficacy of every case management technique.

   d. Pretrial Stipulations. A third tool for narrowing issues is to force pretrial stipulations by the parties. This process is akin to requests for admission, but it involves the court in a more serious and sustained fashion. It is also akin to the preparation of a Rule 16(e) final pretrial order, which usually requires the parties to stipulate to non-controverted facts and admissibility of evidence. As useful as the final pretrial order might be for streamlining the trial, however, it fails as a device to narrow the issues and thus streamline the discovery and pretrial process.

   Perhaps the most famous use of early pretrial stipulations occurred in the mammoth *United States v. AT&T* antitrust litigation. The United States alleged that AT&T had maintained its monopoly for decades by means of scores of illegal practices and actions. Early in the litigation, the government identified 82 distinct episodes of monopolistic behavior, many of which created substantial pretrial difficulties in their own right. The district court therefore ordered the parties to engage in a series of exchanges, first presenting basic allegations and supporting information for each episode in a "Statement of Contentions and Proof," and then winnowing down the actual disagreements through a series of three additional and increasingly detailed statements in which each side was to state each disputed issue and its proofs regarding that issue. The other side was then to admit or deny each issue and proof.[68]

   The system as initially designed did not work well. It bogged down as the parties expanded rather than narrowed their disagreements in the second round of statements. The statements were roughly 2,000 pages per side, and tended to obfuscate and avoid, rather than clarify, the issues and proof. Consequently, in a larger departure from the adversarial ideal, the judge handed over the stipulation process to a pair of special masters, who spent thirteen intensive months negotiating with nineteen teams of lawyers for each side.[69] The process led to the abandonment by the government

chapter, the Seventh Amendment may keep the continental system of continuous trial from completely prevailing. *See infra* pp. 250-53, 259-62.

   68. The system is described in more detail in United States v. Am. Tel. & Tel., Co., 461 F. Supp. 1314 (D.D.C. 1978).

   69. The story, as told by the masters, can be found in Geoffrey C. Hazard, Jr. & Paul R. Rice, *Judicial Management of the Pretrial Process in Massive Litigation: Special Masters as Case Managers,* in WAYNE D. BRAZIL ET AL., MANAGING COMPLEX LITIGATION 103 (1983).

of fourteen episodes; the masters later stated that the process also led to stipulations for 80 to 85 percent of the disputed facts.

A similar stipulation process has been subsequently employed in several other antitrust actions.[70] The success of the process in these cases has never been reported. It appears not to have been widely employed in other types of complex litigation.

Although the district judge in *AT&T* thought that the power to order stipulations resided in Rules 16 and 26, the authority for such an aggressive stipulation plan can fairly be said to lie, if anywhere, in the interstices of the rules, and not their plain text. Moreover, given the lawyers' natural adversarial tendency to admit as little as possible, it seems likely that such a process can be successful only with the strong presence of the judge or a judicial adjunct. Such a presence involves the judge in the pretrial process in a manner more reminiscent of continental than common law procedure. The process also raises questions of cost-effectiveness; judicial bias; departure from the adversarial ideal; and, since the process is used only in some cases, departure from the trans-substantive ideal as well.

Some of these concerns may explain why forced issue stipulation is an infrequently exercised case management power.

4. Summary

As a descriptive matter, the original design of the Federal Rules limited the ability of the parties and the court to narrow the issues during pretrial. Begun as a response to the deficiencies that complex litigation exposed in this design, case management has now reoriented our pretrial system to some degree. But the limits on issue narrowing are still strong — sometimes unavoidably, because of Seventh Amendment constraints, and sometimes prudentially, because of other assumptions and aims of our procedural system. Those who find little fault with a strong adversarial approach during pretrial may be disturbed by the encroachments of case management; those who prefer a less adversarial process may think case management has not gone far enough. The present thinking on case management balances between the extremes. Although this thinking has permeated routine as well as complex cases, some of the techniques we have explored here — such as bifurcation and pretrial stipulations — find more frequent use in complex cases.

As a matter of prescription, the reasons that courts assume these greater powers, and do so more frequently in complex cases, still

---

70. For cases, see TIDMARSH & TRANGSRUD, *supra* n.14, at 1039.

elude us. The relationship between the problems of narrowing issues during pretrial and of aggregation also seems muddled. Does a single thread run through these seemingly different fabrics? Why are judges using case management powers whose source of authority can in some instances charitably be called unclear?

C. DISCOVERING FACTS

Whether the issues are successfully narrowed or not, the lawyers' principal pretrial task is to discover the facts relevant to whatever issues are pertinent to the case. The problem of factual discovery in complex litigation is somewhat different than that of issue narrowing. As we have seen, the drafters of the Federal Rules erred strongly on the side of factual development, and provided a breadth of party-controlled discovery devices unequaled in the history of procedure. The problem is not the scarcity of devices, as with issue narrowing; the problem is the bounty. In many big cases, factual development on a vast scale is impossible. If the case is ever to achieve some closure in a reasonably expeditious and economical way, some constraints on and streamlining of the present discovery system might need to be implemented.

1. The Limited Structural Impediments to Full Discovery

Rule 26(b)(1) states that parties "may obtain discovery regarding any matter, not privileged, that is relevant to the claim or defense of any party"; for "good cause," discovery can also be had "of any matter relevant to the subject matter involved in the action." The basic discovery devices — interrogatories to a party (Rule 33), written or oral depositions of any potential witness (Rules 30-32), production of documents by a party or subpoena of documents from a nonparty (Rules 34 and 45), and physical or mental examinations (Rule 35) — allow the parties to obtain virtually any form of admissible evidence: testimony, documents, databases, viewings of premises, and so on. There are some gaps (for instance, no interrogatories can be sent to nonparties), but they are filled in by other methods for obtaining the same information (for instance, by subpoenaing the testimony or documents of a nonparty).

As originally drafted in 1938, the discovery rules required court approval of certain discovery requests. In stages, however, the Rules extricated the court from this role, and by 1970 discovery was an entirely party-controlled affair. In terms of both the breadth of and the judicial supervision over the discovery process, however, the history of the discovery rules since 1970 reflects a movement back toward tighter control by the court. With regard to breadth of discovery, the 1983, 1993, and 2000 amendments have chipped away at the fringes at discovery's wide scope. For instance, Rule 26(b)(1) now requires that good cause be shown in order to obtain discovery relevant to the subject matter of the case but not directly relevant to a claim or defense. Rule 26(b)(2) requires that discovery be proportional to the needs of the case and conducted in such a way as to be efficient and non-duplicative. Rule 26(g) requires parties to certify that discovery requests and responses are not intended to harass, and are reasonable and not unduly burdensome in light of the needs of the case. Unless leave of court is granted, Rules 30(a)(2)(A) and (d)(2) limit depositions to 10 per side, each to last no more than 7 hours. Likewise, Rule 33(a) limits interrogatories to 25 in number.

Party control over discovery has also been weakened. The great expansion of judicial case management powers in the 1983 amendments to Rule 16(c) included the power to take action to avoid "unnecessary proof" and "cumulative evidence." In 1993, Rule 16(c) was further expanded to give the court powers to control and schedule discovery, and Rule 26(f) was amended to require the parties to conduct a discovery planning conference early in the case. The 1993 amendments also removed some of the party control over discovery, and replaced it with a more inquisitorial process. Under Rule 26(a)(1), parties were required, without an opposing party's request to disclose certain information: the identity and location of witnesses and documents that support the party's claims or defenses, computations of damages, and insurance policies. This process was expanded in some ways and contracted in others in the 2000 amendments. Similarly, under Rule 26(a)(2), the identity of experts, their opinions, and the bases of their opinions must also be disclosed on a mandatory basis, though not usually until 90 days before trial; and under Rule 26(a)(3), parties must disclose the identity of trial witnesses and exhibits within 30 days of trial.

Thus, the present discovery system reflects mixed commitments. There are some efforts to achieve greater efficiency and some movement away from adversarial practices, but the overall orientation remains toward full, party-controlled discovery. For the most part, the judge becomes involved only to resolve a dispute among parties who believe either that the requesting party has asked for too much (i.e., the irrelevant, the privileged, or the disproportionate) or that the responding party has given too little (i.e., by making inappropriate objections or by failing to supply appropriately requested discovery). Judged in full measure, the system is far from an inquisitorial one.

This is true for cases of all sizes. Nothing in the discovery rules makes any distinction between complex and ordinary cases. The size of the case does not itself trigger more restrictive discovery. On one view of the world, that is exactly the problem. This problem comes in two parts. The first part relates to the virtually unregulated flow of information. In some complex cases, that information flow is so great that it becomes impossible for the lawyer to perform adequately the adversarial role assigned to him or her: the sifting and marshaling of evidence that can narrow issues and prepare for the trial or other resolution. There may be millions of pages of documents and thousands of witnesses. With every passing day, documents are destroyed or lost, and witnesses' memories fade. Sheer volume virtually guarantees that, by the time the lawyers begin to sift through the mountains of initial information, other information will be lost or damaged.

To some extent, such a problem can be compensated for by a team approach that uses different sets of lawyers to handle different discovery tasks. But that approach often means that no single lawyer knows the entire case, thus creating inefficiencies. It also means that under-financed litigants can be placed at a disadvantage. The judge might address the problem of information overload through issue-narrowing techniques, but, as we have seen, these techniques raise their own concerns.

Admittedly, this problem of information overload infects only a small percentage of "big" cases. The second part of the problem with discovery's lack of significant limitations is arguably more common. It is a problem not peculiar to complex litigation, though the size of the case may exacerbate it: the strategic use of broad discovery to achieve private ends.

2. Strategic Behavior

Although discovery is designed only to reveal the information needed to proceed to disposition, we have seen repeatedly that rules designed for one purpose can often be used by adversaries for another. Discovery is no exception.

Two separate strategic issues can arise. The first is impositional discovery: discovery or discovery responses in which the primary purpose is not to obtain information, but to impose costs on an opponent. The hope of such discovery is that the cost to the opponent is so great that the outcome of the case will be affected in a manner favorable to the requesting party.

Two examples should suffice. First, suppose that Smith sues XYZ as a result of his exposure to asbestos. His injury has a fair settlement value of $300,000, of which his lawyer would get $100,000 on contingency. Smith sends a document production request for certain of XYZ's documents concerning asbestos, which XYZ has already culled out of its files in prior litigation. Rather than merely giving Smith the documents, XYZ responds that Smith may go through all of XYZ's millions of pages of documents as they are kept in the ordinary course of business.[71] The cost of doing so may be very high — let's say, $50,000. At least until Smith's lawyer starts to undertake the task, XYZ has effectively dropped the settlement value of the case to $250,000; and if it can run up other discovery expenses through a tough-minded approach to pretrial, it might reduce the value of the case to a point where Smith's lawyer decides that it is simply no longer worth the time to pursue the case.

Conversely, Smith could ask for information that would be costly for XYZ to provide, but that would help Smith's case only marginally. Smith may seek to depose all of XYZ's officers and directors about their knowledge of asbestos, or ask for documents that might cost XYZ a great deal of money to find. The information that Smith requests may be sensitive (such as trade secrets), and the risk that this information might fall into the wrong hands is far greater than the value of Smith's lawsuit. Hence, XYZ might be willing to pay more than $300,000 to settle the lawsuit; and even if Smith's suit lacks merit, XYZ might even be willing to pay something just to avoid greater litigation costs, litigation risks, and bad publicity.

These are but two of the many ways that discovery can be used as a tactical weapon in litigation. Such tactical discovery is simply a reflection of three facts: discovery itself is a costly process, costs of litigation can have an effect on the outcome of a case, and discovery has largely been left in the hands of adversaries who have incentives to bend rules to secure favorable outcomes.

A debate exists about whether impositional discovery actually occurs, and, if it does, how serious a problem it is.[72] Even if it does not exist, however, impositional discovery has attained the status of an urban legend, and the legend underlies many of the recent moves to limit various forms of discovery, to mandate initial disclosures, and to require greater case management.

A second form of strategic behavior in discovery is stonewalling — refusing to provide relevant information either by asserting inappropriate objections, by construing discovery requests in an

---

71. *See* F.R.CIV.P. 34(b) (giving responding party the option to produce records as they are kept in the usual course of business or according to the numbered requests).

72. *Compare* Frank H. Easterbrook, *Discovery as Abuse*, 69 B.U. L. REV. 635 (1989) (impositional discovery is common) *with* Jack B. Weinstein, *What Discovery Abuse?: A Comment on John Setear's* The Barrister and the Bomb, 69 B.U. L. REV. 649 (1989) (discovery abuse is absent in most cases).

unfairly narrow way, or by simply refusing to disclose clearly requested information. Like impositional discovery, stonewalling may be more the stuff of myth than fact, but enough anecdotal evidence exists to make people believe in its frequent occurrence. As a potential problem, this seems more intractable than impositional discovery, for greater judicial control over the adversaries can make little headway in the face of determined stonewalling.

Even when impositional discovery or stonewalling does not exist, parties in large-scale litigation are often likely to have a number of disputes regarding the legitimate scope of discovery and the proper construction of discovery requests and responses. Providing an efficient method of dealing with these disputes is a critical part of a streamlined discovery process.

3. Responses

Two types of response might be used to cure the structural and strategic problems of discovery. First, the broad scope of discovery could be more restricted in complex cases than in ordinary cases. Such a bold approach would clearly create a two-track discovery process that creates issues of trans-substantivity. Second, various less radical methods to streamline the discovery process could be attempted.

a. *Changing Settled Rules.* Thus far, there has been no attempt in the case law to change the settled rules of discovery for complex federal cases. Some state courts have instituted differential case management plans, under which small cases that meet certain criteria are shunted into a quick resolution mode, while other, larger cases receive full discovery and pretrial. Thus far, nothing akin to the opposite approach — full discovery in ordinary cases and limited discovery in complex cases — has developed.

This is not to say that the law applied in ordinary and complex cases is invariably the same. The law of discovery is full of standards — relevance, proportionality, good cause, and leave of court — that allow courts to factor the complexity of a case into the decision about whether to permit discovery. For instance, in complex cases, the parties often cannot fully comply with the initial mandatory disclosure requirements of Rule 26(a)(1), and require a measure of relief. Likewise, the court typically relaxes the limits on depositions and interrogatories. The stakes in a complex case may make it difficult for a court to say that even far-reaching discovery is disproportionate to the need of the case. Moreover, complex cases generate a modest set of privileges and related doctrines that are unique; perhaps the most significant are the "common interest" doctrine, in which parties sharing a common interest can disclose to each other privileged material without losing the privilege, and special methods for handling the problem of inadvertent waiver.[73] But these differences in big-case discovery lie mostly at the margin, and they are balanced between more and less restrictive discovery.

We detect no great trends in the cases to restrict discovery in ways that are peculiar to complex litigation. To the contrary, the stakes in big cases are usually regarded as a reason to conduct more, not less, discovery. Moreover, any effort to restrict discovery in big cases would surely run afoul of the trans-substantive ideal to which our system aspires. A more cynical view is that the commitment in the discovery rules is to such individual tailoring that the trans-substantive ideal is mere illusion. In this view, the very "squishiness" of the discovery rules and the discretion given to federal judges to administer the discovery system make the creation of special discovery rules unnecessary.

Indeed, it would be difficult to know what form general restrictions on broad discovery would take. Should depositions be banned in complex cases? That seems draconian. Should parties be forced to justify the proportionality of their every question or request? That seems to create the possibility of so much satellite litigation over discovery that any arguable efficiency gains of restricted discovery would be more than offset. Should judges, rather than lawyers, conduct discovery? This large step abandons the adversarial system; indeed, the hallmark of most inquisitorial systems is the judicial development of evidence. In such a system, the problem of impositional discovery would largely end, and perhaps less stonewalling would occur as well. But can judicial control overcome the problem of the vastness of available information? Does a judge have the time resources, or staff to gather pretrial information? Might close contact with the discovery material bias the judge in advance of trial?

There are some advocates of a more inquisitorial system of evidence gathering.[74] Such an effort would require some source of authority (perhaps, once again, the court's inherent power?) and would have to live with the uncomfortable language of the Federal Rules, which clearly places discovery in the hands of the parties. At present, there is no indication that judges are shouldering an

---

73. For a detailed look at these and other recurring issues of special import in complex litigation, see TIDMARSH & TRANGSRUD *supra* n.14, at 1144-47; RICHARD L. MARCUS & EDWARD F. SHERMAN, COMPLEX LITIGATION 604-23 (3d ed. 1998).

74. The most famous argument for inquisitorial, and against adversarial, information gathering is John H. Langbein, *The German Advantage in Civil Procedure*, 52 U. CHI. L. REV. 823 (1985).

inquisitorial burden in any cases, complex or otherwise. In stream-lining discovery in the big case, less dramatic methods must be used.

b. *Delivering Information More Efficiently.* Numerous tech-niques can streamline the fact-gathering process, at least in some large cases. With respect to documentary evidence, one technique is to set up a common system for the identification of documents. Another technique is to enter a document retention order that prevents parties from destroying records. Still another, which is probably cost-effective in only the largest multiparty cases, is to set up a document depository whose cost is shared by the parties; rather than sending discovery to each party, a disclosing party merely sends the information to the depository, where the information is cata-logued and made available for inspection by all parties.[75] A small-scale version of the depository that is becoming increasingly common (and that may ultimately render the depository obsolete) is to scan documents into a computer and then make CD-ROMs or optical disks available to all parties at low cost.

A fourth cost-cutting measure is to allow parties to have access to discovery materials produced in prior litigation. For instance, in the behemoth *United States v. AT&T* litigation, the United States sought to streamline costs by piggybacking on the work of MCI and Litton Systems, which had previously sued AT&T on comparable antitrust grounds. The United States asked AT&T to produce the documents that it had produced in the *MCI* and *Litton* cases. These documents amounted to a whopping 2.5 million pages, but it was considerably less than the even more whopping 12 million pages from which MCI and Litton had culled the documents. Obviously, the government hoped to avoid duplicating the expense of winnowing out chaff to find wheat. AT&T opposed the request, ostensibly because it would impinge on the work product of MCI and Litton, and might led to the discovery of irrelevant or privileged information. Since neither MCI or Litton objected to the government's request, however, the court made short shrift of AT&T's argument: "'[O]ne of the purposes of the Federal Rules of Civil Procedure was to take the sporting element out of litigation. . . .' It would not advance but defeat the purpose of the rules to require plaintiff in this case to proceed laboriously, and possibly at the cost of several years' delay, to duplicate the document selection process."[76]

---

75. On the power of the court to establish and assess costs for a deposi-tory, see *In re Three Additional Ap-peals Arising out of the San Juan Dupont Plaza Hotel Fire Litig.*, 93 F.3d 1 (1st Cir. 1996).

76. United States v. Am. Tel. & Tel. Co., 461 F. Supp. 1314, 1339 (D.D.C. 1978) (quoting Martin v. Rey-nolds Metals Corp., 297 F.2d 49, 56 (9th Cir. 1961)) (citations omitted).

In some circumstances, however, obtaining the discovery conducted in another case is not possible. This is especially true of grand jury proceedings, where the rules of grand jury secrecy adumbrate still murky limits on the ability of parties to uncover matters occurring before a grand jury.[77]

A final method of streamlining the discovery process is to use targeted, phased, or wave discovery. Targeted discovery focuses discovery just on certain factual or legal issues, in the hope that the resolution of these issues will advance the disposition of the case. In this regard, targeted discovery is much like pretrial bifurcation, and it has similar strengths and drawbacks. It is, however, a bit more informal than bifurcation, and perhaps carries less risk that the judge will become wedded to a particular view of the case.

The idea of phased discovery is to conduct discovery in distinct phases. When the phases are directed to a particular legal or factual issue, we have targeted discovery. But it is also possible to phase discovery in other ways. For instance, the initial phase of discovery might be designed to obtain only the first rough cut of information, from which a better assessment of the merits and needs of the case can be made. Likewise, discovery can be controlled by time period, geographical market, or any other structure that makes sense on the facts of a given case. The obvious drawback, as with targeted discovery, is the chance that steps will need to be retraced in later phases if the early discovery does not bring the case to closure.

Wave discovery had once been *de rigueur* in complex litigation, and it is still used with some frequency. Its idea is to conduct one form of discovery at a time. A standard approach is to begin with a wave of document production, then a wave of interrogatories, then a wave of depositions, and finally a wave of requests for admission. Although this method imposes a generally sensible order on a potentially chaotic discovery process, its problem is that the discovery of facts is often a fluid process; sometimes it is best to take testimony before requesting documents, or to send interrogatories as a follow-up to requests for admission. As a hard-and-fast rule, wave discovery can be draconian and, in some cases, counter-productive; as a guideline only, wave discovery does not seem to improve significantly on a world in which lawyers freely conduct discovery as they see fit.

c. Resolving Discovery Disputes Efficiently. Disputes concerning the entitlement to discovery are likely in cases with vast quantities of sometimes sensitive information. This problem is often exacer-

---

77. *See, e.g.,* Douglas Oil Co. v. Petrol Stops Northwest, 441 U.S. 211 (1979); TIDMARSH & TRANGSRUD, *su-* *pra* n.14, at 1113-16; MARCUS & SHERMAN, *supra* n.71, at 632-35.

bated because the usual penalty for the inadvertent disclosure of privileged information is severe: The disclosing party is deemed to have waived the privilege not only for the disclosed material but also for any other material for which the same privilege could be claimed.[78] Given the number of documents to which a waiver might extend, the incentive to take a cautious approach to discovery is great.

Hence, an important component in the efficient working of big-case discovery is the prior design of a process for the resolution of discovery disputes. One commonly used process is the "umbrella protection order," under which the parties are allowed to designate all or certain documents as confidential, but then share them with their opponents.[79] In return, opposing lawyers usually are ordered not to use the documents for any purpose other than the present litigation; and the distribution of documents to others (sometimes including the lawyers' clients) is curtailed or barred. If another party wishes to use disclosed material as evidence, parties retain the right to assert appropriate objections. The idea behind an umbrella protective order (also called a confidentiality order) is to reduce discovery disputes; the hope is that, in the end, most of the documents will turn out not to be relevant, or else the case will settle and the disputes will be avoided. In either event, very costly document-by-document wrangling will have been eliminated.

Although umbrella protective orders seem sensible, they are somewhat controversial. A leading treatise on pretrial litigation in big cases, the *Manual for Complex Litigation (Third),* takes a lukewarm approach to the device.[80] Umbrella protective orders do not work well in cases with a significant amount of information that the parties will refuse to disclose even with a guarantee of limited use (for instance, think of the government's state secrets privilege). Furthermore, there is some sense that litigation, as a public enterprise, should not work behind veils of secrecy. The Supreme Court has held that the public has no First Amendment right to obtain discovery materials, and has upheld a state protective order against constitutional challenge.[81] But the gnawing feeling that the court system should not participate in secretive enterprises remains. Indeed, a number of courts that issued confidentiality orders later

---

78. For a general discussion of waiver and courts' response to it, see TIDMARSH & TRANGSRUD, *supra* n.14, at 1145-47; MARCUS & SHERMAN, *supra* n.71, at 593-604.

79. The source for such an order is F.R.CIV.P.26(c)(7). *See* Zenith Radio

Corp. v. Matsushita Elec. Indus. Co., 529 F. Supp. 866 (E.D. Pa. 1981).

80. *See* MANUAL, *supra* n.8, § 21.432 (1995).

81. Seattle Times Co. v. Rhinehart, 467 U. S. 20 (1984).

removed the protection of the order, and allowed the public to have access to the discovery.[82] Parties considering entering into confidentiality orders must therefore be wary.

Other techniques to resolve discovery disputes efficiently are also sometimes available. If the case contains many potentially privileged documents, the court can establish in advance the criteria under which a privilege claim can be made. The court might require parties claiming a privilege to turn over the documents for *in camera* inspection by the court, redact the privileged information, and give the remainder to the opposing party. A court might combine both methods with another, by establishing screening criteria and then placing a special master or magistrate in charge of the *in camera* review process.[83]

d. Using Non-Traditional Methods for Obtaining Information. A final possibility is to find off-book ways to garner information efficiently. If a government has relevant information, the Freedom of Information Act[84] or its state counterpart might be used to obtain it, but it is not obvious that such a request is significantly less expensive than an ordinary subpoena. Moreover, this approach gives only the requesting party access to the information. In some situations, the parties have agreed to have neutral third parties collect information from mass tort claimants in lieu of traditional interrogatories and depositions. The process of negotiating the survey's contents can be difficult and expensive, but evaluators in one case in which the system was used thought that the surveys showed significant overall savings in comparison to traditional discovery.[85] Of course, such surveys move the discovery system into a more inquisitorial mode, and require the agreement of all parties to abandon their adversarial prerogatives. Getting the better-financed party to forsake a chance to impose entirely legitimate costs on a less well-financed party may require a *quid pro quo*. In the case mentioned above, the trade-off was that plaintiffs that twice failed to appear to answer the survey were dismissed from the case — a harsh

---

82. *See, e.g.,* Cipollone v. Liggett Group, Inc., 785 F.2d 1108 (3d Cir. 1986), *cert. denied,* 484 U.S. 976 (1987); *In re* "Agent Orange" Prod. Liab. Litig., 821 F.2d 139 (2d Cir.), *cert. denied sub nom.* Dow Chem. Co. v. Ryan, 484 U. S. 953 (1987); Arthur R. Miller, *Confidentiality, Protective Orders and Public Access to the Courts,* 105 HARV. L. REV. 427 (1991); Richard L. Marcus, *Myth and Reality in Protective Order Litigation,* 69 COR-

NELL L. REV. 1 (1983).

83. *In re* "Agent Orange" Prod. Liab. Litig., 97 F.R.D. 427 (E.D.N.Y. 1983).

84. 5 U.S.C. § 522.

85. Francis E. McGovern & Allen Lind, *The Discovery Survey,* 51 LAW & CONTEMP. PROBS. 41 (Autumn 1988). Professor McGovern had been a special master involved in the design and administration of the survey.

sanction that is at odds with the basic commitment of the Federal Rules to decide cases on their merits. The discovery survey has been rarely used.

D. CONCLUSION

Again, the lesson seems to be that the design of our procedural system ill suits the needs of the big case, but all of the available responses require us to make uncomfortable sacrifices of some of our cherished procedural ideals. We might imagine that, at some point, technology will obviate many of these issues: Information will be largely kept in electronic form, and search engines or newer forms of artificial intelligence will quickly do the research and discovery at the lawyer's direction. Discovery will be simple and cheap, so there will be little need of issue-narrowing devices or lead counsel arrangements.

That day, however, lies in the future.[86] For the present, the chicken-and-egg problem of narrowing issues and discovering facts, and the quandary of our open-book, on-the-merits, and by-the-parties pretrial system, remain our reality. The response to the quandary has been uneven. Case management suggests a more activist, inquisitorial role for the judges, but in its implementation, case management has not resulted in an activist judge entirely different in kind from the passive judge of adversarial lore. The willingness to bend traditional rules and roles is greatest with the appointment of lead counsel, more modest with the use of issue-narrowing devices, and nearly absent with discovery. Alternatives to traditional rules and roles have not sprung forth in a burst of creative energy; virtually every technique is one as applicable in ordinary litigation as in complex litigation.

Perhaps the reason that this is true of discovery is a pragmatic one. Unlike a problem of aggregation that can be solved (or at least controlled) with a single class action certification or anti-suit injunction, discovery requires intensive day-to-day involvement for which the American judiciary is ill-equipped. A far more significant re-orientation toward the inquisitorial system, together with the supporting infrastructure and the appointment of cadres of new judges, would be required to support this involvement. Should such involvement be encouraged or discouraged? Put differently, will a single inquisitorial judge in fact lead to a better discovery outcome

---

86. For an examination of some of the ways that present technology can already assist lawyers and the legal issues that surround this tech-nology, see TIDMARSH & TRANGSRUD, *supra* n.14, at 1173-95; MARCUS & SHERMAN, *supra* n. 71, at 528-31, 536-42.

than a system controlled by the parties' lawyers? The answers to
these questions may hinge on whether judicially-controlled discovery
is ultimately cheaper; whether the problem of impositional discovery
(which is the one discovery issue that a non-adversarial judicial
process would eliminate) is real; whether the outcomes of judicially-
controlled cases would be either more accurate or more acceptable;
and finally, whether the citizenry of the United States would be
willing both to pay the additional taxes needed to support such
judges and to tolerate the inevitable accretion of power to unelected
government officials.

Chapter 7

TRIAL COMPLEXITY

As we observed at the start of the last chapter, one of the central issues — if not *the* central issue — in the design of any procedural system is the trial. Once we know the format of the factfinding process, then we can design both forward and backward in the procedural system.

Our heritage of factfinding is a confused one. On the one hand, we employed the common law trial, in which witnesses testified live and were subject to cross-examination, a lay jury determined factual disputes, and all claims and issues were definitively resolved in a culminating trial event. Factfinding was different in equity, whose ancestry lay in the contrasting civil law tradition: "Trials" were only a series of discrete hearings that resolved issues seriatim, evidence was presented only in written form, and a chancellor (not a jury) made factual determinations.

The Federal Rules of Civil Procedure abolished any formal distinctions between law and equity. In the main, the trial process in the merged system ran like the old common law trial: live witnesses, cross-examination, a single culminating trial event. The Federal Rules also borrowed certain trial features from equity — most noticeably, it allowed a case to be broken up into separate trials "in furtherance of convenience or to avoid prejudice, or when separate trials will be conducive to expedition and economy."[1] But, driven in part by the commands of the Seventh Amendment, the old distinctions between juries, which are the factfinders at law, and judges, who are factfinders in equity, remained relevant. For instance, a Rule 42 order for a separate trial must "always preserv[e] inviolate the right of trial by jury as declared by the Seventh Amendment."

Although equity had its origin in the civil law's inquisitorial tradition, the mature forms of common law and equity had one common feature: a decidedly adversarial flavor in the trial itself.

---

1. F.R.Civ.P. 42(b).

Nothing in the Federal Rules of Civil Procedure or the Federal Rules of Evidence has changed that flavor. The fundamental trial model remains one in which the lawyers are charged with the tasks of presenting evidence and arguments to the law-giver and factfinder, while the law-giver (the judge) and factfinder (judge or jury, depending on the claim) sit passively, listen to both sides, and make a determination without predisposition or prejudice.

In the trials of some (but not all) big cases, the standard model threatens to produce an outcome that is insufficiently grounded in reason. In some situations, the problem may be, as it is during pretrial, the inability of the lawyers to marshal the evidence needed to present effective arguments. More frequently, however, the problem lies with the factfinder, who is expected to make a reasoned decision on the basis of thousands of bits of often technical information delivered over the course of several weeks or months. In these cases, reasoned decisionmaking is threatened, as are the accuracy and acceptability of the judgment itself.

Not every case that presents issues of structural or pretrial complexity also presents problems of trial complexity; conversely, some cases that present no issues of structural or pretrial complexity present serious issues of factfinder comprehension. For instance, if Smith sues XYZ for an asbestos injury, the case might well pose, as we have seen, structural challenges. The case might even present difficult pretrial issues as Smith's lawyer seeks to uncover vast quantities of information describing XYZ's pattern of manufacturing and marketing behavior. Assuming that Smith's lawyer can marshal this information, however, the trial itself would not appear to be exceptionally difficult for the lawyers, the law-giver, or the factfinder. On the other hand, if the structural problems of Smith's case be overcome by aggregating his case with those of thousands of other asbestos victims, enormous comprehension difficulties can occur at trial. In the standard-model all-issues trial, how is the factfinder to keep straight the cacophony of information about different plaintiffs' exposure histories, injuries, and damages, or the defendants' varying behavior over time and among product lines?

In this chapter we examine some of the techniques that have been used to deal with these two problems of trial complexity. We begin by looking at the possibility of restructuring the adversarial model's division of responsibility among lawyers, factfinders, and lawgivers. We then look at the two means through which factfinder comprehension can be increased: either by narrowing the number of issues that the factfinder must consider at one time or by changing the standard trial format to increase factfinder comprehension.

A. RESTRUCTURING THE RELATIONSHIPS AMONG LAWYERS, FACTFINDERS, AND LAWGIVERS AT TRIAL

The adversarial model places the lawyers firmly in charge of presenting evidence and arguments to a passive jury and judge. The passivity of jury and judge ensures, according to theory, the neutrality of the decisionmakers, and allows them to make their decisions on an objective basis of what they see and hear, rather than on a subjective basis of the preconceptions and biases that might overtake a more active jury or judge. The standard model also guarantees the autonomy of each party to present the evidence and arguments as he or she sees fit. In the heyday of common law pleading, in which claim and party joinder was highly restricted, this guarantee rarely caused problems of juror or judicial comprehension. In a modern case governed by the transactional assumption of joinder, individual presentation of evidence and individual arguments for each party threaten to create information overload and to extend trials beyond the capacity of most factfinders to recall adequately evidence from the trial.

As with pretrial complexity, therefore, the first question to consider is whether a restructuring of the relationships among lawyers, factfinders, and law-givers might ameliorate the problem of trial complexity and sufficiently increase the level of comprehension by the decisionmakers. Such a restructuring might move trials in complex cases away from the adversarial system's commitment to individual autonomy. It might also weaken our commitment to jury trial, and to the principle that it is the unique province of the courts to declare the law.[2] Assuming that the answer to this question is "yes," the second question is whether the marginal gains in comprehension are worth the cost of cherished political, constitutional, and procedural ideals.

1. Restructuring the Lawyers

In the last chapter, we saw that courts claimed an inherent power to appoint lead counsel or committees of counsel to work on a group's behalf during the pretrial process.[3] The next issue is whether such a power might extend to trial.

The advantages and disadvantages of such a power would largely be the same as those that were discussed in the last chapter. Since we are now talking about trial rather than pretrial, however, some

---

2.   *Cf.* Marbury v. Madison, 5 U.S. (1 Cranch) 137, 177 (1803) ("It is emphatically the province and duty of the judicial department to say what the law is.").

3.   *See supra* pp. 205-10.

aspects of this power take on a different mein. On the one hand, the appointment of a single trial counsel for a group of individuals eliminates the problem of having 50 or 100 different lawyers all presenting evidence and cross-examining witnesses on behalf of similarly situated clients.[4] On the other hand, the incursion on the autonomous right of each party to present the case in that individual's best interests seems more dramatically infringed during trial. The strengths, weaknesses, and flavor of each individual's case inevitably are lost when a single lawyer blends multiple cases into a smooth, bland consistency.

Whatever the theoretical propriety of trial counsel arrangements,[5] courts do claim the inherent power to appoint trial counsel, and they use the power with some frequency. For the most part, the parties acquiesce in the power; it is difficult to find cases that challenge an appointment. The only noteworthy case is *In re Air Crash Disaster at Detroit Metropolitan Airport on August 16, 1987,*[6] in which one plaintiff argued that the appointment of a lead counsel for trial "abridged her right to representation by the counsel of her choice." Relying on prior cases appointing lead counsel (most of which actually involved pretrial appointments), the court rejected the argument out-of-hand.

2. *Restructuring the Factfinder*

Unlike the restructuring of counsel relationships, which has a strong affinity to the material on pretrial complexity, the restructuring of the factfinder is a new question for us. As we have already seen, the constitutional cleft of the Seventh Amendment[7] divides factfinding responsibility between juries and judges: Juries generally determine the facts in matters whose heritage lies in the common law, while judges generally decide facts in cases whose heritage lies in equity.[8] Congress can shift the divide by statutorily

---

4. Whether this would occur is far from certain. Presumably good trial lawyers would voluntarily agree to coordinate and limit their presentations so that factfinder confusion, which is often in no plaintiff's best interest, does not exist.

5. For a general criticism, see Roger H. Trangsrud, *Mass Trials in Mass Tort Cases: A Dissent,* 1989 U. ILL. L. REV. 69.

6. 737 F. Supp. 396 (E.D. Mich. 1989).

7. For the text of the amendment, see *supra* Ch.6, n.1.

8. Judges bear a limited factfinding role even in jury-trial cases. Upon proper motion, they ensure that the jury's factfinding is neither unreasonable nor against the great weight of the evidence. If a reasonable jury could determine the facts and the verdict in only one fashion, the court can enter judgment as a matter of law during trial or renewed judgment as a matter of law after trial. *See* F.R.CIV.P. 50(a), 50(b). The court can

authorizing jury trials in otherwise judge-tried cases, but it cannot, consistent with the Seventh Amendment, generally transfer fact-finding from the jury to a judge.[9]

When law and equity remained separate, determining the identity of the factfinder was a simple matter. After the merger of law and equity in the 1938 Federal Rules of Civil Procedure, however, the matter became far more complex. All transactionally related claims, whether legal or equitable in the old nomenclature, could now be joined and heard togther in a single action. Should a judge or jury now decide the facts relevant to both claims?

Numerous solutions to this problem are possible. One idea is to let the judge decide the facts relevant to the equitable issues and the jury decide the facts relevant to the legal issues, with each making an independent determination on overlapping facts. This idea, however, violates normal rules of issues preclusion (according to which the first actually litigated factual determinations are binding), is inefficient in its use of factfinding resources, and may lead to the spectacle of judges and juries disagreeing about facts that are based on the same evidence. Another possibility would be to determine whether the action was "primarily" legal or equitable. Another would be to determine whether the legal or the equitable aspects of the case were filed first. Yet another approach would be to hand the entire case over to the jury once some jury-triable issues exist.

The Supreme Court has rejected all of these approaches. To begin with, the Court has stated a preference for jury factfinding: When facts are relevant to both legal and equitable claims, the jury must determine those facts and thus bind the judge to them. Since the jury also decides the factual issues relevant only to the legal aspects of the case, the judge is left to decide those facts relevant only to the equitable aspects of the case.[10]

But this preference does not answer the logically precedent question of what is a "legal," as opposed to an "equitable," claim. What, in other words, is the exact reach of the Seventh Amendment? In *Ross v. Bernhard*,[11] the Court sought to answer this question by a three-part test: "first, the pre-merger custom with reference to such questions; second, the remedy sought; and third, the practical abilities and limitations of juries."[12] The first issue has subsequently been understood to refer to the practices of equity and law in 1791,

---

also order a new trial if the verdict is against the evidence's weight. *See* F.R.CIV.P. 59(a).

9. There is an exception to this rule in certain "public rights" cases. *See* Granfinanciera, S.A. v. Nordberg,

492 U.S. 33 (1989).

10. *See* Beacon Theatres Inc. v. Westover, 359 U.S. 500 (1959).

11. 396 U.S. 531 (1970).

12. *Id.* at 538 n.10.

the year in which the Seventh Amendment was adopted. The second issue hinges on whether an injunction (the usual relief in equity) or damages (the usual relief at law) is sought. Of the two issues, "the second stage . . . is more important than the first."[13] The third issue has, at least in more recent cases, been understood to mean that Congress can statutorily authorize a judge to determine facts that would otherwise be jury-tried in "public rights" cases — cases in which Congress has the authority to delegate the factfinding to an administrative agency.[14]

Application of these principles is not always easy,[15] but for our purposes the main points are simple. First, sometimes a jury will determine the facts, and sometimes a judge will do so. Second, the division of responsibility is largely controlled by the Seventh Amendment, a fact that makes it difficult to restructure factfinding responsibilities when a jury is involved. Finally, the volume and often technical nature of the evidence in complex cases can make it difficult for either a jury or a judge to perform adequately the factfinding function. Since the functional constraints are somewhat different for a jury and a judge, we consider separately the restructuring of the jury's and the judge's factfinding responsibilities.

a. *Replacing the Jury.* One of the great academic procedural issues, for which more trees have given their lives than nearly any other, is whether there exists a "complexity exception" that allows a judge in a complex case to strike the jury and determine the facts on his or her own. The argument for such an exception is straightforward. Certain complex cases present such a vast quantity of information, or else information of such a technical nature, that a lay person cannot be expected to understand, process, and recall it. In these cases, the lay jury process leads to irrational decisionmaking in which jurors will make decisions based on whim, prejudice, or misinformation. This state of affairs leads to uncertainty in commercial affairs, and encourages meritless lawsuits. The jury must be replaced by the judge, who can determine the facts without falling victim to these problems.

Granting the accuracy of this argument for the moment, the difficulty lies in finding a way to give the argument any legal effect. The Seventh Amendment speaks in categorical terms, and contains no complexity exception. Does this mean that efforts to substitute rational for irrational factfinding are constitutionally forbidden?

---

13. *Granfinanciera*, 492 U.S. at 42.

14. *Id.* at 51-55.

15. To make matters more complicated, there are a couple of important refinements that we do not mention here. For a short synopsis, see JAY TIDMARSH & ROGER H. TRANGSRUD, COMPLEX LITIGATION AND THE ADVERSARY SYSTEM 1216-19 (1998).

A few courts and many commentators have thought not. Their arguments have run on two tracks. The first is to suggest that the Seventh Amendment itself contains a complexity exception. Some commentators have located the exception in the history of law and equity. They argue that equity opened its doors to parties whenever a serious deficiency in the courts of law could be shown. According to this argument, had an allegation of jury incompetence been successfully proven in 1791, equity would have intervened to hear the case without a jury. One problem with this argument is that, although claims of defects in the jury system had over time led equity to take jurisdiction over certain cases, no cases around 1791 in fact made a claim of incompetence-creating complexity. Nor are there any definitive indicators that equity would have acted as the commentators have predicted. A second problem is the Supreme Court's more recent pronouncements that the second *Ross* factor — the nature of the relief requested — carries more weight than the history of jury trial in 1791.

A somewhat different argument, albeit still on the "complexity exception" track, seizes on *Ross v. Bernhard*'s modern construction of the Seventh Amendment — especially on the third "practical abilities and limitations of juries" factor of footnote 10. According to this argument, juries do not possess the practical ability to decide certain complex claims in an acceptably rational manner. In these cases, this third factor outweighs the other two, and the jury must therefore be stricken. Problems with this argument include the fact that this third factor, which was dictum in *Ross v. Bernhard*, had no prior precedential support, and has been subsequently construed and limited by the Court in a way generally inconsistent with this argument.[16]

The second track concedes that the Seventh Amendment does not bar juries in complex trials, and argues instead that the due process clause of the Fifth Amendment requires the jury to be stricken. The argument runs as follows: One component of the due process clause is the guarantee to litigants that the decisionmaker will use reason, and reason-enhancing procedures, to arrive at an outcome.[17] When the jury is not capable of coming to a rational decision because of a case's complexity, due process is offended. In the battle between the command of the Seventh Amendment and that of the Fifth, the Fifth wins; the jury must be struck. The fundamental problem with this argument is evident: Each step of the argument's syllogism is a premise that is neither obviously nor intuitively correct.

---

16. *See supra* n.10, n.14 and accompanying text.

17. *See* ch.1, n.4 and accompanying text.

Despite the academic interest in the issue,[18] only a modest half-dozen federal cases have ever stricken a jury in a complex case. Of this number, all but one has relied on the Seventh Amendment,[19] and the other has used the due process clause.[20] A host of cases has rejected the arguments.[21]

Perhaps the greatest flaws in the jury-striking arguments are the assumptions that (1) a jury is not capable of rationally deciding certain cases, and (2) a judge is more capable than a jury. The available empirical, anecdotal, and psychological evidence suggests that, contrary to the legal culture's myth, juries generally do quite well at determining facts, and even have certain abilities (such as the benefit of multiple perspectives — twelve heads can sometimes be better than one) that a judge does not. Little of this data, however, was taken from complex cases, so the institutional capacity of the jury in these cases is still unclear. But a lack of clarity is far from the type of showing of jury incompetence that should undergird a decision to overlook a constitutional command.

Likewise, it is far from obvious that a judge is a better factfinder in a complex case than a jury. The judge has some notable advantages: years of factfinding experience, the ability to deliberate at a more thoughtful and leisurely pace, the presence of law clerks, and the ability to re-open the evidence in the event a stumbling block is reached. But years of experience do not necessarily make the judge a better factfinder, or make the judge's experience more valuable than that of jury members. One study reports that judge-jury agreement on the outcome is 63% of the complex cases in the data set, with judges tending to favor plaintiffs when disagreement exists. Other studies suggest that judges and juries have similar problems in assessing difficult technical evidence.[22] Moreover, no studies have yet examined whether increased contact by the judge during pretrial case management might skew the factfinding of the judge, but that risk remains. As for the remaining advantages of a bench trial, many litigators and judges would say that the discipline and enforced simplicity of a jury trial makes the trial run better and smoother in the long run.

---

18. For a small sampling of articles, see TIDMARSH & TRANGSRUD, *supra* n.15, at 1240.

19. *See, e.g., In re* Boise Cascade Sec. Litig., 420 F. Supp. 99 (W.D. Wash. 1976); ILC Peripherals Leasing Corp. v. Int'l Bus. Mach. Corp., 458 F. Supp. 423, 444-49 (N.D. Cal. 1978); Bernstein v. Universal Pictures, Inc., 79 F.R.D. 59 (S.D. N.Y. 1978).

20. *In re* Japanese Elec. Prods. Antitrust Litig., 631 F.2d 1069 (3d Cir. 1980).

21. *See* TIDMARSH & TRANGSRUD, *supra* n.15, at 1233-34.

22. For a general summary of empirical evidence or jury performance in civil cases, see *id.* at 1237-39.

At the end of the day, therefore, most courts have sought ways to make the jury's task easier, rather than to eliminate the jury altogether. Before we examine some of these methods, we stop to examine possible ways to restructure the factfinding process when a judge acts as factfinder.

   b. *Assisting the Judge.* One of the assumptions underlying the striking of a jury in complex cases is that a judge would be a better factfinder. As we have discussed, judges have some institutional advantages as factfinders, but they too lack the expertise to decide many technical questions. If judges can seek assistance with such questions, then perhaps they will have the type of strong advantage over juries that will both make judges better factfinders in complex bench-tried cases and make a stronger case for striking the jury in otherwise jury-tried cases.

   One option — to appoint an expert to finally determine disputed technical facts — is certainly out of bounds. The essence of adjudication by the bench is that the final factual decisionmaker is an Article III judge, and any efforts that undermine judicial decisionmaking violate the Constitution. That point was made in *La Buy v. Howes Leather Co.*,[23] an antitrust case in which the trial judge, facing a six-week bench trial, referred the trial to a special master who was to recommend findings of fact and conclusions of law. The stated reasons for the referral under Rule 53 were the congestion of the court's docket, as well as the complexity and length of the trial. As we discussed in the last chapter, *La Buy* affirmed the issuance of a writ of mandamus against the trial reference, which it thought amounted to "an abdication of the judicial function."[24] The Court emphasized that the district court had become familiar with the litigation during pretrial, and that the complexity of the case was a reason to have a skilled and experienced Article III factfinder, *not* a reason to appoint a surrogate factfinder.

   As strong as the language of *La Buy* might seem, the decision was a limited one. First, Rule 53 still contemplates referrals to special masters in "exceptional circumstances," including equitable accountings. Second, Judge La Buy had appointed an attorney as master — not an economist or business person who might have had technical knowledge of the markets or industry involved. Might a referral to an expert master amount to an "exceptional circumstance" when such technical issues are in play? *La Buy* is not clear on the point. Third, *La Buy* involved a situation in which a master was, subject only to limited judicial review, the factfinder. Might a judge be able to appoint a "technical advisor" or "expert consultant" with

---

   23. 352 U.S. 249 (1957) (5-4 decision).   **24.** *Id.* at 256.

whom to confer, as long as the responsibility for factfinding rests ultimately on the judge's shoulders? Again, *La Buy* is silent.

On this last matter, some courts have appointed a "technical advisor" to assist the court in its factfinding responsibilities. For instance, in *Reilly v. United States*,[25] the district court appointed an economist as a technical advisor when it felt that the defendant had failed to provide adequate evidence to help the court assess the costs of future medical care. The defendant's belated objection to this procedure was rejected by the court of appeals, which did not think that the procedure so manifestly unjust as to overcome the defendant's waiver of the issue when it failed to submit a timely objection.

Underlying *Reilly*'s narrow holding, however, were two points of greater significance. First, the court of appeals affirmatively believed that district courts have the power to appoint technical advisors. The exact source of the power was (once again) uncertain. The court of appeals rejected resort to Federal Rule of Evidence 706, which allows appointment of expert witnesses, because it correctly observed that technical advisors do not testify.[26] The court also declined to hold that an appointment of an advisor was appropriate under Federal Rule of Civil Procedure 53, whose plain language suggests a somewhat different trial role for a master. Instead, the court of appeals located the authority in the district court's inherent power, a proposition for which it cited an opinion, authored by Justice Brandeis, often used to justify trial innovations.[27] *Reilly*'s standard for the exercise of this inherent power — that such appointments are the "exception and not the rule," reserved for "truly extraordinary cases where the introduction of outside skills and expertise, not possessed by the judge, will hasten the just adjudication of a dispute without dislodging the delicate balance of the juristic role"[28] — sounds a great deal like the standard for a Rule 53 reference to a master.

Second, *Reilly* recognized that the use of a technical advisor, whose conversations with the judge are neither subject to examination nor open to the parties, requires certain procedural safeguards. Among them are notice to the parties of the advisor's identity, an

---

25. 863 F.2d 149 (1st Cir. 1988).

26. Although the court of appeals does not mention it, Rule 53 would also appear not to work because the role of the master at trial is designed to be a public one.

27. *See Ex Parte* Peterson, 253 U.S. 300, 312 (1920) ("Courts have (at least in the absence of legislation to the contrary) inherent power to provide themselves with appropriate instruments for the performance of their duties.").

28. *Reilly*, 863 F.2d at 156. The district court's appointment of an advisor under this standard is reviewed only for an abuse of discretion. *Id.*

opportunity to object to the proposed appointment, a requirement that the advisor file a written report, a "job description" for the advisor, and an affidavit from the advisor stating compliance with this job description. Although most of the safeguards were missing in *Reilly*, the court of appeals held that the government had waived its right to object.

The Supreme Court has never decided whether the use of technical advisors is the type of "abdication of judicial function" that infected *La Buy*. The use of advisors certainly suggests a very different role for the judge — and for the lawyers, who now lose the adversarial right to control the presentation of evidence and arguments to the factfinder. Whether technical advisors remain the "way out" for judges who are unable to understand the technical aspects necessary for rational adjudication, or whether the judge must simply insist on better adversarial presentations or court-appointed expert witnesses under Rule 706, remains to be seen.

3. Restructuring the Lawgiver. In the adversarial system, the judge declares the law to which the facts must be applied. Sometimes the cases and literature refer to a case being both factually *and* legally complex. This observation gives rise to a question: When a case presents complex issues of law, can the lawgiving function be restructured (as we have seen the lawyers' presentation function and juries' and judges' factfinding functions restructured)?

The answer seems to be "No." *Reed v. Cleveland Board of Education*[29] pushes the envelope on this issue to its farthest limit. In *Reed*, a school desegregation case, the district judge appointed a constitutional law professor to help him handle thorny legal questions. The professor's communications were *ex parte*, and consisted of drafting orders and consulting with the judge, his law clerks, and the master. As in *Reilly*, the defendant never filed a timely objection to the appointment. Unlike *Reilly*, however, the court of appeals thought that the appointment of an advisor exceeded the court's authority. Because the defendant had not objected, the court of appeals affirmed the award of fees to the professor for the time spent consulting with the master. With regard to advice given to the judge or his clerks, no award was permitted: In conjunction with the briefing by the parties and *amicus curiae*, the court of appeals reasoned, the district court was capable of handling legal issues on its own. To consult with an advisor *ex parte* amounted to "a partial abdication of his role. . . . [T]he adversary system as it has developed in this country precludes the court from receiving out-of-court advice on legal issues in a case."[30]

29. 607 F.2d 737 (6th Cir. 1979).   **30.** *Id.* at 748.

The few other cases considering the issue have flatly rejected the use of legal advisors.[31]

4. Summary

The restructuring of the lawyers' roles in complex litigation is an accepted fact — at least for plaintiffs. The restructuring of the judge's lawgiving role and the jury's factfinding role may be impossible to accomplish. In limited circumstances, the judge's factfinding role can be changed.

In each of these areas, the critical issue is why the court's inherent power permits some forms of restructuring but not others. The facile answer is that the Seventh Amendment's jury trial right, the Fifth Amendment's due process clause, and Article III impose constitutional limits on this power. But such an answer begs the question of what the Seventh Amendment, the due process clause, and Article III require.

Whatever the answer to these questions, the fact remains that complex cases often strain the factfinders. In the rest of this chapter we focus on ways that this process might be made to run more smoothly. These techniques roughly break down in the same manner as the pretrial techniques: those that narrow the number of issues that the factfinder must consider at one time and techniques that help a factfinder to more effectively comprehend the information presented at trial. After we examine these techniques, you might again profitably ask whether we need more, or less, restructuring of the lawyer-jury-judge relationship in complex trials.

B. NARROWING ISSUES

Assume that Smith's case has been aggregated in some fashion with the cases of 1,000 other alleged victims of XYZ's actions. In the traditional common law trial, all of the outstanding issues in the case — from the largely overlapping issues of XYZ's liability to the highly individualized issues of each victim's exposure and damages — should be tried before the factfinder at one time. This prospect seems onerous, to say the least. Lawyers may have difficulty presenting individual proofs and arguments. The factfinder may have difficulty recalling voluminous evidence or comprehending technical, medical, or scientific concepts, thus creating risks of factfinder confusion and the melding of individual claims into a gestalt. One of the ways to

---

31. *Reilly,* 863 F.2d at 157;   (E.D. Tex. 1986).
Young v. Pierce, 640 F. Supp. 1476

avoid these problems is to narrow the amount of information that the factfinder must hear at one time.

1. Structural Limitations on Narrowing Issues

As we have observed, the usual form of the common law trial was to decide all issues at one time; equity's tradition was to break the adjudication into a series of discrete issues and hearings. If the case needs to be narrowed into digestible bits in order to assist the lawyers' presentation of evidence or to avoid factfinder confusion, perhaps the procedures of equity could be applied.

But the problem is more challenging than that; certain realities constrain our ability to abandon the all-issues trial. Some of these constraints are cultural; we must honor certain expectations of what a trial should do and how it should run if the litigants and the society as a whole are to accept the trial's outcome. Some constraints have a more traditionally legal hue. In bench-tried cases, separating the case into discrete-issue trials presents few structural difficulties. In cases in which some or all of the facts are to be tried to a jury, however, the Seventh Amendment again presents an obstacle. The difficulty is not the Seventh Amendment's first clause — the right to jury trial in "Suits at common law" — but rather its second clause. Often called the "re-examination clause," this part of the Seventh Amendment commands that "no fact tried by jury, shall be otherwise re-examined in any Court of the United States, than according to the rules of the common law." This rather odd phrasing has generally been understood to mean, among other things, that the issues in separate trials cannot be broken up in such a way that a second or third jury, in determining the facts relevant to its issues, is able to re-examine and re-determine the factual issues that the first jury found in deciding its portion of the case.[32] Preventing this forbidden re-examination may sound like a simple matter, but as we shall see, it is not.

The first half of the Seventh Amendment might also come into play. Arguably, the right to jury trial can be read to protect the classic all-issues trial of 1791. In its purest form, this view seems impossible to maintain — especially in light of Justice Brandeis's observation that "[n]ew devices may be used to adapt the ancient institution [of jury trial] to present needs and to make of it an efficient instrument in the administration of justice. Indeed, such changes are essential to the preservation of the right."[33] At some point, however, issue-narrowing changes in the structure of trial

---

32. Gasoline Prods. Co. v. Champlin Refining Co., 283 U.S. 494 (1931).

33. *Peterson*, 253 U.S. at 309-10.

may be so radical as to violate the very nature of the individualized adjudication arguably implicit in the right to jury trial.

Third, the same claim might be made more generally as a matter of due process, which governs both jury and non-jury actions. Due process requires not only a commitment to procedures that can rationally adjudicate a dispute, but also a modicum of adherence to traditional adversarial methods. Truly unusual methods for narrowing issues at trial might therefore violate due process.

A final, infrequently mentioned structural constraint is *Erie Railroad Co. v. Tompkins*,[34] which requires federal courts in diversity cases to apply state substantive law and, in some situations, state procedural law as well. A federal court's reworking of traditional trial methods as a means of narrowing issues might have the potential to so skew the outcome or the deliberative process that it could be viewed as a reworking of the substantive law itself — thus bringing a federal court into potential conflict with *Erie*'s command.

2. Strategic Behavior

Any method of adjudication favors some parties over others. Lawyers who wish to maintain the traditional trial form, as well as those who wish to change it, often do so because they believe that the method they advocate will change the odds of a favorable adjudication. In some cases, a party will contend for an all-issues trial precisely to create factfinder confusion or sympathy; this is especially true if the party's case is weak. Even when the case is not weak, however, a party may wish to preserve the traditional method of trial because that method would appear more likely to lead to a favorable outcome, albeit at the expense of an arguably more rational resolution. As we examine the following techniques designed to narrow the issues at trial, we will see concretely what we have stated here in the abstract: how the choice of trial structure is often a matter of strategy as well as a matter of law.

3. Responses

Although there are numerous ways in which the issues at trial can be narrowed,[35] we focus here on three that are the most promising — and the most controversial. They are bifurcation, trial by statistics, and limiting the time for trial. We encountered variants of the first and third methods as pretrial issue-narrowing techniques; the second is new.

---

34. 304 U.S. 64 (1938).

35. For a fuller treatment of

these issues, see TIDMARSH & TRANGS-RUD, *supra* n.15, at 1273-333.

a. Bifurcation. The most obvious way to narrow the issues that the facfinder must determine is to split the case up into a series of discrete trials, in the mode of equity or the continental systems of procedure. This method limits the amount of information that the lawyers must present and the factfinder must consider at any given trial. Moreover, if the issue is chosen well, the determination on that issue might pretermit further proceedings. For instance, if Smith and his thousand co-plaintiffs were exposed to asbestos at a shipyard in Maine, and if XYZ contends that it never sold asbestos to this shipyard, a trial limited to the factual issue of marketing would present a discrete, digestible issue that might otherwise be buried in an all-issues trial. If the jury finds that XYZ did not market asbestos to the shipyard, a much lengthier trial will also have been avoided.

This division of the trial into parts is usually called "bifurcation." "Bifurcation" occurs when the trial is split into two parts, "trifurcation" occurs when it is split into three parts, and "polyfurcation" occurs when it is split into four or more parts; the shorthand term "bifurcation," however, is typically used to describe them all. Unlike its pretrial counterpart, trial bifurcation has clear support in the text of the Federal Rules. Rule 42 permits separate trials "in furtherance of convenience or to avoid prejudice, or when separate trials will be conducive to expedition or economy." Such separate trials must, however, "always preserv[e] inviolate the right of trial by jury as declared by the Seventh Amendment . . . ."

Trial bifurcation suffers from many of the difficulties of pretrial bifurcation, in addition to the new problem of Seventh Amendment compliance. Often there is no easy, dispositive issue like the marketing of XYZ's asbestos; the easy issues are not dispositive, and the dispositive issues are not easy. If the bifurcation does not work, the ultimate conclusion of the trial might be extended rather than shortened, and witnesses who must now testify at two trials will be doubly inconvenienced.

In addition, trial bifurcation has the potential to seriously skew a case's outcome — hence the strategic interest in bifurcation by some parties. The available data on bifurcated trials show that, when a case is bifurcated between liability and damages issues, with the liability issues tried first, the chances for a defense verdict rise substantially.[36] This data is backed up by anecdotes, perhaps the

---

36. The famous study demonstrating this effect is Hans Zeisel & Thomas Callahan, *Split Trials and Time Saving: A Statistical Analysis,* 76 HARV. L. REV. 1606 (1963). An experimental study showing a similar effect in complex litigation is Irwin A. Horowitz & Kenneth S. Bordens, *An Experimental Investigation of Procedural Issues in Complex Tort Trials,* 14 LAW & HUM. BEHAV. 269 (1990).

most famous of which is *In re Bendectin Litigation*.[37] In *Bendectin*, more than 1,100 federal cases were multidistricted. After giving some of the plaintiffs the opportunity to opt out and return to their original transferor forums for trial, the district court ordered the trial trifurcated. The issue of whether Bendectin could cause birth defects was tried first; subsequent trials on the defendant's liability and on individual issues of causation and damages were to be held later. The effect of trifurcation was to exclude from the first jury evidence of the defendant's alleged wrongdoing in the marketing of Bendectin, as well as the horrendous injuries that the plaintiffs had suffered. The trial became, to use the plaintiffs' famous catchphrase, a "sterile or laboratory atmosphere"[38] concerning Bendectin and its possible side effects. After a three-week trial the jury returned a verdict for the defendant, finding that Bendectin did not cause any birth defects. As a result, 844 cases — cases that would otherwise have taken 182 judge-years to try — were terminated after 15 days of trial. Finding no injustice to the plaintiffs but significant overall economy in this procedure, the court of appeals upheld, under an abuse of discretion standard, the district court's decision to trifurcate.

In one sense, the *Bendectin* trifurcation worked exactly as it should have. In another sense, the outcome for at least some of the 844 cases would almost certainly have been different had the jury heard the damning evidence of Merrell Dow's behavior and the sympathetic evidence of deformed children. Whether this fact is troubling might depend on how you one perceives the purpose and nature of factfinding processes. You might also be troubled by the fact that a possibly outcome-determinative procedure was applied just to these cases, and not to other product liability or mass tort cases. You should certainly be troubled by the fact that many MDL Bendectin plaintiffs who opted out of the trifurcated trial received single all-issue trials in the transferor districts, as did most of the plaintiffs in state court. In some of these individually tried cases, plaintiffs identically situated to the *Bendectin* plaintiffs prevailed. A greater breach of our trans-substantive goal, not only in like types of cases but also in virtually identical cases, would be hard to imagine. Without here choosing sides about which procedure was better, a procedural choice, undertaken in the name of economy, appears to have influenced the outcome of individual cases.

Courts have sought to soften these concerns about bifurcation in various ways. One approach, which was popular in asbestos cases, was to "reverse bifurcate" — to try damages before liability. Another is to use "exemplar" or "bellwether" plaintiffs. In this method, the jury determines bifurcated issues for all plaintiffs, as well as all the

---

37. 857 F.2d 290 (6th Cir. 1988).   **38.** *Id.* at 315.

issues for the bellwether plaintiffs. The injection of the claims and
faces of actual plaintiffs makes the trial somewhat lengthier, but
arguably lessens the sterility of a liability-only trial. Should the
defendant prevail on one of the bifurcated issues, the case ends.
Should the defendant lose, it is precluded from relitigating common
issues, it gains good information about the judgment value of the
remaining cases, and it can begin the task of settling them. That, at
least, is the theory. In practice, the selection of the bellwethers,
whether done randomly or through nominations from the parties, can
have an enormous influence over the process.

Even if the practical and policy problems of bifurcation can be
resolved, the Seventh Amendment issue still looms large. Whatever
issues are selected for bifurcated trial must be sufficiently distinct
from the remaining issues that a second jury will not have the need
to determine the same factual issues again. In *Bendectin* the issue
of the birth defects that Bendectin caused would not have been
determined again; assuming that the jury had found that Bendectin
caused certain defects, subsequent juries could have skipped over
that issue and focused on whether an individual plaintiff had that
birth defect and the mother had a sufficient exposure to Bendectin to
cause the defect.

Sometimes, however, carving the case into discrete issues is not
so simple. Suppose that the judge decides that the best way to try
the *Smith* case is to begin by holding a trial to determine the fact of
XYZ's wrongdoing. If the jury finds wrongdoing, subsequent juries
would still need to determine, on a case-by-case basis, issues of
proximate causation and comparative negligence — both of which
require the latter juries to consider in some fashion the issue of XYZ's
wrongful behavior. Would this division of the issues violate the re-
examination clause?

Some courts say "Yes." In *In re Rhone-Poulenc-Rorer Inc.*,[39] a
trial court certified a class of persons with hemophilia who became
HIV-positive as a result of exposure to tainted blood products. One
of the defendants' arguments against certification was that the trial
of more than 5,000 plaintiffs would be unmanageable. Not so, said
the district judge; the general issue of defendants' negligence could
be bifurcated and tried first, with individual follow-up trials on issues
of causation and comparative negligence. The court of appeals issued
a writ of mandamus against the certification, in part because of the
unmanageability of the trial. Its reasoning was that 5,000 individual
negligence trials would indeed be required; hence, the district court's
trial plan violated the Seventh Amendment. Under the district

39. 51 F.3d 1293 (7th Cir.) (Pos-   v. Rhone-Poulenc Rorer Inc., 516 U.S.
ner, C.J.), *cert. denied sub nom.* Grady   867 (1995).

court's plan, the case-by-case determination of the issues of proximate causation and comparative negligence would force subsequent juries to look again at the previously determined question of the defendants' liability, either to see whether the plaintiffs' injuries flowed naturally from the wrongdoing (proximate cause) or to measure the relative culpability of each plaintiff and defendant (comparative negligence). According to the court of appeals, this re-examination was forbidden by the Seventh Amendment.

Rhone-Poulenc can be criticized for an unduly broad view of the subsequent juries' tasks. Under the district court's plan, the first jury would merely have determined the defendants' negligence *simpliciter*. No subsequent jury could, or would need to, re-examine that finding. To determine whether the defendants' fault was proximately related to each plaintiff's injury, or to weigh the gravity of that fault against a plaintiff's own, is a legally distinct matter that may require the second jury to hear some of the same *evidence*, but would not require it to re-determine the *fact* of defendants' liability.

Be that as it may, the re-examination clause does preclude some forms of bifurcation, and the broad view of the clause evinced in *Rhone-Poulenc* may prevent the most sensible method of narrowing the issues in many tort trials. When joined with the other concerns that bifurcation raises, this method for narrowing issues at trial, which had seemed self-evident, turns out to be anything but.

b. Trial by Statistics. Even if the trial in Smith's case can be successfully bifurcated on liability issues, determining the individual issues of proximate causation, defenses, and damages still presents a daunting challenge. If we assume (optimistically) that each trial on these issues will last only three days, the 1,000 trials will take 3,000 days — or about twelve full-time years of the judge's and jury's time. In addition, outcomes among comparably situated people will inevitably vary; maintaining consistency over 1,000 cases and twelve years is impossible.

Enter the concept of "trial by statistics." The essence of trial by statistics is to try some sample of the overall number of cases, and then to extrapolate the results of those trials to the group as a whole. The trial process is greatly shortened, and the entire group receives comparable treatment.

The first attempt to use trial by statistics occurred in an asbestos class action in the Eastern District of Texas. As originally formulated, the district court intended to conduct bifurcated trials on liability and defenses, followed by a second full trial of forty-one class members (fifteen chosen by plaintiffs, fifteen by defendant, and eleven at random). This second trial was to include testimony from a special master, who had conducted a survey (based on discovery responses) of the class as a whole and would have summarized for the jury the demography, injuries, and other relevant characteristics of the class. The jury was then to award a single lump sum to the entire class as damages.

The defendant successfully sought a writ of mandamus against the trial plan.[40] It argued that the plan violated the due process clause, the Seventh Amendment, and *Erie*. Reserving judgment on the first two arguments, the court of appeals held that the substantive law of Texas, which applied to the case, required an individualized assessment of proximate causation. The court held that the attempt to assess damages on behalf of the class as a whole was inconsistent with this law, and thus precluded under *Erie*.

That decision was not, however, the end of the story. The district court went back to the drawing board, and, in a process that consumed years of judicial time, conducted 160 individual trials on damages. The trials included randomly selected plaintiffs who suffered from each of the five disease processes associated with asbestos. At the end of these trials, the court averaged the verdict for each disease type, and proposed to apply that average award to each plaintiff suffering from that disease. The plaintiffs consented to this procedure, and submitted evidence that, to a 99 percent degree of confidence, the average award in each disease category represented the likely average award of individual trials for all members of the class suffering from that disease. The trial court therefore overruled the defendants' objection to the procedure, and proposed entering judgment for each "extrapolation" plaintiff in the amount of the average award for the plaintiff's disease category. Those plaintiffs whose cases were tried, on the other hand, received their actual award. Defendants' share of damages in both the tried and extrapolated was determined not according to whether any given plaintiff had been exposed to their asbestos, but according to their share of asbestos in the relevant worksites.[41]

Defendants appealed. After sitting on the decision for the better part of a decade, the Fifth Circuit ultimately reversed the district court's extrapolation plan. The court of appeals held that the plan violated the defendants' Seventh Amendment right to jury trial. With regard to the cases that had been tried, the jury had never determined, as Texas law and the Seventh Amendment required, that any given defendant's products had caused any given plaintiff's injuries. With regard to the thousands of "extrapolation" cases, the

---

40. *In re* Fibreboard Corp., 893 F.2d 706 (5th Cir. 1990).

41. Cimino v. Raymark Indus., Inc., 751 F. Supp. 649 (E.D. Tex. 1990).

Seventh Amendment required a jury to determine the actual damages suffered by each and every plaintiff.[42]

After the district court's decision but prior to the Fifth Circuit's decision, the Ninth Circuit had approved a plan that was loosely based on the district court's trial plan.[43] The case involved approximately 10,000 victims of the repressive regime of Ferdinand Marcos. The district court randomly chose 137 cases, in which the parties conducted full discovery. A special master then made recommendations concerning the viability of the 137 claims and the damages due for each viable claim. He also recommended that the jury extrapolate from these damages calculation, and award the remaining 9,800 plaintiffs the average award for the type of injury from which they or their decedent suffered. The jury heard additional evidence that the average award in the 137 cases would, to a 95 percent degree of confidence, match the average award in the remaining cases. The jury generally followed the master's recommendations.

On appeal, the defendant did not assert a Seventh Amendment argument, but strongly contended that this trial by statistics plan violated its due process rights. Finding that the plaintiffs, who were the only ones standing to lose from this process, had consented, and that the costs of the individualized trials outweighed any arguable gains in the accuracy of the outcome from the defendant's perspective, the court of appeals found no violation of due process.

Statistics have long been used to prove issues of importance in discrimination, antitrust, and securities trials. But this new form of trial by statistics is different; rather than using statistics to help prove an underlying factual issue in dispute, it uses statistics to avoid the underlying issue of individual harm and to substitute for that issue the different issue of group harm. That shift in focus makes the technique controversial.

Whether the decision in of the Fifth Circuit or that of the Ninth Circuit seems correct may depend on your view of the value of a traditional trial structure. Is the one-on-one adversarial confrontation the essence of adjudication; or is it a costly relic that must be jettisoned in mass disputes? Are the autonomy and individuality implicit in case-by-case determinations the irreducible minimum of jury trial; or in Justice Brandeis's words, may the "new device" of trial by statistics be adapted to preserve the "ancient institution" for modern times? Is the bedrock requirement of American process a remedy precisely tailored to individual circumstance; or is the harm

42. Cimino v. Raymark Indus., Inc., 151 F.3d 297 (5th Cir. 1998).

43. Hilao v. Estate of Marcos, 103 F.3d 767 (9th Cir. 1996).

to the group and the full internalization of that harm to the defendant the central issues?

Like several of the issues we have seen in this book, trial by statistics places the traditional and the progressive into stark contrast. The stakes of this debate are far greater than the structure of trial, since a trial is a rare event in large mass torts. If trial by statistics is ultimately validated in court opinions, it will also provide a powerful impetus to aggregate related cases. As we have seen, one of the reasons that courts are sometimes reluctant to aggregate cases is the unmanageability of the resulting suit. In at least some of these cases, especially mass torts, trial by statistics will reduce or eliminate that unmanageability. It may also spur even more creativity that will uncover still other devices to bring the institution of trial into a new form.

The jury, so to speak, is still out on trial by statistics. Its ultimate fate bears watching.

   c. Time Limits. Like their pretrial counterpart — early, firm deadlines — time limits at trial are an indirect method for narrowing issues. When a party is given only a certain amount of time within which to present a case, a skilled advocate will go for the jugular and strip away the extraneous. Of course, a skilled advocate would do this even without judicially mandated time limits, so a fair question is: Why time limits would be thought necessary? One possible answer is that, as the modern profession has evolved from a group of trial lawyers into one of (primarily) pretrial litigators, the trial experience and competence of the average member of the bar has declined. Perhaps time limits act as necessary compensation for that decline in skill.

Whatever its cause, time limits are often imposed in large cases. Limits can be imposed in different ways, each with certain advantages and disadvantages. One method is to give each side a certain number of hours or days to present its case. The problem with this method is that the opposing party has an incentive to drag out cross-examinations in order to steal time from the opponent's case-in-chief. To counteract this, a second approach is to give each side a number of hours that it may spend as it wishes — on direct or cross-examination, on arguments, or on objections. When the time runs out, even in mid-question, that side's case is concluded. A third approach is to allocate time on a witness-by-witness basis. The second and third approaches also pose numerous administrative problems, including how to determine an appropriate number of hours, how to allocate those hours fairly among the parties (equal time is not always best, for one side's case might be more complicated), and how to measure each side's time accurately.

Within any system of time limits, theoretical issues also loom large. When the evidence is too voluminous or technical for the lawyer to adequately present or for the factfinder to adequately comprehend, do time limits help or exacerbate the problem of achieving reasoned decisions? How do we justify the use of time limits in some, but not all, cases? What effects do time limits have on the outcomes of cases, and is time saving an adequate justification for potentially different outcomes? Might such limits "prevent[ ] a full and meaningful presentation of the merits of the case"?[44] Do time limits constitute an undue intrusion on parties adversarial right to control their own proofs and arguments?

Another nagging question is the precise source of the court's authority to impose time limits, which are nowhere specifically mentioned in either the Federal Rules of Civil Procedure or the Federal Rules of Evidence. One view is that the power inheres in the loosely worded language at the commencement of both sets of Rules, which require that they be construed so as to avoid undue delay and expense. Sometimes other provisions, such as Federal Rule of Evidence 403 or the case management power in Federal Rule of Civil Procedure 16(c)(15), are cited.[45] But none of these provisions speaks precisely to the issue, once again leaving the impression that the court's inherent power to control litigation is driving the decision.

4. Summary

Although there also exist other, less frequently used issue-narrowing powers,[46] these three devices comprise the bulk of the court's special issue-narrowing powers in complex cases.[47] With the exception of bifurcation, whose effects are known (and disquieting), no empirical research has been performed on these techniques to see whether or whom they might favor in relation to the ordinary form of trial, whether they lead to true time or cost savings, and whether (and to what extent) the accuracy of outcomes is affected by their use. Whether the need to innovate — the need to provide some easy resolution to a massive dispute on terms more or less equivalent to

---

44. Newton Commonwealth Property, N.V. v. G + H Montage GmbH, 261 Ga. 269 , 404 S.E.2d 551 (1991).

45. For a general discussion of the uncertain source of this power, and other problems of time limits, see TIDMARSH & TRANGSRUD, *supra* n.15, at 1319-26.

46. These include multiple juries

and the narrative presentation of testimony. *See id.* at 1316-19, 1326-33.

47. A more general issue-narrowing power is the judgment as a matter of law, which is the trial equivalent of a summary judgment. *See* F.R.CIV.P. 50(a), (b). There do not appear to be any special interpretations given to this rule in complex cases.

the terms provided to other litigants in other types of disputes — is strong enough to overcome these doubts remains today an open question. Echoing Justice Brandeis' call to innovation, some courts and scholars are enthusiastic about new issue narrowing devices. Others are not; as one commentator has remarked, "Our civil justice system owes a twelve-year-old girl born with foreshortened limbs after her mother took [Bendectin] the same due process that . . . we routinely afford the victims of many automobile accidents that are tried every year."[48]

C. INCREASING COMPREHENSION

In a classic adversarial trial in America, presentation of the evidence proceeds from plaintiff to defendant, followed by rebuttal by the plaintiff. Evidence comes either from exhibits or from testimony of witnesses, who are subject to direct examination, then cross-examination, then (possibly) re-direct and re-cross. Lawyers make an opening statement and a closing argument. If a jury is involved, the judge instructs it. It must sit passively, ask no questions, and take no notes. The judge rarely comments on the evidence or asks a question; presenting proofs and arguments is the lawyer's job, and there is a fear that comments or questions will unduly influence the jury. In a bench trial, this form is somewhat less strictly followed, and briefs often take the place of opening statements and closing arguments. Even here, however, the lawyers have the primary task of presenting proofs and arguments.

In some cases — those that we have called "complex" — the ordinary form of trial may create a serious risk that the factfinder will not be able to comprehend the information adequately enough to reach a rational decision. The most common problems are the technical difficulty of the information presented, the volume of the evidence, (relatedly) the length of the trial, and the inability to comprehend the legalese in jury instructions.

In response to these problems, various techniques have been developed.[49] Some seem quite commonsensical, such as allowing the jury to take notes or drafting clear and tailored jury instructions. Some make minor changes in the ordinary form of trial, such as trying a case issue-by-issue,[50] using interim statements from counsel

---

48. Transgrud, *supra* n.5, at 87-88.

49. The techniques are explored in much greater detail in TIDMARSH & TRANGSRUD, *supra* n.15, at 1333-84. *See also* RICHARD L. MARCUS & ED-

WARD F. SHERMAN, COMPLEX LITIGATION 816-31 (3d ed. 1998).

50. This method is different than bifurcation. The trial remains an all-issues trial, but instead of being organized by plaintiff's case and then

or interim instructions from the judge, or using verdict forms that focus the jury specifically on each important fact. Some techniques rely on computer technology to animate or illustrate difficult concepts. Some involve greater departures from the adversarial method of party-controlled presentation, allowing judicial or jury questioning, judicial commentary on the evidence, or the testimony of court-appointed expert witnesses or special masters. It is common to see more than one of these devices employed in a single trial.

For many of these devices, there exist scant empirical or experimental data designed to determine their efficacy in increasing comprehension or their potential for affecting outcomes. For others, such as high-tech computer evidence, there are serious concerns about the ways in which wealth and access might skew adjudication by the factfinder. Many of these techniques are now being employed in more routine litigation as well — yet another indication of how complex litigation has influenced ordinary cases.

D. CONCLUSION

The common themes of this book replicate themselves in the materials on trial. One or more of litigation's "players" cannot fulfill the role expected of them by the adversary system. Into the void step new devices, engineered by the judge and threatening the traditional model. The new devices promise greater economy or more reasoned decisionmaking. Whether they deliver on that promise, and whether keeping the promise is worth the prices of individual autonomy, disparate treatment for different claims, and the rise in judicial authority are unresolved questions.

However the answers to these questions might be framed, it should be obvious that the ramifications of the trial structure extend beyond the trial itself. As this book has emphasized, decisions about trial procedure have a marked effect on the entire procedural system. For instance, trial bifurcation naturally lends itself to pretrial bifurcation, and thereafter the entire system starts to blur into continental-style procedure. But it is also true that the trial process can affect the amount of joinder that is possible; the more closely we cleave to the traditional one-on-one paradigm, the less aggregation we can reasonably accomplish. Procedure is a seamless web, and the choice of a particular trial structure also dictates the rough outlines of an entire procedural system. Thus, it is a fair point to ponder whether judges should be allowed to design trials on an *ad hoc* basis,

defendant's case, the case is organized by plaintiff's evidence on issue 1, defendant's evidence on issue 1, plaintiff's evidence on issue 2, defendant's evidence on issue 2, and so on.

or whether stronger guidelines for appropriate and inappropriate techniques would be a better solution.

Chapter 8

REMEDIAL COMPLEXITY

In the study of complex litigation, the issue of remedies often receives short shrift. Structuring a case is intellectually challenging, handling pretrial is vital and intense, and the trial is exciting. Remedies, on the other hand, are mundane. This attitude is a great mistake. A wonderfully executed campaign of aggregation, pretrial, and trial means nothing if the remedy that the lawyer seeks is impossible or excessively costly to obtain. Lawyers must keep their eyes firmly on the prize.

Many cases that are complex in the structural, pretrial, or trial sense do not present any significant issues of remedies. Conversely, many cases that present few challenges in the structural, pretrial, or trial stages present enormous difficulties at the remedial stage; an excellent example is *Brown v. Board of Education,*[1] in which the liability phase essentially ended within three years and the remedial phase has carried on for nearly fifty.[2] Still other cases, such as *United States v. AT&T*, are complex both pre- and post-remedy.

At first blush, remedial complexity would seem to have little to do with the other forms of complexity. Few rules concerning remedies are found in the Federal Rules of Civil Procedure. The issue of the quantum of the remedy seems distinct from the issue of the procedures that should be used to arrive at that point; put differently, the law of remedies is usually regarded as a distinct field of study from the law of procedure.

Real cases, however, care little about the niceties of academic pigeonholing. As we shall see, many of the same themes that we have considered throughout this book find new voice in the field of remedies.

---

1. 347 U.S. 483 (1954) (liability decision); 349 U.S. 294 (1955) (remedial decision).

2. The history is briefly related in JAY TIDMARSH & ROGER H. TRANGSRUD, COMPLEX LITIGATION AND THE ADVERSARY SYSTEM 1401 (1998).

A. STRUCTURAL LIMITATIONS ON DETERMINING AND IMPLEMENTING REMEDIES

The fundamental issue of remedial law is to determine what "a court . . . will do — simultaneously — *for* the victim, *through* the wrongdoer."[3] In American remedial law, the answer that has traditionally been given to that issue is the "rightful position" principle.[4] In essence, this principle holds that a wrongdoer must restore the victim to or maintain the victim in the position that he or she would have occupied if no wrong had occurred. In some cases, when the wrong and its harmful effects have been irreversibly felt, the only option available in our society to give effect to this principle is to provide money. In other cases, when either the wrong has not yet occurred or at least some of the effects of the wrong might yet be avoided, an injunction (or sometimes a declaration) is the appropriate remedy to achieve the rightful position.

1. The Ability to Depart from the Rightful Position Principle

Fundamental issues surround the rightful position principle. The first is the extent to which the rightful position is a necessary aspect of American adjudication, as opposed to a guideline useful in the majority of cases. The answer to this issue is central to our project, for remedially complex cases are usually those in which the rightful position either cannot be easily determined or cannot be easily implemented. If the rightful position principle can be dispensed with in favor of some other principle, the problem of remedial complexity might be overcome.

But what, you might fairly ask, is a satisfactory substitute principle? The alternative that is usually mentioned is, colloquially, the "do good" principle. Rather than committing itself to a precise re-balancing of the world before the harm, the "do good" principle allows a court, once wrongdoing has been found, to make a better world — even, perhaps, to make adjustments in favor of victims that exceed the amount of the defendant's wrongdoing. For instance, if the defendant committed particularly egregious securities fraud, perhaps it might not only be required to compensate victims, but also be forced out of business entirely. The court is capable of determining a fair and appropriate remedy.

The "do good" principle unhinges the violated right from the

---

3. Doug Rendleman, *Remedies — The Law School Course*, 39 BRANDEIS L.J. 535, 535 (2001) (emphasis in original).

4. This is Professor Douglas Laycock's term. The older phrase — the "original position" principle — is sometimes inaccurate.

remedy. The close right-remedy connection is somewhat peculiar to Anglo-American law; continental legal systems generally opt more in favor of a fairness principle. Implicit in the strong rightful position principle is a premise that litigation is essentially private dispute resolution rather than a public dispute process designed to address larger social matters of which this dispute is one manifestation. And implicit in this private view of dispute resolution is the private control and ordering of the dispute — in other words, the adversarial system.[5]

In perhaps the most famous procedural article ever written, the late Abram Chayes argued that in "public law litigation" — a phrase he coined — the right-remedy connection, and the private worldview underlying it, had collapsed in favor of a new paradigm.[6] Among the types of cases that Professor Chayes mentioned as emblematic of this new public law paradigm were large institutional reform cases such as desegregation decrees, litigation over prison conditions, and antitrust breakups. In this paradigm, the violation of a right did not necessarily determine the scope of the remedy. The remedy itself was often the subject of dispute and negotiation, rather than an *a priori* outgrowth of the violation. In defining the remedy, the judge played a large role that was antithetical to traditional adversarial theory.

Professor Chayes had a point. How exactly is a court to determine the rightful position of a school system's African-American children when they, their parents, and their grandparents had been subject to segregation for decades? How exactly is a court to implement a prison reform decree when the legislature refuses to take the politically unpopular step of appropriating the necessary funds? The inadequacy of the rightful position principle to address these problems was patent, and, as Chayes documented, courts were not reluctant to abandon the principle in order to achieve a fair, appropriate, and legitimate outcome.

That observation, however, merely returns us to the question of whether departures from the rightful position principle are permissible, or whether the principle acts as a structural limitation on the court's ability to deal with complex cases. The best guidance on the question has come from the Supreme Court's desegregation cases, which fairly can be characterized as somewhat inconsistent. This inconsistency is perhaps best demonstrated in *Swann v. Charlotte-*

---

5. Perhaps the best-known defense of the right-remedy connection and its relationship to the adversary system is the posthumously published Lon. L. Fuller, *The Form and Limits of Adjudication*, 92 HARV. L. REV. 353 (1978).

6. Abram Chayes, *The Role of the Judge in Public Law Litigation*, 89 HARV. L. REV. 1281 (1976).

Mecklenburg Board of Education,[7] which ultimately upheld busing as a remedy for the past unlawful segregation of a school system. In the course of the opinion, the Court observed, first, that the remedial "task is to correct, by a balancing of individual and collective interests, the condition that offends the Constitution"; and second, that "the nature of the violation determines the scope of the remedy."[8] Both statements, of course, are strongly consistent with the rightful position principle. In other parts of the opinion, however, the Court observed that "[o]nce a right and a violation have been shown, the scope of a district court's equitable powers to remedy past wrongs is broad," that the "district judge or school authorities should make every effort to achieve the greatest possible degree of actual desegregation," and that "[t]he remedy for such segregation may be administratively awkward, inconvenient, and even bizarre in some situations and may impose burden on some"[9] — all statements that could be read to mean that a court may not only correct the wrong but also "do good."

Indeed, one of the primary points that divided the Court in its many desegregation decisions was the starting remedial principle, with cases involving a more conservative approach leaning on the rightful position and cases upholding more liberal approaches emphasizing the ability of district courts to move away from that principle. For the time, at least, the matter appears to have been settled. In *Missouri v. Jenkins*,[10] a bare majority of the Court reversed a set of remedies designed to eradicate the vestiges of unlawful segregation in the Kansas City school system. The discrimination had been long-lasting and clear. At the time of remedial declaration, the school system was performing well below national norms. The district court's stated intention was to turn the system into one of the best in the country — a laudable goal that was designed to reverse the effects of "white flight" and achieve an integrated school system. To accomplish this goal, the district court oversaw the most massive restructuring of any segregated school system in the country. Magnet schools were established, old facilities were repaired and restructured, new facilities were constructed, and new programs were commenced. The total cost of the program ran into the hundreds of millions of dollars.

In 1995, the Supreme Court called a halt to the farther reaches of the program. It emphasized that the only correct remedial principle in such constitutional litigation was the rightful position: The validity of the district court's orders "must rest upon their serving as proper means to the end of restoring victims of discrimi-

---

7. 402 U.S. 1 (1971).

8. *Id.* at 16.

9. *Id.* at 15, 26, 28.

10. 515 U.S. 70 (1995).

natory conduct to the position they would have occupied in the absence of that conduct."[11] According to the Court, the district court's efforts to create excellent schools as a means of introducing natural integration patterns in Kansas City was too distant from the discriminatory wrong to justify the program's continuance.

Although the Court, for now, seems committed to the rightful position in constitutional litigation, it has stopped short of saying that the rightful position is constitutionally compelled, or put differently, that the "do good" principle is unconstitutional. Even if they were, the reach of *Missouri v. Jenkins* is federal constitutional law; it does not directly affect non-constitutional litigation or litigation whose remedial source is state law. Nonetheless, the rightful position appears today to be an entrenched part of remedial law — even more than when Professor Chayes first described its apparent evanescence a quarter century ago.

2. *Constitutional Constraints*

Missouri v. Jenkins also highlights a second remedial limitation. The case involved the specter of an Article III judge attempting to restructure an institution of the executive branch of the state government. In many public law cases, questions of separation of powers and federalism suggest important constraints on the attempt to correct the wrong — whether under a rightful position or a "do good" principle.

One aspect of this problem was squarely presented in an earlier incarnation of the *Missouri v. Jenkins* controversy that also reached the Supreme Court. In that case,[12] the issue was not the scope of the remedy; the issue was the power of the district court to order the State of Missouri to pay a share of the multi-million dollar remedy. Standing squarely in the way of the State's ability to pay was a state constitutional amendment that limited the State's authority to increase tax assessments to pay for education. Since the State was already taxing property at the maximum level, it argued that it was illegal to raise taxes further, and that the federal court could not force the State to disobey its own constitution. In response, the district court suspended the operation of the constitutional amendment in order to allow the state to raise funds to pay for its share of the remedy. Although the district court did not itself impose a tax, its order had essentially the same effect.

By a bare majority, the Supreme Court upheld this order. The majority believed that a federal court must have all necessary

11. *Id.* at 89.   12. Missouri v. Jenkins, 495 U.S. 33 (1990).

powers to uproot the lingering effects of constitutional misbehavior, though it should apply those powers with restraint and due consideration for separation of powers and federalism concerns. The opinion implied that the district court probably would have had the authority to impose a tax, if such a move been ultimately necessary; but it did not need to decide the issue because the district court's appropriate use of the lesser power to order suspension of the amendment turned out to be effective. A strong dissent did not believe that the distinction between a court's suspension of the taxing amendment and a court's imposition of the tax was a meaningful one, and argued that such *de facto* taxing authority violated the boundaries of Article III, offended federalism concerns, and belied one of the founding principles ("no taxation without representation") of our republic. Given changes in the membership of the Court since this case, this dissent might well command majority support today.

Beyond the striking facts of *Missouri v. Jenkins* lies a more general issue. Courts are not generally thought to be institutionally capable of running large institutions. When those institutions are government institutions, separation of powers concerns are inevitable. When, in addition, those institutions belong to state or local government, federalism questions loom large.

The Supreme Court has demanded that district courts be sensitive to these concerns. Once again, the primary vehicle for voicing this demand has been school desegregation cases, though the principle applies as well to public housing or prison reform litigation. The Court has stated that a federal court must consider three factors in selecting a remedy: "the nature of the desegregation remedy is to be determined by the nature and scope of the constitutional violation," "the decree must be *remedial* in nature, that is, it must be designed as nearly as possible 'to restore the victims of discriminatory conduct to the position they would have occupied in the absence of such conduct,'" and "the federal courts in devising a remedy must take into account the interests of state and local authorities in managing their own affairs."[13] The first two factors merely restate the rightful position (indeed, they seem to be alternative formulations of it); the third suggests that separation of powers and federalism concerns may keep a court from achieving even that much.

3. The Jury's Role

A third constraint on adopting the appropriate remedy is our unique history of law and equity. As we have said, damages (the

---

13. Milliken v. Bradley, 433 U.S. 267, 280-81 (1977) (quoting Milliken v. Bradley, 418 U.S. 717 (1974)) (emphasis in original).

usual remedy at law) compensate for irreversible effects of past wrongs; injunctions (the usual remedy in equity) prevent wrongful behavior, or repair the yet-preventable effects of the past wrongful behavior. You might think that choosing the right form of remedy — damages or injunction — is a simple matter. When only damages are available, it is. But when the wrong has not yet been committed or when the yet-reversible effects of the wrong have not been fully felt, the choice is not as obvious: Is it better to let the harm occur and have the defendant pay for it, or try to prevent the harm through an injunction?

Your immediate reaction might be to issue the injunction. With a moment's more thought, however you might accept a somewhat more refined position: Give the best remedy available, which will be the injunction in most cases, but might be damages in special cases.

These reactions, however, neglect a critical fact: Damages mean a jury, while an injunction means a judge. As we have seen, our system has a strong preference for jury trial. Moreover, the long historical struggle between law and equity in England led to the development of certain principles that preserved the independence of law against the encroachments of the crown's Chancellor. These concerns have hardened into a pair of age-old adages: Equity may not intervene when there is an "adequate remedy at law," and equity steps in only when the injury is "irreparable" (i.e., cannot be ameliorated by an action at law).

The inadequacy of a legal remedy and the irreparability of injury might appear to be two ways of saying the same thing, but they are often separately cited in court opinions and they can be given independent meanings.[14] The net effect of the two principles is this: In some cases, we will not provide the equitable remedy that would best achieve the rightful position; a victim must instead suffer the wrong and its harmful effects, and be content with an action for damages. The reasons to accept the second-best damages remedy vary; but a recurring one is the belief that this type of case should be heard by a lay jury and not a judge. This state of affairs is unique to the Anglo-American system; having no experience of a power struggle between law and equity, nor a right of jury trial, other legal systems simply give the best remedy, or combination of remedies, available.

In combination, these limitations — some constitutionally derived and some common law in origin — constrain the choice of remedy. In many cases, these constraints pose no particular

---

14. See DOUGLAS LAYCOCK, MOD-   ed. 1994).
ERN AMERICAN REMEDIES ch.3-4 (2d

difficulty. In some cases — those that are remedially complex — they often do. But these constraints are not the only source of remedial difficulty. Strategic behavior can create additional problems.

B. STRATEGIC BEHAVIOR

Thus far in this chapter, we have discussed the issue of remedies as if it were entirely the court's problem. In any remedial system, however, the most important player is the wrongdoer — the party that is expected to comply with the court's remedial order. When a party willfully fails to comply with that order, the court has various tools available to it to enforce the judgment — executions, garnishments, attachments, and the like for damages, and contempt power for injunctions.

A different, more intractable set of issues arise when a remedy requires the acquiescence or cooperation of persons who are not parties to the dispute. Perhaps, as in *Missouri v. Jenkins*, a legislature refuses to authorize the funds required for a remedy. Perhaps a common council refuses to enact the legislation required to give a consent decree full effect. Perhaps bureaucrats and low-level employees erect roadblocks and fight rear guard actions that threaten the remedy. Perhaps community leaders or activists mobilize against the remedy and undermine its effectiveness.

In these scenarios, the wrongdoer is not the recalcitrant party. Rather, the full realization of the remedy depends on the cooperation of others that have private reasons to oppose the remedy. Even when the remedy navigates through the structural reef of remedial theory, the shoals of practical strategic behavior remain.

C. RESPONSES

As the examples in the last two sections have suggested, the problem of remedies presents itself in two distinct ways. The first is one of determining what the remedy should be — a task traditionally reserved to the decisionmaker. The second is one of implementing the remedy — a task traditionally reserved to the wrongdoer and the victim. As you might expect, injunctive and monetary issues play out somewhat differently in each of these two areas.

1. Declaring Remedies

As long as the rightful position is the guiding principle, the process of declaring a remedy would appear to be simple: determine the position that the victim would have occupied but for the threatened or actual harm, and give just enough remedy to maintain the victim in or to restore the victim to that position. As *Missouri v. Jenkins* shows, however, that position can often be hard to determine or achieve when the wrongful behavior has already occurred and injunctions are necessary to repair the harm.

The problem is not limited to injunctive relief; sometimes the same problem occurs in cases seeking damages. For instance, in *Democratic Central Committee of the District of Columbia v. Washington Metropolitan Area Transit Committee*,[15] a regional transportation system's predecessor was found to have overcharged some of its riders by a small amount on each ride. The aggregate total of the overcharge was several million dollars. Unfortunately, the overcharging had happened in the 1960's, and the fund first became available for distribution in the 1990's. Although the theoretical path was clear — track down the riders from the 1960's and give them back the appropriate number of pennies per ride — the expense and practical difficulties of doing so were prohibitive . On the other hand, simply allowing the wrongdoer's successor to pocket the money created exactly the wrong incentives.

A similar declaration problem sometimes occurs in employment discrimination cases. For instance, in *Dougherty v. Barry*,[16] the defendant discriminated against five firefighters, two of whom should have received promotions that instead went to other persons. In theory, the remedy for a wrongful failure to promote is easy: back pay and benefits that compensate the plaintiff for the value of the lost promotion. The practical problem was determining which two of the eligible plaintiffs would have received the promotions in the counterfactual perfect world, and were therefore entitled to the remedy.

Arguably *Democratic Central Committee* presents a somewhat different problem than *Dougherty* or *Missouri v. Jenkins*. In the latter two cases, the declaration problem derived from the impossibility of knowing the counterfactual world in which no discrimination had occurred. In *Democratic Central Committee*, the problem was the practical difficulty of determining the exact damages that each victims had actually suffered. But all the cases ultimately come to the same frustrating point: the inability of the decisionmaker to provide the actual victims of wrongdoing the exact remedy — no more and no less — that they deserve.

---

15. 84 F.3d 451 (D.C. Cir. 1996).   16. 869 F.2d 605 (D.C. Cir. 1989).

The solutions for this problem are painfully few. One, which we have explored before, is simply to abandon the rightful position principle when continued adherence to it creates insurmountable problems. As we have also seen, that option may be unavailable in federal constitutional litigation involving injunctive relief. Whether it is available in state law or other federal law injunctive claims also remains an open issue.

The point is also controversial in damages cases. Some courts in situations comparable to *Democratic Central Committee* have established a system known as "fluid recovery." Fluid recovery determines the amount of harm done in the aggregate to the victims, and then provides relief in that amount to another group that acts as surrogate for the original victims. To use the facts of *Democratic Central Committee*, a fluid recovery would give present bus riders free or discounted fares until the amount of the discounted fares equaled the amount of harm done. Presumably there would be some overlap between the original victims and the beneficiaries of the fluid recovery, though the harm suffered and benefit received would not necessarily correspond. Fluid recovery achieves the right amount of deterrence, but it invariably results in uncompensated victims and undeserving beneficiaries, thus failing to meet the restorative aspect of remedial law. Moreover, fluid recovery makes the most sense when small injuries are suffered by repeat players in a particular market, so that giving recovery to another set of players in the same market guarantees a modicum of victim compensation. Fluid recovery makes little sense, and has received no use, when injuries are catastrophic and non-repetitive. Thus, reducing the price of XYZ's asbestos or other products as a means of compensating the victims in an asbestos class action is unthinkable. For these reasons, most cases have rejected the concept of fluid recovery.[17]

Among those cases was *Democratic Central Committee*. Instead, the district court chose another method for handling the declaration problem: It decided to use the damages to fund other programs that would be of benefit to the victims of the rate overcharge. But it still needed to determine the nature of the program. Among the options that the court considered were an escheat of the funds to the government for transportation purposes, an escheat for general governmental purposes, the funding of a foundation or watchdog group that would work for the interests of the transportation users, or a flat *pro rata* distribution to the users. The court of appeals ultimately determined that the money should escheat to the wrong-

---

17. The best-known case is Simer v. Rios, 661 F.2d 655 (7th Cir. 1981), *cert. denied*, 456 U.S. 917 (1982) (re- jecting fluid recovery). For other cases, see TIDMARSH & TRANGSRUD, *supra* n.2, at 1414-16.

doer's successor, which was required to purchase new buses and improve services for the areas affected by the original wrongdoing.

In contrast, *Dougherty* adopted the *pro rata* approach. Unable to determine the two firefighters that would have been promoted, the district court had awarded that each of the five plaintiffs the full value of a promotion. The court of appeals reversed, holding that each plaintiff deserved two-fifths of a full award.[18]

The solutions in *Democratic Central Committee* and *Dougherty* possess a certain elegance and a certain common sense. They also have another important effect: They simplify the trial. These solutions have a close affinity to trial by statistics,[19] in which an easier-to-prove surrogate for the plaintiffs' actual harm is also employed. To take a further step back, simpler mass trials make the decision to aggregate plaintiffs easier as well. Thus, these remedial solutions have ripple effects backward through a complex case.

But the solutions are far from clearly correct. Undercompensated victims and undeserving beneficiaries are inevitable. Missing is the precise individualized balance of wrongdoing and correction; neglected is the rightful position principle. Enforcing the rightful position principle with such apparent rigor in equitable claims such as *Missouri v. Jenkins*, while overlooking it in damages cases such as *Dougherty*, is an unsatisfying solution. It is also a great irony — for it is equity, and not the common law, for which flexibility has always been the leitmotif.

A second declaration problem can also occur in some circumstances: The determination of the remedy presents highly technical issues of accounting or, as in the *Marcos* case discussed in the last chapter,[20] massive quantities of information that the factfinder might have difficulty remembering or keeping straight. Really a form of trial complexity, this problem has typically been addressed through a reference to a special master. Since masters have long been used to provide such remedial aid and Rule 53 contemplates such references, the use of the special master here has not so far tended to create the theoretical or practical difficulties that pretrial or other trial references have.[21]

---

18. For a case awarding full benefits to each discriminated class member, see Kyriazi v. W. Elec. Co., 465 F. Supp. 1141 (D.N.J. 1979), *aff'd*, 647 F.2d 388 (3d Cir. 1981). *Kyriazi* shifted the burden of proof, holding that the defendant as wrongdoer must prove that a particular plaintiff was undeserving of a promotion.

19. *See supra* ch.7, nn.40-43 and accompanying text.

20. *See supra* ch.7, n.43 and accompanying text.

21. For a general discussion of and some problems with such references, see TIDMARSH & TRANGSRUD, *supra* n.2, at 1419-22.

2. Implementing Remedies

Once the remedy has been declared, the parties must implement it. In some complex cases, remedial implementation is a difficult enterprise. For one thing implementation may require years of incremental adjustments that re-orient an institution's internal culture or else the creation of an infrastructure to support the changes. For another, the judge is usually unequipped to engage in the functions of administering and overseeing the details of a large prison or school system. It is also a questionable use of precious judicial resources to have a judge determine the eligibility and compensation for each person in a large class; but, if an asbestos class action settles for a lump sum of $10,000,000, how else is the judge to determine the precise share that each plaintiff deserves? Finally, full remedial implementation often hinges on the compliance of third persons, and that compliance may be difficult to attain when these nonparties oppose the remedy.

A number of mechanisms have been developed to deal with these problems. As we have seen, when a party claims a legal obstacle to his or her full implementation of the remedy, the court may be able to enjoin enforcement of the obstacle — though the first *Missouri v. Jenkins* warns us of potential constitutional limits on this power.

When the problem is one of determining proper individual awards in the context of a lump sum settlement or award, courts (either alone or in conjunction with a special master) have often established eligibility criteria for an award.[22] But even when the parties agree on eligibility criteria (as they did, for instance, in the breast implant litigation and the two scuttled asbestos settlements in *Amchem* and *Ortiz*[23]), the separate problem of determining each individual's eligibility and award remains.[24] To respond to this problem, courts have sometimes contracted with special masters or insurance companies to make eligibility and award determinations. In some large cases this has required the creation of temporary bureaucracies employing hundreds of people. The judge serves largely as an ultimate appellate authority over the work of the bureaucracy — a role far removed those of from the factfinder and the lawgiver in traditional adversarial theory.

22. *See, e.g., In re* Combustion, Inc., 978 F. Supp. 673 (W.D. La. 1997); *In re* "Agent Orange" Prod. Liab. Litig., 689 F. Supp. 1250 (E.D.N.Y. 1988).

23. On *Amchem* and *Ortiz*, see *supra* ch.5, nn.100-02, 107, 133-39, 172-76, 179, 200-01, 212-13 & 280-86.

24. Note that the problems of eligibility criteria and individual eligibility and award determinations are avoided with fluid recoveries, discussed *supra* n.17 and accompanying text. As we have seen, however, such recoveries are not favored, especially with one-time catastrophic injuries.

Oversight issues often require patience, pragmatism, and, on rare occasion, hard-heartedness. Since it is often impossible for the judge to oversee every aspect of a large institutional reorganization and inappropriate for him or her to assume the responsibility of running a company, a school system, or a prison, the judge again must rely on a host of judicial adjuncts — special masters, monitors with the organization, and sometimes even receivers that step in to run a truly resistant institution.[25] As with other uses of judicial adjuncts, however, certain concerns arise. Among the most frequently mentioned are the unconventional and often *ex parte* nature of the adjuncts' operations, the creation of a bureaucracy with greater affinity to the administrative than the judicial process, costliness, and abdication of the judicial function.

The last significant problem of remedial implementation is third-party intransigence. In a sense, this problem returns us to where we began this book: the inclusion of all interested parties in a single case. As we learned then, a court usually can issue binding orders only against those who have been joined as parties to a case. Hence, in some situations, the proper response to intransigence is party joinder. But this is rarely an effective solution. For one thing, joinder *after* the establishment of liability usually cannot bind the third parties to the rulings that have occurred before their joinder. For another, many third parties do not have the type of legal interest that permits their involuntary joinder. Under what theory can the influential local pastor who advocates that community's parents disobey a desegregation plan be made a party to the desegregation case itself? Should the pastor wish to intervene, Rule 24(a)(2)'s "impaired interest" test might be inclusive enough to sweep the pastor into the case;[26] but forced joinder of a person with no legal interest in the case is another matter.

In some complex cases, nonparties hold the key to implementation of the remedy. For instance, in *Spallone v. United States*,[27] the City of Yonkers agreed to settle a housing discrimination lawsuit. When it came time for the city council to pass the legislation implementing the agreement, however, a majority of council members balked. The district judge applied direct pressure on the city (by levying ever-increasing fines that bankrupted the city within weeks and left vital services such as garbage pickups suspended) and indirect pressure on the recalcitrant council members (by holding them in contempt for their votes on the council). The direct measures were ultimately successful; one of the council members

---

25. For cases using these adjuncts, see TIDMARSH & TRANGSRUD, *supra* n.2, at 1443-48.

26. *See supra* ch.5 nn.19-26 and accompanying text.

27. 493 U.S. 265 (1990).

switched sides and created a majority to implement the settlement. In a case brought by the council members seeking to void the contempt orders, the Supreme Court held that the district court had no power to hold the council members themselves in contempt, for such a move would create serious separation of powers, federalism, and free speech concerns.

Spallone is an unusual case with highly charged facts, and should not be read to mean that all efforts to apply pressure on third parties are impermissible. Perhaps the classic case is *United States v. Hall*,[28] in which the district court was struggling to enforce an unpopular desegregation decree. Hall was an African-American community activist that vehemently opposed the plan. Eventually the district court issued an *ex parte* order preventing the parties, or anyone else with actual notice of the order, from entering school grounds except in certain limited situations. After having been specifically served with a copy of the order, Hall entered onto school property in order to protest the court's orders, and was held in contempt by the district court.

The court of appeals upheld the contempt sanction. According to *Hall*, courts have an inherent power to make effective their lawful orders. That power extended not only to the parties to the dispute, but also to those nonparties with actual knowledge of the order, when the activities of the nonparties might "disturb[ ] in any way the adjudication of the rights and obligations as between the original plaintiffs and defendants."[29] The court of appeals was also unpersuaded that the *ex parte* nature of the order was, under the circumstances, inappropriate.

In dicta, the Supreme Court has indicated its apparent approval of *Hall's* use of contempt against a nonparty.[30] Even in *Spallone*, the Court broadly hinted that, had the direct sanctions against the city proven ineffective, the court would eventually have been able to hold the legislators in contempt. This apparent acquiescence is difficult to square with the Court's contemporaneous insistence that nonparties cannot be bound to a judgment entered in their absence — even when they are aware of the judgment[31] — and suggests an as-yet untapped route around the usual requirement of party joinder as a necessary precursor to binding a person to a judgment.

---

28. 472 F.2d 261 (5th Cir. 1972).

29. *Id.* at 265.

30. *See* Golden State Bottling Co. v. NLRB, 414 U.S. 169, 180 (1973); Washington v. Washington State Commercial Passenger Fishing Vessel Ass'n, 443 U.S. 658, 693 n.32 (1979).

31. *See* Martin v. Wilks, 490 U.S. 755 (1989); Richards v. Jefferson Cty., Alabama, 517 U.S. 793 (1996); S. Cent. Bell Tel. Co. v. Alabama, 526 U.S. 160 (1999).

D. CONCLUSION

Remedial complexity poses somewhat different issues than the other forms of complexity. Absent, at least in a direct fashion, are procedural assumptions like concerns for transactionalism and trans-substantivity. The jury trial assumption plays a muted theme, and adversarialism comes into play primarily as a modest buttress for the rightful position principle.

Still, important connections to other issues remain. The fear of judicial aggrandizement of power at the expense of other entities reaches its pinnacle in remedial law, as does the unfettered discretion perhaps wrongly associated with the "do good" principle. The need to achieve and preserve rational adjudication operates as powerfully after the trial as it did before. The need to be efficient and fair weaves throughout the various forms of complexity, including remedial complexity.

At the end, therefore, only a single question remains: Is there some set of broader connections within which these various manifestations of complexity can be understood and against which they must be evaluated?

Chapter 9

EPILOGUE

At the start of this book we posed a question: What exactly is complex litigation? We suggested then that the best way to answer the question is to see the ways in which various doctrines, ideas, policies, statutes, and constitutional provisions interact over the course of a complex case, and then to try to find common threads or themes among them.

In the first chapter, we also provided a working definition of complex litigation: cases in which the ordinary rules of procedure (and, as we now know, remedies) do not work well. We can now perhaps see the reasons why they do not work well. Modern American procedure is built on a welter of foundational assumptions that cannot all be fully realized simultaneously. An adversarial system, with its many incentives for strategic behavior, cannot run at the socially optimal level of efficiency. Adversarialism is also in conflict to a large degree with transactionalism. Moreover, what constitutes efficient procedure for the particular case may well create outcome-affecting inequities among similar cases. At some point, individual autonomy, social efficiency, equality of opportunity, and political notions of limited government cannot all peacefully co-exist.

That much seems obvious. The frustrating thing about defining complex litigation, however, is that, over the range of the many doctrines we have explored, each of these ideas seems to have its day in the sun. Sometimes one principle seems to win out, sometimes another. There is no lexical ordering of the principles; all appear to be incommensurable goods. Some rather hard-hearted pragmatism seems to be the only way to make sense of everything — in which case there can be no definition of "complex litigation" at all.

Perhaps that is ultimately the right attitude to have about the problem of complex litigation. Something else, however, may be afoot, something that is powerfully descriptive *and* also predictive of the legitimate stopping point to the wonderfully inventive spirit that animates this field.

Our understanding of complex litigation begins with the
adversarial system — a system that we will not here defend as better
or worse than any other method for organizing proofs and arguments. It is, however, the system that we have chosen by tradition.
Like all such systems, the adversarial system assigns to various
players in the litigation enterprise — lawyers, judge, jury, and
parties — certain roles and responsibilities. Lawyers have the
primary responsibility for organizing the structure of the case, for
developing the issues and evidence, and for presenting the proofs and
arguments at trial. The judge is passive and detached from these
tasks, partly in order to maintain neutrality and partly in order to
preserve the individual autonomy and limited governmental
authority implicit in an adversarial system. The judge's role is to
rule on disputes brought before the court by the parties, to determine
the law applicable to the dispute, and in some cases to determine the
facts. Juries are also passive and neutral; they resolve the factual
disputes that are jury-triable. The parties are even more passive;
aside from supplying information during pretrial and trial, they have
a very limited role until the remedial phase, at which point their role
is to implement the declared remedy.

One theme unifying virtually every doctrine we have examined
is that the roles adversarial theory assigns to the players break down
in the face of the realities of large-scale disputes. The breakdown can
occur in any aspect of litigation — structuring the case, pretrial, trial,
and remedies — and can affect the roles of any of the players
involved in that aspect of the case. In most litigation, the breakdown
is sporadic, rather than across-the-board. Sometimes the breakdown
results from the structural, procedural, or remedial limits of our
adjudicatory system; sometimes they result from strategic, non-
optimal behavior by lawyers or parties. Whatever the cause, at some
point and in some fashion, a breakdown occurs.

A second theme unifying the various issues we have examined is
that the response to the breakdown is a non-adversarial one: In each
situation, the response has been to give the judge greater powers
than adversarial theory suggests. The judge may use the All Writs
Act to force the removal of a non-aggregated case, become a case
manager deeply involved in the shaping of the issues, adopt a
creative interpretation of the Seventh Amendment to prevent jury
factfinding, or assert contempt authority over nonparties who
threaten implementation of the remedy. Whatever the exact
response — and it varies with the nature of the breakdown — the
judge is no longer the passive, neutral, umpireal judge of old.

Of course, the judge is not all-powerful. Important constitutional, statutory, codal, common law, and practical considerations

constrain him or her. Where these constraints hold sway, no available response is capable of avoiding the breakdown. From the inability to maneuver around constitutional subject matter jurisdiction limits to the handcuffs of the rightful position principle, these constraints create the intractable problems of complex litigation.

A third theme also runs through many of these materials. We repeatedly focused on the source of a judge's authority to engage in certain non-adversarial actions, and often found ourselves with no better answer than the capacious language of the All Writs Act or the even more capacious concept of "inherent power." Granting the existence of non-adversarial powers, which it would be feckless at this point to deny, what exactly are their limits? Put differently, why is this authority exercised in some places but not in all?

This book has left some clues about how these themes might be assembled into a coherent whole. Perhaps the largest clues can be found at the beginning of Chapter 2 and the end of Chapter 8. In Chapter 2, we suggested that two different ideas of socially optimal aggregation might be entertained. One was a model of efficiency. The other, which we called "remedial equity," was the idea that aggregation should occur only when a failure to aggregate would deprive someone (whether present plaintiffs, present defendants, or nonparties) of a fair share of a remedy.[1] Throughout the materials on structural complexity in Chapters 2 through 5, we saw that, despite the constant concern for efficiency, efficiency proved a weak predictor of when a judge would assert greater, non-adversarial powers to shape a case. "Mere" efficiency was infrequently the reason that judges fashioned new doctrines that upset the ordinary rules of subject matter and territorial jurisdiction, venue, joinder, and preclusion. The desire to avoid remedial inequity, on the other hand, was a powerful predictor of the judge's successful invocation of non-adversarial powers to overcome standard aggregation patterns.

But this observation demands deeper analysis. What makes remedial inequity a powerful creative force? And, if it is such a powerful motivator, why did remedial inequity seem to disappear in the discussions about pretrial, trial, and remedy?

Both questions can be answered together, once we take a step back from the immediate concerns of complex cases. The essence of adjudication is the use of procedures that create an atmosphere in which rights and liabilities can be determined rationally. Our transactional assumption posits that *all* people involved in a transaction or series of transactions are entitled to a reasoned adjudication of their claims. When the failure to aggregate a

---

1. *See supra* pp.10-11.

transactionally related person in a lawsuit results either in the inability of nonparties to obtain a fair share of a remedy they deserve *or* in the inability of the present parties to hold onto the remedy that they obtained in a prior adjudication, the ability to determine rationally each transactionally related party's rights and liabilities is threatened. When that happens, a court has the power — whether we nominally locate it within the All Writs Act, in the court's inherent power, or elsewhere — to preserve this core of adjudication. Indeed, we encountered exactly this rationale at the end of Chapter 8, in *United States v. Hall.*[2] *Hall* justified the use of the contempt power against a nonparty precisely because this power was needed to preserve the final adjudication of the rights and liabilities of the original parties to the suit.

With a bit of reflection, we can expand this basic idea and see it at work in each form of complexity that we examined in this book. The adversary system is simply one system to adjudicate disputes in a rational manner. The threat posed by the "complex" case is the destruction of the ability of a person assigned a task by the adversary system to complete that task in a way that advances the rational adjudication of the dispute. Thus, at the structural stage, we saw the doctrinal difficulties and strategic choices that led lawyers, who have primary responsibility for structuring the lawsuit in an adversarial system, not to aggregate cases in a manner that would guarantee a fair share of the remedy for all. During pretrial, we focused on the problems of the lawyer in performing the assigned adversarial tasks of narrowing issues and gathering evidence. During trial, we focused on the problem of lawyers in presenting proofs and arguments, and of judges and juries in performing their tasks of rational factfinding. At the remedial stage, the relevant players were the judge, who had difficulty declaring the remedy, and the parties, who had difficulty implementing it. Without the ability of the relevant player to perform these tasks at one or more stages, the ability to adjudicate the dispute fairly and comprehensively was in jeopardy.

In each case, the curative response to the threat was the exercise of greater judicial authority. When that response made no sense — as, for instance, with the lawgiving authority at trial — then no greater authority could be exercised or entertained by the judge. When greater judicial authority made the case run more efficiently but was not needed to preserve rational adjudication, courts usually balked at expanding judicial power. The adversarial system usually held its own against the argument of inefficiency; it could not hold its

---

2.   *See supra* ch.8, nn.28-31 and accompanying text.

own against the claim that the system was defeating the very purpose of transactional adjudication.

If the application of non-adversarial judicial power to meet a threat to reasoned adjudication is a *sine qua non* of complex litigation, as we believe it is, then two further propositions follow. The first is that this power creates unavoidable disparities among cases; in other words, the trans-substantive ideal cannot be fully honored. Since the elegance and simplicity of this ideal is a powerful one in our procedural system, its loss in complex litigation is an unfortunate occurrence. Indeed, trans-substantivity may ultimately impose its own limitations on the ability of a court to invoke non-adversarial power in some, but not all, cases. To use such powers in Smith's case but not to use them in Green's identical case would be deeply disturbing, perhaps even impermissible. To use them in the case of asbestos victims but not in the case of, say, car accident victims may be troubling, but is more likely permissible.[3]

Second, some trans-substantive disparities can be eliminated by shoving ordinary litigation in the direction of complex litigation — a phenomenon that is perhaps most noticeable with regard to the case management movement and other pretrial devices that have recently spread from the complex case to the more ordinary. Whether such a general shift — as opposed to the shift only in those complex cases in which the shift is essential — is a wise idea may depend in part on your views of the adversary system, in part on your views of the importance of maintaining a single consistent system for adjudicating disputes, and in part on your views of other procedural ideals such as efficiency, transactionalism, and federal-state relations.

By synthesizing these concerns, we arrive at a definition of complex litigation. Complex cases are those cases in which:

> (1) the rules, doctrines, or circumstances make it impossible for the relevant player to perform a task that our adversarial process has assigned to the player in a manner that assures the rational adjudication of the dispute,

> (2) rational adjudication can be attained with the curative application of greater judicial power than is consistent with adversarial theory; and

> (3) the result of the application of judicial power is the use of different, potentially outcome-determinative procedures or rules among similarly situated cases.

---

3. For an argument that the trans-substantive ideal may impose such constraints in a limited number of cases, see Jay Tidmarsh, *Unattain-able Justice: The Forms and Limits of Complex Litigation*, 60 GEO. WASH. L. REV. 1683 (1992).

In this definition, there is no happy ending. As we have seen, at times a judge is constrained by Constitution, statute, or policy from applying greater judicial power, with the result that the adversarial system must slog through a case with no guarantee that rational adjudication will occur for all persons involved in the transaction. Even when greater power is available and applied, disparities in outcome among like cases gnaw at us. Nor would a shift to some other procedural system solve the problem, for in any system there will be cases in which the players cannot perform the tasks necessary to achieve rational adjudication for all participants.

Ultimately, this is the story of complex litigation. The inability to attain perfect justice, and the constant striving toward that ideal, are the realities that give complex litigation its fascination, its restless frustration, and its creative energy.

TABLE OF CASES

References are to page numbers.

INDEX

References are to page numbers.